EAST OF BALI
FROM LOMBOK TO TIMOR

Text and photographs by

KAL MULLER

Edited by David Pickell

PERIPLUS EDITIONS

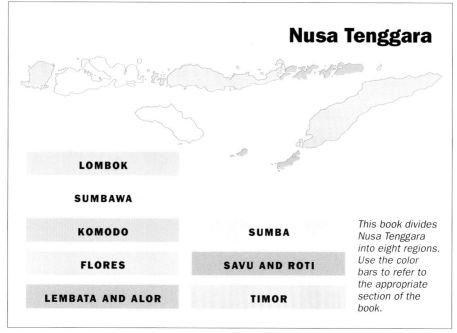

Nusa Tenggara

LOMBOK

SUMBAWA

KOMODO

SUMBA

FLORES

SAVU AND ROTI

LEMBATA AND ALOR

TIMOR

This book divides Nusa Tenggara into eight regions. Use the color bars to refer to the appropriate section of the book.

© 1995 by Periplus Editions (HK) Ltd.
2nd edition.
ALL RIGHTS RESERVED
ISBN 962-593-006-X

Publisher: Eric Oey
Design: Peter Ivey
Marketing Director: Julian Sale
Production and cartography: David Pickell

International distributors:
Benelux Countries: Nilsson & Lamm bv, Postbus 195, 1380 AD Weesp, The Netherlands.
Germany: ILH GeoCenter, Postfach 800830, 7000 Stuttgart 80.
Indonesia: C.V. Java Books, P.O. Box 55 JKCP Jakarta 10510.
Japan: Charles E Tuttle Inc., 21-13, Seki 1-Chome, Tama-ku, Kawasaki, Kanagawa 214.
Singapore and Malaysia: Berkeley Books Pte. Ltd., Farrer Road P.O. Box 115, Singapore 9128.
U. K.: GeoCenter U.K. Ltd., The Viables Center, Harrow Way, Basingstoke, Hampshire RG22 4BJ.
U.S.A.: *NTC Publishing Group (*Passport Guides), 4255 W. Touhy Avenue, Lincolnwood (Chicago), Illinois 60646.

We are always glad to receive comments and additions from readers. Please address all correspondence to: Periplus (Singapore) Pte. Ltd., Farrer Road P.O. Box 115, Singapore 9128.

Printed in the Republic of Singapore

Periplus Travel Guides

BALI

SUMATRA

JAVA

IRIAN JAYA
Indonesian New Guinea

MALUKU
The Moluccas

SULAWESI
The Celebes

EAST OF BALI
From Lombok to Timor

KALIMANTAN
Indonesian Borneo

UNDERWATER INDONESIA
A Guide to the World's Greatest Diving

WEST MALAYSIA
and Singapore

EAST MALAYSIA
and Brunei

Author Kal Muller has explored, photographed and written about Indonesia for over 15 years. His work has appeared in dozens of books, as well as in the pages of *National Geographic, Geo,* and many other magazines. Muller now spends most of his time in Indonesia.

Cover: The color and tying of this man's cloth hat distinguishes him as a Marapu priest.
Pages 4-5: A tapper climbs a *lontar* in Flores.
Pages 6-7: A Muslim Sumbawan woman.
Pages 8-9: Dawn off Moyo island.
Frontispiece: An old warrior from West Timor.

Contents

To Bill Dalton
The dean of Indonesian travel writers

His handbook was my Bible during my first trips to the islands East of Bali. And to **Cody Shwaiko**, my friend and travel companion on my first and latest trips to these islands, and my interpreter before I learned Indonesian.

Acknowledgements

A great number of generous people helped make this book possible. **Dorien Greeven** of Holland kept up a constant flow of "care" packages of background material. **Dr. James J. Fox** checked the manuscript, deleting errors and making pertinent suggestions. But my greatest debt is to the villagers who received me in their homes, wined me on *tuak*, dined me on dog (occasionally), and put up with my highly inaccurate spurts of staining red betel juice.

Contributers

Peter Bellwood is a Reader in prehistory at the Australian National University, specializing in Southeast Asian and Pacific prehistory. His books include *Man's Conquest of the Pacific, Prehistory of the Indo-Malaysian Archipelago* and *The Polynesians.*

James J. Fox is a Professorial Fellow in the Department of Anthropology, Research School of Pacific Studies, at the Australian National University in Canberra. He books on eastern Indonesia include *Harvest of the Palm*, and the edited collections *To Speak in Pairs* and *The Flow of Life.*

Agnès Korb, in the anthropology department of Udayana University, has conducted research in Bali, Lombok and Sumbawa. She graduated in English from the Sorbonne University and the E.S.I.T. Academy of Interpreters and Translators before coming to Bali in 1980 to begin a new career in social anthropology.

Coen Pepplinkhuizen lectures on Asian art and religion in Rotterdam and Utrecht, most recently focusing on the traditional religions of Indonesia. He has traveled widely in Asia, and holds a degree in comparative religion from the University of Amsterdam, and a specialization in Chinese religion from Leiden University.

Brigitte Renard-Clamagirand, who specializes in the social organization, ritual and oral literature of Sumba and Timor, is the author of *Ofarobo, une société Ema de Timor* and has contributed to *To Speak in Pairs.*

PART I

Introducing Nusa Tenggara

In the modern Indonesian state, the next group of islands east of Bali are called Nusa Tenggara, the "Southeastern Islands." To geographers, they are the Lesser Sundas, at least partially because they are smaller than the Greater Sundas—Sumatra, Java and Borneo. There is nothing "lesser" about the region's charms, however. In fact, no other similar sized area in Indonesia—or for that matter, in the world—can lay claim to such a variety of physical and cultural attractions.

From Lombok to Timor, the islands are blessed with deserted white sand beaches, transparent waters and beautiful coral reefs. The three water-filled craters of Keli Mutu, on Flores, provide an almost surreal sight, as minerals have tinted each of the lakes a different hue. Tiny Komodo, nestled between Sumbawa and Flores, is the home of the largest lizard extant, a veritable dinosaur.

And then, of course, there are the people of the Lesser Sundas. In Lembata, men harpoon sperm whales from tiny boats by physically leaping onto their backs. In Sumba, twice a year, hundreds of horsemen gather to fling spears at each other in the ancient, and dangerous Pasola. On Roti and Savu, the people "farm" the *lontar* palm, depending almost exclusively on its nutritious juice, sugar and toddy for their nutritive needs. On many of the eastern islands of the Lesser Sundas, women produce the finest contemporary *ikat* weavings in all of Indonesia.

An island chain

Lying just a few degrees south of the equator, the Lesser Sundas stretch 1,300 kilometers east to west, forming a central link in the 5,600-kilometer Indonesian archipelago. Someone has counted 566 islands in Nusa Tenggara, of which 320 are so small they don't even have names. Of the 42 inhabited islands, five loom largest on the map—Lombok, Sumbawa, Sumba, Flores and Timor—and there are a dozen others worth visiting.

Although overland travel is relatively easy year-round on all the larger islands, it is much more pleasant (if hot) to visit in the dry season, which runs from June through October or November. In the spring, April/May, the islands are a lovely green; by the autumn, they have turned a parched brown.

Time and good humor

Nusa Tenggara is not yet part of the mass tourist circuit, and the lodgings and services here are modest. Travel, particularly to the more out-of-the-way islands, requires initiative, a loose schedule and a healthy sense of humor to deal with the inevitable snags. If you are fully to appreciate the rich cultural life of the islands, leave some flexibility in your plans. Who knows what might turn up—a whip fight in Flores, a boat to little-known Ndao, a circumcision in Bima.

It is very useful, of course, to be able to speak Indonesian. In places you can hire English-speaking guides, but even a limited vocabulary in *Bahasa Indonesia* will prove handy. It also helps to dress conservatively—remember, this is an area where tourism is still new, and the islanders are not familiar with the strange habit foreigners have of parading around nearly naked.

Be prepared to be the center of attention, and to answer the same litany of questions—Where are you from? How old are you? Are you married? Where are you going?—over and over again. And, when you get outside of the major towns, be prepared to eat, sleep and bathe under the most basic of conditions. The reward—a glimpse of one of the most beautiful and culturally rich regions in the world—more than makes up for these minor discomforts.

Overleaf: *A high priest of the Marapu religion in West Sumba scans the shallows for the first signs of* nyale *seaworms.* **Opposite:** *A dancer from Sumbawa gives our photographer the Bronx cheer.*

GEOGRAPHY

Volcanoes and Limestone Plateaus

The islands of Nusa Tenggara, spanning a distance of 1,300 kilometers, connect the Greater Sunda islands in the west to the scattered islands of Maluku, and the large island of New Guinea to the east.

The western islands of Nusa Tenggara—Lombok and Sumbawa—are in many places covered with the luxuriant vegetation characteristic of the humid tropics. When one travels further east, however, the dry season lengthens, and parts of Timor are the driest in all of Indonesia.

The islands of Nusa Tenggara form two distinct arcs. The long northern arc—Lombok, Sumbawa, Komodo, Flores, Lembata—is volcanic in origin. The islands of the shorter, southern arc—Sumba, Savu, Roti, Timor—are formed of raised coral reef limestone and sedimentary rock.

The islands in the volcanic arc are potentially quite fertile, lacking only reliable rain in the east. But the southern islands exhibit barren limestone plains and sparse savannahs, which in places can barely support cattle. Overall, the islands are much less populated than Java and Bali, and villages and cultivated land are widely scattered.

The most productive form of agriculture, like elsewhere in Indonesia, is the cultivation of "wet" rice, in irrigated *sawah*s. In places where farmers have to depend on rainfall, corn, manioc, and tuber crops are grown. On the arid islands of Roti and Savu, the people are supported through the long dry season by the nutritious juice of the drought-proof *lontar* palm.

Turbulent beginnings

The islands of Nusa Tenggara rise abruptly from clear, deep seas as either smoking volcanoes, or as tiers of coralline platforms edging rugged island interiors.

In geological terms the islands are quite young, having been born in the late Tertiary period, some 70 million years ago. Impelled by subterranean currents of magma, the Australian–Indian Ocean plate (sometimes known as the Sahul plate) crept ponderously in a northwest direction, until it collided against the more resistant mass of the Eurasian (Sunda) plate. The Sunda plate, being less dense than the Sahul plate, was scraped to the surface by the heavier Sahul plate. The weight of this crust then forced the Sahul plate downward, where it was compressed and heated.

When it reached a depth of more than 50 kilometers, the rock became molten and, under great pressure, found its way upward through fissures and faults near the shattered margin of the the Sunda plate. When it reached the surface, this molten rock erupted to form volcanoes. Over the millennia, the volcanoes grew in size and eventually merged with the products of neighboring vents to form the northern islands—Lombok, Sumbawa, Flores, and the Solor and Alor archipelagoes.

The magma exploded as ash and cinders, or burst through fissures as viscous andesitic or basaltic lavas. The larger volcanoes typically consist of alternating strata of lava, ash and other pyroclastics of varying thickness.

Mount Tambora, on the island of Sumbawa, produced the greatest eruption of modern geological times on April 5–7, 1815. The force of the explosion was far greater than the better-known eruption of Krakatau, off western Java, in 1883. The Tambora explosion produced an astounding 150 cubic kilometers of ash and pumice, reducing the height of the volcano overnight from 4,200 to 2,851 meters. Depending on the source, from 12,000 to 50,000 people lost their lives. Happily, just 25 or so of the almost 40 identified volcanoes in the region are still thought to be potentially or demonstrably active, although a new one, Anak Ranaka on Flores, appeared as recently as 1988.

The southern chain

The shorter, southern chain of islands—Sumba, Savu, Roti and Timor—form two sides of a neat triangle bordering the Savu Sea. Although these islands contain some old volcanic materials, they are now strictly non-volcanic, and are chiefly composed of geologically young, raised coral reefs, from the Quaternary, and somewhat older Tertiary

Opposite: *The volcanic lakes of Keli Mutu, in south-central Flores, take on different colors from various minerals dissolved in the water.*

rocks derived from marine sediments.

The composition of the sediments ranges from folded and contorted coral limestones, marls and sandstones to peculiar "scaly clays," so-called because of the way they flake when exposed to the air. Embedded in the clays are fragments of all manner of different rock types.

The sedimentary rocks largely derive from the collision zone between the two crustal plates. As the advancing Sahul Plate was forced beneath the Sunda Plate, the relatively soft layer of submarine sediment was scraped off its surface and piled up like a crumpled tablecloth. These sediments, particularly on Timor, have trapped within them fragments broken off the leading edge of the Sunda Plate.

Geological evidence on Sumba points to a different origin. Small exposures of ancient, granitic rocks obscured beneath the younger sediments lead geologists to speculate that Sumba is an island fragment torn off continental Australia and borne northwards on an errant magmatic eddy.

Varied landscapes

Dominating the northern chain are volcanoes of all shapes and sizes, ranging from the massive Tambora caldera, 7 kilometers across, to isolated cones a mere 100 meters high. Most, such as Rinjani, Tambora, Sangeang, Ebulobo and Ile Ape display classical conical outlines. Their precipitous, finely scored upper slopes descend to gentler middle slopes, slashed by deep ravines, and then broaden out to almost level footslope fans.

Several of Nusa Tenggara's volcanoes tower to more than 3,000 meters in height and some contain deep crater lakes. The most famous of these are the mysteriously colored trio of lakes in Mount Keli Mutu, central Flores. The colors derive from dissolved minerals in the lakes, and the varying content of the minerals and shifting light causes the lakes to assume a range of colors: although usually described as light green, turquoise and black, they have been known to appear as sea green, deep blue, even red.

Other crater lakes, like the magnificent 5-kilometer-long caldera lake of Rinjani on northern Lombok, Danau Segara Anak, contain miniature volcanic landscapes of their own, in the form of new daughter cones, complete with fresh lava flows.

A glance at any map of the region reveals contrasting shorelines in the northern and southern island chains. The coast of the northern islands is markedly irregular, twisting in and out of small and large sheltered sandy bays, curving around exposed rocky headlands and liberally sprinkled with clusters of attractive reef-bound islands. The southern islands, on the other hand, possess more regular coastlines. They have long stretches of cliffed coast alternating with nar-

row sandy beaches, guarded by ramparts of inshore or offshore coral reef.

Large parts of the coasts of the southern islands are formed of broad, rolling platforms, or terraces, of reef limestone. These are particularly striking in northern Sumba, and at the eastern and western ends of Timor and Roti. The interiors of Sumba and Timor are rugged and dissected by deep, steep-sided valleys. The highest part of Timor, 2,963-meter Tata Mai Lau, penetrates the clouds; the mountains of Sumba are much

lower, and the highest point is just 1,220 meters. There are few permanent rivers on these islands, and they tend to swell rapidly after rainstorms. Their courses are marked by gravelly beds.

These diverse islands produce a wide variety of soils. The volcanic soils of the northern islands are generally young and productive, although the most recently deposited are too ashy and porous to hold water well, and the reddish clay covering some of the older volcanic rocks is strongly weathered and infertile. The alluvial plains of the northern islands, and the footslope fans built up of rich sediments dropped by mountain streams, are the most favorable to agriculture.

In the southern islands, limestone, marl and calcareous clay are widespread, and on these it is usual to find rather shallow layers of red or brown, clayish soils. In some places, darker soils on these rocks are formed from a clay mineral that swells and shrinks in response to moisture. Where such soils are well-developed, they present considerable engineering difficulties and regularly cause the foundations of roads, buildings and canals to crack.

The driest part of Indonesia

The region as a whole is the driest part of Indonesia. It lies at the edge of the influence of the northwest monsoon, and the southeast monsoon brings rain-bearing winds only to

the southern coasts. The interiors of the major islands, however, are mountainous enough to cause moisture-laden air to be forced upward, to cool, and yield rain, and thus are the wettest parts of the islands.

In Nusa Tenggara, it is the changing wind and rain patterns of the two monsoons, rather than temperature differences, that divides the year into seasons. The intensity of the region's two rainy periods varies with the local orientation of the topography. Still, the rains are not prolonged, and most visitors will remember the islands for their sun and wind.

In south-facing situations, the rainiest months are May to July, when persistent southeast winds from Australia pick up moisture over the Timor Sea. During this period the north coasts, in the lee of the central mountains, remain relatively dry. From December to March, during the northwest monsoon, winds from the Java Sea bring moisture-laden air across the north-facing mountain slopes of Lombok, Sumbawa and Flores in particular. In this season the driest areas are the sheltered southeastern slopes and coastlines.

During both seasons the mountains of the major islands that first intercept the rain-bearing winds receive the greatest rainfall, leaving progressively less for their neighbors downwind. During the southeastern monsoon, eastern Flores, Lembata and Alor, being in the lee of Timor's mountains, are not as wet as the south coast of Timor. Similarly, the mountains of Sumbawa and Flores shelter the northern coasts of Sumba and Timor during the northwest monsoon.

Despite these general patterns, the rain-

Above, left: A fine stand of violet-tinted staghorn coral (Acropora sp.). Above, right: A giant clam (Tridacna sp.). The coral reefs surrounding the Lesser Sunda islands are some of the finest in the world. Opposite: 2245-meter Mt. Inerie is one of several active volcanoes on Flores island.

fall distribution is highly complex and controlled largely by local topography. The higher parts of Lombok, Sumbawa, Flores and Timor can receive more than 3,000 millimeters of rain each year, whereas coastal or sheltered inland plains on the same islands receive less than 1,500 millimeters. Some areas are even drier: parts of Flores' north coast, Solor, Adonara, Lembata, Pantar, Alor, northern Timor, and east Sumba receive less than 1,000 millimeters of rain a year; the driest of these, just 500–750 millimeters.

Most of the rainfall occurs as brief, but heavy showers in the late afternoon. Little rain falls at night or in the morning. Prolonged periods of rain are rare, and the islands are fortunate in that cyclone tracks are largely confined to the waters of the Timor and Arafura Seas, and do not seem to affect the islands west of Timor and Alor.

Warm and sunny

The region is noted for its high number of sunshine hours and fresh winds, ideal for sunbathing and windsurfing. In most coastal areas, there is at least 4–5 hours of sunshine a day from December to February, increasing to 7–8 hours a day from June to October. Timor is the sunniest of all, and even inland areas consistently receive 5 hours, and as much as 10 hours a day. There is less sunshine inland as conditions there are generally cloudier and wetter.

Winds in the northern island chain are fresh most of the year, at least near the coast, being strongest from June to September, and calmest from December to March. Winds along the coast average 9–14 kilometers an hour. On Timor, however, and possibly Roti and Savu, stronger winds are the rule. December to February is the least windy period in these areas, and the most windy is the period from June to August, when the winds averages 24–27 kilometers an hour. On all islands wind speeds are likely to decrease inland. The windiest times of the day are midmorning or late afternoon.

Throughout the lowland regions of Nusa Tenggara, temperatures are high and even all year. Walking and sight-seeing are comfortable activities in the morning and late afternoon, but it can become very hot during the middle of the day. Although October–November is the hottest period, with average highs of 33°C, this means little as temperatures vary just 3°C over the year. Night temperatures, in the coolest period, June–August, can drop to 16°–21°C. Humidity averages 70–80 percent throughout the year, with a slightly greater range in Timor.

Temperatures at higher elevations are refreshingly cooler. This makes moving around during the daytime enjoyable, even invigorating, although the sun can burn quickly. Nights can even be downright cold.

—*David Wall*

FLORA AND FAUNA

Scrublands, Dragons and Coral Reefs

Travelers to the islands east of Bali should not expect to find the kind of exotic wildlife for which Borneo, Sulawesi and Irian Jaya are known—with the very notable exception of the Komodo dragon. These islands, relatively dry and rocky, do not harbor dramatic rainforest ecosystems or a large variety of odd endemic species. They are, in fact, rather sparsely populated with large animals.

The scrublands of Nusa Tenggara support wild deer and pigs, as well as bats and numerous species of lizards and snakes. Few mammals, however, are native to the islands, just one species of wild pig, one shrew and a cuscus. Deer, monkeys, rats and various domesticated animals have been introduced relatively recently by man.

The sulfur-crested cockatoo, as well as parrots, sunbirds, bee-eaters and the unusual mound-building megapode bird can also be found on these islands. Although current figures list as many as 56 endemic species in the region, their numbers are nowhere great in the relatively sparse terrain.

An underwater wonderland

Underwater, the scene changes, and the coral reefs of Nusa Tenggara are one of the richest ecosystems in the world. No place on earth has greater numbers or diversity of aquatic species. A single large reef in Nusa Tenggara can contain almost 1,000 fish species, more than can be found in all the creeks, rivers, lakes and streams of Europe.

In many places, donning a mask and fins reveals a world that is almost unimaginably alive and colorful. Plucky anemone fish defend their living home against a diver's teasing hand until the very last minute, when they dive into the protection of its stinging tentacles. Schools of butterfly fish, as beautiful as their namesake, hover around the reef walls. Stately angelfish patrol the reef in pairs, their names—emperor angel, regal angel—an attempt to describe the elegance of their coloration.

The region is home to large marine mammals, including the sperm whale and dugong, the latter a rather homely, herbivorous creature that somewhat resembles a walrus without the tusks. Large, pelagic fishes can be found at the edge of the reefs—whale sharks, reef sharks and manta rays.

The Komodo dragon

The most dramatic creature found in the islands is the Komodo dragon, the largest lizard extant. Endemic to Komodo and Rinca islands, and nearby eastern Flores, *Varanus komodoensis* is the largest known varanid, or monitor lizard. The monitors are so named because it was thought that they warned of the presence of crocodiles. The name seems somehow inappropriate for the Komodo dragon, however, which itself is as large and voracious as a crocodile.

The Komodo dragon—which can reach 3 meters and 150 kilograms—is a lizard, but has some of the physiology of a snake: a jaw which can be disjointed, allowing it to swallow prey in chunks literally bigger than its mouth, and a flicking, forked tongue that is an organ of both scent and taste.

This animal is one of the best adapted predators known, with a powerful tail for bringing down prey, and strong jaws lined with serrated teeth for eviscerating the hapless victim. The saliva and gastric juices of the dragons are extremely powerful, and they are known to digest the horns, bones and hair of their prey.

Wallacea

Alfred Russell Wallace, who spent from 1854–1862 exploring the archipelago, was the first to notice that in crossing from Bali to Lombok, the forms of large, terrestrial wildlife change markedly. Beginning with Lombok, he found no more elephants and rhinos, or tigers—in fact, he found no more carnivorous mammals at all, except for civets, and no more insectivores, with the exception of a small shrew.

Starting at Lombok and including in its range the islands to the east, Wallace found mound-building megapodes—whose eggs are laid in piles of sand or vegetation to be hatched by the heat of the sun or decomposition—as well as other Australian species, including ground pigeons and the magnificent sulfur-crested cockatoos. He noticed that, overall, the number of Asian species diminished as he moved east, while the num-

ber of Australian species increased.

The division in types of wildlife between two tiny islands—Bali and Lombok—was as great, Wallace noted, as that between South America and Africa, or between North America and Europe. Yet there was nothing on the map that would prove as formidable a barrier as the Atlantic Ocean.

Back in London in 1863, Wallace presented a paper to the Royal Geographic Society in which he drew a red line on a map of the Malay archipelago: it led straight down between Borneo and Sulawesi, and Bali and Lombok. This was to become known as the "Wallace line."

Although he saw no physical barrier here, Wallace reasoned that there must have been one in the past. During the period of heaviest glaciation, the seas fell 180 meters, at which time it was possible to walk to Bali from Singapore—but not to Lombok, because of the deep Lombok Strait.

For many decades, scientists found much both right and wrong with Wallace's theories and lines. Wallace's division persisted to a degree among zoologists, but never caught on much among botanists, as the archipelago shows no sharp breaks in the distribution of its 2,300-odd genera of plants.

Most modern biogeographers attribute the division of wildlife species at least as much to habitat as to the obstacles provided by sea crossings. Asian fauna thrives in the western part of the archipelago because of the high rainfall and tropical forests there, a habitat that matches mainland southeast Asia. In the east, Australian fauna survive because they are adapted to dry, scrubby landscapes.

Although Wallace's theory of impassible straits has more or less been discarded, the region does mark a transition between Asian and Australian animal life. At first, other naturalists drew their own lines, between different islands, but today most simply refer to a zone of transition, rather than a sharp line. In honor of the world's first biogeographer, this zone has been dubbed Wallacea.

Plant life

Except for a few small regions in the west, the vegetation is sparse and made up of dry-adapted species such as various eucalyptus (*Eucalyptus urophylla, E. alba*). White sandalwood (*Santalum alba*), once Timor's major export, is now reduced to a few vestigial stands in remote areas of the island, although the government has recently sponsored efforts to replant the trees.

The fire- and drought-resistant *lontar* palm (*Borassus sundaicus*) is one of the most useful plants in the region, serving as an important source of nutrition.

Above: *A juvenile batfish* (Platax pinnatus) *poses in a grotto.*

PREHISTORY

Bronze Drums, Migrations and Megaliths

The first humans to reach Nusa Tenggara came from the west, undoubtedly from Asia, via Java and Bali, to Lombok. The 3,726-meter Rinjani volcano on Lombok is visible from Bali, so even early humans of about half a million years ago might have gazed at it across the Lombok Strait and wondered. But did they cross the strait to explore further?

This is one of the great questions of Indonesian prehistory. Early humans were in Java about one million years ago; this is now well-known from the finds at Sangiran and Trinil in central Java. However, Lombok lies east of the Wallace line and has probably never been joined by dry land to Bali and the rest of the Sunda shelf, including Sumatra, Java and Borneo. Early humans could certainly have walked from mainland Asia to Bali at such times without getting their feet wet, but there is no hard evidence that they actually managed to cross the 40-kilometer-wide Lombok Strait to Nusa Tenggara until sometime between 30,000 and 50,000 years ago, the age of the earliest traces of mankind found in Sulawesi, Australia and New Guinea.

Indeed, it is very likely that Australia was first settled by migrants crossing from Timor. There have been recent claims that stone tools possibly over 100,000 years old occur in Flores in association with bones of an extinct elephant-like creature called *Stegodon trigonocephalus,* but these finds cannot yet be accurately dated, and no one knows when the local extinction of the stegodons occurred—it might have been well after 100,000 years ago. The issue, however, is an exciting one.

Early Holocene archaeology

So far, the oldest accurately dated archaeological deposits in Nusa Tenggara come from caves in East Timor. Excavations in four caves near Baucau and Venilak have uncovered a stone tool industry of chert scrapers dating from about 13,000 years ago. The Timor finds also include bones and remains of the contemporary native fauna of this region—giant rats, fruit bats, snakes, reptiles, fish and shellfish.

All the larger mammals such as pigs, goats, dogs and even wild species such as deer, monkeys, civet cats and cuscus were probably introduced into Nusa Tenggara from about 5,000 years ago and onwards.

So far, other cave sites in Nusa Tenggara with pre-agricultural archaeological remains have not yet been fully reported, although Indonesian archaeologists have recently made finds of this general period in the caves of Liang Bua in western Flores, and Gua Oelnaik, near Camplong in West Timor.

Presumably at this time the populations of Nusa Tenggara would have shared strong linguistic and biological relationships with some of the populations of New Guinea and Australia. During the last 5,000 years, however, the whole region witnessed a gradual mixing of peoples: Austronesian language speakers entered the region from the Asian mainland via the Philippines and Sulawesi, and Papuan language speakers from New Guinea settled parts of Timor, and Pantar and Alor.

The first agriculturalists

With these new peoples, agriculture, domesticated animals and pottery-making appeared in Nusa Tenggara. The incoming Austronesians probably introduced all of these. Since the Papuan speakers of New Guinea had developed plant cultivation at least 6,000 years ago, however, it is possible that some agricultural practices had existed in Maluku and Nusa Tenggara before the Austronesians. But this is only a surmise.

Clear archaeological evidence of the appearance of agriculture has only rarely been recovered from Nusa Tenggara. The best sites, again, are the Baucau and Venilak caves, which reveal simple pottery, shell beads and bracelets, fragments of trochus shell fishhooks, and bones of pigs—the most important domesticated animals of the region—beginning about 5,000 years ago. The dog, goat, cattle and water buffalo bones are more recent, 3,000 years old or less.

The age of metals

By about 2,000 years ago the peoples of Nusa Tenggara were able to acquire bronze and iron, and perhaps even were able to cast and

Opposite: *A very old Dongson-style bronze drum, dug up by a farmer on Alor, is evidence of ancient trade links to mainland Southeast Asia.*

smelt the metals. Nusa Tenggara was never "Indianized" to the extent that Bali and Java were, so the coastal cultures can be considered to have been essentially prehistoric and fundamentally Austronesian until the spread of Islam in the 15th and 16th centuries. Still, they were on the edge of this influence, and glass, carnelian and agate beads of Indian inspiration, and sometimes even Indian manufacture, were imported through the region.

Metal Age artifacts are known from many localities. Examples of the massive "Dongson" bronze drums, manufactured in Vietnam between about 300 B.C. and A.D. 200, are recorded from Sumbawa, Sangeang, Roti and Alor. The most magnificent specimen comes from Sangeang, a small island north of Sumbawa, and is now in the Jakarta museum.

This drum, called "Makalamau" by the local population, stands 84 centimeters high, and its decorations show elephants, horses, shrines with raised floors, and people wearing costumes which may be Han Chinese and Kushan, from northwest India. Such exotic iconography suggests a mainland Asian manufacture, possibly in Vietnam or Funan (now southern Vietnam) during the first three centuries A.D. No one knows when the drum reached Sangeang, although it could have been long after the date of manufacture.

Other indications of possible trade contacts with Vietnam about 2,000 years ago come from Flores, where a rock carving—the Watu Weti, near Ende—shows a typically Dongson dagger among canoes and bronze axes. An actual bronze dagger of the same type was discovered at Inelika, near Bajawa. The island of Roti has also produced three remarkable ceremonial bronze axes, unique in shape, but with Dongson motifs. They were almost certainly made somewhere in Indonesia, perhaps 1,500–2,000 years ago.

Jar burials and megaliths

Two important Metal Age burial grounds have recently been excavated: Gunung Piring, in southern Lombok, and Melolo in East Sumba. At Gunung Piring, the dead were buried in shallow graves with pots, bronze bracelets and iron tools. At Melolo, the dead were first allowed to rot, then the bones were placed, perhaps after secondary burial rites, in large lidded pottery jars in pits in the ground.

Little is known about the rest of the prehistoric past in Nusa Tenggara, although the practice of erecting stone graves and platforms (so-called "megaliths") still occurs widely in these islands. Some of the most interesting structures are the table-like grave markers of Sumba. These "dolmens" can also be found in Sumatra, Java and Melanesia. When they were first built is unknown, but perhaps they mark some aspect of an ancient, shared cultural ancestry.

—*Peter Bellwood*

HISTORY AND PEOPLE

The Flow of Life in Nusa Tenggara

The three provinces east of Bali—Nusa Tenggara Barat, Nusa Tenggara Timur, and Timor Timur—best demonstrate Indonesia's national motto: Bhinneka Tunggal Ika, or "Unity in Diversity."

The diversity is at first more apparent than the unity, since there are some 50 distinct language groups spoken in the region, and many of these are further divided into a variety of dialects. On the unity side, most of these languages are related to each other, forming part of just a few linguistic subgroups of the Austronesian language family.

The languages

The Sasak language of Lombok and the language of the western half of Sumbawa are fairly close to neighboring languages to the west—Balinese and Javanese. The language spoken in Bima, however, is markedly different. It forms part of a linguistic group that includes the languages of Sumba, Savu, Ndao and western Flores. In the eastern part of Nusa Tenggara—eastern Flores, Timor and Roti—the languages spoken are more closely related to those of the Moluccas.

Scattered in coastal settlements on many of these islands, where they have migrated over the past three hundred years, are the Bajo, a sea-fishing population who speak a Samal language originating from the Philippines. Seafaring traders from Sulawesi—Bugis, Makassarese, and Butonese—have also moved into the region and many have settled permanently.

In addition to these Austronesian languages, the region also includes some non-Austronesian languages. Speakers of non-Austronesian or "Papuan" languages, with affinities to languages spoken in New Guinea, are found at the eastern end of Timor, in one part of central Timor, and on the islands of Alor and Pantar.

From this diversity of languages, one can surmise a number of separate migrations from the north and west, beginning as early as 3,000 B.C. The non-Austronesians, however, do not appear to represent a remnant population, but rather a later intrusion into an already populated Austronesian region. (See "Prehistory," page 26.) The Bajo and other populations from Sulawesi are the latest of these migrant waves.

For trade and communication, Malay has for centuries served as a lingua franca, and now, of course, Bahasa Indonesia is the language of government and education. Distinct dialects of Malay are still spoken, along with modern Indonesian, in the old towns of Kupang and Larantuka.

Marginal islands

For the most part, the islands east of Bali remained marginal to Indonesia's great sweeps of history. No great Indianized kingdoms, like Srivijaya, based in Palembang, Sumatra (8th–13th centuries), or Majapahit in East Java (14th–15th centuries), developed here. In fact, other than in styles of weaving, the force of "Indianization" was little felt in Nusa Tenggara. The later proselytizing sweep of Islam did reach some of the eastern islands, such as Solor, but was basically confined to the westernmost islands in the region, Lombok and Sumbawa.

At various times in this period, some of these outside powers claimed all or parts of Nusa Tenggara, particularly the Majapahit Empire and the sultanate of Gowa in Makassar, now Ujung Pandang. However, these claims represented no more than imperial bluster. Since there was no powerful central authority on any of these islands, real conquest by outside forces was difficult.

Even in the 17th century, when the Portuguese and the Dutch brought their colonial forces to bear on the islands, the Europeans found it impossible to rule absolutely, and sought instead to insure that political control was dispersed enough that they could continue their trade. Through the end of the colonial period, a remarkable amount of local autonomy was preserved.

The sandalwood trade

The biggest attraction in the region for the colonialists was Timor's precious white sandalwood, which for centuries had brought traders to the island. Timor was never as important an imperial or colonial prize as the clove- and nutmeg-producing Spice Islands—Ternate, Tidore, Ambon and the Bandas—but the fine white sandalwood was still much sought after.

Sandalwood was admired as early as 1,700 B.C. in Egypt, where it was used in body ointments and perfumes. (Even today, sandalwood extracts are important in fixing scents, particularly such quickly vanishing ones as jasmine.) The Brahmans of India used powdered sandalwood to mix the pigments they used for caste markings. Since sandalwood is native to India and Sri Lanka, however, the prime market for Timor's product was China.

It is still unclear just how long the trade in Timor's sandalwood has been going on. It was well established by the 14th century, and perhaps even by the 12th, although it may be several hundred years older. The traders exchanged porcelain, beads, silk, mirrors and iron tools for the fragrant sandalwood.

Sandalwood was absolutely required at various rituals, particularly burials, where it was burned to perfume the air. The relatively soft, fine-grained wood is also an excellent material for carving, and Chinese craftsmen excelled in fashioning fans and boxes, which retained their sweet smell for many years.

Colonial period

The Age of Exploration served to create further divisions and allegiances in Nusa Tenggara, as regional traders competed with the Europeans for Timor's sandalwood. The trade was pioneered by traders from Java and Malacca, and they were followed by others from China and elsewhere. These men dealt directly with the rulers of Timor, who controlled sandalwood-felling in the interior.

When Ferdinand Magellan's ship, the *Victoria,* put in on the north coast of Timor in 1522—without Magellan, who died the year before—the Europeans encountered a trading junk from Luzon, in the Philippines. Later, in 1566, when the Portuguese established a fortress on the island of Solor, just east of Flores, in an attempt to control the sandalwood trade, they had to contend with Muslim raiders from Java and Makassar.

The struggle for sandalwood continued for centuries. Portuguese-speaking mestizo traders attracted to the fortress settlement on Solor formed a separate population known as Topasses or "Black Portuguese." When the Dutch East India Company or V.O.C. (Vereenigde Oostindische Compagnie) reached this area in 1613, they forced the Topasses from their fort on Solor to Larantuka on east Flores.

By the time of their ouster, however, the Topasses had managed to establish settlements at Lifao on Timor in what is now Ambeno (formerly Oecussi) on the northwest coast of the island. From there they began to exert an increasing influence in the sandalwood growing areas of central Timor.

In 1642, a Portuguese fidalgo led a small armed force across the island of Timor to conquer the two kingdoms of Timor, and thereby claimed control over the island. To counter Portuguese influence, in 1653 the Dutch established a fortress at Kupang to gain a toehold on Timor, and for the next hundred years disputed the claims of both Portuguese and independent Topasses to control of the island.

To strengthen their position, the Dutch created a network of alliances and trade contracts with various native rulers: Muslim populations who opposed the Catholic Portuguese on Solor, and native rulers on the western tip of Timor and on Roti, Savu and the northern coast of Sumba. Similar contracts extended Dutch alliances to Makassar in the north and Bima in the west.

At this time, the Sultan of Bima was closely allied with the royal families of Makassar and claimed sovereignty over much of western Flores and most of Sumba. Each year Dutch East India Company vessels would sail

Overleaf: *West Timorese woven cloths are a part of everyday dress.* **Above:** *A descendent of the Raja of Sikka, central Flores.*

from Batavia (now Jakarta) to Kupang, stopping at Bima, where the company had a trading "factory," to supply and reinforce its often beleaguered settlement.

Divide and rule

In many of the islands of Nusa Tenggara, political authority was local and dispersed. The tiny island of Roti, for example, was divided into 17 separate domains, each with its own native ruler. The far smaller island of Savu was divided into five such domains. In signing treaties with native rulers, the Dutch bolstered the creation of numerous small states or domains. Timor, for example, became a patchwork of independent territories during the colonial period with changing claims of allegiances to either the Dutch or Portuguese.

The large island of Sumbawa, on the other hand, had already been divided between two sultans, the Sultan of Bima at the eastern end of the island and the Sultan of Sumbawa whose jurisdiction extended on the western side of the island.

The colonial recognition of domains in parts of Flores and of Sumba occurred in the nineteenth and early twentieth century, but both of these islands also include domains with a long history. The domains centered on the old settlements of Sikka and Larantuka date from the early Portuguese period.

Throughout the nineteenth century, the Dutch continued to exert limited colonial authority through these officially recognized "self-governing" territories. Inter-island migrations began in this period, which the Dutch used to stabilize the region. To end local feuding on Roti, the Dutch transferred loyal Rotinese to Timor to assist in the pacification of that island.

The Dutch also supported Muslim traders from Ende on Flores in an effort to develop what later became a thriving export trade in horses from Sumba. Increasing wealth from this horse trade stimulated the development of rival domains on Sumba, and internal warfare broke out. The Dutch were then obliged to suppress the fighting with loyal native troops: Endenese and Christian Savunese. As a result, Endenese and Savunese settled on the coast of Sumba.

In the mid-nineteenth century, the Dutch and Portuguese sought to determine their mutual areas of colonial control. Portuguese territory in east and central Flores was sold to the Dutch and later, in 1915, the two colonial powers fixed their borders on Timor. The Portuguese ceded much—but not all—of the original heartland of the Topasses in central west Timor in exchange for undisputed control of east Timor. Despite these agreements, well into the twentieth century the Dutch and Portuguese were still "pacifying" many areas they had long claimed to control.

Social organization today

Colonial strategies of influence and domination, established by the middle of the seventeenth century, set the pattern of population in Nusa Tenggara to this day. By manipulating the islands' many domains through shifting contracts and treaties, the Dutch insured the maintenance of these traditional political and social groupings. Today, most people still identify themselves with a former domain or ritual community, and display this allegiance through their language, dress, and customary practice or *adat*.

These former domains were generally identified by their ritual center, a feature of their organization that caused particular difficulties for the colonial administration. Colonial administrators were concerned with the precise boundaries between domains, that is, territory. Local populations, however, were more interested in enhancing the prestige of the center of their domain. The influence of their domain would then, they believed, emanate outward in proportion to its eminence.

In most domains, the center or source was associated with the person of a ruler or ritual leader. This person was part of a sacred complex and often subject to numerous prohibitions. Most domains, in fact, contained two figures of importance: the ritual leader, and an executive, who exercised power in the name of the leader.

Colonial administrators often created problems for themselves by failing to recognize this dual leadership. Often they recognized the executive leader of a domain, but ignored the spiritual leader. In other cases they signed treaties with the spiritual leader, without understanding that he had no executive authority in worldly matters such as trade.

For example, the Dutch claimed to have an alliance, dating from a treaty signed in 1756, with the ruler of the Tétun whom they designated as the "Emperor" or "Kaiser" of

Opposite: *Heirloom elephant tusks, originally imported to Lembata to trade for slaves, now serve as part of the bride price. The value of the tusks is determined by their length.*

Timor. To the Tetun, this personage was known as the Nai Bot, "The Great Lord." He was a ritual figure who represented the silent powers of the earth at the center of the kingdom. The Nai Bot exercised his authority through an executive known as the Liurai. When the Dutch attempted to contact the Great Lord some 150 years later, in 1906, they had to fight their way, in a series of pitched battles, to the center of the kingdom. And when they finally presented themselves to the Nai Bot, he would not speak to them directly, but only through a spokesman.

In all of the domains of Roti, there was a division between the "Head of the Earth" and "Male Ruler" and on Savu, between the "Lord of the Earth" and the "Descendant of the Sun." On both of these islands, the authority of the ritual leader, associated with the earth, diminished greatly during the colonial period while the other figure was invested by the Dutch with the full powers of a local raja.

Today, throughout the region, the powers of the once important local rajas have been subsumed with the bureaucratic structures of a modern state. What remains is a remnant respect for past glories and a continuing observance of many of the traditions of the domains.

The ritual and social 'house'

Most domains are composed of clans, and everyone in society belongs to a particular clan by virtue of birth, adoption or marriage. Clans, in turns, are often divided into "houses" or are themselves identified as single houses. In some domains, clans and houses are marked by class distinctions, with some being made up strictly of nobles, and others of commoners. Even in domains with no class distinctions, there often exists a local ranking of clans based on ritual precedence.

Houses are extremely important in the ritual and social life of the community. A house unites many households, and these "house-groups" conduct their rituals not in their individual residences, but at a single ancestral house. Marriages are arranged not between individuals or households but between house-groups, according to specific rules. Marriages are often celebrated at the ancestral house, as are mortuary rituals. The graves of the dead are located near the ancestral house, and the ancestral spirits take up residence there.

In Sumba, Savu and parts of Flores where settlements are concentrated, the arrangement of ancestral houses—frequently on hilltops around a central plaza—serves as a spatial representation of social group relations. In Bima and Sumbawa, the mausoleums of the former sultans were built as houses, and were the focus of special veneration.

In Timor, and in parts of Flores where settlement tends to be scattered, the arrangement of ancestral houses is partially replaced

by the institution of the cult house. Cult centers, with special houses, are (or were) often located at a distance from other settlements. Several groups might maintain a single cult house, and these houses were not always permanently occupied.

In some cases, a cult house might be erected specifically for a periodic ceremony and then abandoned until the next ceremony. Nevertheless, these houses were considered of great social importance. A person might live in a hovel, but the cult house must be renewed and maintained.

The architecture and orientation of ritual houses is elaborate, and thoroughly dictated by tradition. The Savunese house, to take just one example, is built to represent a *prahu,* with its bow to the west and its stern to the east. Internally the house is divided into two halves—the bow side is considered "male" and the stern side, "female." In all domains, rituals are performed in accordance with the spatial orientation of the house. In the Savunese house, men's activities are carried out on the male side, and women's on the female side.

A poetic view of life

A commonality of related customs and general beliefs underlies the diversity of ritual practice in the various domains. All of the populations are concerned with the ritual knowledge of their specific origins which establish-

es personal and social identity, and forms the very foundation of cultural life. The ceremonial communication of this knowledge, which includes the recitation of genealogies and the tracing of ancestral migrations, is a key feature of rituals.

Much of this communication features a special ritual speech that requires the pairing of words and phrases. Even simple ceremonies evoke an extraordinary poetic view of life, which sustains, enhances, and transforms even ordinary activities and objects. In Kodi, at the western end of Sumba, the drum used to accompany ritual oration in ceremonies is addressed as follows:

> You are the bird we set singing
> You are the butterfly we set flying
> So let us walk down the same path
>   together
> So let us ride astride the same horse
>   together.

These metaphoric comparisons pervade all aspects of life. On Roti, for example, young unmarried girls are conventionally compared to "blackbirds and green parrots who sing with soft voices and warble with gentle songs." Young boys are said to go "with bow and blowpipe to hunt and stalk these blackbirds and green parrots."

Throughout the region, there is a belief in the interrelationship of all forms of life. Most rituals are intended to be life-giving—to engender a harmony in human actions that is in accord with the pattern of life in general.

The metaphors that articulate these beliefs are complex but one dominant metaphor is the association of human life with the structure and life of plants. On Roti, for example, the traditional marriage ceremony was performed by splitting a coconut and giving one half to each marriage partner. Then the structure of the coconut serves as a metaphor for a successful union:

> This coconut has five layers
> The husk embraces the shell
> The shell embraces the flesh
> The flesh embraces the milk
> The milk embraces the germ.
> So let it be
> For this young man and woman
> Let one embrace the other
> And one cling to the other
> So that the shoot of the coconut may grow
> And the germ of the *areca* nut may sprout
> So that she may give birth to nine times
>   nine children
> And she may bring forth eight times eight
>   children.

Cycles of life and death

Marriage itself is no trivial matter. It is the way society directs and guides the flow of life. The whole of the region is noted for its elaborate systems for the arrangement of marriage. The purpose of these arrangements is to set a direction to the flow of life so that for any group within society, there is at least one group that "gives" life and another that "receives" life from it. In this way, all social groups are enmeshed in a network of life-giving and life-taking relationships established by marriage.

Death is part of the same cycle, and as a consequence the populations of the region devote enormous attention to mortuary ceremonies. Except among strict Muslims, these ceremonies are not a single event but a succession of rituals designed to conduct the spirit of the deceased to the world of the spirits. Communication with this world of the spirits must be maintained, because it is the spirit world that bestows the blessings of life.

Agriculture and the ritual calendar

This cycle of life and death is also reflected in the rituals accompanying the annual agricultural cycle. Although it is expressed in a variety of ways, there is a set rhythm to the agricultural year. Nusa Tenggara is subject to a long dry season, followed by brief monsoonal rains. Subsistence is more heavily dependent than elsewhere in Indonesia on dryland crops such as maize, sorghum, mung beans, or millet, which are at the mercy of the rains. Rice is planted wherever there are sufficient supplies of water, but in most areas, the rice harvest does not yield enough for daily consumption. Rice is thus a prestige food reserved for ceremonial feasts.

When the seeds have been planted, social life enters a dormant period. In Sumba, this is referred to specifically as the "bitter period." Silence is supposed to reign. No gongs or drums may be beaten and no large public ceremonies should be held. In practical terms, this is also the time when food stocks begin to run low and the population must carefully husband its remaining resources. There are numerous ritual prohibitions to be observed at this time. With the coming of the harvest, these prohibitions are lifted—the ceremonial silence is broken and the rituals of the new year may begin.

On Lombok, Sumba and Savu, the coming of new life is heralded by the swarming of a particular type of seaworm (*Eunice* sp.) generally known as *nale* or *nyale*. (See "The Pasola," page 184.) This seaworm attaches itself permanently to the undersides of reef rocks and, in accordance with a set lunar and tidal rhythm, releases its posterior parts. These free-swimming sexual segments rise to the surface, turning the waters of the shore line into what looks like boiling, slightly greenish spaghetti. It is an orgiastic expression of the coming of new life, and people gather them by the bucketful to eat.

The ceremonial cycle

Travelers to this part of the world who want to witness something of the rich ceremonial life of the islands must visit during the lively period of the year, generally beginning sometime in February and continuing through October. From November through January, there are few ceremonies, and the monsoon rains inhibit local travel.

Whenever one visits, remember that even the simplest of activities is endowed with significance that may not at first sight be apparent. It takes time to appreciate life on these islands.

—James J. Fox

Opposite: *Chin ornaments provide an unusual touch to the costume of this dancer from East Flores.* **Above:** *Smiling after a bout of tears, this little girl from western Sumba models her family's traditional finery, including thick ivory bracelets.*

RELIGION

Visions of Duality and Balance

Official statistics present a rather neat, but somewhat inaccurate picture of Indonesia's religious landscape: 88 percent Muslim, 5.8 percent Protestant, 2.9 percent Catholic, 2 percent Hindu and 0.9 percent Buddhist. A marginal "other" category is listed as those "who do not yet have a religion."

These categories are unevenly distributed over the many islands of the archipelago, but there is a general trend that the further east one goes, the more Christians and "others" one encounters.

In Nusa Tenggara, Lombok and Sumbawa in the west are predominantly Muslim. There is a Christian majority on the islands of Flores, Roti and Timor. Sumba, the last island in the group to come under colonial control, and Savu are still strongholds of local ancestral religion.

Traveling through the region however, one soon becomes aware of quite another religious reality, which seems to belie the official statistics. The visitor meets with traditional religious life of great richness and diversity, only thinly veiled by the uniform drapery of the great universal religions. This is perhaps most pronounced in the ostensibly Christian areas, although there are traditional sects among the Muslims as well, for example the Wetu Telu in Lombok (See "Wetu Telu," page 54).

At first one is impressed by the diverse coloring of local traditions, and the region seems a patchwork of highly distinctive local cultures, each differing even from its close neighbors. But a rather basic pattern can be seen in this bewildering complexity. This pattern provides a key to understanding the religious culture of the region, even in its official vestments.

Guided by a dream

Imagine a group of settlers moving into new territory in Nusa Tenggara. They may have left their village because of population pres-

sure, village wars or internal strife. Whatever the reason, they certainly will carry with them some sacred objects: a sword, a sacred drum, or maybe soil and water from their place of origin. These objects will link the new village with the old one.

Having decided upon a place of settlement, guided by a dream or some other kind of divination, they will have to come to terms with the original inhabitants and spiritual owners of the land: the divinities of mountain, forest and water. These powers are still wild and dangerous, keeping the area "hot" and unfit for human habitation. However, by putting up an altar of "rock and tree" and sprinkling the stone with sacrificial blood, a covenant is made.

The unruly powers of the local landscape are invited or even pressed to take up their "seat" in the altar stones—in this way becoming the divine protectors of the community. The leader of the band of settlers, representing the human partners of the deal, promises to fulfill all ritual obligations. By this procedure, which is repeated when the new fields are laid out, the area is "cooled" and made fit for human activity.

The religious bond between people and landscape is strengthened when the founders and first cultivators have died and are worshipped as ancestors. Their megalithic tombs, enshrining their memory, encircle the village-plaza with the rock and tree, and their deified spirits take their seats in the high-peaked *adat* houses. They mediate between their living descendants and the powers of nature, keeping a close watch on the fulfillment of the specific terms of the founding covenant. At first they are intermediaries, but with time their cult tends to merge with those of the village gods, and they become divine themselves.

The senior living male descendant of the founding ancestor is the Tuan Tanah, "Lord of the Land" in Indonesian. He divides the communal fields for cultivation, initiates the agricultural activities, and officiates at the great fertility rituals. His house harbors the sacred heirlooms of the community and has the most important village altars on its doorstep. As Tuan Tanah he is heir to the "first deal" with the local powers of nature, and acts as the ritual leader of the village.

Presiding over the first deal was a divinity,

Opposite: *Marapu priests in West Sumba ride their horses to the sea to greet the yearly arrival of the* nyale *seaworms and prepare for the Pasola.*

the highest of all, who is the ultimate audience of all prayers and ritual activity. This divinity's name cannot be pronounced. In most of eastern Indonesia he is imagined as double-gendered, the female/male aspect representing the complementary union of "Mother Earth" and "Father Heaven." This double identity, which is shared by the higher powers of nature, is most visibly expressed by the village altar: a tree sheltering the rock, just as Father Heaven shelters Mother Earth.

Inside and outside

The higher gods and ancestors can not be addressed directly. Some kind of mediation is required. Ritual orators, acting as spokesmen for the sponsoring family or village, call first on a long chain of spirit-messengers, village deities and ancestors, before communication can be established with the highest powers. This type of communication makes use of a formalized ceremonial language—the language of the ancestors—which employs twin-groupings of parallel sentences.

The coupled sentences, conveying concrete and vivid images, mirror the double identity of the higher spiritual powers and have been likened to "arrows pointing at a hidden target."

This principle of complementary duality pervades all aspects of life and thought: from marriage relations to agricultural activities and even political structure. It is the main way of ordering the world. The most general and important of these complementary oppositions are those between "female" and "male," and "inside" and "outside." The "mountain/sea" opposition is of special importance for orientation, "cool/hot" is important in a ritual context, and "elder/younger" in a social one. All these envision a totality: a scheme of cosmic dimensions, in which all things are continually born from and return to an underlying unity, their source or origin.

Human beings have a special responsibility for securing and maintaining this circulating flow through ritual. Some, of course, have greater responsibilities than others. The Tuan Tanah is considered the first-born, the elder brother, and he is to stay home and guard the rock and tree of the cosmic parents. His "younger brother," with whom he shares authority and who usually belongs to another lineage, has to go outside to patrol the boundaries of the sacred domain.

The Tuan Tanah is associated with the "inside," cooling the area with fertility rituals, and is as such symbolically classified as "female." His "male" counterpart represents political power, and might, for example, lead the men in a head-hunting expedition to replenish the dwindling vitality of the soil with trophies brought in from the "outside." From a perspective outside the group, however, both men belong to the sacred center,

the source or place of origin, from which fertility and well-being flows out over the whole domain.

The activities of the two leaders, working together in a system of "dual sovereignty," follow the seasonal rhythm of the monsoon. The dry season is the period of the head-hunting expeditions, the village wars and the season of the great hunt. It is a period of "ritual heat," ending with the preparation of the swidden fields by cutting and burning. Only then, after the world has been "heated-up," can one await the cooling and fertilizing rains of the west monsoon.

Sumba: spirits and stone

Sumba is the only island of eastern Indonesia where a majority of the population still follows the ways of their ancestors. The official census-cards even have a special column, making it possible to register as worshipper of *agama* Marapu, "the Marapu religion."

In East Sumba, *marapu* refers only to the deified ancestors of the lineages and clans, who have dispersed over the villages and settlements of several traditional domains. In the western part of the island the term has a more general use: it refers to everything connected with the invisible world of gods, spirits and ancestors.

Traditionally, the ancestral villages of a domain were located on hilltops and protected by thick walls of stone or cactus hedge. Inside, two rows of high peaked traditional houses—the cult-houses of different lineages—face each other across the village plaza. In the plaza are the altars of the protecting deities, the skull-tree for the display of the head-hunting trophies, and the megalithic tombs of the founding ancestors.

In West Sumba the traditional houses are often found in a circular or oval arrangement. These ancestral villages are the "place of origin" for many other villages and hamlets, and come to life only during the dry season, when the dispersed members of the group return to participate in the ceremonies of their "mother house." Usually one recognizes a kind of "capital village," where the cult-house of the founding lineage of the domain is located.

One of the most spectacular ceremonies is the festive dragging of the enormous tomb-stones, which are to shelter the bones of the ancestors and will forever enshrine the "fame" of the sponsoring family. At one time, hundreds of buffaloes and pigs were killed to feed the spirit of the stone and make the long

At this point the tree is still considered 'hot' and dangerous, and is kept covered. Women should take care, as the ngadhu is still wild and lustful, and might rape them!

journey possible. (In 1988 the government set a five-animal limit, to keep families from impoverishing themselves.)

The stone has a shifting identity. When first quarried, it is welcomed as a "young bride," and carried by the "bride-takers" on a kind of boat-sledge to its destination. In the village, the stone switches gender, and he is festively honored as a "victorious warrior."

Finally, after the necessary preparations, the stone is placed as a soul-carrying "male" buffalo over the womb-like cavity of the "female" tomb. Richly decorated with symbols of wealth, the megalithic tomb presents a fitting memorial to the enduring wealth and power of the sponsoring lineage.

Flores: the outside within

The *ngadhu,* a carved wooden post about three meters high crowned by a conical roof of palm fiber, is by far the most distinctive cult construction within the Ngada villages in the Bajawa district of central West Flores. The *ngadhu* carries the name of the male ancestor of a lineage and forms a pair with a little thatched *bhaga* house, dedicated to the female ancestors. Together with the *peo,* a stone sliver about one meter high which serves as a sacrificial stake, they constitute one ceremonial unit.

The *ngadhu, bhaga* and *peo* are placed in a line, along the east–west axis of the village. Ritually, they are connected with the cult house, the tombs and the other megalithic structures of the lineage. Dominating the village square between the two rows of confronting houses, the several *ngadhu*-sets serve as striking symbols of ancestral "inside" protection.

However, the *ngadhu,* for which only the hard, red wood of the *hebu* tree can be used, must be taken from the forest, the very heart of the "outside." This is a difficult, costly and dangerous undertaking, in the course of which many fowl, buffaloes and pigs have to be sacrificed. After a tree has been selected by divination, it is dug out with its roots intact. Then the branches are cut, leaving the "horns" of a two-pronged fork.

At this point the tree is still considered to be extremely "hot" and dangerous, and is kept covered with red cloth. After some introductory rituals, in which the distance between "outside" and "inside" is gradually overcome, the forked post is finally welcomed inside the village by a festive ceremonial gathering.

Women should still take care, however, as the *ngadhu* is still wild and lustful, and might rape them! Only after the trunk has been "tattooed" by carvings, and planted in its foot-covering of stone and earth, is it cooled and tamed. At this stage it becomes worthy to receive the ancestral presence.

Before the *ngadhu* is constructed, the female *bhaga* house has to be built. It shelters the main participants in the proceedings. The *bhaga* functions like a womb, from which the fiery ancestral deity is born. After the complete unit has been installed, the *peo,* with more modest ritual accompaniment, is erected. The *peo* will become the focus of a sacrificial arena, where the blood of many buffaloes is shed to restore the exhausted vitality of the soil.

Timor: milk and semen

Among the Mambai of East Timor, "rock and tree" do not just mark the center of their domain, but constitute the very essence and meaning of their lives.

This altar evokes the union of Mother Earth and Father Heaven, which generates and maintains the flow of life. The altar is a round, tiered structure of rocks and earth, built around a three-pronged altar pole, on which Father Heaven descends at the great seasonal rituals.

The rocks and post are connected with the most important cult-houses, the "Black House" for Mother Earth, and the "White House" for Father Heaven, and also with the great banyan tree which protects and shelters the people of the village. This rather impressive ceremonial complex ultimately centers on a stone crater in the middle of the altar, usually concealed by grasses or ferns.

The Mambai Mother Earth and Father Heaven were formed from the body-substance of a formless and undifferentiated First Being, who kept them inside the hollow of its navel. Impregnated by her brother, Mother Earth was the first to descend from

After being guided to the ancestral mountains, the souls of the dead rise up to the sky, in nebulous exhalations, to gather in the black rain-clouds from which new life is born.

her formless place of origin, and gave birth to the first mountain. The birth fluids then created a primordial sea. Later, Father Heaven reunited with his sister on the top of the mountain, and the first trees, grasses and people were born. Then, Mother Earth fell ill and died.

Her agony was protracted, until she found a final resting place under the rock and tree. Here, she is still watched over and cared for by the ritual guardians of the altar, who in this way repay their debt for the gift of life.

The most important task of the guardians, representing the Mambai as a people, is to re-establish the contact between Mother Earth and Father Heaven, which was broken when the Father recoiled in horror from the blackened and putrefying corpse of his wife. The decomposing flesh of the Mother produced the black and fertile earth, while her white essence was kept untouched and entered as "milk" into the pure waters of the underground.

The sexual reunion of the cosmic pair, brought about by the festive clamor of gong and drum, is thought to result in the arrival of the rains. The eagerly awaited monsoon rains, which usually arrive in November or December, are the cooling and fertilizing "white semen" of Father Heaven. However, each of the two principles that make up a pair are considered the other's essence, thus the semen has risen from the "milky" waters of the sub-soil!

The meteorological cycle, in which the dampness of earth and sea is transformed into life-giving rains, also provides a vehicle for the recycling of souls. The souls of the dead are first guided to the ancestral mountain in the interior and then, after some time, carried by boat to the sea. From there they rise up in the sky, in nebulous exhalations, to gather in the black rain-clouds from which new life is born.

—*Coen Pepplinkhuizen*

Lombok

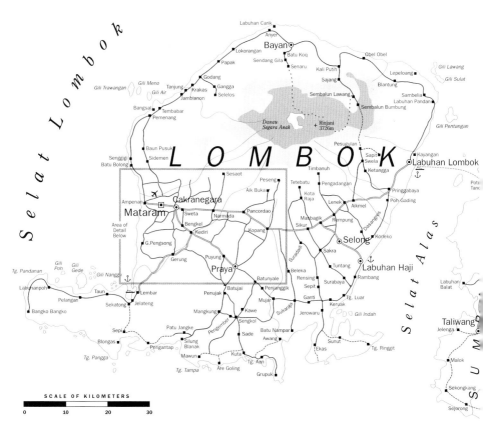

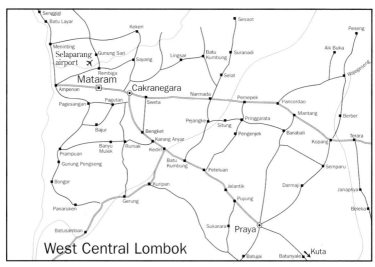

West Central Lombok

PART II

Introducing Lombok

For better or worse, Lombok has become Indonesia's new "in" destination. The more than 100,000 foreign tourists who yearly visit the island represent just a fraction of the number landing in Bali, but this figure is sure to rise as the many new hotels being constructed open for business. All the good beach properties, even in areas that today are only accessible by jeep, have been snapped up by big business interests from Jakarta.

Comparisons with neighboring Bali are inevitable. Lombok's area and population—4,739 square kilometers and 2.3 million people—are both just slightly smaller than Bali's. And there is a cultural connection between the two islands. Some 85,000 Balinese live in West Lombok, descendants of 18th Century invaders. Lombok's Balinese maintain a network of temples and perform rituals like their relatives back home. But other than this minority the culture of the two islands is quite distinct. The natives of Lombok, the Sasaks, are Muslims, and their art and religious life are quite different from those of their Hindu neighbors.

The name 'Lombok' is said to come from a fiery red pepper, used as a condiment in Indonesia, although this may be a folk etymology. The Sasaks call their island Bumi Gora, which means "The Dry Farmland," or Selaparang, which is the name of an old East Lombok kingdom.

With a bit of poetic licence, the bonnet-like shape of Lombok resembles the roof of a *lumbung,* the traditional rice storage barn. The island measures about 80 kilometers north to south and about 70 kilometers east to west. A prominent peninsula extends west from the southwest corner, and a smaller peninsula juts out from the southeast.

There are several clusters of small islands off Lombok's coast, all called "Gili" from the Sasak word for island. Some are inhabited by fisherman and stray cattle, and the best-known—Gili Air, Gili Meno, and Gili Trawangan, off the northwest coast—host hordes of young, mostly European tourists, especially in July, August and September.

The Rinjani volcano

Lombok is dominated by 3,726-meter Gunung Rinjani, Indonesia's highest volcano and one of the highest points in the archipelago (4,884-meter Puncak Jayakesuma in Irian Jaya, Indonesian New Guinea, is the highest.) Rinjani crowns a group of mountains that dominate the north-central section of the island. Most of the rainfall striking these mountains flows south, irrigating a large, rich agricultural area. Elsewhere on the island, the landscape is more barren, and planting is only possible during Lombok's rainy season, the October–March northwest monsoon.

The coastal hills to the south, with average elevations around 500 meters, do not form a watershed, but drop spectacularly into the sea. These cliffs frame beautiful bays and sandy coves. Other than the harbors at Lembar, in the crook of the southwestern peninsula, and Labuhan Lombok, in the northeast, only the south coast is blessed with any decent bays.

The strait between Bali and Lombok marks a very important ecological boundary, first discovered by the great 19th century biologist, Sir Alfred Russel Wallace. In his travels through the archipelago, Wallace noticed that the range of Asiatic animal and plant species, which extends through the Greater Sunda islands of Sumatra and Java, drops off sharply after Bali. The flora and fauna of Lombok, just across the Lombok Strait, bear a greater similarity to species found in Australia.

Wallace drew a line along this boundary, which became known as the Wallace Line.

Overleaf: Topeng *masks show the Balinese influence on Lombok. The Balinese dominated western Lombok for almost two centuries.*

Modern botanists and zoologists have refined Wallace's findings, and now think of a zone of transition, dubbed Wallacea, rather than a sharply delineated boundary. (See "Flora and Fauna," page 24.)

Early history of Lombok

Little is known of Lombok's prehistory. The Sasak language, like most languages spoken in the archipelago, is Austronesian. The Austronesians, originating in mainland Asia began expanding from Taiwan around 5,000 years ago to populate the Philippines, Indonesia and the South Pacific islands.

Lombok is mentioned in the 14th century chronicle of the great East Javanese Majapahit empire as a dependency. The only copy of the chronicle itself, the *Negara-kertagama*, was found in the late 19th century in the small Lombok village of Pagutan, just outside of Mataram. In this period there were undoubtedly many local chiefs in Lombok, each controlling an area with a few villages. Occasionally one of these small-time rulers, who glorified themselves with the title "Raja," succeeded in controlling a larger area, which was soon broken up again. For a while, an "empire" of sorts, called Selaparang, controlled a region in eastern Lombok.

Islam was introduced to Lombok in the first half of the 16th century from Java by either Sunan Giri or Pangeran Sangopati, or both. Pangeran Sangopati was the same man who was known in Bali as Pedanda Bau Rau, and in Sumbawa as Tuan Haji Semeru. These first Muslims preached a syncretic version of Islam, which blended with indigenous animism and Hinduism. Several early accounts concur that Lombok's first and most important mosque was the one still maintained in Bayan, in the north.

In the 17th century, cultural and religious influences reached Lombok from another direction—Sulawesi. The Islamic kingdom of Makassar (now Ujung Pandang), allied with nearby Bima in Sumbawa, held some political control over eastern Lombok.

The Balinese arrive

In pre-Islamic times, the Balinese rajadom of Klungkung exercised a great deal of influence in Lombok. But it was Balinese from Karangasem who first conquered western Lombok, just after Islam was first introduced there from Java. This conquest was aided by Banjar Getas, the *patih* (prime minister) of the Sasak kingdom of Pejanggiq. Apparently the king of the region had seduced his wife

after sending him away on business. After the Balinese victory, Banjar Getas was rewarded with lands and wealth. Later, the Balinese turned against his son and heir who, with his followers, was defeated in what became known as the First Praya War.

Although the Balinese controlled the west, for a long time they remained there are the east was protected by a thick forest, which existed until the early years of this century. In 1678, the Balinese crossed the forest and, with the help of some discontented Sasak aristocrats, laid waste to the Selaparang court. But it was another 150 years before the Balinese established hegemony in East Lombok.

The Balinese introduced their irrigated rice-growing techniques but otherwise had little cultural effect on the eastern Sasaks, who maintained their Islamic faith.

Between 1775 and 1838 the Balinese feuded among themselves, thus allowing the Sasak aristocrats in the east to regain a measure of independence. But in 1838, the Balinese at Mataram emerged firmly in charge. Not only had they defeated their rivals in nearby Cakranegara—whose end was marked by a mass suicidal charge called a *puputan*—but also the rajadom of Karangasem in Bali, the former feudal overlords of the Balinese on Lombok.

The Mataram Balinese then established control of eastern Lombok, ending the period of independence of the Sasak nobility and villages of the east. The peasants of east Lombok were turned into serfs. Used to their autonomy, they revolted—in 1855, 1871 and 1891—and were crushed by the Balinese, who were supported by the Sasaks from the western half of the island.

In spite of his military expenses, the Balinese raja of Lombok became extremely rich thanks to his control over trade, land tax and corvée labor. Between 1850 and 1890, the towns of Mataram and Cakra became filled with spacious palaces, public drinking fountains and illuminated main streets.

Contemporary accounts describe the Raja of Lombok as almost certainly the wealthiest indigenous ruler in the eastern part of the Indonesian archipelago. This information, together with reports—later proved false—of tin deposits, was enough to rouse Holland's interest in the island.

The Dutch in Lombok

The Dutch, who had run trade operations in the region since the 17th century, had signed

a treaty the Balinese rulers of Lombok in which they stated they would never annex the island. Still, in 1894, on the pretext of a Sasak revolt, the Dutch invaded Lombok.

The Dutch army, equipped with modern European weapons, was soundly defeated by the Balinese defenders. More than 100 Dutch soldiers died, including the force's second-in-command, General Van Hamm. It was a total rout. The Dutch could not afford to lose face, nor could they afford to reveal how thinly their forces were stretched across the archipelago. Angry, and with reinforcements, they returned.

Mataram was burned to the ground. Then the Dutch advanced to the last Balinese stronghold, Cakranegara. The crown prince, Anak Agung Ketut, was killed and the old raja sent into exile to Batavia. But the Balinese were still tough opponents, and many expired in a suicidal *puputan* rather than submit to the Dutch.

The victory was not easy for Holland, and the Dutch forces suffered several hundred casualties. But the survivors were well rewarded for their pains by looting the raja's treasure chamber. Measuring three by five meters, this room was 60 centimeters deep in rijksdaalers. A smaller vault was filled with gold coins, precious stones and a number of priceless ornaments.

The Sasaks, who had requested the Dutch intervention, found themselves ruled by new masters, who were much harsher than the Balinese. Taxes were heavy and the Sasak men were forced into the heavy labor of road construction. Colonial rule in Lombok led to unprecedented economic exploitation and the impoverishment of the majority of the peasants. Many were dispossessed of their lands and became paupers.

The Dutch ruled Lombok indirectly, through Balinese and Sasak aristocrats, who had to give up most of their revenues to the colonial powers. Still, the collaborating rulers were able to concentrate land ownership.

Thanks to corvée labor, the Dutch built a series of nine dams which greatly increased rice production. But the population grew fast, and the peasants' average daily rice intake actually declined—from 400 grams in 1900 to 300 grams in 1940. The Balinese rajas had always required 50 percent of the rice harvest as tribute, but the Dutch by 1940 were insisting on 80 percent, and this was just one among a host of taxes. Things got even worse during the Japanese occupation, when the Sasaks faced starvation and terror.

After Indonesia's declaration of independence in 1945, Lombok became part of the Dutch-controlled East Indies Federation,

Above: *Deserted beaches stretch along Lombok's south coast. Access is difficult because of the cliffs, but the best have been bought up by speculators betting on the current tourist boom.*

which covered the eastern part of the archipelago. In 1949, when Indonesian independence became effective, Lombok was made part of the Lesser Sunda province. In 1951, the province of Nusa Tenggara Barat was created, with its capital at Mataram. Today, Lombok is split into three political districts, or *kabupaten*—West, Central and East—with their capitals at, respectively, Mataram, Praya and Selong.

Sasak art and culture

The Sasaks never developed the arts to the same degree as their Balinese neighbors. There remains some good traditional craftwork—weaving, basket-making and pottery—but nothing that approaches the handicrafts of the Balinese. Nor have recent attempts at the modernization of the crafts industry, to produce items for sale to tourists, produced outstanding pieces.

Lombok has been famous for its *ikat* cloth, but since tourists are not willing to pay the cost of a fine piece of cloth, hand-spun thread and natural dyes are being abandoned in favor of cheap, ready-made replacements.

A low-tech program to market local pottery—partially funded by the government of New Zealand—has enjoyed a measure of success, putting added cash income into the pockets of the three villages selected for the pilot program. The island's potters are considered excellent craftsmen. Also among the best of the local crafts in Lombok are baskets, finely woven from strips of rattan, banana leaves and other vegetal fibers.

Sasak dances and ceremonies also seem somewhat less splendid that the lavish ceremonies of the Hindu Balinese. The main right of passage for a Sasak boy is his circumcision. During this ritual, he is dressed in finery and carried about on a large wooden horse. Muslim weddings, most of which take place after the harvest when funds are plentiful, are also lavish affairs. (Harvest time varies. Rice is planted in October or November, and the new short-season rice is ready 3 months later; the traditional tall, long-grain rice is ready in 5 months.)

Circumcisions are often performed in the Muslim month of Muhammad's birthday. (See "Travel Advisory," page 239, for information on the Muslim calendar.) The ceremonies are often accompanied by ritual fights, called *peresehan* or *berempuk.* In these, men face off, armed with tough rattan staffs and buffalo skin shields.

Blood flows freely in these exciting battles, which are not for faint-hearted spectators. *Peresehan* fights are also held in conjunction with national or local celebrations and, occasionally, as part of an agricultural ritual asking for rain.

Milder versions of the fights are sometimes put on for tourists, and in these the men limit themselves to whacking each

other's shields. Although there is lots of noise, there is no bloodshed.

The Wetu Telu

Most of the people of Lombok are Muslims, but one group, traditionalists to the core, have refused to give up their ancient ways. Their religion and culture goes under the name of Islam Wetu Telu, which roughly means "Three Times Islam." There is no agreement as to what the "three" refers to, although many explanations are given.

Wetu Telu is not one of Indonesia's "official" religions, so no statistics on the total number of practitioners are available. Many are concentrated in the northern part of the island. One estimate suggests that there are 5,000 in the Bayan area, 6,000 in the Tanjung/Gangga district, 10,000 in East Lombok and 7,000 in Central Lombok. Government sources usually list a number between 0 and 3,000.

Although the Wetu Telu are sheltered somewhat by their partial acceptance of Islam, they face a great deal of pressure from the more orthodox Sasak Muslims to conform (see "Wetu Telu," page 54).

Farming and development

Some of Lombok's inhabitants have begun to benefit from the jobs and increased craft sales resulting from the recent tourist boom, but the vast majority remain subsistence farmers, perpetually facing land shortages and fearing inadequate water supplies. In spite of the widespread government birth-control program, the island's population density remains extremely high. Indeed, Lombok surpasses even Bali in number of inhabitants relative to arable land.

The transmigration program, in which some of Lombok's excess population is shipped to underpopulated islands, has helped reduce population pressures, but there are still too many people for the land to

support. Lombok leads the nation in the unenviable categories of infant mortality and illiteracy. Many of those who receive some education go to Islamic schools, which are fine for teaching religion and Arabic, but do little to prepare young men and women for opportunities in an expanding economy.

The government is making commendable progress in some areas. A pilot children's vaccination program against the prevalent hepatitis B shows signs of progress even among conservative rural people. The quality

of the drinking water is being improved, in an effort to reduce the number of cases of cholera. And malaria, which has been a widespread problem, particularly in the north, has begun to receive attention. The number of clinics and trained personnel staffing them are steadily increasing.

Health programs are not immediately visible to casual visitors, but other government programs are: rural electrification, the construction of dams and, especially, the fast improving network of paved road on the island. While some of the new roads aim to provide easy access to tourist areas, many others link out of the way villages to main roads and markets.

The heartland of Lombok, an irregularly shaped triangle with its base on the west and its apex around Pringgabaya in the east, has always been the island's rice bowl and regularly produces a large surplus. The area is rich in rice paddies or *sawah*s, and the landscape looks a lot like Bali or Java. Irrigation developments are slowly adding to the hectarage of *sawah*s. New varieties of high-yield-

Opposite: *A woman refreshes the exposed leaves of her* kangkung, *a tasty vegetable here being grown in the Jangkok river in Ampenan.* **Above, left:** *Transplanting young rice shoots into a flooded* sawah. **Above, right:** *High grade tobacco, grown in the dry south, is Lombok's most lucrative cash crop.*

ing, fast growing rice help boost production, but locals prefer the taste of the old, slow-maturing variety. In the markets, the old rice sells for a premium price.

Thanks to government advice and encouragement, most farmers now practice crop rotation, planting soybeans after one or two crops of rice. In the drier areas, especially to the south of the fertile triangle, many fields are now planted in high-grade tobacco, which is dried in local kilns and sold to a large company for export to Java and abroad. Tobacco has become Lombok's largest cash crop. The island's farmers also export *areca* nuts, beans, chili peppers, cinnamon, coffee, onions, plants used in herbal medicines—and recently, cloves, pepper and vanilla.

Exports and tourism

In value, high grade pumice leads all of the island's exports, fetching $1.4 million during just the first six months of 1990. The pumice boom started in 1985, and much of the production is shipped to Hong Kong where it is used in making stone-washed jeans, as well as cosmetics and floor-scrubbing material.

There are several pearl farms in Lombok, which are run as joint ventures with the Japanese, who first discovered years ago how to "seed" pearl oysters then keep them alive. The yearly value of Lombok's pearl production is over $1 million.

One of the newer crops is seaweed, which is processed into carrageenan. Carrageenan is used to add creaminess to foods and cosmetics. Sprigs of the seaweed *Eucheuma* sp. are tied to strings and staked to the bottom or to floating frames in the quiet shallows just offshore. Although the price varies with the world market, because of the importance of processed food, this ecologically sound crop has proved a reliable source of local income.

Most of Lombok's fisherman serve the local market, but the crop from shrimp farms is exported, and milkfish fry (*Chanos*) are netted and sent live to Java to grow out in the rice paddies. *Trepang* (sea cucumbers), collected on the reefs, are dried and sent to Singapore, Hong Kong and Taiwan, where they provide an important ingredient in Chinese haute cuisine.

Although agricultural and sea products bring cash to Lombok's economy, tourism has given the island its major boost. The construction industry is booming. Crafts sales—pottery, woven cloth, baskets—both for local sale and for export to the tourist markets of Bali, have also grown.

So far only the Senggigi Beach area has sprouted full scale resort hotels, but the Kuta beach area is slated for star-ranked hotels soon. Several spots along the south coast of Lombok, now still hard to reach, offer beautiful scenery and white sand beaches, and the big boys from Jakarta have already bought up all of these paradises, on which they plan to build deluxe accommodations—or just to speculate on the price of the land. And no one buys just a few hectares—it's all sold in 100-hectare chunks.

In order to fill all the expected hotel rooms, the government is planning a huge international airport, probably to be located southeast of Praya. Construction is slated to begin in the mid to late 1990s.

The land-sale boom has put unheard of sums into the pockets of a few locals, and many now sell to finance an expensive pilgrimage to Mecca. (Current cost: about $3,000 a head if organized by the government, two to five times higher if handled by a travel agency). Although many return as respected hajis, having sold their land they face poverty.

Visiting Lombok

Most foreign visitors currently settle in the west coast beach resort of Senggigi, or on one of the "Three Gilis" a bit further north. Tourists are also beginning to discover the Kuta beach area of the south. Although there are several mountain resort areas on the south slope of Gunung Rinjani, most tourists head for the beaches.

You can see the "essential" Lombok in a one-day tour offered by several travel agencies and free-lancers out of Senggigi. This usually includes a look at a couple of Balinese temples, weaving at Sukarara village, pottery at Penujak, the traditional village-for-tourists of Sade and Kuta beach with the adjacent bay at Tanjung Aan. While this suffices for the visitors who have trouble tearing themselves away from the beach, there is a lot more to Lombok. Seeing the rest of the island, however, requires a bit of initiative.

The roads of Lombok, most of them already paved, are improving fast. The best road, wide and smooth, connects the Lembar harbor with the three-city urban area at Mataram, then heads east across the island to the ferry port of Labuhan Lombok.

A road of similar quality connects the Central Lombok district capital of Praya with the east–west trunk highway. The East Lombok capital of Selong is also connected to

the highway by a good road, which continues to the small fishing village of Labuhan Haji on the east coast, whence the pilgrims to Mecca used to depart.

Cidomos are the main traffic problem on the roads of Lombok. These horse-drawn passenger and freight carts are ubiquitous, and often hold up cars and *bemos*. By some miracle, the poor horses seem to survive all the swerving vehicles. In my many travels around Lombok, I saw only one dead cart horse, which had just been struck by a hit-and-run truck. The cart-driver's face was a pitiful sight as he struggled to hide his despair. A good *cidomo* horse can cost around $175, and most drivers rent the horse and cart—for which they are personally responsible—from the owners.

The term used for these contraptions, *cidomo*, comes from the first two letters of three different words: *cikar,* meaning a hand-drawn cart in Sasak, *dokar,* from the more common Indonesian word for a horse-drawn carriage, and *mobil,* from automobile, for the two car tires used.

The paved back-roads of Lombok are often potholed and narrow, but work is progressing in many areas to improve and widen the surfaces, along with the building of lateral drainage canals. It's on these roads, where your vehicle has to travel more slowly, that you become the target of the children's especially shrill "Turis! Turis!" This unwanted attention is the price you pay to visit places off the tourist track. There's no sense in getting agitated. Just grin and bear it.

Small as it is, you will need several days and lots of driving to see all of Lombok. Vehicles, mostly 4–6 passenger mini-vans, are widely available for rent, with a driver and an English-speaking guide. These vehicles can reach most areas of Lombok, but to see some sections of the rugged south coast, where the island's best coastal scenery lies, you will need an experienced driver and either a jeep (locally called "hardtop") or a Kijang (a locally assembled utility vehicle) in good shape.

Organization of this section

The travel section following has been divided to roughly correspond to Lombok's three districts: West, Central and East. If a particular road cuts across a district boundary, we follow it to avoid confusion. We have also added a jeep-or-Kijang section, dusty and bouncy, but rewarding for the adventurous.

You can see the island by making a series of day-trips from Senggigi or the Mataram area or, to avoid backtracking, sleep in *losmen* along the way. If you choose the second alternative, you will have to pay for your driver's and guide's accommodations and food.

Above: *Traditional fights with rattan sticks result in more than just bruised egos. In many areas, the fights accompany ritual celebrations.*

DANCE AND MUSIC

A Rich Performing Arts Tradition

Visitors to Lombok should expect neither the vibrant dance and music of Bali nor the cultural refinement of Java. In Lombok, artistic activity is strong in certain villages and rare in others, but cultural performances are far less frequent than in Bali. In the few remaining traditional villages of Lombok, the performing arts are considered important community contributions, but they are not encouraged in modern or strongly Islamic villages.

Although Lombok seems culturally impoverished when compared to Java and Bali, it is rich in arts when compared to the other islands of Nusa Tenggara. And for its size, the variety of dance, music and theater forms found in Lombok is remarkable.

A variety of influences

Dance and music are directly tied to cultural identity in Lombok. They are used in many ritual settings and believed to embody religious values. Some Sasak traditions are associated with the minority of nominal Muslims known as the Wetu Telu (see "Wetu Telu," page 54) and others with the majority of orthodox Muslims, called Wetu Lima. Religion and performing arts have become deeply intertwined, which has caused heated arguments about the arts, Islam, and tourism as the orthodox population tries to eliminate the arts and culture of the Wetu Telu.

The Sasak received various artistic influences over the last millennium, first from the Javanese, who brought Hinduism, Islam, the shadow play and poetry. Later, during the period of Balinese colonization (1740–1894), the Balinese brought theater, dance, new musical instruments, and a new tonality in music. Together, the Balinese and Javanese influences constitute a very important stream of cultural concepts which have affected not only the performing arts of Lombok, but also the island's architecture, agricultural practices, and *adat* (customary practice).

A second stream of influence came through Sumatra, Malaysia, and the Arab world; this was a later arrival and is the origin of the different religious literature and theater forms. These two streams remain alive today. Balinese influence can still be seen in new music and dance forms, and Middle Eastern influences continue to evolve musical forms associated with Islam. Virtually all Sasak music and dance traditions reflect these two streams of influence, adapted to the environment and identity of Lombok.

Lombok's performing arts are often divided into "traditional" and "contemporary," the latter meaning "Islamic." The traditional arts are associated with an early form of religious practice combining elements of ancestor worship, animism, and Hindu/Buddhism with Islam. Because of pressure from orthodox Muslims, these arts rapidly declined and would likely have disappeared entirely if not for government policy, which has sought to support traditional arts to retain cultural identity and entice tourists to Lombok. Traditional music now consists of various forms of *gamelan* orchestras and sung poetry, the *tembang Sasak.*

The large Balinese minority in West Lombok retain their temple festivals and performing arts. Chief among these are the ritual *canang sari* dance performed only at temple festivals, and the *gamelan gong kuna,* a ceremonial orchestra unlike any in Bali.

Pre-Islamic *gamelan* and dance

The instruments of Sasak *gamelan*—large gongs, gong-chimes with rows of kettles, double-headed drums, cymbals—are clearly related to the Java-Bali stream of influence and especially to Bali. The names of the instruments, the style of play, the interlocking musical parts, the scales used, and even the musicians' costumes are similar to those found in Bali, yet are not Balinese.

The basic traditional *gamelan* is the *gamelan oncer,* also called *kendang belek.* These *gamelan* play instrumentals, accompany vocalists, and accompany theater, but they are particularly famous for the *tari oncer* or *kendang belek* dance in which two musicians play single large drums and dance together. The dance is non-narrative, but the dancers strike dramatic poses and confront one another, while dancing with large steps and heightened energy as in strong Balinese

Opposite: *Large drums are featured in the* kendang belek *dance, in which two men strike dramatic poses and confront each other.*

dance. Then, as the intensity rises, they play rapid, interlocking parts on the drums until the gong stroke, whereupon the energy relaxes and the dancers again move slowly.

Some ritual *gamelan* similar to the *gamelan oncer* exist in remote communities. In villages of the Boda, who are ancient Sasak Buddhists, the sacred *gamelan jerujeng* is used to invoke the ancestral deities for religious festivals. In Bayan, a northern village known for its rich *adat,* the sacred *gamelan* Maulid performs only on Muhammad's birthday. These ensembles, which play slow, sedate music, can neither be seen nor played outside of their religious contexts.

The *gamelan tambur* or *gamelan baris* of Lingsar in West Lombok is another sacred ensemble. This *gamelan* features the *tambur* drum and is used to accompany the ritual *batek baris* dance.

Stately processionals

Batek baris is a military processional, performed in Lingsar and several other villages, featuring dancers wearing old Dutch army costumes and carrying wooden rifles. A stern "commandant," barks orders in a combination of Sasak and Dutch. The *batek baris* dancers lead a procession, including *batek* and *telek* dancers, to sacred springs.

The *telek* dance, though loosely based on a legend concerning a princess in love with a commoner, is usually non-narrative when performed and features the simple hand, eye and feet movements characteristic of Sasak dance. At Lingsar, *telek* has been incorporated into a dramatization of a king's retinue, including two "front" warriors, a prime minister, and a king, danced by young women and accompanied by a *gamelan baris* and a vocalist.

The *preret,* a wooden oboe with a powerful, piercing note, is also heard at Lingsar and just a few other villages. The instrumental performance of sacred poetry by the *preret* invokes the deities and instills a sense of reverence among the attendants of the temple festival. Although also part of many ensembles, the *preret* and its ritual repertoire form one of Lombok's unique traditions.

Two more common processional ensembles are the *gamelan tawa-tawa* and *barong tengkok*, used to announce life-cycle ceremonies (birthdays, circumcisions, weddings), community celebrations, or national holidays. The *gamelan tawa-tawa* features eight sets of cymbals affixed to lances, as well as gongs, kettle-gongs, cymbals, and drums. The music produced by this *gamelan* has a marching quality well-suited for processions. The lances are decorated with tassels, and when the cymbals are played in the standard interlocking fashion, the tassels appear to be dancing.

The *gamelan barong tengkok* features kettle-gongs placed within the body of a *barong* figure—a mythical lion—similar in appear-

ance but lacking the symbolism of the Balinese *barong*. This ensemble accompanies wedding processions in Central Lombok, in which the bride and groom are hoisted onto hobby horses and paraded around.

Love, trance and drink

Gandrung (literally "love") is a dance in which the female *gandrung* dancer selects male partners from the audience for short duets. This dance is known in East Java and in Bali, though in Bali it is a female impersonator who dances with male partners. The *gandrung* dances and sings solo, then taps a man with her fan who joins her in spontaneous dance that, depending on the dancers, can be theatrical or erotic.

The man gives the *gandrung* a small amount of money, usually 100 rupiah, and the audience roars in laughter at the impromptu dances. Although opposed by religious leaders, *gandrung* keeps appearing throughout the island and is being seen more and more in tourist performances.

Gandrung is accompanied by *gamelan oncer, gamelan grantang,* or *gamelan gong* Sasak. While the *gamelan grantang* is a rare ensemble of bamboo xylophones, the *gong* Sasak is a modern combination of the *gamelan oncer* and Balinese *gamelan gong kebyar.* It looks and sounds like Balinese *gamelan;* in fact some of its repertoire is derived from *gong kebyar* pieces, the most common on Bali. This ensemble is quite popular and is the sole modern music form not associated with Islam. Most newly created pieces in Lombok use the *gong* Sasak because of its dynamic sound and range.

Two other dances well worth seeing are *tandang mendet* and *paresean. Tandang mendet* is a military processional of Sembalun Bumbung, a village which maintains early Islamic traditions in a high valley on Mount Rinjani. This strong and well-choreographed dance, performed at the spectacular *alip* festival which takes place just once every three years, leads a dramatic procession to the grave of a Majapahit ancestor.

Paresean is a ritual mock battle between two warriors with staves and shields. These battles can be seen at family and community celebrations throughout Lombok. In most settings, the performance is not concluded until one of the combatants draws blood.

Two trance dances are still known among the Sasak, though they occur very infrequently. The *suling dewa,* a tradition of northern Lombok villages featuring flutes and

singing, functions to invoke deities into a shaman who blesses the village. *Pepakon* is a trance dance in East Lombok performed to cure illness. The sick become possessed, walk through fire, and then their sickness is forcibly removed from them using sticks.

Song and recitation

Cepung is a unique Balinese and Sasak form of "song," which combines recitation and singing from the *lontar monyeh* ("monkey manuscript") concerning the East Javanese Prince Panji. The *lontar* is written in Kawi—the Old Javanese court language—as well as Balinese and Sasak. The singers are accompanied by two instruments, a bamboo flute (*suling*) and a bowed lute (*redeb* or *rebab*), and a group of men who imitate the sound of a *gamelan.* As the members of the chorus get progressively more drunk from palm wine (*tuak*), they start dancing wildly. Not surprisingly, religious leaders have never approved of *cepung.*

Tembang Sasak, Sasak songs, reflect Java-Bali influences. Many of these songs use Javanese poetic meters and language. Another form, *pantun* rhyming couplets, is found throughout Lombok and used in courtship songs at the annual *bau nyale* festival in southern Lombok. This festival is initiated by the yearly spawning of colorful sea worms and draws more than 100,000 people to flirt and watch a modern dance drama based on the Putri Nyale or Mandalika legend—a princess, with too many suitors, throws herself into the sea, where she transforms into the *nyale* seaworms. (See also "The Pasola," page 184, for a ceremony in Sumba also based on the appearance of the seaworms.)

Pepausan, groups which sing *tembang Sasak* from *lontar* manuscripts, often congregate at different ceremonies to solemnize the event and offer ancient wisdom contained in traditional literature. A similar tradition reflecting Sumatran and Arab influences is *hikayat,* in which *lontar*s based on the "1,001 Nights" fables, written in Arabic-scripted Malay, are sung and then translated into Sasak at ceremonies.

Other Middle East–inspired forms include readings from the *Barzanji,* a book of Arabic poetry concerning the lives of Muhammad and Islamic saints. These readings often take place in the mosques on Thursday evenings. Some *Barzanji* passages are incorporated into *zikrzamman,* a call and response song form. The soloist is supported by the mosque's congregation, who move together, often with their eyes closed to more fully concentrate on God.

Islam and art forms

In strongly Muslim villages, Islamic praise songs have replaced *tembang Sasak* and sometimes even *hikayat,* and new ensembles have replaced traditional *gamelan.* Religious leaders banned traditional music ensembles because the instruments are made of bronze, sometimes called "the voice of the ancestors," and because of their association with non-Islamic practices. In their place have arisen orchestras without any bronze instruments whatsoever.

The *gamelan rebana,* developed around 100 years ago, was the first example of an "Islamic" ensemble, using *rebana* drums introduced from the Islamic world. Since it was only the bronze and not the music that was the problem, the repertoire of traditional *gamelan* has been incorporated into the *gamelan rebana* and the different drums, numbering as many as 20, imitate the sound of bronze *gamelan* instruments. Even Balinese compositions are played by many *gamelan rebana* groups. Another ensemble that grew out of this restriction is the more rare *gamelan klentang,* which consists entirely of iron metallophones.

Two other ensembles developed by local Muslim artists are *kecimol* and *cilokaq,* nearly identical ensembles featuring *preret, suling,* plucked lutes, violins, and *rebana*-style drums with vocalists who sing popular Sasak poetry. These ensembles are found in many Central and East Lombok villages, as are similar ensembles which accompany *rudat* (see below). The unique and festive *rudat* folk ensembles include violin, *gambus* lutes, a large *jidur* drum which keeps the beat, sometimes a plucked dulcimer called "mandolin," and even conga drums.

No theater or dance forms are normally associated with the orthodox Muslim populace. There are two, however, that exhibit some Islamic influences. *Kemidi rudat* is based on the "1,001 Nights" fables, uses colorful stock characters (good and bad kings, princesses, clowns), and features platoons who perform martial movements in unison while singing Arabic poetry. This dance drama has its roots in Sumatra and is scripted in the Malay language. *Kemidi rudat,* once banned by religious leaders, is now experiencing a resurgence throughout the island.

Wayang Sasak—a shadow puppet play using flat, leather puppets derived from the Javanese *wayang kulit*—is based on the *serat menak* stories. These concern Muhammad's uncle Amir Hamza (also known as Jayaprana), who was sent to prepare the world for Islam. Like Javanese and Balinese *wayang,* the figures include refined and coarse kings, princesses, demons, and of course, clowns. Performances run about five hours.

Wayang Sasak, which uses abstract puppets similar to those seen in Cirebon, Java, was apparently introduced from Java during the 17th century to help spread Islam. Ironically, this was one of the forms banned by fundamentalists due to its depiction of human forms, prohibited by Islamic law.

Other Sasak theater forms are mostly indigenous, with certain conventions borrowed from the Balinese. Among these are *Cupak Grantang, Amaq Abir, Amaq Darmi, kayak sando,* and *wayang wong.* Most of these theater forms use masks, although the masks only rarely specify precise characters and are often crudely carved. These forms are often called *teater kayak,* named for a type of poetry—*kayak*—that is used to express experiences of sadness. In fact, most of the local songs and poetry are considered sad, which distinguishes Sasak songs from those of the Balinese and Javanese.

—*David Harnish*

Opposite: *Bronze kettle-gongs are an integral part of the Sasak gamelan orchestra.*

WETU TELU

Mix of Islam, Traditional *Adat* Practice

Islam Wetu Telu is a religion that mixes elements of Islam with older threads of animism and ancestor worship. The number of practicing Wetu Telu on Lombok is hard to calculate because the government has not officially sanctioned the religion, and thus does not keep a census of its practitioners. One reasonable estimate suggests about 28,000. (The government, for its part, typically states there are just a few thousand.) The orthodox Sasak Muslims are sometimes called Wetu Lima.

Relations between the Wetu Telu and the more orthodox Wetu Lima, particularly the conservative Nahdatul Wahtan sect, have never been good, and the Wetu Telu have at times faced heavy pressure to conform to a more "respectable" form of Islam. As a result, the religious component of the Wetu Telu has been driven underground, and fearing sanctions, very few will admit their adherence.

Bali-Hinduism, Buddhism, Catholicism, Islam and Protestantism are the only five religions formally recognized by the Indonesian government. The first of the government's Five Principles is "Belief in one God" and non-monotheistic religions—such as ancestor worship, animism and Confucianism—have been officially discouraged. Bali-Hinduism is a special case; through some doctrinal legerdemain, the usual Hindu pantheon has been gathered under a single God, dubbed Sang Hyang Widi.

The Islam Wetu Telu remember 1965, the so-called "year of living dangerously." In the overreaction following an attempted communist coup in Jakarta, many Indonesians throughout the archipelago were suspected of being communists and killed. In some areas, those who did not belong to one of the "acceptable" religions were considered atheists, thus—perforce—followers of communism, and killed. During the 1965 terror, some of the strictly orthodox Sasak Muslims classified the Wetu Telu as an "unacceptable" religion and its followers paid the price.

Intolerance and Islam

Understanding the Wetu Telu requires some history of orthodox Islam on Lombok. Elsewhere in Indonesia where there were—and still are—large concentrations of non-recognized faiths, such as in West Sumba, Kalimantan and Irian Jaya. But there were no fanatics in these places to direct the slaughter, and thus no murders.

The 19th century purist reforms in the Arab world were brought to Lombok by Sasak hajis, pilgrims to Mecca and Medina. Dismayed by the slack adherence to Islam by their fellow countrymen, the hajis attempted to purify the faith by stamping out any lingering traces of animism and extolling strict adherence to the Koran. In Lombok, Islam had a political side as well, helping to unite the Sasaks of the east against the Balinese rulers in the west.

Around the turn of the century, when the Dutch took over Lombok, the colonial administrators served to check the more fanatical element of the Sasak Muslim population. The Muslim reformers of the late 19th and early 20th centuries could only try to convince their fellows by peaceful means. They channeled their energies into the Muhammadiyah religious school system, which imparted the strictly orthodox teachings of Islam. Some of these schools opened on Lombok.

After the war and independence, a local Sasak movement called Nahdatul Wahtan was founded, based in the East Lombok district capital of Selong. This organization, led by Haji Zainuddin Abdul Majid, was created specifically to combat the Wetu Telu religion. Haji Zainuddin and his religious organization gained much influence when, during the drought of 1966, he helped feed the starving with rice from productive land owned by his group. With his cooperation, the government party—Golkar—won convincing victories in 1971 and 1977.

Wetu Telu practices

Islam Wetu Telu mixes traditional *adat,* or customary practices and beliefs, with a rather superficial overlay of Islam. The religion incorporates a high degree of respect for nature and her gifts, as well as for village ancestors and other spirits. The most important ritual occasions include the opening of fields, births, circumcisions, marriages and funerals. Although the basic belief systems of all Wetu Telu are similar, there is considerable variation in particulars, as traditions in different parts of the island differ.

None of this sits well with Lombok's orthodox Muslims. Nor does the fact that, by general agreement, Islam was brought to the island through Bayan, one of the principal centers of Wetu Telu. Nor does an ancient palm leaf manuscript (*lontar*) describing the adventures of the missionary who brought Islam to Lombok.

According to the *lontar,* Pangeran Sangopati brought Islam to Lombok and his oldest son founded the Wetu Lima, while his younger son founded the Wetu Telu. The followers of the oldest son, however, were stuck by all kinds of accidents, disease and famine. The younger son's followers prospered. So, according to the manuscript, it was decided to lock the Wetu Lima teachings in an iron chest which was thrown into the sea. Everyone was then blessed by Allah, and prospered thereafter. According, that is, to the ancient text.

Doctrinal complaints lodged by the Wetu Lima include that the Wetu Telu do not pray five times a day and that (some) observe just three days of fasting during Ramadan. The Wetu Telu tend to do things in threes; they believe in three cardinal rules of life (obeying God, the community leaders and one's parents) and three essential stages of life (birth, life, death).

Pak Raden Singaderia

According to the *penghulu* (a religious leader) of Bayan, Pak Raden Singaderia, the ritual life of the Wetu Telu revolves around ceremonies honoring ancestors, the naming of children, weddings, funerals, the building of new houses, and the opening of *sawah* (rice paddies). Once a year, there is a celebration of Bayan's ancient thatched mosque, called Bayan Beleq. The exact age of the mosque was not known by the *penghulu,* but he suggested consulting a man named Raden Kosari, in Jakarta, who could tell the age of things by smelling them.

The Wetu Telu ritual cycle lasts eight 12-month years, and the most important ceremony during this cycle is the Alip festival, in which the Supreme Being is honored. This festival is described in Dutch anthropologist J. van Baal's *The Alip Festival in Bayan.* The most important yearly celebration falls on Maulid, Muhammad's birthday.

Pak Raden Singaderia showed me a document that listed some of the particulars of Wetu Telu *adat.* For example, the bride price of a woman of noble birth requires the following: 650,000 *kepeng* (old Chinese coins with a square hole in the middle), 7 water buffalo, a large basketful of rice with 244 more *kepeng,* and 24 spears.

This fascinating text lists three classes of offenses against morals or community standards, the least serious punishable by a fine of 10,000 *kepeng,* and the more serious by fines of up to 49,000 of the old coins. One "misdemeanor" offense listed was entering a woman's quarters without permission; another was a woman speaking with anyone other than her husband on their wedding night. "Felonies" included a man harassing a woman to the point she has to shout for help; a man caught with a woman not his wife; and parents putting undue pressure on their daughter to marry the man of their choice.

Wetu Telu and the Balinese

Shortly after the introduction of Islam to Lombok in the 16th century, some of the inhabitants who did not want to accept the new faith fled to the mountains to continue in the ways of their ancestors. Called Boda, these people were influenced by both indigenous ancestor worship and Hindu precepts, and settled in the mountains of north Lombok, as well as a few villages in the south. Perhaps the Boda were the spiritual, if not physical, ancestors of today's Wetu Telu.

When the Balinese took control of western Lombok, beginning in the 18th century, the local Sasaks were integrated into various levels of the ruling society. The Wetu Telu participated in Balinese rituals, which were much closer to their own than Islamic rituals, intermarried with their conquerors and willingly adapted to the *subak* system of controlling water for irrigating the rice paddies.

Even today, there are striking similarities between the Bali-Hindu religion and Wetu Telu. Offerings to and worship of ancestral spirits, including salient features of the landscape—mountains, certain large trees, springs, waterfalls or unusual rocks—and harmony with nature. Some Wetu Telu, as well as members of the Balinese minority on Lombok, consider Mt. Rinjani the dwelling place of the ancestors and the most powerful spirits, including the Supreme Being.

The Balinese make offerings to the caldera lake, and some Wetu Telu faithful spend three nights on Rinjani at full moon periods to gain spiritual strength. Both groups worship a sacred stone at Pura Lingsar and wage a battle with each other there using banana-leaf packets as missiles.

THREE CITIES

Ampenan, Mataram and Cakranegara

The population center of Lombok is an urban sprawl in the west made up of three contiguous cities spreading inland from the coast: the old port town of Ampenan blends into the administrative city of Mataram, which blends into the commercial town of Cakranegara. Just a bit east of Cakra is Sweta, the site of Lombok's biggest market as well as the island's bus terminal. The combined population of the three cities approaches the quarter million mark, about 10 percent of Lombok's total population.

Mataram is the capital of Nusa Tenggara Barat province (incorporating Lombok and Sumbawa) as well as the capital of the West Lombok district. The island's two other regional capitals, Praya in Central Lombok and Selong in East Lombok, seem tiny and provincial in comparison.

A wide, 8-kilometer-long one-way street through the three cities insures a smooth flow of traffic. This is the only area where the horse-drawn *cidomo* carts are not allowed, which greatly improves movement along the thoroughfare. This roughly east–west road begins as Jalan Langko in Ampenan, becomes Jalan Pejanggik in Mataram, and ends as Jalan Selaparang in Cakranegara. At Cakra it turns into the main cross-island trunk road to Labuhan Lombok, ending at the Lombok–Sumbawa ferry landing at Kayangan, 77 kilometers from Mataram.

Each city has a very different personality. Ampenan, with its maze of small streets, old buildings, Chinese and Arab quarters and decaying port, has the most character and life. Mataram, the administrative capital, has modern government buildings and little of interest to the visitor. Cakranegara has craft shops, weaving, and points of interest from the days of Balinese domination.

Ampenan: old port town

The bulk of Ampenan lies between the Berinyok River to the south, and the Meninting River to the north. (See map page 259.) Most of the population is concentrated on the coast along the Jangkok River, which cuts through the center of town.

From a bridge over the Jangkok, you can see carpets of *kangkung* growing in the shallow water. This leafy vegetable—with the awkward name of water convolvulus

(*Ipomoea aquatica*) in English—is popularly known as Asian watercress or Asian spinach. The Chinese have the most poetic name for the tasty green: *kong xin cai,* literally "empty heart vegetable," so named for its crispy hollow stems. *Kangkung* is among the most popular vegetables in Indonesian cooking. From the Jangkok bridge, you can see women splashing water on the *kangkung* leaves, especially in the early morning and late afternoon.

At the mouth of the Jangkok River, hundreds of colorful outriggered fishing canoes line the beach. Most of these are taken out at night, to fish with pressure lamps. These graceful boats glide like water-spiders under triangular sails of every hue, a spectacle that remains Lombok's most memorable sight.

You can observe the boats leaving in the late afternoon from the port area next to the new Pertamina oil storage tanks. On clear days, Bali's Gunung Agung can be seen in the background. As the sun sets, men fishing from the piles of the old dock are silhouetted in the sea's golden reflection of the setting sun. Bring your camera!

Ampenan's main street, Jalan Yos Sudarso, is lined with ethnic Chinese–owned shops, and there is a *pekong* or temple close to the sea. Also close to the beach, north of Yos Sudarso, is the Arab quarter, a little enclave of narrow streets barely wide enough for a vehicle. The faces here still show Arab features. Unfortunately, the section of the Arab quarter nearest the sea was bought by Pertamina and torn down to make room for huge, gleaming oil tanks.

Ampenan's Malay quarter, inhabited mostly by descendents of migrants from Java and Sulawesi, is south of the Chinese shops. It spreads all the way to the Jangkok River. Just a bit inland, around the Ampenan *bemo* terminal, is Kampung Sukaraja, the Sasak quarter, home to members of Lombok's main ethnic group.

Antiques and sights

North of Ampenan proper, along the main road to Senggigi, is the town market. A bit north of the market is Sudirman's Antiques, perhaps the best place on the island to find genuine articles without hunting around yourself in the small villages. Pak Sudirman has received a presidential award for his efforts to revive Lombok's traditional crafts. He is responsible for introducing the brightly painted wood horses of varying sizes, found in all the crafts shops, modeled on the prototype used to carry the boys prior to their

Muslim circumcision ritual.

Right next to Sudirman's, a paved road leads to Pura Segara, a Balinese beachside temple. (See "Balinese Temples," page 60.) Fishing canoes line the beach here, and stands sell snacks and drinks.

From Pura Segara to the Meninting River is a huge, old Chinese cemetery. The cemetery spreads over a wide area, and all the tombs face east. Many Chinese, accused of communist sympathies, were massacred on Lombok after the attempted coup in 1965. There is another Chinese cemetery south of the Jangkok River, but the tombs there— some quite colorful—lack the character of those at the old grave site.

Across the Meninting River, a beach by the same name hosts another fleet of fishing canoes. spread on either side of the Sasaka Beach Hotel, once Lombok's best but now decaying. The hotel, however, is scheduled for renovation and expansion. (For points further north, see "West Lombok," page 62.)

To the east of this area and about 6 kilometers north of Mataram, the village of Gunung Sari, on the old road to Pemenang, is full of craftsmen making "instant antiques" out of wood, leather, bone, horn and bamboo.

Opposite: *Batik-clad women carry coconuts, corn and firewood to the Ampenan market.* **Above:** *A proud mother and her healthy baby stand in front of pottery packed for the truck ride to market.*

It is much cheaper to buy these goodies here than in the art shops, and nobody will try to trick you into thinking they are genuine antiques. You can watch the friendly craftsmen work and, if you have time, they will even teach you how to make the items yourself.

Mataram: museum and offices

Leaving Ampenan along Jalan Langko, you pass the regional tourism office, just before the traffic light at Jalan Suprapto which marks the legal border with Mataram. Turn right and head south at the light, and the Nusa Tenggara Barat museum is a half-kilometer away on the right.

The highlights are the cloth collection, the fine *kris* knives and a small Dongson drum, and there are good displays of tools and craftwork. Most of the displays have English captions. One showcase holds "mystical" paraphernalia with amulets used to acquire supernatural force, immunity from weapons or to foretell the future.

There is a good arts shop, Lombok Asli, at Jalan Gunung Kerinci 36, near the University of Mataram. The Balinese owner, Gede Bandesa, and his New Zealand partner, Ann Woodroffe, have encouraged craftsmen to improve the quality of their traditional work and designed new items for both the local tourist market and for export. These new items include colorful modern masks and silk clothing with traditional Sasak patterns. The store has a wide range of stock and can pack and ship for you.

Mataram proper is a city of government offices with nothing of interest to visitors. The large governor's office building incorporates a bit of traditional Sasak architecture, but it is imposing only because of its size. The building is hard to miss, and it is on the main street, Jalan Pejanggik, at the corner of Jalan Cokroaminoto, which heads north toward the airport.

The end of Mataram comes after Jalan Pejanggik crosses the Berinyok River at the intersection where Jalan Bung Hatta heads north, and Jalan Bung Karno heads south. The best hotel in town, the Granada Hotel with its aviary and tropical gardens, is just a couple blocks south on Jalan Bung Karno.

Cakra: weaving and crafts

The city becomes interesting again as you move through Cakranegara, locally just called Cakra. The main street changes name to Jalan Selaparang and, heading east, passes the Cilinaya shopping center, where there is

a good little supermarket, a travel agency, a car rental agency and the Jabal Rahma bookstore. The Jabal Rahma is about the only place in town to get *Time* magazine, which arrives every two weeks or so and is quickly sold out. The *Jakarta Post* arrives daily around 4–5 p.m., but get it fast as it is almost always sold out by 7 p.m.

Just southeast of the shopping center is a row of shops selling crafts and faux antiques. In back of these shops, in an area called Karang Jangkon, is a Balinese temple with a cremation site out front. In back of the *pura* is a small plot. This is the grave of General van Hamm, killed during the Dutch defeat by the Balinese in 1894. The two marble plaques, giving the particulars of the man, were stolen a while back. (For the two important Balinese temples in Cakra—Pura Meru and the Mayura Water Palace—see "Balinese Temples," page 60).

The Rinjani weaving factory—and its sales outlet—is just across the street from the shopping center. Here, women work foot- and hand-operated looms (rather than the more traditional backstrap looms), slowly weaving traditional and new patterns.

There are two other weaving factories and outlets in Cakra: The Slamet Riady, is on a back alley, Jalan Tenun/Ukir Kawi, just northwest of the Mayura Water Palace; and the Sari Kusuma, on the main street past the gas station. If you want to see lots of women weaving, it's best to visit the factories between 9 a.m. and 12 noon.

The traffic light on Jalan Selaparang, where Jalan Hasanuddin heads north and Jalan Gede Ngurah heads south, marks the heart of Cakra. Four long blocks south on Jalan Gede Ngurah, turn left (east) onto Jalan

Above: *A healer, who came along with the young man for just this kind of emergency, gives a jockey some first aid.* **Opposite:** *Horses streak by at the Selakalas racetrack in Cakranegara.*

Pertanian to the blacksmith center of Getap.

The blacksmiths, *tukang besi,* work from around 7 a.m. to 4 p.m., but not during the Friday noon prayer time. They feed their fires with bellows made from huge sections of bamboo and pound scrap steel, usually from junked cars, into agricultural tools.

Heading north at the light on Jalan Hasanuddin, you cross the Jangkok River and, a couple of hundred meters to your left, reach the crafts center of Jangkok Rungkang. Here just about everyone is busy churning out well-made craft items either for sale in a large shop at the entrance, or for export to Bali. Most of the items are made from various parts of the sugar palm tree. The prices are very reasonable. East of Hasanuddin, before the river, is a twice-weekly (Tuesday, Thursday) livestock market.

Horse racing

A bit further east of the market, on Jalan Gora, is the Selakalas horse racing field, which often hosts events on Sundays and various holidays. Even if you are not a race fan or horse fancier, it's worth watching at least part of a race to see the boy jockeys, 5–11 years old. Retirement is compulsory at age 12, so that the jockeys are always too young to be corrupted into holding back their mounts by the unscrupulous behind-the-scenes gamblers.

The kids, either tough, 10-year-old veter-ans or innocent rookies, wear ski-masks and helmets (spills are not uncommon) in their special colors. They whip their red tasseled mounts around the track to the finish line, the winners beaming and the dirt-spattered losers with tears in their eyes. An entire village's pride rides with the little ones. Horses also have their pride, and it is not unusual to see one bite a passing competitor.

Horse racing had been traditional in Lombok, partially due to the ubiquitous *cidomos,* but organized races had lapsed until the government stepped in around 1988, offering prizes like TV sets, motorcycles, bicycles, cattle and goats.

The horses, really ponies, are matched according to their height at the shoulder, the big boys reaching just 150 centimeters (15 hands). The largest and fastest animals, classified as "super" or "XL" can be worth more than $4,000. The distance run varies with class, the smaller horses going around the 1,000 meter track once, the biggest ones doing 1,400 meters. The track record for the longer race is a respectable 1:07.

The night before the race, the villagers massage the animals, keep the mosquitos away and sometimes help the steeds relax with *gamelan* music. Of course, the horses are fed with the choicest grains and grasses, along with delicacies such as eggs, honey and ginger. In the morning, they are given a nice bucket of sweet coffee.

TEMPLES

Balinese Culture on Lombok

The tourist department of Lombok, capitalizing on the popularity of neighboring Bali as a tourist site, at one time used the motto: "You can see Bali in Lombok but you can't see Lombok in Bali." The phrase has been dropped, which is a good thing as it really is better to see Bali in Bali. Still, there are some 87,000 Balinese in Lombok, over 95 percent of whom live in western Lombok, and they maintain a number of temples to serve their community's spiritual needs.

It is not always easy to visit these *pura,* and unless there is a ceremony going on, most places are locked up. Finding the man with the key can be a frustrating endeavor. Only the few tourist-circuit temples are open most of the time. The most important rituals are usually held at the full moon (*purnama*) during the various months of the Balinese calendar. Check at the Bali section of the Department of Religion (Kantor Agama) in Mataram.

The temples

Gunung Pengsong, about 6 kilometers south of Mataram, offers some of the best views in Lombok on clear days: Mt. Rinjani in the early morning, Bali's Mt. Agung during the late afternoon, and an extensive overview of rice fields all day long. The small shrine is located on top of a steep hill, which can be reached by walking up lots of stairs, escorted all the way by chattering monkeys looking for a handout. One of the altars holds a large, egg-shaped stone firmly cemented in the seat of honor.

An important harvest ceremony is held here around March or April. It is said that during this ritual a water buffalo is led to the top to serve as the main sacrifice. By far the most important ceremony here, called Anggara Keliwon Prang Bakat, is held once every other cycle of the Pawukon, the 210-day Balinese ceremonial calendar.

Pura Segara is north of Ampenan, right on the beach. (Turn left off the road to Senggigi on the paved road next to Sudirman's Antiques.) This is a typical Balinese temple, but the setting is most of the attraction: the temple is surrounded by innumerable outriggered fishing boats, some of them with their sails unfurled, like birds drying their wings. There are several food stalls here for drinks and snacks.

Batu Bolong is further up the coast, just before Senggigi Beach. The temple sits on rocks jutting out to sea. In clear weather, there are good views of Bali's Gunung Agung at sunset. Unfortunately for tourists, virgins are no longer thrown to the sharks from here. A large hole in the rock next to the temple gave it its name: *batu* means stone and *bolong* is hole.

The Mayura Water Palace is right in the middle of Cakranegara. As its name implies, the palace, built in 1744 to serve the Balinese court, centers around a large rectangular pool. Mayura was the location of an important battle between the Dutch and the Balinese, who were supported by Sasak allies. After Holland's invasion of Lombok in 1894, the Dutch army camped at Mayura, which proved to be a tactical blunder. The Balinese, with firearms, sneaked up to the compound's outer walls and picked off the defenders. Several cannon, next to Balinese statues, are reminders of the victory—or defeat—depending on your sympathies.

A large open pavilion, the Bale Kembang, sits in the middle of the pool, accessible by a causeway. This court of justice and meeting hall is an island of tranquility next to Cakra's busy main street. Boys fish from here while others cool off, swimming in the pool. Hopefully the garbage in the water will have been removed when you visit Mayura.

To visit the religious shrines east of the pool, you must wear a temple sash. One of the shrines, surrounded by frangipani flowers and colorful crotons, faces the water. The full moon of Purnama Keempat, the fourth month of the Balinese lunar calendar, is the date of Mayura's most important ceremony.

Pura Meru, the largest Balinese temple on Lombok, is just across the main road from Mayura. Built in 1720, under the orders of Anak Agung Made Karang of Singosari, the complex is made up of three courtyards and holds over 30 shrines. The three main *meru* shrines—dedicated to Siwa, Wisnu and Brahma—are all slender and multi-roofed, with 11, 9 and 7 tiers. The temple is the site of one of Lombok's biggest Balinese rituals.

Narmada is about 10 kilometers east of Pura Meru, just to the right of the main road heading to Labuhan Lombok. The centerpiece here is a large artificial lake whose shape resembles Anak Segara in the caldera of the Rinjani volcano. It was built in 1805 by the raja of Mataram after he became too old to climb Rinjani to deposit offerings in the sacred lake there.

The replica of the volcano's lake served for the raja's offerings, but a malicious rumor has it that he really built the place so he could watch the village girls bathe—then take his pick of the local lovelies.

Most of the large Narmada complex is now secular, complete with food and drink vendors—you can even get a cold beer! For 30¢ an hour, you can paddle large swan-shaped boats around the lake. Above the lake is a large swimming pool, open daily from 8 a.m. to 5 p.m., for a 15¢ entrance fee. The place gets very crowded on weekends.

One part of the Narmada complex, the Pura Kalasa, is still used by the local Balinese. This is the focus for the yearly Pujawali ritual, in which offerings, including live ducks, are made to the artificial lake. (The ducks are soon caught and kept by the local boys.) Some Balinese climb Rinjani to Lake Anak Segara to deposit gold trinket offerings there in a ceremony called Pakelem. This is during the full moon

(Purnama) of the fifth Balinese lunar month (Kelima).

Lingsar Temple, a few kilometers north between Cakra and Narmada, is the most important one on the island for the Balinese and the local Sasaks who adhere to the Islam Wetu Telu religion (See "Wetu Telu," page 54). The main temple complex at Lingsar, built in 1714, is divided for the two religions, with the Balinese sector located higher and to the north.

Once a year, the Pujawali ritual takes place here, a week-long series of events centered around Purnama of the Balinese lunar month Kenem (late November–early December). The highlight, which occurs late afternoon before the night of the full moon, consists of the two sides—Balinese and Sasak—pelting each other with *ketupat*. These are tightly packed, leaf-wrapped missiles of steamed rice which can cause more than bruised egos. Cockfights follow.

There are two small pools at the entrance of the temple, and a lake just below the temple complex. Here sacred eels are kept, and hand-fed eggs.

Opposite: *A roast pig offered to the gods by Lombok's Balinese.* **Above, left:** *A stylized Balinese elephant guards the Narmada Water Palace.* **Above, right:** *A sculpture and cannon at the Mayura temple, where the Dutch suffered a humiliating defeat to the Balinese in 1894.*

WEST LOMBOK

Senggigi, the Gilis and the Peninsula

With the Three Cities area, the airport and the greatest concentration of hotels, West Lombok is the logical settling down place for the visitor. The popular Gili islands are in the district, as are all the major Balinese temples, the center of the Wetu Telu and Mt. Rinjani.

Our first route heads north from the Three Cities to Senggigi beach, the Gilis, the Wetu Telu area around Bayan, and finally the foothills of Mt. Rinjani. The second route heads south to the quiet beaches and surfing areas of the southeast peninsula.

Senggigi beach

Heading north from either the airport or Ampenan, the road rises over two small hills and then drops down to the coast at a long, curved beach. (See map page 42.) On mornings following moonless nights, these hills offer the best panoramic view of a sea dotted with colorful triangular-sailed fishing catamarans returning home to the beaches north of Ampenan. The fishermen take their craft out at sunset in a long line, their lamps forming a beautiful display visible from many of Senggigi's beachside hotels.

The first of the small hills, Batu Layar, holds the sacred grave of one of the Muslim holy men (*wali*s) who brought Islam to Lombok. Locals pray at a roadside shrine here, a short walk up from the road. From the top of the second hill you can walk down to the seaside Balinese temple at Batu Bolong, literally "Holed Stone." (See "Balinese Temples," page 60.)

Senggigi's row of hotels grows by the month, creeping northward along the coast. They line a seaside road all the way to Pemenang, 20 kilometers from Batu Bolong. This road follows the coastline, although it does climb some hills which offer splendid views of coastal coconut groves and the sea. The old road to Pemenang runs further inland. It starts out at Mataram, passes Rembiga village and Gunung Sari, which has a busy week-long market, then begins climbing around Sidemen village.

Sidemen is famous for its red palm sugar, made by boiling down the sap of the sugar palm. The sugar—*gula merah*—is sold at market in hemispherical lumps. The sugar palm sap is also drunk fresh, just after it is brought down from the tree tops in bamboo tubes. This sweet sap is called *tuak manis*; if it is left to ferment into a frothy, slightly alcoholic toddy, it is called simply *tuak*.

You can stop at the village to watch the sugar-making process, or drive up to the mountain pass at Pusuk, where there is a pleasant coffee house which offers a good view, in clear weather, of the Gili islands. From Pusuk, the road drops down to Pemenang, past roadside bands of monkeys waiting for a handout from passing cars.

The Gili Islands

At Pemenang, a 1.5-kilometer side road leads to Bangsal, which is the embarkation point for the three Gili islands, just offshore. A hired car will drop you off right at Bangsal, but the public *bemo*s stop at a side road. There is a money changer here, and a *cidomo* that will take you to Bangsal for 15¢ a head.

Which of the Gilis to visit? All three offer white sand beaches, inexpensive bungalow-type accommodations, and clear waters for snorkeling. The only real hotel on the islands is the Indra Cemana on Gili Meno. If you have the time, charter a boat for a day ($20) and take a look at all three islands. This might be more crucial in the high season, June through early September, when all the accommodations could be full and the beach might be the only place to sleep.

There is also talk of limiting the number of *losmen* on the islands, as freshwater supplies are already strained and there are no septic tanks. When evaluating bungalows, note the following: toilet facilities, mosquito nets (essential during the November–March rainy season), and dining facilities.

Gili Air: most populous

Gili Air is the closest to Bangsal and the "mainland," and has the highest local population of the three: 1,000 people (See map page 263.) Most of the people live in the south of the island, and the bungalows are concentrated in this area as well. Here, and on all the Gilis, the principal economic activities other

Opposite: *Large ferries shuttle back and forth between Padangbai, Bali and Lembar, Lombok.*

than tourism are coconut growing, fishing and small-scale cattle and goat raising. Gili Air has a small, bare-bones clinic, and each of the islands' villages has a mosque and a primary school.

The beach runs all the way around Gili Air's 100 plus hectares, and the best sunbathing and snorkeling areas are located out on the southern shore.

The waters off Gili Air are crystal clear, but snorkeling is marred by dynamite-blasted coral, a limited number and variety of fish, and the seasonal visit of stinging jellyfish, tiny critters but bothersome enough at times to drive you from the water. The best snorkeling is at the edge of the reef, which encircles the island, where the coral slopes down to the 14–20 meter bottom. The west coast of Gili Air is pretty barren, but you might be lucky and see a school of 1–1.5 meter Napoleon wrasse (locally called *anke*).

Gili Meno: hotel and blue coral

Only 350 people live on Gili Meno, the middle island, and there are the fewest *losmen* here as well. All the drinking water is brought from Lombok; the wells here produce a brackish mix with a salinity close to seawater, not much good even for bathing. The Indra Cemara, the only star-rated hotel in the Gilis, has its own desalinization plant to produce bathing water. Just inland from the west coast is a large salt lake, its surface marked off into sections for collecting salt during the dry season.

Cholera occasionally strikes Gili Meno in the dry season, May–October, and the rest of the year brings bothersome malarial mosquitos. Take your pills and sleep under a mosquito net.

The hotel and bungalows here are on the southeast coast, and all offer great views of Gili Air and Gunung Rinjani to the east. The best snorkeling is off the northeast coast, in front of the Blue Coral *losmen*, which takes its name from the beds of branched, blue-tinted staghorn coral found here. The reef offers a good variety of coral species and clouds of colorful little fish.

Gili Trawangan: boisterous crowd

Gili Trawangan, the furthest offshore, is also the largest, covering 3.5 square kilometers. Many of the 700 people here, as on the other Gilis, are descendants from Bugis migrants from South Sulawesi. They now have intermarried with the local Sasaks, and speak the Sasak language.

In 1891, Gili Trawangan was a penal colony. With all his prisons filled, the Raja of Lombok exiled 350 Sasak rebels to the uninhabited and undesireable island. Today, barebreasted European women and other western hedonists crowd the 18 *losmen*/bungalows on Trawangan.

At the height of the tourist season, July

and August, many of the 200 or so tourists who head out daily from Bangsal end up sleeping on Trawangan's beaches. All the *losmen* are located along the east coast; some provide a disco to entertain their young guests. The Paradisia and the Trawangan have the loudest and liveliest atmosphere.

The young, mostly European tourists who come to Trawangan or the other Gilis pass their days bronzing on the beach. Snorkeling and frisbee tossing are the favored daytime sports. Many places have masks, snorkels and fins for rent. The reefs off the east coast of Trawangan are decent, but be careful about swimming out too far as the currents can get quite strong when the tides change. A walk around the island takes no more than about 4 hours.

The Albatros scuba club, well-equipped and with its own boat, is the most experienced operator going to the Gilis and provides the best dive trips. The club can provide everything from easy dives for novices to drift dives in the strong current off Trawangan's west coast. At the latter site divers can see giant *Tridacna* clams, sharks, turtles, manta rays and blue-spotted stingrays.

The northwest: alternative tourism

On the coast road, about two kilometers past Pemenang, a dirt road winds to Sire beach.

There is good snorkeling here, and Sire is the site of a star-rated hotel. From Sire north to Tanjung (where there is a big Sunday market) and beyond, the beach is black, volcanic sand. Anyer (which also has a Sunday market), the head of the Bayan subdistrict, is 35 kilometers from Tanjung.

Along the way, there are a couple of roadside pumice collecting operations. The road cuts through coconut groves alternating with *sawah* and vegetable gardens, which in places stretch a kilometer to the sea. There are short stretches where the road crests a couple of low hills, which offer views of the sea. As the road swings inland, it passes Muslim cemeteries, marked by gnarled frangipani trees.

Three villages between Pemenang and Anyer have been marked for "alternative" tourism—Jambianon, Krakas and Godang. These places are off the beaten track, and free of tourist hype. The people are friendly, and lead quiet, traditional lifestyles.

Jambianon village, 2 kilometers south of Tanjung, lies on a beach-lined bay. Although the water is clear, much of the nearby coral has been dynamited, although there are still a few good spots left where fishermen will take you for a very moderate fee. (Figure $3 for a half day to the boatman; if an outboard is used, add the cost of fuel). Local fishermen can also take you south to Sire for snorkeling and a look at the seaweed farming areas. You

can even hire a ride to the Gili islands.

A Balinese temple, Pura Medana, is located on a hilltop to the west of the bay with a great view; the sunset over Bali's Gunung Agung is spectacular. Perhaps best of all, the children in Jambianon have been taught in an experiment not to beg, stare or shriek "Turis! Turis!" at the sight of tourists. They will politely chat with you in Indonesian or accompany you on walks around the area.

Krakas (short for Karang Kates) is about 4 kilometers past Tanjung. It is a fishing village, but with a difference. The village's drinking water comes from an offshore spring. About 400 meters from the shore, 10 meters down, a spring spouts cold, clear drinking water. Fishermen come here to collect their families' water supply. They will take you to the spring, and even dive with you on the reef, teaching you how to use their homemade spear guns, which use a rubber strip to propel a steel missile.

Godang, a bit past Krakas, is the point of departure for a stroll to the beautiful Tiu Pupas waterfall and seven nearby caves. You can find a guide in Godang to the waterfall and caves, which are on the way to Keruak hamlet. From Godang, a good 6 kilometer road snakes inland to Selelos village. The road passes the village of Gangga, which is one of the most important centers of the Islam Wetu Telu religion. (See "Wetu Telu," page 54.) An important ritual is held periodically in the nearby sacred forest of Bebekeq.

Just before reaching Anyer, near Sukadana village, is a hamlet called Segenter. Here, the people have kept to their traditions in both building styles and Wetu Telu customs, thanks to their relative isolation. They are friendly, and not at all closed to visitors, although most do not speak Indonesian. Bring a Sasak-speaking guide, or communicate in sign language.

Bayan: Wetu Telu stronghold

Bayan village is just five kilometers from Anyer. Just before Bayan, a road leads due south to Batu Koq and Senaru, the points of departure for the climb up Rinjani. (See "Mount Rinjani," page 68, and "Climbing Gunung Rinjani," page 271.) There are several *losmen* in the area, and from here it is less than an hour's hike to the high Sidanggala waterfall, the source of irrigation water for the extensive *sawah*s east of the village.

Bayan is one of the biggest Wetu Telu strongholds, and the local *penghulu*—a religious leader—lives next to a homestay just north off the main road. The Wetu Telu followers live on the north side of the road, and

Opposite: *The hand-weaving industry had almost disappeared until tourism revived the craft. Hand-spun threads hold dye much better than machine-made thread.* **Above:** *Lombok is known for its simple, but high-quality earthenware pottery.*

the orthodox Muslims live on the other side. Islam is said to have first arrived on Lombok at Bayan, and Bayan's mosque, 300 years old, is thought to be the oldest on the island.

About 10 kilometers east of Bayan, a road rises and falls over steep coastal hills, bringing you to Kali Putih. This is a dividing point of sorts, and the roadside sign indicates 90 kilometers to Mataram by heading west (the way we have come) and 126 kilometers by heading east, then south to Labuhan Lombok, then west across the middle of the island.

From Kali Putih, a road heads south up into Rinjani's foothills, ending at Sembalun Lawang, 18 kilometers away. It is possible to climb Rinjani from Sembalun Lawang, but it is easier and more pleasant from Bayan. Some 5 kilometers before the village, you can see steep, bald mountains with vegetation creeping up their slopes. The village entrance is marked by a large monument to garlic, a not so subtle clue to the area's main product. Sembalun Lawang is at the north end of a steep valley planted in garlic, and Sembalun Bumbung, the south end.

The rich volcanic soil here produces bumper crops of garlic and shallots, and these two villages are considered Lombok's wealthiest. The people from the Sembalun area believe that the brother of the "Raja of Majapahit" lies buried nearby. Be that as it may, this area shows a marked Javanese influence in its language, music and dances.

The two Sembaluns are linked by a 2.5-kilometer road in an awful state. From Sembalun Bumbung, it's 16 kilometers and an easy 4–5 hour hike south of the mountains to Pesugulan, where frequent public transportation will whisk you on the cross-island highway to the Three Cities area.

South: the port of Lembar

Heading south from the Three Cities towards the port of Lembar, you have a choice of two possible routes. The main road heads south at Cakra, then west at Kediri, and stays good all the way to Lembar. Alternatively, you could take a small, potholed road that leads south from Ampenan through back-country *sawah*s. This road passes the Balinese temple at Gunung Pengsong (see "Balinese Temples," page 60). Doubling back slightly, the road heads west, past Rumak, to rejoin the main road at Karang Anyar.

Just a bit east of Rumak is Banyu Mulek, a little village known for its open-fired earthenware. A variety of items are on sale here. Back on the main road, you soon reach Kediri, where you head southwest on a good road to Lembar.

There are usually several large Bugis schooners anchored in Lembar's harbor, graceful vessels with the lines of a sailing craft, but the diesel motor of a modern cargo ship. These are a contrast to the ungainly, but efficient ferry boats from Padangbai, Bali.

From just south of the harbor area, you can charter a motorized outrigger for an hour ($5–$6) for the ride along the coast to Gili Nanggu. Here there are great bungalow-cottages, sitting on stilts next to a beautiful beach, and clear, turquoise waters. Snorkeling is a disappointment, however, because of the extensive damage to the reef from dynamite fishing. A delightful stroll around the island takes just 20 minutes.

Scuba divers are sometimes taken to Gili Genting, a short ride from Gili Nanggu. The dive here is off a steep rock face. We found the visibility awful, with only a few fairly good formations of hard and soft corals. The best of the reef was near the surface, at easy snorkeling depths, where there were good coral formations and lots of colorful fishes.

The southwest peninsula

To reach Lombok's southwest peninsula, take the turnoff just before reaching Lembar. This road heads south, then circles the bay before climbing a steep hill and heading inland. A 9-kilometer side road here sticks

tight to the bay, offering a full view of the port area and a great view of the bay.

Here the water is dotted with *bagan*s, stationary fishing platforms poised over the smooth surface of the water like spiders. After sunset, the fishermen lower their huge nets and use pressure lanterns to attract schools of fish. Two or three times in the course of the night, the nets are hauled up and stripped of their catch of tiny fish.

The side road continues, past the shrimp farms lining the bayside, and rejoins the main road at Jelateng (Thursday market). A few kilometers further on the main road is Sekatong, the political center of the *kecamatan* that includes the entire peninsula. At Sekatong Tengah, a dirt road heads south to Sepi (see "Lombok by Jeep," page 78.).

The road west, partially paved, hugs the peninsula's north coast, and occasionally sends side roads to the sea. The waters here are quiet, and all the beaches are covered in beautiful, white sand. Most of the seaside dwellings are simple thatch huts, with red tile roofs. There are many islands just offshore, and coconut groves and stands of mangrove alternate with the beach.

The only public transportation to and from this area is on the back of open trucks, but *bemo*s should be available once the pavement is finished.

In the west Sekotong district (Sekotong Barat) is a little Balinese hamlet, Batu Liong,

with a small shrine and temple offshore.

Pelangan village has a great beach, and good snorkeling just offshore. A Japanese-run pearl farm lies offshore in this area, towards Labuhan Poh. The people of the area are friendly; you can stay in their homes as a guest and participate in village life. Even as a guest, however, you should pay for your stay. The villagers are very poor, and your visit will put them out financially, although they will never admit this. Also a little cash income will really help them with necessities such as medicines and clothing.

Bangko Bangko: surfing

The peninsula road ends at Bangko Bangko beach, 3 kilometers past the last little hamlet (where the pavement currently stops), 78 kilometers from the Lembar turnoff. The beach has sprouted some bungalows, which will perhaps be open by the time you read this. There is good surfing just past the end of the road, which is stopped by a sheer cliff. The snorkeling is lousy, however, as the shallow coral gives way quickly to a sandy bottom. A few large sea eagles patrol the skies, swooping down for an occasional snack of fresh fish.

Opposite: *A fishing boat at anchor in the clear water off Gili Air.* **Above:** *Extracting salt from the salt lake on Gili Meno represents an important source of cash for the people of the island.*

MOUNT RINJANI

Trekking up Lombok's Great Volcano

Slogging up the steep slope in the cold mist, I was nursing a bloody nose. Eyes to the ground, I foolishly had kept going when my guide, Salim, carrying the food ahead of me on a bamboo pole, had stopped. The cut edge of bamboo can be very sharp indeed. Bamboo knives are still used for circumcision in Lombok, and now I knew why.

Darkness began to fall, and Salim chose a spot to camp. He and our two porters started a fire, and stretched some plastic sheets which we hoped would protect us from the inevitable rain.

Salim and his helpers whipped up a quick meal of rice and dried fish, liberally overlaid with an evil-looking red sauce. I was starved, so I wolfed down my portion. Soon my mouth was on fire, my eyes streaming and my nose dripping. I was used to hot, spicy Mexican food, but this was far beyond anything my palate had yet encountered. Although it scorched my mouth, the food also warmed my soul.

Just as darkness was closing in, the clouds and mist cleared a bit, revealing a tantalizing glimpse of the panorama from the highlands of Lombok. Then the curtain shut and the rain fell. We huddled under the plastic, close to the fire and passed a cold, wet and miserable night. It was one of those times one asks oneself, Why am I doing this?

The next morning my doubts left with the dark. Just before dawn the lightening sky revealed a breathtaking sight. Off to one side, the peak of Gunung Rinjani shot straight up. Some 900 meters below, a large tranquil lake, Segara Anak, filled the volcano's caldera. Looking east, the sun was just edging over Sumbawa Island, the yellowish ball almost directly over Gunung Tambora. This glorious morning justified three days of tough hiking and bone-chilling rains. (There are faster ways up, I took the long route for reasons of my own.)

We started up Rinjani's steep slope, but a half hour later the clouds and mist moved in again. By the time we reached the top, visibility was down to one meter. The morning panorama was to remain the highlight of the trip. We returned to our overnight camp, unburdened ourselves, and scampered down to the lake. There we found a volcanic vent, which warmed some hot, sulfurous springs nearby. We let the near boiling water soak away all of our aches and were warmed to the very marrow.

A trip to Rinjani

The top of Mt. Rinjani, 3,726 meters, is one of the highest points in Indonesia outside of Irian Jaya. The name "Rinjani" may come from an old Javanese term for "God" or "All Great." According to Sasak legend, a princess named Anjani, daughter of the Supreme God, lives on the mountain. And it is likely that in old times the Sasak believed that the most important spirits lived on Rinjani, a belief adopted by the local Balinese as well.

The view from the tip of the caldera on Mt. Rinjani can definitely be the highlight of a trip to Lombok and perhaps all Indonesia. The climb is not easy, but neither is it particularly difficult. Even a 50-year-old chain-smoker made it up just fine. If you're not at the peak of fitness, take an extra day or two. The usual time for the round trip, including a descent to Lake Segara Anak in the caldera, is three days and two nights.

With even a little bit of conversational Indonesian, you can organize your own climb. But if you don't want to bother, just leave all the logistics to a reputable travel agency or a free-lance guide. The travel agency will definitely be more expensive, but the guide could be less efficient. (See "Climbing Gunung Rinjani," page 271.)

The easiest and most convenient route to the peak is the path leading south out of Bayan. (See map page 270.) There are three permanent shelters (in need of repairs), water (still, bring your own), and shaded forest full of monkeys. The path west from Sembalun Lawang is longer, has no shelters or drinking water, and almost no shade. The only drawback to the Bayan route is the lack of frequent public transportation to Bayan. Buses and *bemo*s are much more frequent to

Opposite: *The sun rises over 3,726-meter Gunung Rinjani, which dominates Lombok island. Rinjani is the highest volcanoe in the Indonesian archipelago. The photograph here was taken from the island of Gili Meno.*

the wealthy, garlic-growing village of Sembalun Lawang, whence they head to Labuhan Lombok, and the ferry to Sumbawa.

If you find the Bayan route too comfortable, you can always return to Sembalun Lawang in the east. There is no problem making this alternate descent, as long as you have brought along camping gear, and you are willing to pay your guides and porters for their transportation back to Bayan. They can take back your rented sleeping bag and tent.

To Bayan for the climb

It's not too hard to catch a *bemo* from Sweta to Anyer, especially on Sunday mornings, the weekly market day there. From Anyer you can wait for a truck heading towards the base camp area south of Bayan, or you can charter a vehicle for yourself—if anything is available. Or walk, and start whipping yourself into shape for the climb.

You follow the paved road out of Anyer towards Bayan for about 3 kilometers, then as the road curves east, the trail to base camp, rough and dusty, heads due south. This trail has been asphalted a couple of times, but it has always washed out. At the moment, the road is being worked on again. Some 4 kilometers up this road, you reach Batu Koq, and a bit further up, three *losmen*. At any of these three places you can make arrangements for the climb: rental of tent and sleeping bag, buying food for the trek, hiring porters and guides. (See "Climbing Gunung Rinjani," page 271.)

A couple of kilometers from Batu Koq, you reach Senaru, a village of thatch-roofed huts. The elevation here is already 600 meters, and this is the last village along the trail. There are no *losmen* here, but floor space is available. A good vehicle and driver can reach Senaru during the dry season, usually from May/June to October/November, which is the only time you should attempt to climb Rinjani.

If you have made all the arrangements for the next morning's departure, and still have daylight, time and energy left (or if you are of a masochistic bent), visit the dramatic Sindanggala waterfall, about an hour away. The hike is downhill on the way out, and uphill coming back. The top of this waterfall is visible from the road near Batu Koq.

An early start

The first day is the toughest and you will want to rest as often as possible—get the earliest possible start. Depending on your physical condition, it will take anywhere from four to nine hou*s to reach the camping spot, a couple of hours below the caldera rim.

Insist on setting your own pace. Don't let your guides get ahead of you, at least until mid-afternoon when, you can keep one with you and let the others go on to get a head start setting up camp. If you can afford to,

hire enough porters so that you don't have to carry anything yourself. The climb takes you through silent forests, and chances are you will enjoy the trek even if you are not in top physical shape.

A series of markers begins at Senaru village, the first one marked "1" and the last, at the rim, "200." Some markers are missing, but there are enough for you to be able to chart your progress. From Senaru to the crater lake is a total of 12 kilometers. With a bit of luck, some stagnant water should be available at markers 114 (Pos II campsite, about halfway up) and 185 (Pos III, at 2,100 meters, just short of the tree line). But don't count on this, and have enough water with you, at least three liters per person.

Once you reach your campsite, your porter-guides will pitch your tent and whip up a meal before you collapse into sleep. When packing, remember that on the hike you will welcome special tidbits of food, and a bottle of booze will help to keep the chill away. Also, some kind of light mattress could be the difference between an uncomfortable night and a great rest.

It gets cold on the mountain, and a sweater and jacket are essential, particularly in the evening and at dawn. The shelters at Pos II and III are similar—a roofed platform with one end walled off, making a small room that will sleep 6–8 bodies. The structures, plundered for firewood, are fast deteriorating. There is lots of litter around.

Try to get an early start the second morning as well. The best views are at dawn, and once you get past the tree line, it can get awfully hot when the sun is up. It will take you anywhere from one to three hours to reach the caldera rim, which is at 2,600 meters. Steps and railings help at the steepest parts. At the rim, take a good rest and lots of photographs.

The clarity of the view, and how far you will be able to see, depends on the amount of atmospheric haze on any particular day, but under good conditions it is possible to see Sumbawa to the east, and perhaps even Gunung Agung, in Bali, to the west.

At the point where the path crosses the rim, you are still about 1,100 meters below Rinjani's 3,726 meter top. Good boots, and lots of energy and water are needed to reach the very top. Few hikers even attempt it. If you want to try it, add an extra day to your plans. The air gets thin, and loose stones make for lots of lost footing. There is a rough shelter of sorts at around 3,000 meters.

The lake and hot springs

From the rim, it's a couple of steep, muddy hours down to the kidney-shaped crater lake, Segara Anak, at 2,030 meters, inside a caldera roughly 8 kilometers by 6 kilometers. The lake itself is 3 kilometers at its widest, and is said to reach 250 meters in depth. The rocks along the path are covered in graffiti. Sheer cliffs behind the lake reach 500 meters, and there are stands of pine trees nearby.

The spot breathes magic as well as beauty. It is no wonder that both Wetu Telu and Balinese consider this the dwelling place of spirits. The Balinese come here during an annual ritual held in conjunction with the Narmada temple east of Cakra, and throw little gold trinkets into the lake. The large artificial lake at Narmada was built to resemble crescent-shaped Segara Anak.

The Wetu Telu come to the mountain to pray on full moon nights, bringing with them mystically powerful objects—such as a *kris* knife wrapped in white cloth—which then acquire an extra measure of potency because of the visit here.

The lake has recently been stocked with carp and tilapia, and the pilgrims can now engage in the secular activity of fishing.

Lake Segara Anak, literally "Child of the Sea," takes on bluish-green color in strong sunlight. It is often obscured by afternoon clouds which settle into the large crater. Gunung Rinjani has for the most part behaved itself since 1901, but in 1942 a mini volcano formed from a vent under the lake. This little island reaches 145 meters above the surface of the lake, and is called Gunung Baru, "New Mountain." Every now and then Gunung Baru coughs and emits a puff of smoke.

Hot springs reward

A river called Kokok Putih (or Lekok Putek), flows out of the lake and cascades downward in a series of spectacular waterfalls, reaching the sea just beyond the turnoff from the north coast road to the Sembalun villages. The water, because of sulfur and other dissolved minerals, is milky and opaque.

The best spot for your weary body is in a network of hot-spring pools. These are believed to hold curative powers, which is easy to believe, because after the shock of the initial stinging heat wears off, the water sure feels great. Some of these springs pour out of Gua Susu, "Milk Cave," so called for its sulfur-based milky yellow deposits.

The local people who come up here have little notion of the western concepts of ecology: litter carpets the ground at the hot springs. The corrugated steel sheet shelters and cooking pits do little to enhance the scenery. From the camp spot by the hot springs, count on a long 8–10 hours back to Senaru.

The climb from Sembalun Lawang

To climb Rinjani from the east, you set out from Sembalun Lawang village. Sembalun Lawang, and its sister village, Sembalun Bumbung, are the onion and garlic growing capitals of the island. The villages mark, respectively, the north and south ends of a large fertile valley northeast of Rinjani.

There is frequent public transportation to Sembalun Bumbung from Labuhan Lombok, and from there you can hike the 2.5 kilometers to Sembalun Lawang, whence you set out for the caldera.

A perhaps more pleasant way to get there, however, is to hike from Pesugulan village, which you can reach by turning off the main east–west trunk road at Aikmel, northeast of Masbagik. Before reaching Pesugulan, the rice fields provide a perfect foreground for Rinjani, looming in the background.

The 16 kilometer, 4–5 hour hike to Sembalun Bumbung from Pesugulan leads through beautiful mountain scenery. The walk starts out through gently rising mead-ows, then you get a full view of Rinjani. When you arrive at Sembalun Lawang, the Wisma Cemarasu can help you organize for the climb. But they have no tents or sleeping bags available for rent—you will have to bring your own.

From Sembalun Lawang, the climb is not difficult, although it is hot and there is no water. You reach the crater rim at a place called Plawangan II (Plawangan I is where the trail from Senaru reaches the rim. Plawangan means "door"). The view from this side is better, and fewer hikers take this path—perhaps a few dozen a year, as opposed to the more than 1,000 who hike up from Senaru every year.

The ascent from this side is also better if you intend to climb to the very top of the mountain, as your first night's camp is already at 2,900 meters, just 700 meters or so below the summit.

The climb to the summit can be disappointing, however, as early morning clouds can reduce visibility to nothing, which is exactly what happened to me when I first climbed Rinjani in 1978. At that time there was no road to the Bayan area and Sembalun Lawang was the only logical point of departure for the climb.

Above: *Porters returning from Gunung Rinjani. Although the track is easy to follow, a few friendly porters make the trip much more pleasant.*

CENTRAL LOMBOK

Earthenware, Cloths and Seaworms

Central Lombok is the tourist heart of the island. The region includes the traditional villages featured on most one-day itineraries, all near the Three Cities area, and the south coast: Kuta beach, which is the site of the *nyale* seaworm festival, and Tanjung Aan, with beautiful beaches and good waves for surfing. These areas are easy to reach, and many operators run day trips there.

But before following the busloads of tourists, think about trying something different. If you have more than a passing interest in Sasak culture, stop at Batu Kumbung village, which has been suggested for "alternative" tourism (see "Lombok Practicalities," page 258). Batu Kumbung is a traditional Sasak village just 3.5 kilometers north of the Narmada water palace. Some of the village's women still weave *ikat* using traditional backstrap looms, and there is a creek here with healing powers.

The village has acquired a measure of local fame for its music and dance groups—a *gandrung* ensemble and a *kendang belek* group. The troupes perform in the village, and in other nearby villages at events such as weddings. This is pleasant country for walks. If you like it here, you can learn the local dances, or how to play an instrument. It is possible to arrange for homestays at Batu Kumbung.

Southeast to Praya

The tourist route zips towards Praya (Saturday market), turning off just before reaching this district capital to head for the weaving village of Sukarara. There are five weaving centers here along the main road through the village. All but one of the centers (which is a normal house) consist of traditional raised wooden platforms, protected by a thatched roof. You are welcome to take photos. Each has an attached shop selling local cloth, without high-pressure sales pitches. Some bargaining is possible.

Another turnoff from the main road leads to a pottery-making area centered around Penujak village. At the Pottery Promotion Center in Penujak, craftsmen are often at work making large water receptacles with lizard or frog decorations ($14) for the local market, and "tourist" items, such as flower vases or lidded containers ($3 each). The objects are built up from coils of wet clay, then pounded with a flattened stick. The day's production of earthenware is usually fired, in open air straw fires, around 4 p.m.

Examples of all items are available at a shop in the center, which can also arrange for shipping. Good luck with your big water container! Six nearby hamlets also feature pottery works. At Kampung Tenandon, gas ovens are used for firing, allowing the craftsmen there to create stronger, thinner-bodied items. Most of the small pottery objects here are glazed.

Sade: traditional houses

Continuing south from Penujak, you pass through the little town of Sengkol (Thursday market) before reaching the village of Sade, all traditional houses and rice barns. The building code here prohibits "modern" touches like red tile roofs.

Little boys, some of whom have picked up a good bit of English, will escort you around their village, explaining whatever they think will interest you. In 1989, the government put in a concrete pathway—apparently too many elderly tourists were falling down. Women with an entrepreneurial spirit have set up little stands selling *ikat* cloth along the path. These are serious saleswomen, so keep your cool as you walk the gauntlet of high-pressure sales pitches.

The traditional houses enclose an interior platform raised about a meter off the ground, and made of a mixture of clay, dung and straw, that has been polished to a high gloss. The roof is thatch, and the walls are bamboo or palm leaf ribs. Sade also has many of the pile-supported, bonnet-shaped rice barns—*lumbung*s—which have become the symbol of Lombok. About 150 families live in the village, all farmers in the nearby fields.

Kuta: the nyale ritual

From Sade, it's just a short hop to the south coast at Kuta village (Sunday market) and

Opposite: *Traditional rice barns, called* lumbung, *have almost disappeared from Lombok. The few remaining are now tourist attractions.*

beach. Although the area is slated for hotel development in the near future, so far there are just a few simple *losmen* and restaurants here. The scenery along the 8-kilometer coastal road from Kuta to Tanjung Aan and Grupuk, which hugs the bayside beach, is nothing short of spectacular.

Kuta beach hosts one of Lombok's most extraordinary yearly events, the Bau Nyale. Each year, 5–7 days following the second full moon—usually February but sometimes March—a bottom dwelling seaworm (*Eunice viridis*) begins a reproductive cycle by sending sperm- and ovum-containing sections to wriggle to the surface and produce fertilized eggs. The same phenomenon takes place elsewhere in Indonesia, notably Sumba, where it marks the beginning of the Pasola ritual. (See "The Pasola," page 184.)

The people of Lombok, like the Sumbanese, believe that the relative number of these *nyale* "worms," along with other aspects of their behavior, have a direct bearing on the abundance of the upcoming rice harvests. There is a legend of a beautiful princess who despaired over the many suitors fighting to marry her and threw herself into the sea. Her exquisite hair became the *nyale* worms. (There is a similar legend among the people of Sumba.)

Just before the appearance of the *nyale,* thousands of people camp out on Kuta's beach. When the worms are seen, the ritual is opened by the *mangku*, the leader of traditions. The fertility aspect of the ritual takes a form particular to Lombok, a conservative society where young people of marriageable age have little opportunity for contact. At the *nyale* festival, parents loosen their holds on their daughters, and young people are allowed unsupervised contact, albeit in groups. Courting is permitted, but only in public. Some restraints still apply.

Young men and women, dressed in their best, form separate groups and go strolling around to see what's available. Flirting takes place through poetic songs and subtle wordplay; just the opposite of macho posturing. A light, gay atmosphere prevails.

At dawn, the youths go out in boats to collect the worms, which will be prepared for eating later in a variety of ways: raw, mixed with grated coconut; grilled; salted and partially fermented, and preserved in bamboo tubes. Some believe that eating *nyale* worms produces an aphrodisiac effect.

In the past few years, with an eye to making the *nyale* ritual more attractive to foreign tourists, the government has commissioned paid actors to put on a beachside play re-enacting the drama of Princess Nyale. This seems an unnecessary interference in a traditional event, and hopefully the idea will be dropped. The "play" belongs to the show floors of tourist hotels, not Kuta beach during the local celebrations.

Tanjung Aan: gorgeous bay

From Kuta beach, the coastal road continues to Tanjung Aan, a kilometer-wide, horseshoe-shaped bay. Big waves crash with impressive booming sprays on the rocky islets at the opening of the bay. Tanjung Aan's wide sand beach encloses turquoise waters, where seaweed is grown on bamboo frames. A long, steep peninsula juts out to sea on the west side, giving access to great panoramic views.

An almost completed hotel sits by the beach. The building was closed before it even opened, as it apparently violated a regulation against building so close to the water. Be that as it may, a star-rated hotel is scheduled to rise from the ashes at this very spot.

The coastal road continues a couple of kilometers past Tanjung Aan, to Grupuk village, where the recent introduction of seaweed cultivation, for agar, has put much needed rupiahs into local pockets. Nearby, there is supposed to be excellent surfing at a place that has been baptized "Desert Point" by Australian surfers.

A little before Tanjung Aan, a 13-kilometer dirt road leads to, and ends at, Awang village on the shore of a large bay. Few people take this road, which is a bit rough, and the hamlets here are still quite traditional. The hilltop, just before the road drops down to Awang, offers a view of the bay.

There are many bamboo rafts of seaweed here. The owners tie colored flags to them so that they can be identified.

From Awang, you can charter an outboard-powered canoe to Batu Nampar at the head of the bay (15–30 minutes, about $3). A good road heads north out of Batu Nampar. Also, three *bemo*s a day connect Sengkol with Awang.

Unless you have to head back to your hotel because you are on a day tour, we suggest spending one night (or more) in the Kuta area and returning by a different road. If you want the best overview of this area, take a short—but steep—hike to the top of the hill just west of Kuta. A paved road heads west and soon goes into a steep climb to the top where a small hotel was under construction when we visited. The view is stupendous, so bring your camera.

Batu Nampar: traditional villages

After Kuta, head for Batu Nampar via Sengkol, Mujar and Ganti. Shortly after the turnoff from Ganti to Batu Nampar, there is a large village called Batu Rintang. The village has only traditional thatch huts and lots of *lumbung* rice barns. Almost no tourists come this way, and the people of Batu Rintang are very curious about the ways of westerners.

The village just across the road has the none-too-reassuring name Mata Mailing, "Thief's Eye." In several areas of central and south Lombok, thieves are admired—as long

as they steal (usually cattle) from another village and share the proceeds. This dates back to the days of frequent hunger. Clever rustlers were proud of their title: "Master Thief." Better hang on to your wallet when visiting Mata Mailing.

There are extensive salt works outside Batu Nampar, along with the floating seaweed frames in the bay. Bugis and Mandarese immigrants, who favor the stilted houses of their home islands, now outnumber the Sasaks here. Some of these perched houses sport walls with colorful, geometric motifs. From Batu Nampar you can charter an outboard-powered canoe down the coast to Awang, or across the bay to Ekas. The ride to Ekas takes about one hour and will set you back $6.

Tanjung Luar: Bugis settlement

Heading north from Batu Nampar, turn east at Ganti toward two coastal settlements: Ekas and Tanjung Luar. To reach Ekas, turn south, past Jerowaru (Thursday market), and follow a good dirt road to the little village on the eastern shore of Awang Bay.

The road passes salt ponds and crosses low coastal hills. There is lots of seaweed grown in the area, and good scenery along the way. At Ekas, you may be able to find a motorized canoe to take you back to Batu Nampar or Awang.

To reach Tanjung Luar, keep going east from Ganti, through Keruak, and on to the coast. Tanjung Luar is a large village of Bugis immigrants from south Sulawesi. Most of the people here are fishermen, and they catch a great deal of squid, particularly from October to April.

Hundreds of little outriggers line the long, curved, black sand beach, and some larger boats anchor off to the right of the pier. People go out on the flat reef at low tide to collect shellfish, but if you want to watch the operation, be prepared for shrill cries of "Turis! Turis!" Also, be very careful when you walk on the beach: it serves as the village's toilet.

You can rent a boat from Tanjung Luar for the one-day round trip to Tanjung Ringgit ($15–$30) on the far tip of the southeast peninsula. There is little of interest along the coast north of Tanjung Luar.

If you return to the three cities through Keruak, look for the traditional canoe-making operation there. The craftsmen are on the south side of the road, just before the crossroads at the center of town.

Beleka: crafts and tobacco

From Batu Nampar, you can also return to the east–west trunk highway through the crafts village of Beleka (Wednesday market). At the Gadin Mas Handicraft Center, craftsmen create rattan and bamboo baskets; carved wooden items; and seashell-decorated pottery. There are many items on sale in their shop. Much of the center's production is shipped to Bali, where it will fetch much higher prices.

The dry countryside around Beleka is typical of south and east Lombok. The main crop grown is tobacco, which requires little water. Several dams seem to serve no purpose other than to provide a place for people to bathe and wash their clothes. It's slow going on this road on the late afternoon, when the water buffalo are driven home.

After passing through Besun (Thursday market) you reach the main road at Kopang. From here, or from Ganti to the south, you can begin your explorations of East Lombok. Or, if you are worn out, head back to join the sybarites in Senggigi.

Opposite: *Women tying sprigs of seaweed to lines that will be floated in rafts just offshore. After harvest, the seaweed is dried and exported to be processed into carrageenan.* **Above:** *Even in these times of peace, the formal dress of a Sasak nobleman is not complete without a* kris *knife tucked into his waistcloth.*

EAST LOMBOK

Mountain Resorts and Empty Plains

Except for the crafts area around Kota Raja, the eastern portion of Lombok is largely a blank on tourist maps. The area is not really geared for foreign visitors. But, in addition to the crafts area, we suggest a visit to the areas around Selong, and the coast between Labuhan Lombok and Kali Putih, to see Mt. Rinjani, deserted shores, and the dry, empty countryside characteristic of this region.

Tetebatu: cool resort

Heading east from the three cities on the cross-island highway, you cross into the East Lombok district soon after Kopang. A short way past the town of Sikur (Friday market), a paved road heads north to Kota Raja. This area has the most decorated *cidomos* and horses, which trot along in a colorful display. Kota Raja hosts a large Monday and Wednesday market. The area is known for handicrafts, blacksmithing, and brick-making.

The vicinity of Kota Raja is a conservative area, children attend Islamic schools and most men wear sarongs rather than pants. The boys dress in sarongs and wear the black *peci* hat; the girls wear long skirts and the *kerudung*, a cloth that covers the head and upper body, leaving only the face bare.

Traditional blacksmiths in Kota Raja forge a variety of farming implements, and nearby Loyok village specializes in bamboo and palm leaf handicrafts.

Tetebatu village, a couple of kilometers north of Kota Raja, has become something of a mountain resort with several *losmen* and homestays. The best and oldest of the lot, Wisma Soedjono, has been expanded around a guesthouse built by the Dutch in the early 1920s. Its open sided restaurant overlooks *sawah*s and forest with a good early-morning view of Rinjani.

There is a "monkey forest" nearby, just past the hamlet of Orang Gerisak. It is just a short walk to a small waterfall, called Joben. A really big one, 50 meters high, called Jeruk Manis or Air Temer, is 12 kilometers away. At the hamlet of Kemban Seri, traditional music and dances can be arranged. The Soedjono rents vans and motorcycles, and also has English-speaking guides for hire. It is cool here at night, so bring a sweater and jacket.

Selong: cattle market

Back on the main road, continue a short way to Masbagik (Monday market), and then head southeast along a good road to Selong. On Mondays, about 2 kilometers along this road, is the island's largest cattle market, which hums with activity. Goats and water buffalo contribute to the weekly cloud of dust raised here. Continuing along this road you reach Selong, the center of an area where some conservative Wetu Telu adherents live uneasily with equally conservative orthodox Muslims of the Nahdatul Wahtan (Rebirth of the Nation) sect.

The good road continues to Labuhan Haji, so-named because this is where the pilgrims used to depart for their haj to Mecca. There are many Bugis in this little town, and their colorful canoes line the black sand beach, facing a barrier reef 100 meters offshore. There was a thriving Chinese community in Labuhan Haji until 1965, when—during the bloodbath following the attempted communist coup—some 40 Chinese were killed, and all Chinese-owned houses burned. The survivors fled to western Lombok, and this marked the end of Labuhan Haji's days as a commercial port.

The dry countryside west of Selong has several Muslim cemeteries marked by the characteristic large, gnarled frangipani trees. This area produces the long, hot red chillies called *lombok,* along with sweet potatoes which are grown in raised rectangular beds. Their edible leaves end up in the local *gado-gado* salad.

Lenek village: traditional dance

About 2 kilometers east of Masbagik is a producer-controlled pottery center, like the one at Penujak, established with the help of the New Zealand government. Further east on the main highway is Lenek village, which has an excellent music and dance ensemble.

This ensemble performs at local events, and on Sundays at the Senggigi Beach Hotel and other fancy venues. With two days' notice, you can have them perform locally for

Opposite: *The tiny port of Labuhan Lombok is of only minor importance in inter-island transport.*

you for $20–$60. Contact their leader, Pak Rahil. In fact, even if you don't want a show, you should try to talk to Pak Rahil (If you speak Indonesian).

The old man has had so many wives that he can't remember them all—nor can anyone else. People say once he fell in love with his own granddaughter, until someone told him who she was. His daughters and granddaughters are among Lombok's most beautiful women. He is still strong, black-haired and very opinionated.

Pak Rahil is an expert on Lombok history as written in the *lontar*s, and is considered the most powerful mystic on Lombok, even by the Wetu Telu people, no slouches themselves in this fine art. Pak Rahil heads the local Kebatinan movement, a sort of mystical sect which originated in Java. The country's president, Pak Harto (Suharto) is an unofficial member.

Aikmel: mountain walk

Aikmel (Wednesday market) is northeast of Masbagik on the main road to Labuhan Lombok. On the way, closely terraced rice fields form a perfect foreground to Mt. Rinjani looming in back. A road north of Aikmel leads to Pesugulan, the point of departure for the 16 kilometer, 4–5 hour hike to Sembalun Bumbung through beautiful mountain scenery. The walk starts out through gently rising meadows, then you get a full view of Rinjani.

Past Aikmel, near the 60 kilometers marker from Ampenan, the highway passes through a lovely long tunnel formed by trees and tall bamboo lining both sides of the road. Past Pringgabaya (Saturday market), the landscape changes dramatically from rice paddies to dry, desolate plains with few trees and mountains rising in the background.

Labuhan Lombok: port town

From Mataram you can reach Labuhan Lombok, 74 kilometers away, in about 1.5 hours if you do not stop on the way. The town is centered around the beginning of a 2-kilometer stretch from the market to the Sumbawa–Lombok ferry landing.

The road north from Labuhan Lombok heads along the coast through dry, rugged country, with an occasional oasis provided by a *sawah,* or a grove of coconut or fruit trees. The dry stretches feature a few *kapok* trees, whose pods yield a fluffy white fiber used to stuff mattresses and pillows.

At the village of Labuhan Pandan, just as the road curves left, a short side path leads to the sea. The local fishing boats are neatly aligned on a carpet of green leaves covering the hot black sand. From here you can charter a canoe to several offshore islands for $12 a day. The islands have white sand beaches, but you have to bring your own water.

LOMBOK BY JEEP

Exploring the Island's Rough Back Roads

Although most of Lombok's roads are now paved and work is proceeding on upgrading others in many places, there are still three areas along the south coast—which offer the island's best seascape scenery—where the roads are too poor for a *bemo* or car. Here, you need an all-wheel-drive jeep, called a "hardtop" locally, or, at the very least, a Kijang (a brand of utility vehicle) in good shape with a driver who knows what he's doing on rough roads.

Don't attempt most of what's described below during the rainy season in any kind of vehicle except perhaps a large, twin-axle truck. It would be a lot less trouble, and maybe even faster, to hike it.

Sepi area: rough, but beautiful

The first stretch of our bumpy route starts in Sekatong Tengah past the port of Lembar, on a partially paved, 10-kilometer road running due south across the peninsula to Sepi. The road winds through dry hills, where you can see terraced garden plots on impossibly steep slopes.

Just before Sepi, a very steep downgrade leads to the sea, offering the first of a long series of spectacular vistas. From Sepi, a ragged little fishing village, you can rent an outboard powered canoe ($12) to the white sand beaches at Blongas, on the far side of the bay. There is supposedly good snorkeling and scuba diving near Blongas, as the coral there has not been ruined by fish bombing. Divers have reported 2-meter sharks, turtles and large fish in waters with good visibility.

An occasional *bemo* makes it to Sepi, but no further until the road ahead improves. From Sepi onward, almost all the houses are traditional, with the occasional red tile roof saved for the village mosque. During the dry season the road is dusty.

Pengantap village is 8 kilometers further east, inland on a peninsula. Somewhere in this area is Lombok's oldest archaeological artifact, a 1.5-meter-high *menhir* said to have been erected some 3,000 years ago. The stone, called Batu Pujaan ("Stone of Worship") retains its mystical powers, and many rituals connected with birth, a child's first haircut, circumcision, marriage and death are still held here. People of the area also go to the stone to meditate, and to concoct traditional medicines and magic brews. It is said that shamans gather at Batu Pujaan once a year to share trade secrets.

About a kilometer past Pengantap, you can drive or walk across the fields to the sea for a great view as far as Silung Blanak, your destination. A small low island, about 250 meters offshore, could offer good scuba diving—if you can get all your gear this far. Local boatmen say that there are lots of fish, some of them big ones, lurking out there around the island.

Just past the lookout, the road heads inland over a steep hill which again gives a great, wide view of the area. From here, however, it's a boring, albeit somewhat less bumpy 18 kilometers to Silung Blanak, through hilly country with few villages.

We saw not a single vehicle between Sepi and the village of Patu Jangke (Wednesday market), which sits just before the pavement begins for the short downhill stretch to the sea. The little fishing settlement at Silung Blanak (Sunday market) sits just off a wide, dazzling white sand beach running along a huge bay. The water is various shades of blue, turquoise and green. A couple of stalls here sell drinks and snacks.

Kuta area: best view in Lombok

The short coastal stretch between Kuta and Mawun offers probably the best seascape scenery in Lombok. It is faster to get to Mawun along the 11-kilometer road from Pengember, but only the rough 10 kilometers from Kuta offer the scenery.

The first section of the road west from Kuta is paved. It meanders low just a bit before rising very steeply to the hilltop, giving a splendid view to the east: Kuta beach and Tanjung Aan lie, magnificently, at your feet. When we last visited, a small hotel (perhaps a restaurant) was under construction at the best viewing spot.

From here the road cuts a bit inland, the pavement stops and the surface degenerates. You pass a limestone cliff, riddled with caves on three sides. Over a hill and you are in an oasis of palm trees and creek-fed ricefields. A bit further on, a tough 1.5-kilometer side

road leads to Are Goling, another great beach, this one fronted by Nusa Tanjung, "Cape Island," which you can easily walk to at low tide.

A marine biologist working here predicted that snorkeling and diving would be good from September to April, after which the waves come up and visibility could be a problem. Surfers could try it the rest of the year. Along with the fish, there are lobster and small abalone here as well.

This beach and the one at Mawun, white, curved and as lovely as they come, have already been bought up by a speculator. Work is proceeding to extend the road to Tampa, a beach cove about 2 kilometers west of Mawun.

The southeast peninsula

The south coast of the peninsula jutting out from southeast Lombok has beaches and scenery to match and perhaps even surpass those on the Kuta–Mawun leg. From Ekas (see "Central Lombok," page 72), an awful dirt road runs 6 kilometers to the peninsula's south coast. The last stretch of this road is covered in choking brown dust.

On the beaches here the Big Boys from Jakarta are playing speculator's Monopoly; buying 100 hectare chunks of beachfront at a reported $20,000 per hectare. (The price of beachfront in Senggigi—if anyone there is willing to sell—is at least 20 times higher.)

But the price is worth it to whoever manages to put up a hotel. The coast is a series of half-moon bays, every one of them lined with white sand. The small bays are separated from each other by low cliffs and capes, allowing a view of the beautiful water and the fringing reef, some 100 meters offshore.

The first beach ends in a bold island, which raises its rock straight out of the sea: Gili Anak Ewok, "Orphan Island." You can walk here from Ekas if your vehicle can't make it—but bring plenty of water.

On the way back from Ekas, about halfway to Jerowaru, a 20-kilometer dirt road, said to take about one hour to negotiate by jeep, ends at Tanjung Ringgit. You can also reach this little seaside village by outboard from Tanjung Luar.

Tanjung Ringgit is thought to be something of a magically charged place. There are said to be spirit caves nearby, and the Wetu Telu leader of Bayan, on the northern tip of Lombok (and as far as you can get from Tanjung Ringgit and still stay on the island) says there is a mystical connection between his area and the tip of this peninsula.

Above: *The rugged limestone cliffs of Lombok's south coast, seen here through a fish-eye lens, alternate with great expanses of white sand beach. Access to these splendid beaches is difficult, requiring a four-wheel-drive vehicle, but the beauty and isolation is worth the trouble.*

PART III

Introducing Sumbawa

In a certain sense Sumbawa is the western-most island of East Indonesia, that is, the first of the islands that never felt the direct influence of the Indianized cultures of Java and Bali. Here, despite the dominance of Islam, *adat* remains strong. From Sumbawa eastward in Nusa Tenggara, one encounters a belief in traditional ancestral religions. In some cases, the professed Islam or Christianity exists only as a thin veneer.

Sumbawa is really two islands: Sumbawa Besar in the west, and Bima in the east. In fact, although outsiders call the whole island "Sumbawa," on the island this term is only used for the west. The two parts of the island are divided by both geography and language—that spoken by the Sumbawanese being more like Sasak; that spoken by the Bimans being more like the languages of Flores and Sumba. This division has been further reinforced by the historical influence of the Balinese in the west, and the Makassarese of South Sulawesi in the North.

Although Sumbawa is three times the size of Lombok, it holds just one-third the population—approximately 800,000 people. The island's terrain is rough and mountainous, and Sumbawa is blessed with no fertile plain like the one gracing south-central Lombok. On a map, the outline of the island is contorted by capes, peninsulas and deeply cut bays. The 15,600-square-kilometer island stretches 280 kilometers east–west, but its width varies from 15 kilometers to 90 kilometers.

Some 85 percent of Sumbawa is too mountainous to farm, but the rich volcanic soil of the river valleys yields bumper crops. These valleys were the site of many petty states, the island's first political units.

The Great Explosion

Sumbawa is part of the volcanic northern chain of Nusa Tenggara, and while activity took place over the eras, no single explosion seems to have been as dramatic as the Mt. Tambora eruption of 1815. According to *The Guiness Book of World Records,* this one was the greatest in known history. Over 150 cubic kilometers of rock and ash, including the top third of the volcano, were propelled upward, leaving Tambora truncated, the now 2,851-meter cone holding a huge caldera.

An estimated 10,000 people died in the blast, and perhaps another 30–40,000 (some estimates run as high as half the island's population) died of starvation afterwards when a 5-centimeter-thick layer of volcanic ash smothered all plants in a wide area. The devastation was such that there are stories of parents at the time selling their children for three kilos of rice.

In 1845, a Dutch geologist found large areas still completely buried under 50 centimeters of debris. The explosion obliterated the Sanggar and Pekat sultanates, located on opposite sides of the large peninsula holding Tambora. Although Tambora has since behaved, the island's volcanic tradition is by no means a thing of the past. In 1985, Sangeang Island's Gunung Api ("Fire Mountain") turned active and forced the evacuation of its 3,000 inhabitants.

Early history

It is thought that the first Austronesians reached Sumbawa approximately 2000 B.C., introducing agriculture to the island. While no extensive archaeological work has yet been carried on in Sumbawa, decorated stone sarcophagi found here firmly anchor the island to the chain of megalithic cultures strung out unevenly throughout Indonesia.

Written letters—probably of Pallawan or Sanscrit origins—were recently discovered, incised in a rock formation at the mouth of

Overleaf: *Water buffalo head home after a long day's work in the rice fields of west Sumbawa.*
Opposite: *A bridesmaid at Tepal, a traditional village in the mountainous interior of Sumbawa.*

Bima Bay. Accompanied by Hindu-style carvings, these date from perhaps the 7th century. Bronze Dongson-style drums found on the island, including a fine one actually cast by Dongson craftsmen found on Sangeang island, confirm that the northern coast of Sumbawa was part of the east–west maritime trade route to the spice and sandalwood islands to the east.

The East Javanese Majapahit Empire, which at its height in the 14th century was Indonesia's greatest, traded with and perhaps exercised a small measure of political and military control over Sumbawa Island. After Majapahit collapsed in the face of Islam, the Balinese kingdom of Gelgel, through marriage relations and a military expedition, controlled West Sumbawa for a short while.

In the 15th and 16th centuries, the kingdom of Bima claimed Flores, Timor, Solor, Savu and Sumba, but it is doubtful if this amounted to much beyond an occasional military foray to obtain slaves and some control over trade.

The Bima district

With its large, hourglass-shaped bay, protected year-round from the monsoon winds, Bima has always been the island's preeminent town. This harbor was the logical place for traders to stop to take on water, rice and other foodstuffs, and to buy local cloth and sappanwood, which is used in dye-making.

The island's written records accord the greatest importance to Bima as well, which is understandable since the only sources are the "Bo" manuscripts of the Bima dynasty. Written on *lontar* leaves, first in a local adaptation of Sanscrit, then, after Islamization, in Arabic, these record the early history of the island.

According to the Bo, Maharaja Pandu Dewata, the Lord of the Heavens, had five sons, one of which was Sang Bima. An inveterate traveler and ladies' man, Sang Bima met an unusually beautiful maiden, and did what gods usually do in these circumstances. The brief affair resulted in a daughter. On a subsequent trip, Sang Bima met the daughter, and fell in love again (although, to his credit, Sang Bima did not know he was sleeping with his own daughter.)

But even gods are not supposed to commit incest. When he discovered her identity, Sang Bima told his daughter that when her twin sons are born, she must abandon them (Moses like) on a raft in the river. She carried out her father-lover's instructions.

With perhaps a bit of divine intervention, a childless *ncuhi,* one of the early clan leaders, found the boys and took them into his care. One of the boys, named Indra Zamrud, founded a dynasty, which he named after his father: Bima. The other, Indra Komala, founded the Dompu kingdom, just west of Bima. The Bima palace records show 16 descen-

dants of Indra Zamrud ruling successively until the line switched to Islam in 1630.

The coming of Islam

In the early 17th century, a family feud between two brothers for the throne of Bima resulted in a civil war. The conflict was initially won by Salisian, who in subsequent palace records is called "the usurper." After his initial defeat, the "rightful" heir, Ma Batawadu, sailed to Makassar in South Sulawesi for assistance. There he was told he could have all the military help he needed—and a royal princess to boot—but only if he converted to Islam. (The terms of the bargain, however, do not appear in the palace records.)

This agreed to, Ma Batawadu returned with an army of tough Bugis and Makassarese warriors, and defeated his brother's forces. In 1630, Ma Batawadu became a sultan (instead of a Hindu-style raja), taking the name of Abdul Kahir. From this time on, palace records cite Bima's "ties of blood, religion and law" to South Sulawesi.

The Syara, the Islamic code, became the law of the land—until the Dutch forced rulers to tone things down in 1908. Although Bima is still heavily Islamic today, the government does not tolerate fanaticism. (A group from Bima once tried to assassinate President Sukarno for his allegedly anti-Muslim views, succeeding only in killing some school girls.) But Saturday-night discos had to be closed, although it was two kilometers outside of Bima proper.

Sumbawa Besar's succession of hereditary rulers was not as smooth as Bima's. The royal lineage ended in 1820, when a Muslim adventurer from the Banjarmasin Sultanate in South Kalimantan seized the royal heirlooms and the throne. The line he established ruled until Indonesia's independence.

The colonial period

For the most part, the Dutch colonial authorities left Sumbawa Island alone. They did try to monopolize trade, particularly in the local sappanwood, but with varying degrees of success. Only in the early 20th century did Holland assert control, and although there was spirited resistance, the Europeans' superior weapons and organization won out.

The influence of the Dutch was short-lived, lasting only until World War II, when the Japanese invaded. Still, it had an effect on the local aristocracy, members of which were allowed to attend Dutch schools. Even today, many of the older members of the aristocracy are still fluent in Dutch, although the younger generation studies in English.

In 1929, the Sultan of Bima arranged for

Opposite: *These onion fields in the Bima district require hand irrigation. The farmers splash water on their plants from twin buckets, which they carry slung over their shoulders on a pole.*

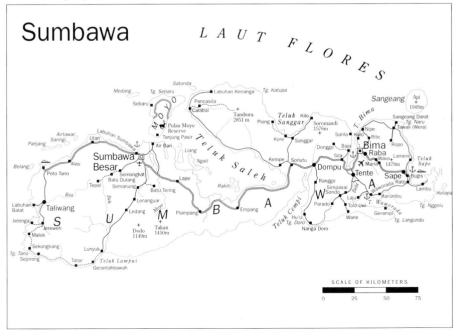

his daughter to marry the daughter of his counterpart in Sumbawa Besar. This royal intermarriage was the first ever between the two leading sultanates. When the young people met for the first time on the eve of their marriage, they could communicate only in Dutch. Nyonya Kaharuddin, who survived her husband by many years, told me that her dowry included many slaves. It was only in 1959 that her husband signed a decree freeing the few remaining ones.

The Japanese were at first welcomed on Sumbawa Island, but they soon inspired hatred for their indiscriminate killings, robbery and rape. After the war, and a short period within the Dutch-imposed Federated States of Indonesia, Sumbawa was integrated into today's Republic of Indonesia. The island's three districts—Sumbawa Besar, Dompu and Bima—correspond to the sultanates which survived prior to colonial control. In 1951 Bima's 13th sultan, Salamuddin, having ruled since 1913, gracefully gave up his powers to the central government. His heirs have held high government positions in both Bima and Jakarta.

The Dou Donggo

There are two main ethnic groups on Sumbawa Island: the Tau Samawa (or Orang Sumbawa) in the west, and the Dou Mbojo (or Orang Bima) in the east. The Samawa (a distortion of whose name yielded "Sumbawa")

are by language close kin of the Sasaks and Balinese to the west. The Bimanese language—Nggahi Mbojo—belongs to the eastern part of Nusa Tenggara. Because of contacts with Sulawesi, the coastal population includes Bugis, Makassarese and Bajau settlers. There are also several thousand Balinese in the west, and a few hundred in the east.

Some of the original inhabitants of the island retreated to the mountains to preserve their traditions in the face of coastal influences, perhaps even before the arrival of Islam in 1630. In western Sumbawa, traditional communities—the Tau Tepal—live in the areas of Tepal and Ropang. In the east, a traditional people called the Dou Donggo live around the southern flank of Mt. Soromandi, and in the area of Wavo, just east of the Bima–Sape highway.

Eastern Sumbawa's Dou Donggo people still follow the leadership of the *ncuhi* clan heads, and maintain many of their ancient rituals connected with ancestral spirits, and agricultural and life cycles. Their Trinity consists of the Sky, the Water and the Wind. Their belief system is called Marafu, similar in both name and expression to the Marapu of Sumba. The Donggo sacrifice water buffalo, goats or chickens (according to their social standing) to curry favor with the spirits for bountiful harvests and good health. A general fertility ceremony is held around the November planting date.

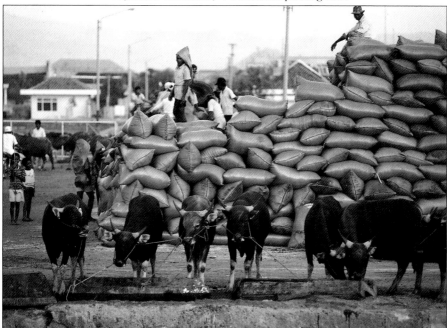

The Donggo are divided into two groups. The Donggo Ipa—"Yonder Mountain people"—some 5,000 strong, live in the highlands of the peninsula west of Bima Bay. The Donggo Ele—"Eastern Mountain people"—more influenced by Islam, live in the highlands to the east of the airport and bay, in the Wavo Tengah subdistrict.

The Bima court today

Although the cultural life of the Dou Donggo has survived, the Bima court has not kept up the spectacular festivals of the past. Economic constraints, and pressure from orthodox Muslims, have preempted spectacles such as the week-long, day-and-night Ua Pua. This yearly event—held in the Muslim month of Rabi'ul Awal, following Maulid—was first staged in the 17th century by the religious teacher of the second sultan.

Abdul Khair Sirajuddin, alias Lambila, had been slack in his faith, mostly because he had spent so much time on his love of the fine arts. To woo his attention back to religious matters, his Muslim teacher organized a spectacular celebration to commemorate Muhammad's birthday. The event's highlight was a giant pavilion, containing 99 egg-flower arrangements (symbolizing Allah's 99 names) which was carried in a procession featuring brightly dressed dancers and an orchestra. The celebration was splendid enough to convince the sybaritic sultan that Islam did not need to be boring.

Thus, Lambila ordered the festival to continue forever on a yearly basis. His orders were followed until 1950, when the influence of strict Muslim reformers became strong enough to have it stopped. The event has been staged just once since, in 1981, but was not repeated—mostly because of the great expense involved. Today, there is talk of reviving at least a part of the Ua Pua celebrations, to be financed with funds from the department of tourism.

A revival of the court dances created in the 17th century under Sultan Sirajuddin's patronage is also taking place. Rehearsals are often held at the former palace—now the district museum—in Bima, with public performances held on some Sunday mornings.

Entertainment at the village level has seen less of a decline. Held in conjunction with local celebrations such as weddings, there are mock fights—with or without weapons—based on the *pencak silat,* an Indonesian martial art. Other events include a whip fight called *parise* adopted from western Flores, and the most distinctive Bimanese-style fighting, *ntumbu,* in which men charge each other with lowered heads and bang together, in the style of rams.

Opposite: *Bags of sea-salt and livestock ready for export at Bima harbor.* **Above:** *Dancers in front of the old sultan's palace at Sumbawa Besar.*

TRADITION AND MAGIC

Shamans, Spells and a Mighty Punch

A haji—a Muslim religious leader who has made his pilgrimage to Mecca—in Tepal, Sumbawa Besar once told a curious anecdote about the soldiers fighting for Indonesian independence.

There was a village nearby renowned for its powerful *sanro.* This shaman, he said, could make men bullet-proof by rubbing magical oil into their heads. Before releasing his "patient," the *sanro* would test his work by whacking the man in the neck with a sharp-edged machete. If any blood came out, he repeated the application of the oil until the man's skin was completely impervious to blade—or bullet.

Before departing to fight with the nationalist army, young men flocked to see this *sanro* to gain magical protection for their bodies. Once they received the treatment, they prayed to Allah and went off to fight.

Whether or not the bullets actually bounced off the bodies has not been recorded. But the story illustrates an important point about the Sumbawanese: beneath a strong belief in Islam lies a perhaps equally strong belief in the old magic.

Many of the ritual events of the old ways are still performed, although no longer in a ritual context. Water buffalo are still raced across the paddy fields, and young men still participate in the *berempuk,* a ritual boxing match in the past designed to spill blood to appease the spirits. These events no longer are performed as part of an animist planting or harvest cycle; but they still are surrounded by magic and the work of the *sanro.*

In a few parts of Sumbawa——among the Dou Donggo in Bima, and the people living in Tepal and Ropang in Sumbawa Besar—the traditional ways continue without apology. In Tepal, marriages still follow elaborate patterns that involve wearing and displaying traditional heirlooms, protecting the bride and groom from the work of evil *sanro,* and the payment of (symbolic) bridewealth.

The buffalo races

Thundering across the flooded rice paddies, two matched pairs of water buffaloes closed in on their target: a bright piece of cloth tied to a stick. The crowd of spectators roared. Despite the efforts of their jockey, riding a flimsy wooden sled, one of the pairs of ani-

mals veered off to the edge of the paddy, just 15 meters before the goal.

The other pair then slowed down and, carefully guided by their driver, approached to within a tantalizingly two meters of the goal. Then, out of the blue, one of the animals decided he had had enough. He just stopped. The other kept going for a second, then—caught by his partner's leash—was pulled tight and stopped. The driver tried pleading with the beasts. No avail. He beat them wildly on their huge buttocks with a switch. Nothing.

Throwing up his hands in frustration, the driver fell backwards off his sled, landing in the water and mud of the rice paddy. He then showered his buffalo with a number of not very endearing names. The spectators laughed. The driver gave up, and let his once more docile animals off into the field.

The water buffalo race has a very practical beginning. Before it receives a new crop of seedling rice, a *sawah* must be "plowed"— the mud must be chopped up and churned to aerate the soil. The easiest way to do this, in Sumbawa and other parts of the Lesser Sundas, is the use the local tractor, the water buffalo. In Sumbawa, this task has turned into a spectator sport, and an occasion for the work of the shaman.

Magic and money

Pak Mustakim, my friend and unofficial guide, as well as the head of the local office of culture, stood up from his seat and walked over to where I had been standing to photograph the event.

"Dr. Kal" he said, "the magic of the *sanro* hired by the owner of the rice paddy was stronger than the magic of the *sanro* who controlled the water buffaloes. That is why neither was able to reach the *puin kayu* (the 'goal-post,' which must pass between the winning pair of buffaloes)."

I told him that I thought everyone in Sumbawa followed Islam, which has no place for "black magic."

"Ah, yes…well, that is the theory."

In practice, Pak Mustakim said, the farmers, though good Muslims, still adhere to many of their ancient traditions and beliefs. They learn their prayers in Arabic and attend services at the mosque. But for many things, they rely on their *sanro*. Even the *sanro,* who manipulate magical forces, consider themselves to be good Muslims, he said.

There was plenty of magic in the air that afternoon. Time after time, the normally well-trained water buffaloes would just refuse their drivers' pleas, whacks and urgings. But a lucky few did make it to the target. For these, another series of races was held, this one timed with a stop-watch.

The fastest pair won a prize of $250, representing about 6 months' income in Indonesia. In addition to the cash prize, the owner of the buffaloes' investment just about doubled in value as well, for the prize-winning beasts were now worth about $800 each. Everyone agreed that most of the credit should go to the team's *sanro,* who had rubbed the animals with special oils and chanted powerful mantras to the team of buffalo the night before the race.

Ritual boxing

Traditional boxing usually accompanies the rice harvest. What we saw were young men whacking each other with much more enthusiasm than style, often drawing blood. Their efforts also attracted admiring glances from the young ladies in attendance.

Opposite: *Water buffalo races across flooded sawah require more than just skill and strong animals—magic carries the day for the winners.*
Right: *Ubiquitous in Bima a decade ago, Muslim headscarves, locally called* rimpu, *are now worn more loosely or in some cases not at all. Although most Sumbawans are devout Muslims, a belief in the power of magic is prevalent and strong here.*

Young men gathered in two groups, one on either side of an open arena. There were no rules or round-robin matches. When the mood struck, a youth would rip off his shirt, gather up a bunch of rice stalks in each fist, and do a little show-off dance, prancing around the arena.

Usually within a few seconds he would have an adversary, who then began strutting around and posturing himself. Then two free-lance "referees" would appear, and check the opponents' hands, removing watches and rings—and making sure that there were no stones in the clenched fists.

After these preliminaries, the boxing would begin. It was really more like flailing—a series of wild, roundhouse punches from right and left fields, most flying way off the mark but the occasional one landing with a resounding, skin-splitting whack. Once the adversaries had exchanged a few punches, they would usually come in close, trading punches rapidly with absolutely no regard for defense or fending off blows. At this point, they would have to be pulled apart by the referees, who usually received a few wild punches for their effort.

Because there were no judges, each of the combatants would naturally assume he had won, and would thus prance triumphantly around the arena before retiring to his cheering side.

The 100-ton punch

That neither technique nor style was very important was illustrated in one of the fights. "Look at the young man who just came out," said Pak Mustakim. "He has trained as a real boxer." Indeed, he seemed to be more solidly built than the others, and his movements were more studied and deliberate. But when the fight began, his unskilled opponent connected with a couple of wild punches, and knocked the "boxer" down. More than coordination and training, it was magic again that played a predominant role.

Pak Mustakim pointed out a young man with a very slight body. Still, he said no one is willing to fight him. This is because they all know he packs a "100-ton punch" that a clever *sanro* helped him prepare. Indeed, as I watched, no one from the opposite side took up the challenge.

Tepal: traditional mountain village

Although the inhabitants of Sumbawa originally settled on the coast, successive waves of immigrants pushed the aboriginal settlers

into the less fertile, and less accessible, interior. The coast was where new philosophies first arrived, and it took a long time for them to reach the inland.

Thus, to witness the traditional life of Sumbawa, my guide and I trudged six weary hours to a village called Tepal. It was certainly off the beaten path. I had read that this was the center of the old culture on Sumbawa. Since I also knew that the first people to inhabit Sumbawa were called "Tau Tepal," my hopes were high.

These were quickly dispelled when I arrived in the village. We were told that we were the first westerners to visit, but there was nothing in the physical appearance of the village or the inhabitants to distinguish them from the coastal dwellers, with the notable exception of a lack of television antennas.

Tepal's 1,000 inhabitants live in thatch-covered houses raised on stilts. The village has been built a couple of hundred meters above a river, its hillcrest position perhaps having served some strategic purpose in the past. Most of the villagers wore store-bought sarongs, and some of the men wore pants.

Above: *Traditional boxing is part of the rice harvest celebration. Strong bodies are less important than the magic applied by a skilled* sanro, *a Sumbawanese shaman.* **Opposite:** *A form of ritual fighting with stout clubs ends in a jubilant celebration for the winning side.*

There is an elementary school here and a mosque, both of which are well-attended.

Our initial disappointment was dispelled somewhat by the news that a wedding was scheduled for the next day. Our interest was further piqued when we were told that the *sanro* who had originally chosen the date for the wedding (two days before our arrival) had changed it when he heard about the foreigners' impending visit. He decided that the wedding would suffer no ill influences if it were to be postponed to coincide with our short stay in Tepal.

A traditional wedding

Preliminaries to the wedding included all-night singing and tambourine playing, at both the bride's and groom's houses. On the big day itself, the women attendants put on all of their family heirlooms—brocades and exquisite antique jewelry as well as traditional head ornaments.

The main event began with a procession from the groom's house to the house of the bride. The parade was led by the village elders and dignitaries, who were followed by the resplendent girls. The groom, mounted on a small horse and surrounded by his friends, closed the procession.

Throughout the entire ceremony, the groom kept a handkerchief over his mouth. I asked Pak Mustakim to find out why, and he held a quick conference with the elders. He explained:

"It seems that there may be some other young men in love with the bride. It is only natural that they would be jealous at this moment. Either on their own or with the help of a *sanro,* they could be casting an evil spell on the groom at this time, his most vulnerable moment, when he is out in the open.

"Of course it is known that a magic spell enters most easily through the mouth. That is why he must keep his mouth covered throughout the procession."

At the bride's house, the bride washed the groom's feet, an act symbolizing faithfulness. The pair then sat under a colorful awning and each ate of a special dish of glutinous rice covered by thin layer of palm sugar.

The couple pecked absently at their food—obviously, their minds were on other things. This symbolic act of eating together was the final phase of the traditional wedding ceremony.

Unlike some other parts of the Lesser Sundas, there was only a symbolic bride price in Tepal. Elsewhere, bridewealth could include herds of water buffalo, antique elephant tusks or prehistoric bronze drums.

The symbolic offering to the bride's family consisted for the most part of contemporary Indonesian coins. It did, however, contain one unusual item: a large silver 5-franc piece, dated 1833, with the inscription "Louis Philippe I—Roi des Français."

WEST SUMBAWA

Taliwang, Moyo Island and Tepal

Most people who visit Sumbawa skip right over the western part of the island in their rush to get to Bima. This is too bad, because the west offers some interesting destinations, and they are not on the usual tourist circuit. The area around Taliwang and along the south coast is blessed with superb, deserted beaches and quiet little fishing villages. Moyo island, in the north, offers a game reserve, and some of the finest undisturbed reefs in the region. Tepal, in the highlands southwest of Sumbawa Besar, is one of the few remaining traditional villages on the island.

There is a catch. Some of these sites require traveling in a four-wheel-drive vehicle or strong truck over rough roads—or a motorcycle, if you are capable—or hiking. And there are no star-rated accommodations along the way. This kind of travel requires a flexible schedule, and you have to be resourceful, and speak some Indonesian or bring along an Indonesian-speaking guide.

South to Taliwang

When you step off the Lombok ferry at Poto Tano, in West Sumbawa, you have two basic choices: head south to Taliwang, or head east to the area around Sumbawa Besar, and on to the Bima district. Buses south usually head as far as Taliwang from the ferry landing, and trucks cover the rest of the way to the south coast, leaving Taliwang early each morning. But it is still best to hire a jeep or Kijang, a locally built utility vehicle.

As you leave the ferry landing area at Poto Tano (Poto means "harbor" in Samawa), you are greeted first by long, rectangular houses, neatly aligned and perched on stilts. It's 10 kilometers to the main road, and then another 33 kilometers to Taliwang.

The first half of the ride leads through dry, empty country with only very occasional glimpses of the sea in the distance. The first sign of life is Setelek village, and its people, fields and animals are a welcome sight. At the

nearby village of Rempe there are said to be some archaeological remains. Eight kilometers from Taliwang you get your first view of Lake Lebo, a large shallow lake with stretches of water lilies, lotus and other surface plants. The road follows the lake shore for 4 kilometers, then veers off. Just before you reach Taliwang, you cross the area's lifeline, the Brang ("River") Rea.

Taliwang is not a very attractive town, there are lots of dogs and several nondescript mosques. If you have your own vehicle, and it's early enough, keep going. If you came by bus, you'll have to stay overnight and catch a truck south the next morning. The locals here make rattan furniture, and perhaps you can watch them work. This is the last town with *losmen*, and if you are going further south, stock up here on supplies.

The Taliwang speak a distinct dialect. Many have emigrated west to Lombok, bringing with them their taste for *ayam* Taliwang, a delicious type of spicy chicken.

About one kilometer south of town, turn west, and at the end of an 8-kilometer road you'll find Labuhan Balat, a wide, curved beach of yellowish sand. The beach is walled in by high cliffs. There are a few huts and fishing canoes here, and a big, crumbling, colonial port building. In Dutch times, before the main road was built, Labuhan Balat was the shipping center of southwest Sumbawa.

The local economy around Taliwang reflects that of the whole west Sumbawa area. Towns and villages grew where land was flat enough, and there was enough water, for growing rice. Corn, soybeans, and beans are grown to supplement the rice, and groves of coconut trees are common along the coast. The farmers also raise livestock—goats, water buffalo, and Bali cattle, a domesticated form of the *banten*. Other than Taliwang's cottage industry in rattan furniture, there are few crafts here.

Labuhan Lalar: Bajo village

Six kilometers south of Taliwang, the road leads to Poto Batu, on the sea at the head of a long, wide estuary. The place is popular with the residents of Taliwang on weekends, and there are a couple of good stretches of beach—you can follow the sand all the way to Labuhan Balat. The waves can sometimes be rough, but the sunsets are beautiful on clear days. There are a couple of thatch-roofed

Opposite: *Bride and groom meet in a traditional wedding in the mountains of West Sumbawa.*

shelters, and with certain tides, a nearby "geyser" is supposed to shoot up to a respectable height from a hole in the coral.

Labuhan Lalar, a Bajo village of huts perched on black sand, is 3 kilometers further. This is the only seaside Bajo village in the area; the rest of the people here are inland farmers. Boats occasionally make the run from here to Lombok, and during the morning hours, delicious fresh fish can be bought at Labuhan Lalar's small market.

The little town of Jereweh, 15 kilometers from Taliwang and just across the Tiu Punje river, is the last one before the road becomes terrible, and the scenery becomes fantastic. There is a fairly well stocked store here for last minute supplies. If you are around just prior to planting, ask if there are any water buffalo races (*kerapan kerbau*). It's worth staying around for, or returning for the event.

Sekongkang: turtle beach

If you have your own vehicle—you might also be able to rent a motorcycle—try the 7-kilometer road that leads directly from Jereweh to Jelenga village, on the sea. Some 250 part-time farmers, part-time fishermen live next to a bay ringed with a white sand beach. There are coconut groves here and you can always buy a goat. No tourists come here. The people will definitely want to check you out.

Outside of Jereweh the "main" road is flat, and fairly good, but not for long. Soon you start climbing steep hills on a rocky trail, and if asphalt was ever applied here, there is no trace remaining. Another 12 kilometers and you reach the sea again at Benete village, where there are some seaweed plots.

Five kilometers from Benete is Malok, frequented by a few very dedicated surfers and their camp followers. The ones we met had suffered close encounters with coral, and were recovering from wounds that would have won a purple heart in any war. The waves break on the reef's edge, about a half kilometer from the shore. The people of the village where the surfers stay are mostly farmers, and do very little fishing.

Sekongkang Atas, 8 rough kilometers from Malok, is the end of the road for all but trucks and four-wheel-drives. Just before the village, a road west leads to Sekongkang Bawah, and from here, another rough 2 kilometers leads almost to the beach and bay. From this point, a narrow trail, difficult at high tide, leads to a superb, deserted bay, divided into two halves by a high coral formation. Bring your own snorkeling gear and everything else. The waves and coral and colors are simply stunning. This is a turtle-spawning beach, and the locals occasionally gather the eggs here. Being good Muslims, however, they don't eat turtle meat.

Beyond the Sekongkangs, the last 12 kilometers to the Sejorong/Tetar area are even tougher than what you just went through.

Informants called the beach at Sejorong "tremendous," and locals affirmed that it was also a turtle-spawning ground. From Sejorong, you can trek through big hills to Tetar, rest, then go on the Lunyuk—3 hours by road to Sumbawa Besar.

Once you are back in Taliwang, it is a long haul—115 kilometers—to Sumbawa Besar, with little to see along the way. It is worth stopping, however, at the old harbor and ferry landing at Alas. Just offshore here is Bungin island, crowded with the stilted huts of Bajo fishermen.

Bungin island

Bungin island, 15 minutes by motorboat from the old ferry landing at Alas, is said to be the most densely populated place in all of Indonesia. Actually the "island" is nothing but a coral reef, which originally was exposed only at high tide. Some 200 years ago, the Bajo fishermen in the area used it as a place to dry their nets. Then, fearing attacks from the Samawa on the mainland, they moved to this islet, where they built a whole village on stilts in the Bajo style. They have been there since then, living off the sea, and trading their fish and *trepang* in Alas markets for tools and staples like rice.

The houses are packed together, all with their backs to the sea. There is no area left on the island to build, so when a man wants to marry, he must first enlarge the island, stacking coral rubble in a shallow area to serve as a support for his new house. Vegetation has almost disappeared from Bungin, and the goats raised by the inhabitants must satisfy themselves chiefly with scraps and even fish.

The people of Bungin fetch firewood, and bury their dead, on Pulau Panjang, an island further west. Until recently, the Bajo were quite isolated—they spoke only Bajo and married among themselves. Girls, especially, never went out before marriage. Things have changed considerably, however, and now there are even electricity and water facilities on the island.

Sumbawa Besar: district capital

The district capital of the western part of the island is a large town with just one redeeming feature for the visitor: an old palace, built in 1885. Sumbawa Besar's palace was partially restored a century later, with the only aesthetic blunder being a concrete apron in front of the main entrance. The palace is worth a short visit, just grab a horse-drawn *dokar* from anywhere in town. There is also the large Seketeng market-cum-*bemo* station, at the eastern edge of town.

Moyo island

Pulau Moyo Island, to the north east of Sumbawa Besar, offers some of the very best snorkeling we have seen in Indonesia. Beautiful, untouched coral. Out by a drop-off, there were even a couple two-meter sharks, which proved harmless if a bit inquisitive. Moyo also offers birders a number of species to see, and there are deer, boar, *banten* (a beautiful species looking like something between a cow and a water buffalo), fruit bats, snakes and lizards.

Although approximately two-thirds of Moyo Island is a state reserve, almost half the entire island has recently been monopolized by the Amanwana resort, a self-contained luxury resort featuring special tents with air-conditioning and king-sized beds.

The resort is not cheap, and you must book through Aman international's office in Bali, or from abroad. It is almost impossible to book locally. For one of their premiere "Ocean Tents," this outfit charges U.S.$400/day, although the "Jungle Tents" are less. The resort offers diving, sailing, windsurfing, and other water sports, and its facilities include restaurant, bar, shop and even a library. (See "Moyo Island," page 278.)

Also, access to the rest of the island is now controlled by a private company, which has set up simple accommodations and a restaurant at the old conservation department camp at Air Manis. The company sells packages including transportation by boat, entrance fee, and lodging. (See "Moyo Island," page 278.)

On the north coast of the island, outside of the reserve, there are a couple of villages—Labuhan Aji and Sebotok—and several hamlets. The farmers here raise water buffalo, horses and goats, and all the inhabitants do some fishing. Coconuts and bananas are the most important crops.

Getting to Moyo

Tanjung Pasir on the southern tip of Moyo is a two- to four-hour ride by outboard from Sumbawa Besar. The Hotel Tambora can arrange the trip, or you can go to Air Bari, a fishing village just across the water from Tanjung Pasir on Moyo, where P.T. Moyo Safari Abadi has a counter. Air Bari is 30 kilo-

Opposite: *A pretty musician from West Sumbawa.*

meters—most of it dusty and pot-holed—from Sumbawa Besar. Brave *bemos* make the run, however.

Air Bari

If your boat doesn't leave right away, you might want to look around Air Bari village (the name means "Salty Water"; despite this, the well water here is quite drinkable—make sure it's been boiled—but if you're fussy bring some bottled water from town.)

You can hang out or even spend the night at the house owned by Pak Abdulahi and Ibu Hanipah; and if there's any available, Ibu Hanipah will cook up some delicious fish.

Go for a swim or take a look around the little village—278 people at last count, a mixture of Samawa, Bajo and Bugis. They are poor, no TVs or motorcycles yet, and eke out a living from the sea and dryland farming of manioc, mung beans and corn. They are all friendly. Their homes are a jumble of styles, reflecting the heterogeneous ethnic mix, although all are Muslims.

Tanjung Pasir

At Tanjung Pasir, there are accommodations available at Labuan Cedal (old Air Manis camp) from P.T. Moyo Safari Abadi. These include six tents, and a basic restaurant.

The island is full of game, and we could watch wild pigs foraging for shellfish at low time right from where we stayed. To see more game, trek inland with one of the staff. You can arrange excursions of from an hour to several hours. One possibility includes a visit to a couple of caves, inhabited by several species of bats, plus the usual game. Hat and water are essential.

During a short stay we only spotted some frigate birds, but the guards told us of some megapode bird nests close to camp. The birds rebuild the old nests in October, in the late afternoons. One man, obviously a seasoned birder, wrote with pride in the old Conservation Department guestbook that, in addition to more common species, he had spotted brahminy kites, great billed herons, the little striated heron, an imperial green pigeon, white-bellied sea eagles, and what was perhaps a helmeted sandpiper.

Snorkeling off the island

While the land animals of Moyo are easy to see and interesting enough, the main attraction lies just under the sea's surface. When we visited there were no scuba diving facili-

ties (the Amanwana resort now offers diving) but a short snorkel just west of the dock at Tanjung Pasir led to a wonderful encounter with a pair of reef white-tip sharks. They were about 12 meters down just off the edge of the coral beds. A surface dive attracted their attention, but they wouldn't let us get closer than about 5 meters.

If you can live without this sort of thrill, just stay in the shallows. There's an incredible variety of soft and hard corals, including some blue-tinted staghorn coral. There were anemone fish, schools of damselfish, box fish, several large batfish, reef trout, and a variety of surgeonfish and parrotfish. No dynamite has yet touched these reefs, thank Allah.

The snorkeling east of Tanjung Pasir, where we hoped to see some big pelagic species, was a disappointment. The waves were too high, and the surface water was just too churned up. This was around the end of September, and the guards said the seas were quietest here during the rainy season—November/December through April/May. According to our informants, when conditions are right one can see moray eels, groupers, blue-spotted stingrays, sharks and even manta rays.

Don't swim right off the tip of Tanjung Pasir. The currents here are very strong, and sometimes form whirlpools. Also, stories circulate of a 5-meter-long shark coming up to the edge of the beach for a look around. For what? Tourist flesh?

Tepal: traditional village

Moyo island is the right place for lovers of nature and the underwater world. But for those seeking a look at the traditional village life of Sumbawa, the hilltop village of Tepal, where many pre-Islamic beliefs are honored, is the place to visit. (See "Tradition and Magic," page 88.)

Reaching Tepal requires an 8-hour walk from Batu Dulang, which is southwest of Sumbawa Besar, at the limit of vehicular traffic. The trek is pleasant enough, much more so than riding horseback on either awful or non-existent saddles.

To make the walk more enjoyable, hire one or two porters to carry your gear. At Batu Dulang, you can often hook up with men from Tepal returning home from a shop-

Opposite: *This wide beach near Sekongkang in southwest Sumbawa attracts spawning sea turtles. Beautiful beaches line this coast.*

ping expedition in Sumbawa Besar. Or, for a reasonable fee, hire an English-speaking guide at the Hotel Tambora who will take care of all the details.

Tepal village, located on a hill above the river used for bathing, has maintained its traditions in great part due to its isolation. While no Japanese tour groups have yet invaded the village, the occasional foreign traveler makes it to Tepal, so the people are accustomed to strange ways and faces. It's no problem to find a place to sleep—check in with the *kepala desa,* the village head. Very basic food is available, but bring whatever goodies you can't live without—and share them with your hosts. Pay about $5 a day for room and board—the village can use the cash income. With a bit of luck, you could catch a wedding or some other traditional ritual.

Batu Tering: sarcophagi

Archeology buffs won't want to pass up a visit to the area around Batu Tering village, to see the remains of an extinct megalithic culture. Batu Tering is about 7 kilometers from the main road to Lunyuk. About 2 kilometers before reaching the little town of Semanung (18 kilometers from Sumbawa Besar), head east along a dirt road (being upgraded). On the way, you can see a group of kilns which are making lime to be used for construction.

At Batu Tering, check in with the village chief, fill out your particulars in their guest book and ask for a guide to take you to a place called Airnung or Ai Renung, 7 kilometers and a couple of easy hours away. At presstime, a motorcycle track was planned.

The large stone sarcophagi at Airnung, which used to hold the rulers' remains, are covered with high relief carvings of lizards and people. These items are a part of a megalithic culture, now extinct in Sumbawa, that seems to have been very similar to the one still extant in Sumba.

Closer to the village is Liang Petang cave, which holds breast-shaped stones, and others with magical properties. The cave is dark, and there are stalactites and stalagmites. Bring a flashlight.

Continuing on the main road to Lunyuk, the well-surfaced road ends at Lenangur, 40 kilometers from Sumbawa Besar. A decent road continues a few kilometers further to Ledang village. Just before Lenanguar, a side road supposedly leads to a place called Ai Kawat where a solidified coil is said to form around a stick thrust in the water. We asked around but couldn't find the place.

The transmigration area of Lunyuk lies on the south coast of Sumbawa, a bit over 90 kilometers from Sumbawa Besar. On our last visit, the second half of this road was still unpaved. Settlers here include Balinese, Sasaks, and Javanese. There are white sand beaches nearby, and the closest one— Lampui—is a nesting place for sea turtles.

ACROSS SUMBAWA

Sumbawa Besar to Bima Town

The 250-kilometer stretch of road between Sumbawa Island's two regional capitals has recently been upgraded to a wide, well-surfaced highway. With a car and driver you can cover the distance in 5 hours—without squashing any stray chickens, dogs or goats. Things have changed since the mid 1970s when this was a hot, dusty journey on a dirt road, taking the better part of 11 hours.

The regular buses take about 7 hours. Traveling east from Sumbawa Besar to Bima, the first part of the ride is relatively boring, but the second half offers much better scenery. Try to get a front seat on the bus or, failing that, a place by one of the left windows—the best scenery will be on this side, which faces the coast.

Leaving Sumbawa Besar

If you've hired your own car, you might want to stop and see *songket* weavers at Poto village, just as you leave Sumbawa Besar. *Songket* is cloth into which silver threads have been worked. The cloth itself is handwoven on backstrap looms.

If the women had nothing else to do in life it would take 45 full working days to create a single one of these cloths, which are only worn on ceremonial occasions. So the $80–$90 they charge does not seem at all out of line. There are also cheaper pieces available, but these are of inferior quality.

Take the left turnoff from the main highway around the 6-kilometer marker, head towards Moyo village on a badly paved road, then continue 2 kilometers further to Poto. There are usually several women weaving in their homes, or they could so on the spur of the moment for the sake of a demonstration. On arrival, ask: Dimana ada orang tenun kain songket?—"Where is there someone weaving *songket* cloth?" Someone will show you.

Back on the main highway, the first stretch leads through dry, monotonous countryside. Some cone-shaped hills relieve the tedium around the 40-kilometer mark, but you have to wait until you've gone 78 kilometers from Sumbawa Besar to catch your first glimpse of the sea, at Labuhan Bontong. Here, there are lots of little fishing boats, and you can see Mt. Tambora in the background. After just 2 kilometers, the road swings inland again, to the town of Empang.

The coastal stretch

Then at around the 100 kilometer mark, you begin a long, wonderful coast-hugging ride, beginning with the stilt-perched fishing village of Labuhan Jambu. Lots of little outriggered sailing canoes, and bigger craft, including the double-hulled *bagan,* a type of mobile fishing platform.

From Labuhan Jambu, the 40-kilometer coastal stretch offers fine views over huge Saleh Bay with Mt. Tambora always looming in the background. The road climbs coastal hills and cuts across the base of many peninsulas jutting out into the bay. Troupes of monkeys wait by the roadside for a snack thrown from a passing vehicle; a colorful wild rooster might fly across the road.

Toward the end of the bay, the vegetation becomes thicker and greener as you approach, then start climbing, the hills. This was the last stretch of the road to be completed. A bus plunged over the side here a while back, resulting in a reported 40 deaths. Don't think about this while you're riding, concentrate instead on the breath-taking scenery. Here you get a bird's eye view of the innermost coves of Saleh Bay, the Kowangku islands, and the *bagan*s sailing across the deep blue water.

The Dompu plain

The road cuts across the mountains and drops to a hill-ringed, rice growing plain centered around the crossroads at Soriutu. Here a 90-kilometer road follows the south coast of the huge peninsula formed by Mt. Tambora.

This scenic roads ends at Calabai, a coastal timber town. From there, it's a short way to Pancasila, where you can hire guides for the tough, 2–3 day, 15-kilometer Mt. Tambora climb. It's easier to take a boat from Sumbawa Besar to Calabai; but there are two or three buses a day there from Dompu, and they cost only a couple of bucks. (For more information on climbing Tambora, see

Opposite: *A man relaxes with a strong hand-rolled cigarette, which provides a far more satisfying smoke than the store-bought variety.*

"Climbing Tambora," page 279.)

The road to the north of Soriutu quickly reaches Sanggar Bay, where it branches: a passable road west to Kore and Piong, and a scenic, but worse road northeast to Kilo.

Back on the main highway, the road continues east over the hill to Dompu plain, rich and green, the first large cultivated area since Sumbawa Besar. Here you begin to notice woman wearing the *rimpu*—a sarong wrapped around the women's head and shoulders, leaving only the face bare. This is the local equivalent of the usually white sewn *jilbab* (Arabic) or the *kerundung* (Indonesian), worn by girls attending Islamic schools. Even just a few years ago the *rimpu* was wrapped in conservative Muslim fashion, revealing only the eyes, but things have loosened up.

The town of Dompu, the bulk of which lies off the main road, offers several *losmen,* and several of the newer ones are quite clean and comfortable. Few travelers stop in Dompu—most keep going to Bima, except for the mostly Australian surfers, who head south through Ranggo to the Hu'u area, some 40 kilometers away.

Hu'u is at the southeast side of the entrance to Cempi Bay. The waves here can be fine during the southeast monsoon season, especially in June, July and August. *Losmen* catering to surfers have mushroomed in this area since around 1987, when word got out that the surf was up in Hu'u.

But it ain't Bali's Kuta Beach yet. There are no crowds on the waves. Buses make the run daily from Dompu to Hu'u. The waters close to shore looked too cloudy for snorkeling, but the surfers said that it clears up further out, where the waves break on the outer edge of the reef.

On to Bima

From Dompu, the highway winds down from the hills through terraced rice fields, then to the salt flats around Bima Bay. The low dikes around the flats are opened up, seawater guided in with large paddles, and left to evaporate. Then the salt is bagged in bright blue plastic sacks. The merciless sun allows salt to be harvested every five to seven days during the four-month long season, June through September. One hectare yields some two tons of salt during this period.

You round the southern end of the bay just before reaching the airport, 17 kilometers from town. The road then closely follows the bayshore, and here you can see fishermen in small canoes and large *bagan*s. You arrive in Bima after crossing an elevated causeway, with salt flats on both sides and a Chinese cemetery to your right.

A Balinese temple crowns a small hill at the entrance to town, near the "6 kilometers to Raba" roadside marker. The large bus terminal and the downtown area welcomes you with daytime traffic and bustle.

BIMA TOWN

Muslim Heart of Eastern Sumbawa

Bima town has an undeserved bad reputation with foreign travelers. One always hears that the place is full of Muslim fanatics who hate foreigners. As usual in eastern Indonesia, appearances are deceiving. Granted, local mores of privacy and politeness are quite different from western etiquette. For example, in the west, no one would think twice about not wearing a bra; in Bima, not even a prostitute would dare dress that way.

There are stories—12, 15 years old—of stones being thrown at "indecently" dressed western women, but things have changed with the great numbers of tourists who now stop in Bima on their way to Komodo. This is not to suggest that you shouldn't dress modestly. You could probably get away with it now, but why offend your hosts?

Visiting Bima town

One's first impressions of Bima, a small crowded town choked with horse-drawn carts—now called "Ben Hur" after the movie—do not inspire one to linger. You could visit one of the several compounds of Raba, notably Ntobu and Rada Dompu, where women weave *ikat* on traditional backstrap looms. Bargain if you want to buy something.

Otherwise, hop into a Ben Hur and be trotted to Bima's port, 15¢ per person for the 2-kilometer ride. On the way, you might see girls attending Muslim schools playing volleyball or badminton in full religious garb: long skirts and the *rimpu,* a head-and-shoulder scarf. While the strict Muhammadiyah system still requires white *rimpu,* a profusion of colors are now in style. If you spot a girl in a yellow *rimpu,* she's a member of the nobility; only the sultan's daughters are allowed to wear green ones.

The port is usually a beehive of activity, with graceful wooden freight schooners and ungainly iron ships tied up at the docks. During the dry season, bright blue bags of salt destined for Java and Kalimantan are stacked on the docks and, occasionally, water buffalo and cattle wait here for boats to Surabaya and Jakarta. Truckloads of garlic, soybeans and especially shallots—the Bima district's chief agricultural export—are shipped to Java. Also sent out from Sumbawa's most important port: dried seaweed, to be processed into agar and carrageenan, fingerling milkfish (*nener*) to stock rice paddies, and huge quantities of dried squid.

The sultan's palace and tombs

The Sultan of Bima's palace, built in 1927 and restored in 1973, is now a museum. Unfortunately, its architecture pales in comparison to Sumbawa Besar's fine old wooden palace. Because of a lack of funds, the contents, in number and quality, are dismal. All the best pieces—and they are really excellent—are kept by the sultan's family, because the museum cannot their safety.

Although it's difficult, the museum director, a member of the sultan's family, might be able to arrange a look at the fabulous family treasures. The diamond-studded gold crown, acid-burnished in places to set off the intricate design, is a wonderful item. The sultan's collection of fine *kris* knives, also studded with jewels, are as fine as any that were produced for the courts of Java.

The palace museum also hosts dances, and you might be able to watch a rehearsal there in the late afternoons, or one of the frequent Sunday performances, which last from about 10 a.m. until noon.

The grave of the first sultan, Abdul Kahir, who reigned from 1630 to 1640, is on a hilltop southeast of town. The Islamic simplicity of the grave's architecture contrasts sharply with the palace's sacred regalia. The grave is covered by a hemispherical stone structure, and has a small doorway.

The hill, called Dana Taraha, offers an excellent overview of Bima, especially in the early morning or late afternoon. A road to the base of the hill leads straight from the bus station. You can also walk there along a footpath from the front of the Parewa Hotel.

Although they are not in such an exalted location, the tombs of Sultan Nuruddin and his Islamic teacher Umar al-Bantami are much more interesting architecturally. These tombs lie neglected in a dusty Muslim graveyard northwest of town, next to a dirt road off Jl. Sulawesi, behind a school. A rusty barbed wire fence does nothing to keep out cattle. Each of the two large graves is constructed as a pyramid set on a raised square

base, the whole covered with a double roof of thatch. The small doorways, located under the massive mausoleums, face south.

Kolo village

Kolo is a little fishing village on the eastern shore of Bima Bay, near the neck, just north of Bima town. Just offshore from the town, the reef offers some decent snorkeling. It is also said that the surfing is good here during the rainy season. Otherwise, there is nothing particularly special about the village, but the ride offers a nice view of the bay.

Take Jl. Sulawesi, past the graves of Sultan Nuruddin and his teacher, cross a small bridge, and head north. The road runs along some rice fields, then along Bima Bay's eastern shore. As the road rises over the low hills towards the neck of Bima Bay, there are excellent overviews of the bay, with Mt. Soromandi on the far side. Five kilometers from Bima, you pass the Songgela Beach Club, popular with some of the local elite.

You can also reach Kolo village by small passenger boat, departing once or twice a day from the edge of Bima's dock. The ride is cheap, but takes a long time. From the same part of the dock, you can charter a boat to explore Bima Bay for about $15. Sailboats occasionally skim by, and there's some good snorkeling on the south side of the little bay on the west side of the neck of Bima Bay, marked by a beacon.

Wadu Pa'a: stone carving

Wadu Pa'a—"Stone Carving"—is a Hindu archaeological site on the west side of Bima Bay, across from Kolo. It is past the bay's narrow neck, and the water gets choppy here during the November–March monsoon. The carvings are next to Sowa village.

There are actually two sites at Wadu Pa'a, Kompleks I and Kompleks II. A keeper has the key to a door through a fence of thorn bushes. Kompleks I, next to a rice field, is a disappointing, graffiti-covered rock overhang with a small altar and a bit of decorative carving. The graffiti is in three languages: Indonesian, Chinese and Bugis.

Kompleks II is about 50 meters away, just above the waterline. It is more interesting, and has not yet been vandalized. First excavated by Balinese archaeologists in 1984, the rock face displays a series of faded, but distinct, relief sculptures including Ganesh (the elephant) and a phallic carving. A nook holds what was probably the principal shrine. The writing, as yet undeciphered, shows 7th century Pallawan/Sanscrit characters.

Just offshore, a freshwater spring wells up into the sea, the probable reason the shrine was erected here by devout Hindu traders, on their way along the spice route.

Above: *These Bimanese girls, following the Muslim code of dress, reveal only their sparkling eyes.*

BIMA DISTRICT

Scenic Coasts and Villages of Fishermen

The eastern part of Sumbawa, the Bima district, is marked by beautiful coastal scenery and stilt-perched fishing villages. After taking a look around Bima town, you can explore the Dou Donggo villages across the bay from Bima, or take either of two nice drives to explore the region: a trip to the south, or a swing along the north coast. You really would want to try only one of these in a given day, as with a couple of spontaneous side trips, the tour will fill the daylight hours.

The Dou Donggo

The name Donggo is given to the people scattered in 11 villages on the clouded highlands West of Bima Bay and on the south slopes of Mt. Soromandi—Bajo, O'o, Rora, Punti, Sowa, Mbawa, Kala, Doridungga, Palama, Sai, Sampungu. There are also less traditional Donggo living around Wavo, just off the main highway from Bima to Sape. The Donggo fled to the hills in the 17th century to escape the Islamization of the Sultans of Bima, and have to some extent maintained their traditional religion to this day.

The Donggo worship a Trinity consisting of a Sky God, "Dewa Langi," a Water God, "Dewa Oi" and a Wind God, "Dewa Wango." Their society is divided into numerous totemic clans, led by hereditary, charismatic leaders called *ncuhi*. The *ncuhi* preside over the great religious festivals, such as the Kesaro, a fertility rite. Traditional Donggo houses, especially those of the *ncuhi*, are single-room "A-frames" with high thatched roofs. Some of these are still standing amidst low-land style stilted houses.

The Donggo are also known for their coarsely-woven, indigo-dyed fabrics called *tembe sangga*, with which they make their traditional clothing: tunics (*kababu*) and trousers (*deko*), or sarongs (*tembe ala*).

Islam and modernization have spread to many of these Donggo villages, and relatively few now keep the old traditions. Generally speaking, those on the peninsula south of Mt. Soromandi are more traditional than those around Wavo southeast of Bima.

South: Wane village

Wane village, on the south coast some 2 hours' drive from Bima, has an excellent white sand beach. (See map page 85.) The

first part of the ride is smooth enough, as you head towards Sumbawa Besar on the main highway. Just beyond the airport, at Tente, you leave the highway and head south towards Parado. This road is almost as good as the highway. The good pavement ends about 17 kilometers away, just past a fertile valley, at the little town of Simpasai.

After Simpasai, you start bumping along on a potholed surface for 5 kilometers, towards Sondo village. On our last trip, the pavement stopped a few kilometers before the village. Go straight through Sondo, and after 4 kilometers of awful bumps you reach Tolo Uwi. Turn left, and after 7 kilometers of much better road, you land in Wane.

Two bays, separated by chunks of black rock, greet you. Each is lined with a white sand beach. The area is quite a sight during the southeast monsoon (May–September) when the waves are up. During the northwest monsoon the water is quiet, and the bays are fine for snorkeling and bathing. The people here, farmers who also fish a bit, remember just one foreign visitor, an Aussie surfer who came at the wrong time of year for the good waves.

West of Wane, several peninsulas can be seen projecting out to sea. These probably shelter additional isolated beaches. A walk to the east leads over a hill, and past boulders and chunks of raised coral. The walk ends at a large bay, where the few local fishing boats are kept. The beach section here is covered with seaweed, but the far side of the bay is swept with white sand.

The tide pools nearby are full of corals and darting fish. Their precarious habitat is refreshed by the splash of breaking waves. The big waves crash 100 to 150 meters out in a broken fringe.

Waworada Bay

There are several routes to take back to Bima. By the time you read this, a road will

probably be opened from Parado to the surfing haven at Hu'u (see "Across Sumbawa," page 98). The easiest way is to go back the way we came, through Sondo, to Simpasai, and then north to Bima.

Alternatively, you can turn right at the crossroads outside of Sondo village, and head northeast along a dirt road, smooth at the beginning. The road skirts the west, then north, shore of Waworada Bay, a long U-shaped bay whose relatively narrow opening makes it quiet most of the year. A short way

along the road, you encounter a long jetty protruding incongruously into the bay.

This is where manganese ore is shipped out. The mining is a small-scale, on-and-off operation. Ore-bearing rock occurs on the surface, and it is broken down by hand, by a group of several dozen men, some of whom put their wives and children to work as well. Soon after the manganese works, the road degenerates into a series of rocks and tidal flats as you round the north-west corner of the bay through the villages of Laju and Waworada. This awful (for now) road is not really worth the torture.

If you want to see Waworada Bay, it's best to return to Simpasai, and then almost to Tente, where a good dirt roads heads east and then south. The road reaches the water at Waworada village, just after the junction with the rough track to Laju. From here, a 45-kilometer road to Sape follows the northern shore of the bay for about 20 kilometers, crossing the village of Karumbu. At Karumbu, stilt-perched villages crowd the shore, displaying their sailing *bagan*s and

Opposite: *A Bimanese dancer, in traditional conservative dress, during Independence day celebrations.* **Above, left:** *The royal crown of the Sultan of Bima, studded with diamonds. The gold fretwork has been acid-etched to the color of copper.* **Above, right:** *The handle of the sultan's* kris *represents the founder of the royal line.*

other fishing craft. Live trees and weathered stumps jut out of the quiet water, and a few small islands lie close to shore.

Traditional house

About 8 kilometers east of Karumbu, on the right side of the road, was the largest traditional Bima house we had ever seen. Bima-style houses are thatch-covered, and rest on stilts. Just beyond this house is the So Rore beach, a spot that attracts locals on weekends. There is a well here, and a couple of thatch-roofed platforms. Snack and drink sellers are out here in force when the people come to play. The waters are shallow and quiet, and some frames tied with seaweed float nearby.

Six kilometers east of So Rore, the road climbs into the dry hills above the bay. A few small fertile valleys punctuate this otherwise barren land. Only a very occasional truck transits the stretch from Karumbu to Rato, where you reach the southern portion of the rich Sape valley.

If you still have any time and energy left, a fairly good dirt road (scheduled for pavement) runs from Rato to almost the end of the hefty peninsula that forms the southern shore of Sape Bay. Almost as soon as you leave Rato, the road climbs into the hills, offering a panoramic view of the Sape valley, with a large coconut grove in the foreground. After winding through the hills you drop down to the bayshore. The road follows a thin, grey sand beach, then leads up over a hill, offering an overview of Sape Bay.

Lambu: Bajo village

Lambu, 11 kilometers from Rato, is the only village on this stretch of coast. The people of Lambu are Bugis and Bajo fishermen and dry farmers. Only a very occasional *bemo* makes the trip from Sape by road, so the people here usually travel to the biggest local town by boat.

Five kilometers beyond Lambu is the reason the road was built in the first place: a large pearl farm, owned and operated by P.T. Bima Sakti Mutiara. It is located on Solato inlet, an offshoot of the large Sape Bay. This pearl farm, like the one at Labuhan Lalar on the other end of the island, was originally set up as a joint venture with Japanese interests. Now, Japanese experts pop into town only to accomplish the delicate— and closely guarded—process of inserting the nuclei on which the pearl will form.

This pearl farm is just one of a dozen similar ones established in eastern Indonesia (the only one in the west is at Lampung,

Above: *A small boat chugs across Bima Bay after a long day's fishing.* **Opposite:** *Young dancers of the royal family of Bima perform a court dance, wearing heirloom gold jewelry and embroidered cloths. This is a sight rarely seen today.*

Sumatra). Several operate on Lombok and off Flores. These quiet, clean sand-bottomed tropical waters are ideal for pearl oyster aquaculture. The oysters are grown on coral ledges 7–10 meters deep. The sandy bottom makes it easy to find oysters that have fallen off the ledge. The water must be extremely clean, and local boats are banned from the site. It takes 18 months for an oyster to produce a pearl of the ideal size.

Visitors are not welcome at this (or any) pearl farm, but the situation could change in the future. You might even be able to rent their scuba gear for an underwater look-around. There are good coral formations here, with lots of colorful reef fish, Spanish mackerel, dolphins and, just outside the inlet, sharks. In the rainy season, there are whales off the point here.

North coast

Along the north coast of the Bima district, beautiful bays with many-hued water shelter fragile-looking, stilted fishing villages. Inland, an occasional irrigated valley, with deep green *sawah*s, contrasts markedly with the dry, barren hills. Just offshore looms Sangeang island, the steep sides of its barely dormant volcano reaching 1,949 meters to twin peaks.

The coastal villages in Bima are settled by Bugis, Bajo—former sea nomads—or ethnic Bimans. All live in houses set on piles near the water, and fish. Where there is enough freshwater, they also farm rice, corn and soybeans as well.

The road north of Bima passes the Jati Baru bus terminal. If you are taking public transportation, a *bemo* to the terminal costs 15¢, and buses leave Jati Baru to follow the northern route to Tawali. After the terminal, the road follows the side of a rice-growing valley, and rises steeply into the hills. After a boring stretch, a wonderful view appears: a series of snaking *sawah*s, following the course of the Nangaraba River.

Rite village

Soon the road drops, and crosses the river at the picturesque village of Rite. Rite has a mosque, and all the houses here are traditional Bima-style, with rice granaries called *lengge*. There is a little store along the road, and its concrete block construction clashes with the architecture of the village. You follow the edge of the fields, passing more little villages with only a few modern roadside houses of the local elite. You reach the sea at Nipe village. A short dirt road leads to a coral beach with few fishing boats and a good view across the mouth of Bima Bay to the mountains of the Donggo region.

As the coast road begins to round the peninsula, Sangeang Island, massive and double-peaked, surges into view. Sangeang will accompany you for much of the rest of the

journey to Sape, peeking over the hills every time the road cuts inland. The road here follows the beach, which is coral sand but dark and unattractive. After 15 kilometers, the road swings inland, to the little town of Tawali, the capital of the Wera subdistrict.

From Tawali, a dirt road heads due south, leading 12 kilometers to the villages of Nunggi Ntoke and Ropo, until very recently quite isolated. Another dirt road, at the far end of Tawali, heads north, to the coastal village of Sangeang Darat, 7 kilometers away. Along this road, not too far from Tawali, is Goa Wera, a cave with stalactites and stalagmites. Some kind of mystical thread connects this cave to the volcano on Sangeang.

Soon after leaving Tawali, you pass a large valley growing rice and red onions. Men irrigate the onion fields here by hand, using sets of two hemispherical buckets called *boru* balanced on a pole across their shoulder. As they walk along the rows of plants, they tip a bit of water out of each bucket.

Sangeang village

Sangeang Darat village (*darat* means "land"), with a population of 3,000, is brand new. The people here were all resettled under government orders beginning in 1986, after the Sangeang eruption. Although the volcano is quiet now, the people are not allowed to settle again on the island, as volcanologists fear for their safety. They do, however, work their old fields on the volcano's slopes.

The best view of the volcano is from the beach at Sangeang Darat, where fishing craft make a perfect foreground to the island. If you are an avid climber, you can hire a ride to the island and climb Sangeang. According to locals, it takes about 3 hours to scramble up the almost 2,000-meter volcano. That seems a little quick to us.

It is commonly believed in the district that the Sangeang islanders practice all kinds of occult arts. One technique, using special oil, is to punish thieves by causing their houses, and all other houses in their village, to mysteriously burn to the ground.

Coastal fishing villages

The 50-kilometer road from Tawali to Sape is paved only by bits and pieces, except for the last 13 kilometers, all of which is paved. Still, all the steep parts have been paved, and traffic can thus pass even in the rainy season.

The good scenery ends at Lamere, the largest of the seaside villages. Lamere is off the main road, at the end of a short, but awful road full of stones and either dust or mud, depending on the season. Dozens of large fishing craft pose gracefully in the crowded bay. The inhabitants are Bugis, descendants of immigrants from South Sulawesi.

Bima town to Sape

Hurrying to catch the 8 a.m. ferry to Komodo, the sleepy traveler often misses the scenery along the 50-kilometer stretch from Bima to Sape. Just outside of Bima, the road cuts through Raba, the administrative capital of the region, but not nearly as lively as Bima. The district capital was established here by the Dutch in 1908, well away from the sultan's palace.

From here the road climbs next to a winding, fertile valley, full of rice fields and groves of banana trees, and then leads past a string of highland villages.

Outside the villages are clusters of *lengge,* traditional granaries. These were relocated outside of the villages after a number of fires destroyed the harvest. Although unguarded, no thief would dare to touch the rice, as it is protected by strong magic. The magic would ensure that the thief would not be able to find his way out of the complex.

The road tumbles down through the western branch of the large Sape valley, following rice paddies and onion fields irrigated by an army of bucket-carrying men.

Sape town

The center of Sape town is about 4 kilometers from the harbor and ferry landing. The busy downtown has an old market, stores and little restaurants. The road continues past the Anda and Frendsip *losmen,* located diagonally opposite each other, and reaches the bus/*bemo*/Ben Hur station.

Only a few buses and private vehicles and Ben Hurs are allowed to go down the remaining 2 kilometers to the harbor. After an empty tidal stretch, the road is lined with the houses of the port area's fishermen. This is where they dry their small fish, and it smells accordingly.

Everything here, including the mosque, sits on stilts over the water, or just above the waterline. Television antennas extend from the house tops, and there are even a couple of satellite dishes.

Opposite: *This young man, watching a group of dancers with interest, is wearing an outfit that in the past had been reserved exclusively for performances at the Sultan of Bima's court.*

PART IV

Introducing Komodo

The Komodo dragon, the largest lizard on earth, is found only on the islands of Komodo, Padar and Rinca, and parts of western Flores. Locally called *ora,* the dragons are most numerous on Komodo, which together with nearby Rinca has been set aside as a park. The lizards are one of eastern Indonesia's biggest tourist attractions, and in recent years, with improved transportation and promotion, Komodo island has turned into a minor zoo of gawking tourists, particularly in July and August.

The Komodo dragon

It is said that the Komodo dragon, because of its great size and ferocity, and fire-like tongue, served as the original model for the Chinese dragon. Perhaps this is so, but to the men of science, *Varanus komodoensis* is a lizard. It is huge—the largest recorded specimen was more than 3 meters long and weighed over 150 kilos—but it is still a zoologically describable animal.

The dragon is the largest known monitor lizard (*Varanus* sp.), a genus whose members are distinguished by their voracity and opportunistic feeding habits. Monitors, also called goanna lizards in Australia (probably a corruption of the Spanish "iguana," which is a strictly New World species), received their name because it was believed that they warned of the presence of crocodiles.

Although lizards, monitors have some very snake-like characteristics. They possess a flicking, forked tongue, which is an organ of taste and smell, just like that of a snake and unlike most lizards. Also, their jaws are not firmly jointed; that is, their lower and upper jaws can disjoint, allowing the animal to swallow large chunks of prey.

The genus is distributed from Africa to Australia, with just one species in northwest Africa and more than 20 in Australia. Other monitors can also reach prodigious sizes—Gray's monitor from the Philippines grows to 2 meters, and the so-called "tree crocodile" (*V. salvadorii*) of New Guinea, is perhaps even longer, but not heavier, than *V. komodoensis.*

A recent discovery

The scientific world knew nothing of the Komodo dragon until 1911, when van Hensbrack of the Netherlands Indies Army "discovered" the huge animals. The scientific description of the lizards followed in 1912, when P.A. Ouwens, the curator of the zoological museum of Bogor in Java, described and named the species.

Although the uniqueness of the animal was recognized early on, and it was immediately protected by legislation, the survival of the *ora* is not a foregone conclusion. The greatest danger now comes from organized illegal hunting parties with dogs which arrive periodically from Sumbawa and Flores to kill deer, the *ora*'s principal prey. Direct poaching of the animals is not a threat, as their skin is rough and dermal bones prevent it ever being turned into supple leather.

Adult lizards are not bothered by the island's population of feral dogs, but those descendents from stranded or runaway animals from hunting parties do eat the dragon's eggs. Wild dogs also compete with smaller lizards for prey, and can drive a juvenile *ora* from its kill. The population of dragons on Komodo is slowly increasing. In 1985 there were 1,400; the 1989 census shows 1,700. There are also perhaps 600 on Rinca and an unknown number on Flores.

In 1987, a 12-year-old boy was killed by one of the dragons on Rinca. The offending dragon was exiled to Flores but returned on its own, swimming back. An adult woman

Overleaf: *The Komodo dragon is one of the most efficient eating machines ever designed by nature.* **Opposite:** *Komodo island is rugged, dry and barren, and appears a perfect setting for its seemingly Jurassic-age inhabitants.*

was also bitten recently by a dragon on Rinca, but she survived. On July 18, 1972 an 84-year-old Swiss tourist, Baron Rudolf Van Biberegg, was killed by dragons.

A born predator

The first year of a dragon's life is spent living in the trees, where it preys on insects, then small rodents and birds. When it reaches about a meter in length, the young dragon becomes too heavy to continue an arboreal existence. Once on the ground, the lizard's list of prey animals extends to wild pigs, horses, water buffalo and, most of all, deer of the species *Cervus timorensis,* which can weigh over 150 kilograms.

The adult *ora* is omnivorous, devouring anything from insects to large game, from putrefying carrion to members of its own species. Its acute sense of smell can detect carrion from 8 kilometers away, but it is also a good hunter. The dragon locates its quarry by sight as well as smell, then uses stealth to bring it down. The *ora* catches its prey while it is asleep, or ambushes it along game trails. An *ora* has been seen gulping down a new born foal while its mother, too exhausted from the delivery to protect her young, looks on helplessly.

The vegetation of Komodo tends toward open savannah and scrub, with some woodlands. The drier hills are dominated by *lontar* palms. Cover is essential for the Komodo

dragon, for it is too large to sneak up on its prey in the open. Although they aren't usually known to run down their intended prey, on at least one occasion an *ora* has been clocked at more than 30 kilometers per hour—and this for several hundred meters. The hunt is over as soon as the dragon clamps its jaws on any part of the prey. In the rare case that the hunted animal is able to wrench itself free of the strong jaws, it will likely soon die anyway of its wounds, and the infection brought on by the *ora*'s powerful saliva.

Evisceration is the brute's favorite killing technique. Massive bleeding occurs when the dragon rips out the stomach wall. The *ora* then often buries its head in the animal's abdominal cavity, ripping out and swallowing the internal organs.

A tiny, rugged island

Komodo Island and neighboring Rinca are between Sumbawa and Flores, approximately 500 kilometers east of Bali. The shape of the island is very irregular, its 340 square kilometers spread over a number of peninsulas and promontories. The dry hills, which rise to 735 meters, sprout skinny *lontar* palms. The plankton-rich seas around Komodo and support amazing reefs, and a range of large marine life, including whales and dolphins.

There is just one village on Komodo, and the 600 or so Komodo Islanders cling precariously to the eastern shore. Despite the small

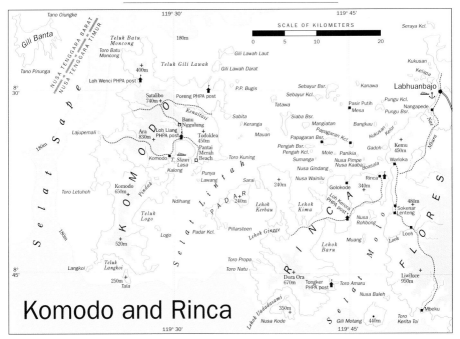

Komodo and Rinca

size of the community, they have developed their own distinct dialect. They make their living by fishing at night with pressure lamps from graceful, twin-hulled catamarans called *bagan*s. Squid is their most valuable catch.

Visiting the reserve

The Komodo Reserve falls under the jurisdiction of the Ministry of Forestry, and particularly the administrative branch for reserves, called the PHPA—Perlindungan Hutan dan Pelestrian Alam, or "Protection of Forest and Conservation of Nature."

Before the PHPA set up its facilities on Komodo, the occasional visitors to the island saw dragons by buying a goat at the village (or a mess of old fish) and then hanging the bait it in a tree until the dragons showed up. This process could take several days. When Loh Liang was set up in the late 1970s, the PHPA took over this system, establishing a regular feeding site in a dry creek bed at Banu Nggulung, about 1.5 kilometers inland. The high embankment, and a wire mesh fence, offered protection. When tourists showed up, the PHPA men bought a goat from the village and took it up to the site.

All this may be coming to an end, however. As we were going to press, the head of the PHPA had announced that the feedings would be stopping "soon." The dragons have become dependent on the feedings, and when they were recently cut down to try to wean the animals off this artificial schedule, at least 12 of the large adult "regulars" at the feeding hole started to grow a bit surly, ambushing the rangers on the way up to the feeding site, demanding their goat. This kind of behavior does not produce a good reaction from more faint-hearted tourists.

One alternative being considered is setting up a blind at a water hole. The previous method, though artificial and creating dependencies and behavioral changes in the animals, did at least guarantee that tourists would see a dragon. Seeing a dragon at a waterhole blind is probably not a sure thing, which may bring pressure from tour operators to continue the feedings.

There are many walks—along designated trails and always accompanied by a guide—through the dragon's territory, and you might be able to see one the old-fashioned way. If not, you will still behold incredible views of the emerald and blue seas and coral reefs off Komodo, especially if you head up towards Mt. Ara.

You could also walk to Pantai Merah—"Red Beach"—east of Loh Liang or ride to Pulau Lasa, an island near Komodo village. The snorkeling and swimming at these sites is superb. Don't forget to bring your mask and snorkel along.

Opposite: *About 600 people live on Komodo island, in a little fishing village.*

ENTER THE DRAGON

Visiting the Island of Dinosaurs

It was back in the 1970s, and almost every time I heard the story the nationality of the traveler varied—German, American, French, New Zealand, Australian. But the essence of the tale remained the same: after weeks of intensive search, all they found were his camera and glasses. And the advice: be careful.

I understood as soon as the first Komodo dragon lumbered into sight, its thick, battle-scarred body propped up by short, muscular legs. Over two-and-a-half meters long, weighing perhaps 110 kilos, with long, sharp, mean-looking claws, the giant lizard looked like he just stepped out of the Jurassic.

"You are lucky, we didn't have to wait long," my guide said to me in Indonesian. "It's because this is the end of the dry season, and the lizards are hungry." The vegetation, which usually hides them when stalking, has dried, he explained, and they find it harder to sneak up on deer, their favorite prey.

"Is that one unusually big?" I asked.

"Around average."

He called the lizards *buaya darat,* "land crocodile" in Indonesian. In the local language the dragons are called *ora.*

"Can we get closer?"

"Yes, but be careful."

As soon as moved forward, the lizard stopped eating and looked in my direction with its long yellow tongue flickering rapidly. I knew that it could not hear well but that its sense of smell through the tongue was quite acute. Apparently the rotting flesh of the goat tied as bait was more alluring than my sweaty human smells. And we were on top of an embankment, thus temporarily out of its reach.

Ripped into chunks

Hunger was obviously the dominant impulse as the lizard chomped down on the dead goat like a vise. Shaking its head back and forth violently, pulling with all its weight and tearing at the carcass with its huge claws, the *ora*

succeeded in ripping out a large chunk of the goat. The lizard's teeth are large, and saw-edged. In a couple of seconds, the huge bite was swallowed whole—hair, bones and skin—to be dissolved by powerful gastric juices. In just a few moments, the whole goat was gone, hoofs, horns and all, in several great gulps.

The *ora* has been observed to swallow the hindquarters of an adult deer whole, in one great bite. In another instance, a 50-kilogram lizard ate a 40-kilogram wild boar in a quarter of an hour. There was literally nothing left.

For larger prey, such as water buffalo, the lizards have been known to cut the Achilles' tendon with their sharp teeth, bringing the animal down to the ground so it could be eviscerated.

And if you still have any lingering affection for the lizards, consider that one of the park's larger monitors consumed a 9-month-old fawn in one bite. So much for their table manners.

The feeding dragon had been an impressive display which I had watched with morbid fascination. I was so awed that the next day I purchased another goat for a repeat performance. This time the scenario was quite a bit different.

Another feeding

After the goat was killed I had him strung up in a tree and we waited. Soon the huge dragon of yesterday appeared, his yellow tongue eagerly darting out to smell his new meal. But the goat was out of reach, so he had to content himself with circling. In a few minutes another *ora,* about one-and-a-half meters long, slid into the open river bed. Alert and light on his toes, he presented a striking contrast to the ponderous larger animal.

The young *ora* gave the impression of speed and agility, so different from the brute, massive strength of the other dragon. But the bigger *ora* was clearly in charge—a quick lunge and a heart-stopping hiss reminded the smaller lizard who was the boss. And the "little" guy seemed instinctively to know that his big brother was not at all averse to eating one of his own kind.

We continued to wait, and after a couple of hours there were six hungry, salivating dragons checking out the suspended bait. The guide was feeling a bit nervous by now, so I went with him as he climbed down a tree, leaning on the embankment, to the dry gulch bottom. He lowered the goat, and quickly staked him to the ground. Then we both

made a fast getaway up the tree to the top of the embankment.

At first the big lizard ripped out the intestines, and a few other easy, succulent chunks. Then, as he busied himself detaching the tougher pieces, the other *ora* would dart in for a quick bite. Once we even noticed some cooperation in the feeding. As the big lizard was struggling with a tenacious chunk, a smaller *ora* would bite at the meat and tendons holding the big piece to the carcass, until the large dragon was able to rip it out.

Up the tree fast

While the carcass was still being chewed up, I decided to climb down the tree to get closer shots of the *ora*. My guide was far from pleased. He warned me to be careful, and I remember him saying that the younger *ora* could climb trees. To me, the lizards looked too bulky for such things, so I scrambled down the tree to the dry riverbed. I took a few photos, but then I started feeling a bit nervous. I backed up towards the tree—with an *ora* following me!

Clutching my cameras, I set a new world's record for the tree climb. I stood breathless at the top, as we watched the dragon, using his tough claws, scamper right up the tree. As soon as he reached the top, the guide and I made like we were going to attack him, and he retreated a bit—but he didn't really seem frightened. On the contrary.

I whacked the ground between us with my heavy belt, feeling a bit ridiculous as a dragon-tamer. Then the guide remembered that we had kept the goat's liver, planning to eat it for supper. He tossed the meat to the dragon, and we both beat a hasty retreat.

Many dangers

The Komodo dragon, although the island's most famous creature, is not the only dangerous one. I was reminded of this by my guide, who told me, before my swim, to be careful of sharks, sea snakes and local saltwater crocodiles, which can reach 7 meters—as well as the occasional Komodo dragon out for a swim. Indeed, they have no fear of water and have occasionally been observed swimming quite far offshore.

I felt safer back on board our boat, headed toward Labuhanbajo, Flores, in a phosphorescent sea. Every time the boat surged forward, a fireworks of sparklers exploded from under the hull. As the dark shadows of islands glided past I imagined myself jettisoned 100 thousand years back when our ancestors, with primitive tools, had to outwit such great animals to stay alive.

Above: *Komodo dragons disembowel a goat, hung by a park ranger in a dry gulch. The organized feedings, in which visitors watch the grisly show from the relative safety of a high embankment, may soon end.*

PART V

Introducing Flores

Flores is a long, narrow rugged island with dramatic volcanoes, beautiful mountain lakes, grassy savannah and even some mountain forest. The landscape is beautiful in an untamed way, and yet it is one of the least-visited parts of Indonesia.

There are 1.4 million people living on Flores, of which 85 percent are Roman Catholic. Ethnographically, however, the island is very diverse. Like most of East Indonesia, the older animist beliefs coexist with, or are just barely hidden by, the new creed. The mixed population is made up of Bimanese, Bugis, Makassarese, Solorese and Savunese as well as ethnic Florinese—Lio, Ngadha, Sikka, Soa and others.

The island seems to mark a transition in the archipelago, and the people of Flores—particularly in the east—show the dark skin, curly hair and strong builds characteristic of the Melanesian populations of the islands further to the east. Apparent in a few faces is Portuguese blood, as the arrival of the Iberians created a mestizo race called Topasses.

Flores is 360 kilometers long, and varies from 12 to 70 kilometers wide. Although the rains here are often irregular, the high mountains insure a fairly constant supply of water. Most of the farming takes place on *ladang*—dry fields prepared by the slash-and-burn method—rather than *sawah*—flooded paddy fields—although wet rice has been grown since the early part of this century in some areas with sufficient water. Elsewhere, the people depend on manioc and corn.

History of Flores

Few written records are available of early Flores history. The Chinese are known to have traded for sandalwood on Timor since at least the 12th century A.D., and probably earlier, and the trade route passed by Flores. It is unclear, however, whether there was any contact. The 14th century chronicle of the Majapahit Empire of East Java notes a claim on Flores, but this probably amounted to little more than occasional trade contacts.

After rounding the cape of Africa, and establishing a base on the coast of India, the Portuguese made their way to Southeast Asia, conquering Malacca—the crossroads of the India–China route—in 1511. The very next year, the Iberians sent the first ships east along the archipelago in search of spices, which at the time were almost unimaginably valuable in Europe.

Flores had no spices, but the early Portuguese chronicler Tome Pires noted in 1515 that the island was an exporter of foodstuffs, including tamarind, as well as a considerable amount of sulfur. The sulfur, probably mined near one of the island's volcanoes, was shipped to Cochin China (South Vietnam), via Malacca.

In 1544, the captain of a subsequent Portuguese expedition to the Spice Islands named the easternmost peninsula of Flores "Cabo das Flores," Flower Cape, whence the island's current name. But early Portuguese texts refer to eastern Flores—including Sikka, Larantuka and Solor—as Solor Novo, "New Solor," while they called the region around Ende, Solor Velho, or "Old Solor."

Although Flores itself offered little of economic benefit to the Iberians, Timor's sandalwood was valuable, and Flores lay at a strategic point along the ocean route between Malacca and Timor. The Portuguese built a fort at Solor in 1566, which provided a haven for traders away from the malarial coasts of Timor. It also provided a good anchorage where they could wait out the changing monsoon winds.

Catholic missionaries accompanied the Portuguese, and by 1570, there was already a religious school in Larantuka, in East Flores.

Overleaf: *Dawn off Flores.* **Opposite:** *A dancer from eastern Flores, wearing heirloom beads that may date back to the days of the Majapahit.*

Flores

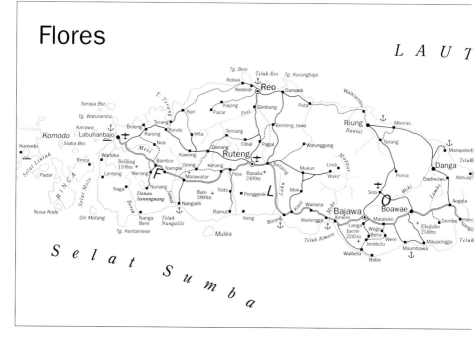

Although the traditional Bugis and Gowanese traders resented Portugal's intrusion into the trade, they were kept at bay by the Iberian's superior ships and weapons. In 1602, the Muslims besieged the fort at Solor with a force of 37 ships and 3,000 men. They would likely have driven out the Europeans, but for the chance arrival of an armed Portuguese man-of-war fleet.

The settlement at Ende

When the Portuguese discovered Eru Mbinge (now Ende Island) in the late 16th century, it was an entrepôt for sandalwood and slaves, with Malay, Arab and Chinese merchants settled there. There was also a local weaving industry, as the dry areas east of Ende supported cotton, and the cloths served as a kind of currency up until the end of the 19th century.

The Portuguese built a fort at Ende, but were ousted in 1630 by furious Endenese after a rather sordid triangular love affair involving a priest, the fort's captain and a native princess. Indonesia's first president, Sukarno, wrote a *sandiwara*—a type of Malay play incorporating song and dance—about this incident while he was in exile in Ende, sent there from Java by the Dutch. Some of the surviving Portuguese settled close to Ende, in Paga and Sikka.

The Portuguese won the loyalty of the Raja of Sikka, Dom Alesu Ximenes da Silva,

who was "educated" by a priest for four years at the Iberian court of Malacca. Before he was sent home, he was awarded with some valuable paraphernalia, some of which survives to this day: a gold helmet (stamped with the year 1607), a gold-tipped baton, two heavy gold chains, a *kris,* a wooden Christ statue and 70 elephant tusks.

Da Silva's efficient administration—helped by the strategic gift of the elephant ivory, which was extremely valuable in the area—led to a partial hegemony of Sikka over the surrounding area. As a sign of loyalty, the Portuguese flag was defiantly flown in Sikka until the end of the 19th century, even during the period of Dutch rule. The last of the rajas of Sikka, Dom Sentia da Silva, gave up his political power after the independence of Indonesia. His family and descendents still retain a large measure of prestige, and still own the regal paraphernalia.

Dutch interests in Flores

Because of Portugal's union with Spain under the crown of the Holy Roman Empire from 1580 to 1640, and Protestant Holland's ongoing fight with the Catholic empire for independence, the Portuguese and their trade were fair game for the Dutch when they arrived in the region in the early 1600s.

In 1613, a Dutch force under Apollonius Scotte executed a successful assault on the Portuguese fort at Solor. In 1621 the Dutch

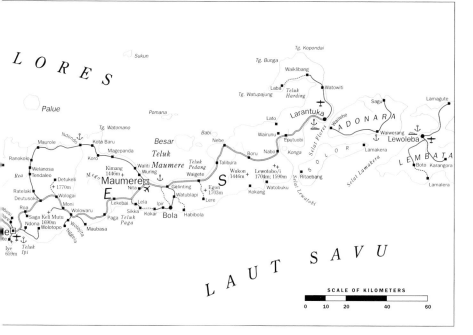

tried to capture Larantuka and failed, but the Portuguese also failed the same year to retake Solor, now defended with Muslim help.

In 1641, however, the port of Malacca fell to Holland. Some of the defeated Portuguese fled to Macassar (now Ujung Pandang), to live and trade under the Sultan of Gowa. Others made their way to Larantuka. Then, in 1667, the military arm of the Dutch East Indies Company defeated the Sultan of Gowa in the famous Battle of Macassar, and Larantuka welcomed another lot of refugees.

In 1859 the Dutch bought Portugal's remaining claims to the island, although one proviso was that the area would remain Catholic. The arrival of Dutch Jesuit missionaries after 1865 brought a revitalization of interest in Catholicism on the island. At this time, only 3,000 nominal Catholics were left on Flores, concentrated on the eastern part of the island.

The newly arrived priests, according to one Dutch missionary, found the faithful divided into two groups: "animists with a sprinkling of Catholicism, and Catholics with a dominant belief in animism." The characterization of a later cleric was more cynical: "baptized heathen."

At first Holland had little interest in maintaining tight controls over Flores. However, unable to stop the slave trade which was centered in Ende, in 1838 the Dutch sent an expedition that destroyed the town and burned 50 Endenese trading ships.

In 1890, a Dutch survey team looking for tin was driven back from the interior of Flores by hostile Florinese. The team returned with a military expedition, leaving hundreds of dead. Still, they found no tin.

Sporadic resistance to the Dutch continued when Holland began ruling Flores directly in the early 20th century. The Catholic raja of Larantuka was Holland's principal nuisance, and his banishment in 1905 quieted that area. Although most of people of Flores bristled at Dutch control, there was never any organized resistance on a large scale: the mountainous terrain and many language and cultural differences made it impossible for the Florinese to coordinate their efforts.

The Church today

Once the island was "pacified," Catholic missionary activity took off in central and west Flores. The first mission was established in Ruteng in 1917, and within a single generation western Flores was completely Christianized. In part, such rapid conversion was possible because open-minded Catholic missionaries allowed the Florinese to continue their traditional dances and customs.

Today, the Church has put heavy emphasis on promoting the well-being of its flock, through education, health services and agriculture programs. They offer no objections to the government's birth control program.

LABUHANBAJO

Quiet Fishing Village on a Pretty Bay

During the summer tourist seasons, Labuhanbajo, on the far west coast of Flores, is overwhelmed by tourists. Although all the *losmen* and homestays are full, ferries kept bringing more bodies from Sape, and buses disgorged more visitors overlanding from Ruteng. There is lots of talk of new *losmen*, even hotels.

With all this tourist traffic, in "downtown" Labuhanbajo, where the two most popular *losmen* are located right across the street from each other, people have now stopped staring at foreigners. Even the kids have grown tired of shouting "Turis! Turis!" and "Hello meester!"

During the mid- to late 1970s, a tourist in Labuhanbajo was an alien from another planet. Things have changed, for better and worse. Bikini-clad Italians now get off the ferry and saunter through town, shocking the sensibilities of the local Muslim fishermen. And during my recent visit to Labuhanbajo, not one rat tried to explore my hair at night—an experience of about 15 years ago that I would rather not repeat.

A beautiful harbor

Even with all this newfound attention, Labuhanbajo is still basically a quiet fishing village. Most of the 3,000 people here make their living on the water, and the bay is full of spidery trimarans, canoes of various sizes, single-hulled sailboats, and inboard motor craft. The island-filled bay, dotted with such a wide variety of watercraft, remains one of Indonesia's most beautiful.

The best in-town location for viewing the bay is from the Sunset Restaurant or from the dining room and top floor of the Losmen Mutiara. Since the Mutiara is raised up over the water, the garbage floating in the water and piled up around the buildings does not interfere with one's view of the spectacular sunsets.

For the very best panoramic view of the harbor, climb Pramuka hill, just south of town. The scenery below can be absolutely spectacular at sunset. Walk up from the road on the north side for easiest access.

A longer jaunt north takes you past the end of the paved road, where you turn right to a dirt road which crosses a group of houses on stilts before climbing a bit and heading north 10 kilometers along the west coast to Cape Waturamba. This peninsula, capped by Seraya Besar Island, forms Flores' extreme northwest extension. Walking is the best way to enjoy the island-filled seascapes here.

Just as you leave town and gain a bit of altitude from the Golo Hotel, there is already a good view of the boats anchored to the north of town, along with the perched houses. A series of changing perspectives unfold to your left until you reach the halfway point, about 5 kilometers away from Labuhanbajo.

A hill in back of the Waicicu cottages, gives a dual perspective onto the seas to the east, where you can see a pearl farm and to the by-now familiar islands and sea to the west. From here it's another 5 kilometers or so to land's end.

A booming town

Even though the mosque's tinny loudspeakers still awake faithful and infidel alike before 5 a.m., the character of Labuhanbajo is changing rapidly. Not all of this is due to the tourist boom, which is mostly made up of Europeans on their way to Komodo. With the completion—and paving—of the 136-kilometer road to Ruteng, this formerly isolated village is now linked to the district capital. Several buses shuttle back and forth between Labuhanbajo and Ruteng daily (4–5 hours each way), and they are always full.

Reo, on the north coast, is still the Manggarai district's chief port, but the development of the Labuhanbajo area is progressing steadily. Health services are improving (particularly to combat the prevalent malaria here), and clean water and electricity are being provided. Primary schools—Catholic, Muslim and government—are steadily becoming more numerous.

Some Roman Catholics, the majority in the Manggarai district, have moved into Labuhanbajo as a result of the new road services. Some come as administrators to the expanding subdistrict, others as farmers who have been resettled from the crowded, isolated highlands with government help. There is even a new market, about 3 kilometers outside of town, next to the main road.

Local farmers grow rice, manioc and corn, and are beginning to experiment with cash crops: oranges, jackfruit, *salak* (a crisp palm fruit), cacao and cashew nuts.

The Catholics who have resettled here have hit upon another source of cash income: performing whip fights for tourists. These are staged in Kaper village, 5 kilometers from Labuhanbajo on the road to Ruteng. The fights are surprisingly well done with musical accompaniment.

A fishing village

Until the road came, there were few farmers living here, just a few Bimanese who sold their crops locally. The majority of the inhabitants were fishermen. In fact, the town is named for its Muslim fishermen: Labuhan (Harbor) Bajo (or Bajau). The fishermen here are ethnic Bajau and Bugis.

The favorable season for the fishermen comes during the northwest monsoon, October to March, when they catch huge quantities of squid which are salted and sent to Singapore. Much of the year, fishing takes place on dark nights, and pressure lamps are used to attract the fish over a fine-meshed net that has been dropped below.

When a large enough school has collected under the lamps, the net is hauled up. The nets are carried by vessels called *bagan*s, bi- or tri-hulled, movable fishing platforms with motors and a cabin for sleeping. The *bagan*s

catch a variety of mostly small fish.

Fishermen also sometimes gather trochus shells to supplement their incomes, and there are two pearl farming operations, one on Rinca Island, and on mainland Flores, another 25 km north of Labuhanbajo.

A petrified forest

Petrified trees lie in great chunks in the hilly country south of Labuhanbajo, at a place called Dataran Lemes. Getting to the site is definitely not half the fun. It's either a two-hour walk, or about $40 by chartered jeep. The road leading to the site is a rough, 10-kilometer dirt track that leads off the main road south of Labuhanbajo, heading off to the right, about 8 kilometers south of town.

Just after the turnoff, you cross the Wai Capi River, and for a while the road is not too bad, passing Kampung Capi and Tanah Dereng villages. An irrigation network has opened some 4,000 hectares here for *sawah* rice production. After this flat area, the jolts start, and you pass two more small villages, then Kampung Benteng—so named because it was the site of an ancient fort (*benteng* means "fort"). Only a low stone rubble in the village remains of the fort.

Above: *A boulder-sized chunk of petrified wood graces a small hill south of Labuhanbajo. The site, called Dataran Lemes, is littered with pieces of the old mineralized wood.*

The petrified wood is another kilometer or so further. You see bits and pieces among the plain old rocks on and beside the track, and just a bit further, some larger trunks lie on the left of the road. The best piece, which looks like a single tree trunk in several sections, sits on a hilltop.

Only one chunk remains with its "original" bark, as visitors from Labuhanbajo have chipped off bits as souvenirs. If you want to see the petrified wood, take a guide, available through the Losmen Bajo Beach. Otherwise you could spend a lot of time looking only at chips and small pieces.

The 'Mirror' caves

A much easier jaunt, and perhaps more rewarding, is a trip to the Batu Cermin—"Stone Mirror"—caves. The caves are at the end of a 4-kilometer paved road that branches off to the left just a couple of kilometers out of town, on the main road to Ruteng. This road was built specifically to facilitate access to the caves. From the parking lot, past new, but non-functioning guardhouses (no water), it's a couple of hundred meters to the two cave entrances.

Large, partially open chambers soar above, and in places the stalactites and stalagmites unite into huge pillars. Where the roof is broken away, trees have sent down long, straight roots to the cave floor. It is quite an impressive formation.

You must walk to the end of a dark, 50-meter-long passageway—a flashlight is essential—to reach the eponymous "mirror rock." Here an opening from above sends a beam of sunlight down a long, narrow shaft to reflect off the mica-bearing rock forming the "mirror."

The sun is right only briefly, sometime between about 9:30 and 10:30 a.m., so be sure that you are on time for the show. The cave attracts crowds of local residents on weekends. There is some graffiti, and the floor of the cave is scattered with litter, but the spectacle is still worth seeing.

Snorkeling and white beaches

The islands just off Labuhanbajo offer good snorkeling, swimming and just lazing on the beach (bikinis are permitted on these isolated islands). They are just 15–20 minutes away from the harbor by boat.

Serious divers head for the Sebayur Islands, an hour away, where there is the distinct possibility of seeing reef sharks, sea turtles, and larger pelagic species. For snorkelers, however, the white sand beach of Bidadari island is quite sufficient. The reef here has a good variety of inhabitants, including some lionfish and large parrotfish. A rocky mini-island, about 100 meters offshore, is home to a pair of large Napoleon wrasse.

You could even swim to Pulau Sarang, a small, rocky island about 250 meters offshore. (But check the currents first!) The vertical rock faces extend several meters underwater, and some sport a plethora of colorful tunicates. Although the coral and fish are limited in numbers here, there are several interesting shallow caves on the west side, 2–3 meters down and, the most fun of all, a couple of places where you can actually swim all the way across the island through narrow, underwater tunnels.

Opposite Sarang is the semi-circular, white sand beach of Pulau Sakure's southwest coast. Here there are a variety of soft corals, some *Tridacna* clams, and a few interesting fish. This is the only good snorkeling spot on Sakure island, as elsewhere dynamite fishing has ruined the coral and, consequently, much of the marine life.

From Labuhanbajo, Sakure Island looks like part of Pulau Bajo, the closest to the north. It's only when you putter past that you see that there is a break between them.

A small offshore island west of the harbor—Pulau Monyet, "Monkey Island"—takes its name from the crab-eating macaques who sometimes feed there at low tide.

On the other side of the bay, there is a hilly, bare cape. Several islands emerge from the sea here at varying distances from the harbor, their slopes covered with dry grass and few trees.

Getting to Labuhanbajo

The first leg of the ferry ride from Sape, Sumbawa to Labuhanbajo has little to recommend it. But the trip from Komodo to Labuhanbajo is stunning, as you pass island after island rising from the sea.

Flying from Bima is also a delight, as it costs little ($35) and takes just 30 minutes. As it flies over Komodo and Rinca, the little plane reveals seas dotted with islands. The seas here are remarkably colorful, turquoise over the sandy bottoms, light blue over the reefs, and dark blue over the deep waters.

Opposite: *A Florinese woman watches a whip-fight with interest. The scars raised by the whips are considered an essential feature of a man's physical attractiveness.*

RUTENG

The Fertile Rice Bowl of Flores

Ruteng is the capital of the Manggarai district, which is the largest by far on Flores, taking up most of the western third of the island. The district capital lies at the base of a tall mountain range, and at the head of an intricate network of valleys that makes up the island's largest rice-producing area. The district is also one of the largest coffee-growing areas in all of Indonesia.

Ruteng is a small town, overwhelmingly Catholic, with a busy area of shops and markets. The local commercial activity is dominated by ethnic Chinese families. The relatively high elevation keeps the climate cool.

For a great view of Ruteng town, the mountains and the surrounding rice fields, stroll up Golo Curu, a hill north of town. Take the road to Reo to about one kilometer past the Agung *losmen,* then, just as you cross a bridge, keep going straight instead of following the main road, which curves left. Continue until you reach a church—Santo Fransiskus Assisi.

'Welcome Mountain'

A dirt road at the back of the church leads to the top of Golo Curu, which means "Welcome Mountain." From the church, it's about 20 minutes of walking to the top. (A motorcycle could drop you off part of the way up, about where the Stations of the Cross begin.) Best to make this trip early in the day, as clouds often hide some or all the mountains in the afternoon.

The view is best at sunrise—around 6 a.m.—and for about an hour or so thereafter. From part way up the mountain, looking towards town, you see in the foreground three cemeteries, one for Catholics, one for Chinese, and a small one in between the others for war heroes.

From the very top of Golo Curu, the vegetation blocks the view of the rice fields, but from lower down you can look out over the surrounding *sawah,* as neat and orderly as

they can be in such contorted countryside. Just a short distance west of the hill spreads one of the very few *lingko randang,* a traditional field layout in which wedge-shaped gardens are arranged like slices of a pie around a central point.

Above the entrance to the top part of the hill, you pass through a gateway marked "Ave Maria," and there is a shrine to the Virgin in the back. It seems that a while back, a local farmer saw a bright light on the hilltop and was told by a supernatural voice that a shrine to the Virgin Mary should be built there. So the church complied—but so far there have been no miracles, according to our informants.

Traditions in flux

With pride and perhaps a little regret, the people of Ruteng consider themselves modern Indonesians, having abandoned most of their traditional way of life. But the most spectacular practice of the ancient religion remains popular—whip fighting. *Caci* (pronounced "chachi") in which combatants flail each other with buffalo hide whips, is an integral part of the traditional wedding, which still accompanies church weddings. (See "Whip Fighting," page 128.)

The wedding "season" runs from the end of June until the end of August. Until there is an official source of information, the best way to find out if one is being held, is to ask around the market (in Indonesian) or, better yet, have someone fluent in the local Manggarai tongue ask around for you.

It's well worth the effort to seek out such an event, as not only will you get to witness the exciting fight, but if you are well-dressed and behave properly, you will also be wined and dined as an honored guest.

Kampung Ruteng, an important ritual center in the past, still displays the *compang,* a stone ancestral altar. The hamlet is just outside of Ruteng, about 2–3 kilometers north. The *compang* is a ring-shaped stone platform surrounding a solid circle of stones. Unfortunately, the people here charge an "administrative fee" of $1.50 just to look at the altar, and ask twice that much if you want to take a photo.

The Lamaleda District, northeast of Ruteng around the village of Benteng Jawa, is considered the best remaining Manggarai

Opposite: *After the Dutch introduced rice to the region some 70 years ago, the highlands around Ruteng grew to become the rice-bowl of Flores.*

weaving center. The cloth, called *songke* (Indonesian, *songket*) is woven with a supplemental weft using local homespun thread and—sometimes—natural color dyes. You can purchase a *songke* sarong for about $20–$50. The weaving area is a bit over 50 kilometers from Ruteng, almost to Reo. Public transportation is available through Benteng Jawa, and it's a 5-hour ride on a rough road, each way.

Climbing a volcano

If volcano-climbing is your sport, try Gunung Ranaka, 2,400 meters, next to and just a bit lower than Mt. Namparnos, which is topped by a bright red-and-white telecommunications tower. The Ranaka crater erupted slightly in 1989, and was still smoking in the early 1990s. A four-wheel-drive jeep can make it almost all the way to the top. Otherwise, public transportation can take you to Robo village, whence you begin a steep, and not particularly easy, 10-kilometer ascent to the crater.

Another local site, especially popular with weekend fishermen from Ruteng, is Rana Mese (Big Lake). The lake, more than a hectare, is surrounded by tree-clad slopes and holds a great many carp. It is about 24 kilometers from Ruteng, some 3 kilometers after the road crests the pass to the south coast. The lake is only 200 meters off the main road to Bajawa.

The road to Reo

Reo is a little town on the north coast, due north of Ruteng by a paved, but still rough road. Many trucks and buses ply the route, which takes 2–3 hours ($1). Great views of the terraced rice fields begin just 5 kilometers out of Ruteng, and continue all the way to Pagal village, 21 kilometers from the district capital.

The area around Pagal, the Cibal subdistrict, is known for its weaving. The villages east of Pagal do their weaving from May to October, and those to the west from October to March. A couple of kilometers out of Pagal, at a place called Golongorong, there is a good road leading west. This road runs along a ridge giving views of both the north coast and the Manggarai Valley.

Cibal village lies a few kilometers along this road. A stone slab "altar to the ancestors" dominates an open space at one end of the village, and whip fights are held after weddings. Cibal sees few visitors.

From Golongorong, the main road drops 37 kilometers to Reo, almost on the coast. The picturesque port-village of Kedindi is just 5 kilometers northwest of Reo. The walk there is a pleasant one, as the path leads through rice fields. At Kendindi, sacks of coffee destined for Antwerp, and water buffalo destined for Surabaya, are loaded on ships and sent off.

WHIP FIGHTING

Stinging Whips at the Wedding

The women quickened the beat of the drums and the young man moved to the attack. Holding high his bullwhip, a vicious weapon made of buffalo hide, he jumped straight up, and on landing, began to move in on his opponent. His opponent, stationary but well-protected with a buffalo hide shield and bamboo baton, was at this point restricted by tradition to defense.

After a fast series of feints, the attacker caught the defender with his shield out of position. The whip slashed in, raising a long angry welt on the defender's exposed back. All fell quiet. With a shout and a smile, the stricken defender threw off his wooden buffalo mask, turned to his nearby clansmen, and began a chant to the spirits.

The *caci* ritual

Whip fighting, called *caci* (pronounced "chachi") is the most exciting surviving ritual of the Manggarai district in West Flores. The performance of the *caci* serves as a kind of offering to the ancestral spirits. But the welts and scars that result have their own compensations—the women much admire whip-scarred backs and arms, as they consider smooth skin on a man to be effete.

The whip fights take place at traditional wedding festivals. Even though the people of Manggarai are now Roman Catholics, a church wedding is not sufficient to unite a couple. The marriage cannot be consummated until the bridewealth has been paid and the *adat* or traditional rituals taken place. It was my good fortune to have been invited to one of these events.

A traditional wedding

When I first arrived, I was given a traditional drink of rice wine, symbolizing acceptance into the host's family. Handsome, brightly dressed girls knelt in front of us and prepared *sirih,* the betel chew. This traditional welcome offering consists of a sliver of *area* palm nut wrapped in a betel pepper leaf with a little slaked lime. The betel quid is chewed like tobacco, and produces copious reddish saliva that one squirts expertly between the floorboards. Or not so expertly in my case, to everyone's delight. The alkaloids contained in the *area* nut, absorbed through the gums, produce a mildly narcotic effect.

Soon, I heard the sound of gongs, and a general bustle announced the arrival of the groom's boisterous party. For the next few hours these guests were wined and dined—with the host's clan carefully keeping track of what was consumed. After the festivities there was to be a "reckoning" of the bill, where it is customary to charge the groom's party twice the store prices for all the items they have consumed: drinks, cigarettes, food and even sleeping mats.

The hosts try by all means to squeeze as much money as possible out of their guests, who have to keep their wits to stay solvent. For example, the groom's clan said that since their guests have come from far away and the weather was cold, wouldn't they like some woven cloth to stay warm? Knowing that they must pay a horse for each cloth accepted, the guests quickly opened their shirts and started fanning themselves, saying that thanks, but on the contrary they were quite hot, and—oh no!—not cold at all. However there was not much resistance to offers of alcohol and cigarettes.

A bag of coconuts

Humor plays an important part in the negotiations over bridewealth. When the groom's party made a ridiculously low offer, the bride's spokesman said that the amount was barely enough to buy a bag of coconuts. Well what do you expect, replied the groom's spokesman, the girl is about as pretty as a bag of coconuts.

In addition to hard cash, the bride price generally includes several horses and a few water buffalo. If a groom is considered ugly, an extra water buffalo must be paid. In fairness it must be said that there are gifts as well from the bride's clan, usually consisting of cloths and perhaps pigs, and about half of the money they receive is spent setting up the household for the newlyweds.

By the time sleep overcame the party, the groom's party had offered their absolute maximum of 125,000 rupiahs (around $200 at the time), whereas the bride's party demanded an absolute minimum of 250,000. I despaired of seeing the *caci* the next morn-

ing, when a member of the bride's household told us he didn't think the wedding would take place.

The final offer

I should have know better. The proceedings could not have advanced so far if the two parties were not determined to carry it through. Sure enough, in the morning the elders of both parties sat down for a few minutes of determined negotiations and it was soon announced that bridewealth of 175,000 rupiahs had been agreed upon. At this point the bride was produced, and she sat next to the groom. Both were equally nervous, and the groom in particular looked like he wished all the preliminaries would quickly end.

The *lea boku,* a knowledgeable elder, started to sing in a deep, resonant voice, asking that the ancestral spirits bless the young couple. A squealing pig was produced, and its throat was cut and liver removed. The elder and two of his savvy old cronies gathered around for a close look, considering the liver from all angles. He then formally announced what everyone wanted to hear: the markings of the liver showed that the ancestral spirits had accepted the offering, and were favorably disposed to the marriage.

The groom's party then formed a chanting procession, which eventually arrived in the center of the village. Here there was a large open space dominated by the *compang,*

or raised stone funerary mound. The groups started to sing—and drink—to build their fighting spirit. The men of the bride's clan formed a circle on the other side of the funerary mound, and started their own song.

Experience triumphs

In Manggarai, every young man adopts a fighting name for himself which he uses whenever he performs in the *caci*. These colorful names include "Wild Boar," "Rearing Horse" and "Naughty Rooster." A mouthful, but full of hubris, was "Gone Around the World and Have Yet to be Bested."

Suddenly, a wiry elder man with a whip jumped out of the bride's group and immediately assailed a man of the opposing side. The young man tried to defend himself, but the experienced older man was not to be denied. The whip lashed in, raising a small but vicious welt on the young man's chest. Throwing off his protective headgear with a smile, the young man shouted cheerfully at his group. They sung back "Even though we are wounded, we feel no pain! We *like* it!" The *caci* had officially begun.

Above: *The Manggarai district whip fights, an essential proof of manhood in the days of warfare, continue to enliven wedding celebrations today. The contest pits one man with a stout bullwhip, the attacker, against another man with a shield and a bamboo baton, the defender.*

BAJAWA

The Island's Traditional Center

The Ngada District, with its capital at Bajawa, has retained its traditional ways more than any other part of Flores. The people are almost all Roman Catholics, but at the same time villages maintain their megaliths and paired *ngadhu,* an ancestral male-identified sacrificial post, and *bhaga,* female–identified shrines.

Few travelers seem to know of the cultural richness of the villages in and around Bajawa, and most zip straight through on their way to Ende, or at most stay overnight in the capital. If you are interested in the religion and culture of the Ngada district, however, you should stay at least a couple days.

Langa village: ritual shrines

Quite close to the small town of Bajawa, population 12,000, are two traditional villages: Langa and Bena. You can walk to either in a day, or a half-day by vehicle. Try to get an early start, because the top of dramatic Inerie volcano (now extinct) tends to become obscured by clouds by around 10 a.m. From Bajawa town, go to the main trans-Flores road, 3 km away. Next to the bus stop, a badly paved road leads 2.5 kilometers to Langa, in which there are 16 hamlets.

In several of them, open squares hold neat rows of five *ngadhu* and four *bhaga.* Mt. Inerie provides a magnificent backdrop. The *ngadhu,* representing a clan's male ancestors, looks like thatch-roofed beach parasol, some 3 meters high, with a thick tree-trunk, decorated with carvings, as its pole. The shrine is topped by a human figure, often wearing a headband and holding a *parang* (machete) in one hand and a spear in the other. There is a circle of stones around each shrine.

The *ngadhu* trunk comes from a special kind of tree which has to be dug up with its roots intact, and carried in a straight line to the village. The *bhaga,* the female partner to the *ngadhu,* is a small thatched hut, sometimes with carvings under the doorway and

around the bottom planks. (See "Religion," page 36.)

When clan elders die, funerary rituals are held by the appropriate *ngadhu* or *bhaga* requiring the sacrifice of a water buffalo tied to a stone stake called a *peo,* which represents future generations. In the past, dozens of water buffalo were used, but a government regulation now limits the ceremony to one—thus preventing the impoverishment of the deceased's family. On other occasions when ancestral help is required, a pig is slaughtered and offerings of betel nut and food are made to the clan ancestors.

In Langa, the annual six-day Reba ceremony kicks off on January 15 with a Misa Kudus ("Holy Mass") followed by dances and various rituals in traditional costumes.

Bena village: cult houses

A 10-kilometer rough dirt road leads from Langa and circles the base of Mt. Inerie. About 2 kilometers out of Langa, a vertical grassy wall offers a spectacular foreground to Mt. Inerie's bare, smooth cone. Then the road drops to Bena village, offering a bird's eye view of Bena's cult houses, *ngadhu, bhaga* and *peo.*

Bena is the central village of the area's traditional religion, and there are no tin roofs here yet. Upon arrival, you register in a guest book and contribute 50¢. Then you are free to wander around the village and photograph

to your heart's content. Similar fees apply in other traditional areas as well.

The annual *reba* cycle begins in Bena, on December 27, and then moves to other villages in the area. A number of other rituals are held in conjunction with the agricultural year: the Zoa planting ritual, in September–October, and the Keti Kua harvest ritual in April–May. Another event, called the Umamoni or Anakoka, is a celebration of the ancestors who first planted here and requires that a water buffalo be sacrificed.

The traditional houses of Bena village have steeply pitched, high thatch roofs. Most are topped by a martial figure, wielding a spear and *parang,* similar to those found on the *ngadhu.* There are also several large groups of megalithic stones—meeting places, where village elders make decisions affecting their relations with the supernatural. It is believed that the stones were all brought to their present location by a muscular supernatural being named Dhake, sometime before the first humans came to Flores.

At the far end of the village, on a small hill, is a shrine where the Virgin Mary sits under a huge, contorted tree. The view from behind the Virgin includes the Savu Sea. There is a guesthouse at the entrance to the village, and it may now be possible to overnight here. Figure about $4–$5, including simple meals.

Old Wogo: megaliths

From Bena, a dirt road slightly better than the one from Langa runs to the main Ende–Ruteng road, which it reaches at Mangulewa village, some 10 kilometers away. Head east, towards Ende, and you soon reach Mataloko village, right on the main highway. Just as you reach Mataloko, a dirt road leads south, to Wogo village. Here one of the district's best sets of *ngadhu* and *bhaga* sit, amidst bright green electrical poles.

Another kilometer or so further on this road, a 200-meter path to the left leads to Wogo Tua, "Old Wogo," the original village site. The people of Wogo moved from here about 30 years ago. At Old Wogo, large megaliths stand weathering, some cleared, others choked by tall grass. The deserted stones look eerie and sad in the frequent afternoon fog.

Soa: traditional boxing

The Soa area, where the airport is located, is 26 kilometers north of Bajawa. There is frequent transport between the two cities, usual-

ly trucks, on Wednesday evenings and on Thursday, which is market day. A little restaurant just off in back of the market serves dog, locally called "RW," pronounced "air-way," a euphemism based on the Indonesian initials for "fine-haired." Not bad.

The Soa region is quite traditional, but with a ritual schedule that differs somewhat from that of the villages around Mt. Inerie. The year's most important ritual here, the Paruwitu, lasts a month, from around mid-October to mid-November. Deer hunting is the cycle's most important event, and men on horseback down the animals with spears. Women wash their hands in deer blood to boost their fertility. Traditional boxing, called *sagi* in the Soa area, is also part of these rites.

This boxing—in which plenty of human blood flows—is also practiced in the region of Boawae, 41 kilometers from Bajawa, on the highway to Ende. In the Boawae area the boxing is called *etu,* and it is supposedly held every year around June 10–20. Boawae, the former seat of the district's most powerful raja, holds heirlooms that include a large carved wood horse. The inauguration of this sculpture required the slaughter of over 100 water buffalo.

Opposite: *Old megaliths lie untended in a field at Wogo Tua. Offerings are still made here to the spirits.* **Above:** *A* ngadhu *shrine in Langa village. The Inerie volcano looms in the background.*

RIUNG

Snorkeling, Fruit Bats and Dragons

Riung, on the coast north of Bajawa, offers beautiful coral gardens in the Seventeen Island National Reserve, as well as thousands of flying foxes and—perhaps—a glimpse of a Komodo monitor. However, be warned: there is malaria in and around Riung. (See "Travel Advisory" page 243, for malaria information.)

Nangamese, better known as Riung, with about 1,500 people, is the biggest village in the subdistrict. Although there have been a few tourists here, the place feels a lot like Labuhanbajo did 20 years ago, before dragon watching on Komodo island became such a popular spectator sport.

Riung village

The people of Riung are a mix of Muslim Bugis and Bajau, and Roman Catholic Bajawanese. The sub-district was originally a string of coastal fishing villages, settled by the Muslim migrants and the animist Bajawanese living inland, scattered in mountain hamlets. The corn and rice grown by the Catholic farmers is supplemented by the Muslim fishermen's catch.

The farmers export copra, shallots, coconuts and kapok, and the fishermen send out trochus shells, *trepang,* dried fish, yellowtail tuna and skipjack. The women of the district weave and embroider typical Bajawa style sarongs, with yellow and red flowers on a blue-black background. (Around $20–$25, depending on the decoration.)

If you are interested in seeing the lizards, as soon as you get to town ask the owner of of your *losmen,* to find a dog or goat to slaughter for lizard watching bait. You need to do this right away, because it will take a couple of days or more for the carcass to develop a noxious, lizard-attracting stink. The bait will cost you $8–$30, depending on the size of the animal. Set it out with one of the local park rangers right away ($3 a day, plus the cost of the boat) so it can begin to attract lizards.

Seventeen Islands

Next step after arranging for the lizard bait, is to find a boat—about $10–$20 a day, depending on its engine and size. You will have 2–3 days to snorkel and enjoy the beaches before your bait gets results. The cheaper boats are outrigger canoes with motors and names like "Crime Hunter." If the water is at all rough, we recommend a boat called *Sentra Riung,* which can take a half dozen foreigners comfortably. Take young coconuts to drink—80¢ for a dozen.

The area off Riung makes up a national park called Pulau Tujuhbelas (Seventeen Islands). There are in fact more than 20 islands, but, in a gesture of patriotism, the number was declared to be 17, to conform to Indonesia's Independence day, August 17.

Some of the smaller islands are just rocks sticking out of the sea. The larger ones, especially Pulau Ontoloe, the biggest of the bunch, are hilly, covered with short grass and a few trees, and fringed with mangroves. On Pulau Bampa Barat, where some fishermen have a temporary residence, you might be able to buy fresh fish for a quick grill. If not, bring lunch for an all-day ride. The *losmen* will provide you with a *nasi bungkus.*

Local rangers say that the greatest threat to the marine reserve are Taiwanese boats that catch shark, yellowtail and skipjack tuna.

Underwater wonders

The reefs off the islands are very healthy, with hard and soft corals in good variety, and lots of colorful fish. Visibility, as well as the ease of traveling around the islands, depends on the wind. The Flores Sea here is quietest for two periods during the year, April–June, and September–November. There are plenty of white sand beaches for sunbathing and swimming.

In the shallow water just offshore, among fields of sea grass, there are numerous reddish starfish, covered with black bumps, and—watch your step!—spiny sea urchins.

At the inshore edge of the reef, 1–2 meters down, are the brilliant turquoise mantles of *Tridacna* clams. Stony corals and brilliantly colored soft corals grow in excellent variety. Nearby, an orange-fringed batfish glided, unperturbed. In one spot off Rutong Island we observed at least a dozen varieties

Opposite: *Fruit bats called flying foxes, disturbed from their daytime sleep by a boatload of tourists, swarm out of the mangrove trees near Riung.*

of soft coral over a mere 1.5 meter vertical length of reef face. Scientists have counted 47 species of coral around Rutong island alone.

With mask and snorkel, take a close look at the underwater portion of the mangrove roots: you might see thin, needle shaped schools of fish just below the surface, while just a bit further down are small spiny fish with big eyes, probably poisonous as they are completely unafraid of divers, daring you to grab them. Your boat will either run up on the beach, or anchor off the reef edge, where it's not at all easy to get back on board.

Flying foxes

Unless you have a lot of time, you are not guaranteed to see the big lizards. But there is a surefire daily spectacle not to be missed. On the north coast of Ontoloe Island, the largest of the "seventeen," the large fruit-eating bats called flying foxes mass in the mangrove trees. At high tide, your boat can get quite close to shore, where the bats hang upside down in the trees, thick as flies.

A few shouts send them flying, and you can see thousands of the bats—with reddish fur and black wings—take off from the trees and wheel around in the sky before setting down again. This is a magnificent spectacle. Although they are the bane of anyone with a backyard mango tree—savvy growers cover the ripening fruit with a paper bag—fruit bats are essential pollinators and seed dispersal

agents. The bats in this colony are said to forage every night as far away as Bajawa and Ruteng.

Monitor lizards

The recommended spot for dragon watching is on mainland Flores, next to Damu Bay. A Japanese torpedo boat, sunk by the Allies in World War II, is supposed to lie about 30 meters down in this bay. After a few days of hanging in a tree, your animal carcass should begin to attract lizards. Contact the local conservation department (PPA) to arrange your viewing expedition.

It is a little bit unclear what your bait might attract. The lizard I saw, though small, looked pretty much like the Komodo dragon, *Varanus komodoensis*. Photos of a captured specimen that the rangers displayed, however, showed a patterned yellowish body with black feet. Definitely a monitor (*Varanus* sp.) but not a typical Komodo dragon: it had a long, thin tail, and a thin, elongated neck. Locally called *mbou,* it is probably another species of monitor.

Getting to the lizard-viewing spot depends on the size of your boat and the tides. At high tide, any craft can just run up onto the beach. At low tide, if the boat is large it might have to park a bit down the coast, requiring a long wade though the waist-high water and a couple of hundred meters of clambering through the brushy shoreline. Good luck!

ENDE

Old Port, Volcanoes and Fine *Ikat*

Ende is the largest town on Flores, with about 60,000 people. The town is set on the island's south coast, nestled in the crook of a small peninsula. There is a port on either side of the narrow peninsula; most of the shipping activity is concentrated at Pelabuhan Ende, which faces west and offers a good view of the wide Ende Bay. The new dock, Pelabuhan Ipi, is on the east side, and here the large ships call, including the *Kelimutu.*

Dramatic volcanoes

Ende is set amidst several volcanoes. From the old harbor, around sunset, if the day is clear, you can get a great view of Ebulobo standing out among the mountains west of Ende Bay and Ende Island. If you miss this view, look south, at nearby Gunung Meja. Meja's flattened top gave this extinct volcano its name: Table Mountain. Further out on the peninsula is Gunung Iye, which is still smoking somewhat. If you fly in or out of Ende, Meja and Iye add a definite element of excitement to take-off and landing.

From the Ipi harbor, a 4-kilometer road leads to Gunung Meja, then to Tetandara village, the site of a volcanology station. The station keeps an eye on Iye, which last erupted in 1969. The volcano makes a fairly easy climb. (See "Flores Practicalities," page 285.)

Downtown Ende

The area south of the old port is Ende's most lively, with lots of shops crowded together into narrow streets. There are several inexpensive *losmen* in this area, frequented by Indonesians and foreign travelers on a very, very tight budget. It's certainly worth a look around, although as a foreigner you will still attract some attention.

Check out the large morning market at the far southern end of the downtown area, bustling every day from dawn till around noon. The "Hello Mister!"s are now much more infrequent than in years past, and you can see wander around with the *ikat*-wrapped women shopping for fruit, vegetables and other staples. The fish section—just off the beach—is perhaps the most interesting, with meter-long tunas, large manta rays and plenty of small sea creatures for sale. We were told that a few years ago a fisherman brought a 6-meter hammerhead shark here for sale. The size is no doubt an exaggeration, but even so it must have been impressive.

Just outside the downtown harbor entrance, several large stands display and sell *ikat* cloths from this region, as well as from the rest of Flores and other islands. Expect to pay about $20 for a sarong-sized cloth from the Ende area, after bargaining of course. You can also buy *ikat,* and watch the weaving process, at the nearby villages of Woloare and Ndona.

Nuabosi: bird's eye view

For a spectacular bird's eye view of Ende and vicinity, go up to Nuabosi village, 9 kilometers from the main highway to Bajawa. The road to Nuabosi starts at the outskirts of Ende, and is paved most of the way, although there are a couple of rough stretches. Even in the beginning the view is good, but be patient—the best view is from the top.

About 3 kilometers from the turnoff is Wolare village, well-known for its traditional blacksmiths, weaving and bamboo work. There is a spring here that comes up among the roots of a large tree, and the Balinese who live in Ende come here to pay respects.

Nuabosi has a *rumah adat,* a traditional clan house, in front of which is a raised crypt. Here stones, topped by a flat slab, serve as an altar upon which water buffalo, horses, pigs and cattle are sacrificed during funerary rituals. (Also goats, for Muslim guests.) The *rumah adat* was recently roofed with tin to catch rainwater, as the hamlet's supply is a steep 300 meters away.

A short dirt road leads out of Nuabosi to the shell of a Dutch-colonial era guesthouse. The spot was well chosen: the view below is absolutely magnificent. A harvest festival is held here around April–May. There is some *ikat* weaving by the women here, while the men work a valley in back of the village where vanilla and many of Ende's vegetables are grown.

Wolowona: Mt. Wonge

For a different view of the area, head out of Ende on the road to Maumere, stopping just 4 kilometers away at Wolowona village. A road leads to the right from Wolowona, and immediately crosses the Wolotolo river. If you continue straight ahead, you reach the weaving village of Ndona, some 5 kilometers away. Just after the bridge, however, a paved road to the right leads through rice paddies to the mouth of the Wolotolo River. Boat building nearby, at Nila. From here, the peninsula, with Gunung Meja and Gunung Ipi, lies just across the bay.

Koa Island, just offshore, is said to be the top of Gunung Meja, chopped off when it got into a fight with another mountain, Gunung Wonge. The big knife Wonge used broke, and fell into Ende bay where it is now a small island near Ende Island.

Wonge Mountain, in local lore, is said to have had five pillars corresponding, in one version, to Indonesia's five major religions: Islam, Buddhism, Catholicism, Protestantism and Balinese Hinduism. Another version says the pillars represent the nation's "Five Principles," the Panca Sila. While Sukarno, who later became Indonesia's first president, was exiled to Ende, he regularly came to this spot to meditate.

Just west of the mouth of the Wolotolo River is Tangga Alam—"Stairs of Nature," a black-sand beach popular with Endenese on weekends. A footpath here climbs over a natural stairway and comes out on a long stretch of beach. The road continues to Wolotopo village, where there is good *ikat* and traditional houses. Just past Wolotopo, a promontory overlooks seas said to be shark infested.

Nggela: weaving village

The well-known *ikat* weaving village of Nggela, located at the end of an awful dirt road overlooking the sea, has been visited by too many tourists. As soon as the saleswomen see a foreign face, they spread out the weavings in the center of the village. So far, not too bad. But the selling techniques are downright rude: You want to take a photo? Buy a sarong first! You want to look at a sarong? Buy one first!

A quick stroll around will acquaint you with the various stages of the various stages of the *ikat* process—unless, of course, the women are all busy trying to flog their cloths. If you want to take photos, you might well have to pay for the privilege. Nggela is famous because only hand-spun thread and natural dyes are used, although the same is sometimes true of the other villages.

The prices of Nggela's weavings vary from $55 to $150, and you can probably get them cheaper at the shop attached to the Jawa Timur Restaurant in Wolowaru. The owner of the Jawa Timur knows when and how to buy the Nggela *ikat* as well as those of the several villages on the way, all of which produce these fine weavings. (He periodically takes a big batch to stores in Bali.)

Ikat has become Nggela's principal source of cash income. The village's 1,300-odd inhabitants cultivate enough rice, corn, manioc and other vegetables for their needs, supplemented by a bit of fishing. But there is little surplus for sale. Weaving provides cash for all the necessities. Each year, some 2,000 *sarung*s are woven here, of which perhaps a quarter or more end up with foreign buyers.

The easiest way to reach Nggela is from

Wolowaru, on the main road between Ende and Maumere, perhaps 40 kilometers from Ende. Daily passenger trucks run to Nggela, on the coast, from Wolowaru for 50¢. (They are more frequent on Friday and Saturday.)

You can hike it also, the Wolowaru–Nggela round-trip taking 6-7 hour and about that many liters of water. You can stop for a refreshing drink of coconut water at either Jopu or Wolojita, along the way. You can also buy *ikat* at either of these two villages.

Above: *To prepare the weft threads for* ikat, *they are wrapped around a frame, and the pattern is painstakingly tied into them with small bits of string. Only the untied threads will take the dye.*

KELI MUTU

Stunning, Three-Colored Crater Lakes

It's dark and cold, everyone bundled up in jackets or blankets, and we are all casting anxious glances at the sky. Not one damn star in sight. We shiver and wait. After more than an hour, the sky begins to lighten and, a while later, we encounter the awful, disappointing truth: we are smack in a cloud bank and the colored lakes of Keli Mutu are completely obliterated from sight.

A shout out of the mist: "Konderatu!" And again, "Konderatu!"

It's an older man, Pak Carolus. He organizes the truck that every day takes tourists to Keli Mutu from Moni. "Konderatu," he shouts again, "Let the clouds part!"

He elaborates: "Lots of people have come from far countries, let them see the lakes." I walked over to him, and asked "Who is Konderatu?"

"He, and his wife Bobi, are the owners of this place," Pak Carolus said. "We must ask them to be allowed to see the lake."

An hour or so later, whether by Konderatu's grace or for some more prosaic meteorological reason, a corner of one of the lakes appeared below us, through thinning clouds. But just as everyone reached for their cameras, the clouds moved in again. For the next half hour, we caught tantalizing glimpses of the turquoise lake, which was playing hide and seek with this eager bunch of tourists. Finally, slowly, the clouds and mist parted to reveal the full splendor of the scenery below.

The colored lakes

Keli Mutu, in southern Flores about 40 kilometers from Ende, consists of three volcanic craters, each filled with a lake of different color. What we saw when the clouds opened up was a large lake, filled with pale turquoise water, then a smaller lake, deep green and finally another, with water so dark it was black. The landscape surrounding the lakes is barren and grey, and in this setting the col-

ors are nothing less than astonishing.

It's no wonder that this spot—1,690 meters high—was formerly an important ritual site. Only 50 years ago, in deference to the Catholic Church, did the large-scale water buffalo and pig sacrifices stop. For it was—and is still—believed that the souls of the deceased find their eternal resting place in these lakes.

In fact, visitors to Keli Mutu might well be advised to bring offerings to Konderatu and Bobi if they want a clear morning in which to view the three lakes.

The locals who maintain the road to Keli Mutu—landslides can cut off the upper portions of the road, especially during the rainy season— are sometimes hurled into the mud or have their tools mysteriously grabbed away from their hands.

When this happens it is time to make offerings to calm down Konderatu. A large pig, rice, *tuak,* betel and some fake gold jewelry are usually sufficient to placate the spirit. It is also said that the spirits of the dead sometimes come out of the lake at night to wander around the mountain.

Visiting the lakes

Base camp for an assault on Keli Mutu is Moni village, right on the main Ende–Maumere highway. A decade ago, the only way to go up to the lakes was by trekking or on horseback, either of which required a 2 a.m. departure—a tough 3–4 hours to the top. Only nostalgic masochists still do it this way—particularly by horseback, which on the bare-backed ponies is far more torturous than walking. (By the way, don't try it without a guide, because unless the moon is full, you will very likely get lost.)

Today, trucks with benches pick up "climbers" in Moni around 4:00–4:30 a.m. for the 45-minute ride to within 1 km of the lake-viewing spot ($1.50). Walking down is pleasant enough after the clouds have closed down the lakes, around 10-11 a.m. Before you leave Moni, check the weather, but try anyway. Figure it this way: you're already up, and the clouds might lift later. If they don't, try again the next day.

Whether you ride or trek, by 5:30 a.m. you should be at the top vantage point—an awful chunk of concrete at the top of a convenient set of steps from the parking area below. It can get really cold up there, and sweaters, jackets and blankets are worth their weight in gold. People with really amazing foresight bring a thermos of hot coffee.

An otherworldly setting

On a clear morning, Keli Mutu is one of the world's most spectacular sights. The pre-dawn light seeps slowly into the sky, the stars fade and the stunning mountains, rising in all shapes and sizes, come gradually into view. Some are piled on top of each other, others are separated by narrow valleys.

Cheers and clicking cameras welcome the sun when it finally rises over the horizon, close to Mt. Egon, an extinct volcano which dominates the scenery to the east, near Maumere. To the south, the dark, oval peak of Keli Bara—1,731 meters—looms above Keli Mutu's flattened top. In spite of the sun, the cold wind reaches right down to your bones for another hour or two, while people wait for the light to reach the lake in front of the vantage point.

The sunshine brings out the nearest lake's beautiful turquoise, broken by a few yellowish streaks on its surface, a thin scum of sulfurous foam. By the time the shadow from the lake's eastern crater wall casts its distinct jagged shadow across the water—around 8:30 or 9:00 a.m.—it's time for a stroll around the other craters.

A good footpath follows the western crater top of the green lake, then continues much of the way around the turquoise lake, ending on its eastern rim. From the path, you can cast cautious glances at the two lakes far below, separated from each other by a low, thin rock wall, perhaps 15 meters high and 10 meters thick. The sun sparkles off the lakes, which look cheerful set against the dead rock walls. The blue-green lake's southern and western rims provide the best vantage spots for morning photography.

If the lakes stay clear of clouds, you might want to remain in this otherworldly setting until the afternoon, but there is no water or food available at the moment. A hat and some water are recommended for the 6-kilometer walk down to the conservation department guard house. There you will be expected to enter your particulars into their guest book and pay a very modest fee.

From this post, a shortcut passes through several hamlets and reaches the Ende–Maumere road just outside of Moni. The path is easy to follow in the daylight, and leads past Manukako, Koposili and Nuadepi before coming out onto the the road.

While you are in the Keli Mutu area, you might want to visit the weaving village of Nggela, on the coast (see "Ende" page 134).

Above: *The colored crater lakes of Keli Mutu. Dawn and early morning, before the clouds roll in, is the best time to visit the mountaintop. The colors of the three lakes are constantly in flux, because of the varying mineral content of their waters, although they appear to most visitors as turquoise, deep blue, and black or even maroon.*

MAUMERE

The Visitor's Capital of the Island

After the devastating 1992 earthquake which left 2,500 dead, Maumere is slowly reclaiming its former status as the visitors' capitol of Flores. The town lies at the island's hub of communications, there is a good range of accommodations, and many of Flores' attractions can be covered in day trips from here. Within range of Maumere are snorkeling and diving—once among the best in Indonesia, and now still recovering from the quake—traditional weaving, great scenery, ancient regalia from Portuguese times and the island's only museum.

You can even visit the colored lakes of Keli Mutu from here (see "Keli Mutu," page 136) instead of Ende. In fact, although Ende is a larger town, we suggest staying in Maumere, especially if you can afford one of the better hotels outside of town. The mountain scenery and the traditional villages in the Bajawa district are the best on the island, but transportation around Bajawa, which is high in the mountains and far inland, is not as reliable or comfortable as around Maumere.

Also, if you have to get sick on Flores, you are advised to do it in Maumere: the Catholic hospital, with its western-trained staff, is perhaps the best in eastern Indonesia.

Watublapi: weaving village

Maumere is on the north coast, near the narrowest part of the island. Just southeast of the town, Flores thins out to just 18 kilometers wide by road. To see this spectacular, mountainous neck, go to Gelinting village, about 10 kilometers east of Flores on the main road to Larantuka, and head south. The best time to catch a public *bemo* or bus to Gelinting without a long wait is on Fridays, after 10 a.m., when the market at Gelinting begins to wind down.

The Gelinting market is the largest weekly market in the Kewapandai district, and many men and women from villages in the interior come here on Fridays. The women wear beautiful, hand-woven sarongs. The crowd and merchandise of the market spreads out behind a line of roadside shops in town. There is lots of activity here, and nobody minds your taking pictures—although you'll get giggles and stiff poses. The fresh fish market is on the other side of the main road, which cuts through town, just off the shoreline.

From Geliting, it's 10 kilometers south to Watublapi village. On the way you can look back and see the Bay of Maumere to the north, and terraced fields on steep slopes where corn and vegetables are grown. To the west a couple of conspicuous rounded peaks appear, while to the east higher, if less spectacular mountains hide Egon, a still-active volcano. During the rainy season, there could be patches of mud just before Watublapi, but otherwise the road is quite passable.

Watublapi is well-known for its *ikat* weavings, and also offers a great overview of the landscape. Ask someone to show you the path to Blarinsina, an open field less than 100 meters from the road, where weaving is sometimes demonstrated and dances performed for tour groups. From Blarinsina you have an unimpeded view of both the Savu Sea to the south and the Flores Sea to the north, with verdant mountains to the east and west.

From Watublapi village, you can continue on the paved road to the south coast. All around the village, and all down the slopes to the east and west, are groves of cacao trees, the region's most important cash crop. Smallholder plantations of coffee and cloves line the road. The delicate coffee trees are shaded by tall *kanari*, which themselves produce a valuable, oily nut.

During the cacao harvest season, April through August, heaps of the beans can be seen drying or fermenting around Watublapi. As you move down to the south coast, coconut groves replace the other cash crop trees, as on the wide coastal plain to the north. One can also see many cashew trees, which produce the most important cash crop after copra along the coast.

Ipir: traditional coast village

About 6 kilometers from Watublapi, the road reaches Bola, a large village dominated by an imposing hillside church, and then drops 2

Opposite: *Three Dutch divers relax in the pool at the Sao Wisata, a resort near Maumere. The resort runs scuba diving jaunts to the world-class reefs on the islands and coastline off Maumere.*

kilometers to Ipir on the coast. Ipir stretches along the sea to the east, where a wide coral break absorbs the shock of the heavy waves, which are often quite spectacular in this area. The paved road continues east along the coast for 15 kilometers to Habibola village. A kilometer or so past Habibola is Pantai Doreng, a fine, 4-kilometer-long beach of golden sand.

Ipir village used to own a large beachside wooden cross, said to have been made during Portuguese times. This cross disappeared in 1947, however, and has been replaced by a plain one at the same location.

Although the people of Ipir are all Catholics, the village has kept at least the outward appearance of tradition. Just about all the huts and small houses are thatch roofed, with walls constructed of cracked bamboo. Most of the women and even the girls wear locally woven sarongs, displaying a distinctive pattern found only in this area. Indeed, weaving is an important cottage industry here, bringing cash to the village as well as supplying the people's own needs.

Whenever the seas calm down a bit, the men set out to fish in tiny outriggered canoes flying small, ragged sails. The economy here relies heavily on copra, although the narrow coastal area at the base of the hills and mountains does not permit the extensive coconut groves found in the north. Cashew trees provide additional income.

The villagers also tap palms for *tuak,* a beverage made lightly alcoholic by natural fermentation. But don't take the "lightly" too lightly: drinking enough *tuak* will get you as roaring drunk as whiskey, with the same regrets.

In Ipir, aside from drinking *tuak,* you can watch the women tying off threads in frames for their *ikat.* All the cloth here is made with hand-spun threads, and the dyes are made with bark, roots and leaves. They weave on backstrap looms, while chatting with friends. Should you feel a bit more ambitious after a look around the quiet village, there are good coral formations and underwater scenery about one kilometer past Ipir village. Ask someone about water conditions, and don't try it against his recommendations. The seas can get very rough here. Your instinct for self-preservation will probably hold you in check anyway.

If you wish to spend a day or more here, the village chief—*kepala desa*—can arrange for a homestay. There are no commercial accommodations. His house is on the beach, just behind the wooden cross. Figure on $5 a day for a mattress and full board of local victuals, which tend to be bland and monotonous, unless a recently caught fish has found its way into the kitchen. A local chicken, should you wish to vary your diet, costs about $2.50–$3. It might be a good idea to bring some of your own food if you are plan-

ning on spending a few days in the area.

There is no running water in the houses, so bathing takes place next to one of several concrete-lined wells equipped with buckets. Manners dictate that the women bathe in full sarongs, while the men douse themselves wearing shorts or underpants. Trucks, crammed with passengers and merchandise, run between Ipir and Geliting several times a day and will charge less than $1 each way to haul you along.

The north coast

To return to the north coast from Ipir you can either take the same road—through Watublapi—or take a track that starts from Bola village, and crosses the mountains to the west. The first 3 kilometers of this road are unpaved, but passable year-round, while the remaining 17 kilometers are surfaced. The road cuts through several villages before reaching the main coastal trunk road some 2 kilometers west of the way to Watublapi. Although you catch only glimpses of the Savu Sea from this road, the views onto the Flores Sea and Maumere Bay with Besar island are spectacular along this route.

In this same direction—although not on the Bola road—is Dobo village. Dobo is some 7 kilometers on a paved road which starts from the main Maumere–Larantuka road, west of Geliting. Lying right on the divide between north and south, Dobo offers views of both the Flores and Savu Seas.

Hidden in the house of its keeper here is a 40-centimeter bronze canoe, complete with paddlers and warriors. We have never seen a piece like this, in a museum or anywhere else. It is unique and worth the hassle to have a look. Informants say the canoe was brought to Dobo during Majapahit times, some 600 years ago.

Offerings have to be made to the canoe—betel nut and other small odds—before it can be brought out of its hiding place and shown to visitors. If the proper offerings are not made, disastrous floods will result. The Dobo villagers also occasionally perform a war dance, and play bamboo flutes.

Northwest of Maumere

The 42-kilometer coastal road west from Maumere to Kota Baru, paved in 1989, reveals splendid, golden hills on the left and beautiful turquoise seas on the right. Several pocket valleys along the way are filled with irrigated rice paddies, and groves of coconut, *lontar* and banana trees. Otherwise the coun-

tryside is barren. Very few foreigners wander out this way.

Hire your own transportation for this stretch or you might face long waits for public *bemo*s or trucks. This road often serves as a detour for public transportation when the rains cut the main road between Maumere and Ende, as a paved road of some 75 kilometers exists between Kota Baru and Deutosoko to the south, about 37 kilometers from Ende, past the landslide area.

Wuring: Bugis village

Wuring, populated almost entirely by Muslim Bugis, is 4 kilometers west of Maumere, just off the paved road. All of their houses sit on stilts in the traditional style, over the high tide line. Some boat construction takes place here, but the carpenters build smaller craft only, not the large *pinisi* schooners for which the Bugis are best known.

Christian women from the hills in back of Wuring come in small groups here, clad in their distinctive sarongs, to sell tiny piles of vegetables in order to buy fish to take home. The people here are friendly, and photography is no problem—but you might be escorted by a throng of children, all simultaneously vying for your attention.

West of Wuring the road passes a government-run cotton gin and hillside rows of dreadful, perfectly aligned little houses built by the government. These were constructed to lure the locals out of their remote and even more barren mountains so they would be closer to government services like schools. The men from these resettlement projects still return to their former lands to hunt deer and wild pigs with spears, bow-and-arrows, and trained hunting dogs.

Around kilometer 14 you catch the first real glimpse of the sea. Set in the fringing mangroves is the village of Waturia, a little Bugis enclave by the sea, with government houses on the hillside for the mountain folks. A few kilometers further, the road climbs some low coastal hills for some great bays and other panoramic views, along with the first of several fertile valleys. Here water buffalo are used to churn up the soil prior to planting rice in the flooded plots.

Ndete: tasty fish

Some 30 kilometers from Maumere is the small seaside village of Ndete, its many little fishing craft testifying to the chief occupation here. Fish, from tiny fry to tuna, are set out to dry in the sun. They will later be sold in

Maumere. At Ndete you can buy a delicious fresh grouper or snapper in the kilogram range for less than $2. Cook it yourself, or have someone grill it for you.

At Magepanda, just a little further, the road cuts across the neck of the Tanjung Watomano peninsula and leaves the Sikka (Maumere) district to enter the Ende district. The paving of the road to Kota Baru should be finished by the time you read this.

The people on the last stretch of the road, unable to afford the ugly corrugated metal sheets of their wealthier neighbors, live in pretty bamboo and thatch huts that stay cool in the tropical heat.

South of Maumere

The villages south and west of Maumere offer a gamut of attractions: a regal treasure of 17th century elephant tusks, the only real museum in the province, splendid views onto the Flores and Savu seas, *ikat* weaving, and a sacred spot reserved for ancestor worship. While you can travel by extremely crowded (but very cheap) public transportation, this is a tiring and time-consuming way to see this area. If you can afford it, we recommend hiring a vehicle.

Start out on the main road to Ende. Some 6 kilometers out, on your right, is a recreational park with a swimming pool and cabin-style accommodations on a hilltop. The view is splendid.

Blikon Blewut museum

Four kilometers further is the large Roman Catholic seminary at Ledalero, run by the international order of SVD fathers. The only one on the island, the seminary trains some 300 Indonesians for the priesthood, although some only take advantage of the excellent educational facilities. The seminary also boasts of a small, over-stocked museum called Blikon Blewut. The exhibits have been lovingly assembled by elderly Father Piet Petu, who first began collecting the items in the 1960s.

The Blikon Blewut features an assortment of fine *ikat* cloths from Flores and other islands in the province, tools from the stone age, fossil bones from a stegadon, an extinct elephant-like mammoth that once inhabited Flores, Chinese ceramics and local pottery, utensils and shells, weapons, gems and carvings plus an assortment of odds and ends. These last include fascinating albums of photos taken by missionaries during the early decades of this century.

There are lots of things to see, but too many objects are squeezed into too little

Above: *A proud mother shows off her baby at Wuring, near Maumere. The seaside village is a settlement of Bugis from South Sulawesi. People come here from the surrounding hills to trade produce for the fish caught by the Bugis.*

space, and nothing is labeled in English. The museum is open every day from 7:30 am to 2 p.m. except Sunday, when the museum opens at 10 a.m. A contribution, say 30 cents or more, is expected.

Two kilometers past Ledalero, on the edge of Nita village, is a Catholic training school run by the local diocese. The weekly Thursday market, located at the end of a 50-meter-long dirt track, is off to the right of the main road. If you want to see the market, get there before 10 a.m., as by noon most of it has been packed away.

Raja of Nita's heirlooms

If you make prior arrangements, it is possible to see the heirloom treasures owned by the descendants of the last raja of Nita. These include several ancient elephant tusks (the largest measures 23 centimeters and weighs 33 kilos) and other royal paraphernalia. All are housed in a picturesque colonial-style house built in 1934.

The "Young Raja," H.E. da Silva, takes care of the heirlooms. If he is around, or you have given him some notice, the house can be opened for you—with a contribution expected afterwards. Offerings to the family ancestral spirits, consisting of betel and various kinds of food, are periodically placed in front of the ancient tusks. The spirits are represented by stones that rest on the same mat as the tusks.

This is not an official museum and opening it depends on Pak H. E. da Silva's good will. Should he be amenable, there are many more heirlooms, mostly jewelry for princes and princesses, some of gold. But to prepare all this for display requires a minimum of two or three days' notice.

Koting: beautiful scenery

For some of the best views onto both the north and south seas, as you leave Nita, instead of continuing on the main road to Ende which swings right, continue straight ahead to Koting village.

Koting is actually a series of hamlets. Unless your driver knows what he is doing, have him stop and ask for directions to Koting-Diler. How far you can drive depends on the state of the road and your driver's skill. At the end, expect a 2-kilometer trek up a steep road to Kampung Wutik, although you might be able to drive all the way.

The road ends at the school in Wutik, and the best spot for a panoramic view, locally called Gajut, is nearby. Mornings are the best

for photography. Should you feel ambitious, follow the path to Hokor village, about 3 kilometers away on the road to Bolao, which locals claim offers even better views. The footpath is a good one, with some—but not too much—climbing on the way. (There is a paved road from Koting to Maumere, but it is frequently blocked by fallen trees, and consequently public transportation is quite difficult to find on this road.)

Back on the main road to Ende, 7 kilometers from Nita and 19 kilometers from Maumere, is Hapang, where the turnoff to Lela and Sikka branches off south. It's 4 kilometers downhill to Lela, located on a large, picturesque bay. From Lela, it's 4 seaside kilometers to Sikka, driving along a black-sand beach, strewn with boulders.

Sikka: weaving center

Thanks to its weavers and pleasant seaside location, Sikka is the most-visited village in the area. Moments after you arrive, word spreads like lightning and dozens of women spread out their *ikat* cloths for your appraisal ($20–$25). All fall quiet, and look at you expectantly. Pick your merchandise, and expect to bargain a bit.

Demonstrations of the *ikat*-weaving process can be arranged here, and the price depends on how many stages of the process you wish to see. This is perhaps $1 to just see a woman weaving, and $30–$50 or more to follow several women through the whole process: spinning the thread from local cotton, tying off the pattern, the complex dyeing process with several root-, bark- and leaf-based colors, then the weaving itself. All of this can be seen for free—but not all at the same time—at Bola village, where more women seem to be engaged in the various phases of the *ikat* than in Sikka.

Sikka also boasts of a fine big old church, dating from the end of the last century. The wall behind the altar, as well as a strip along each side of the long church, is painted in local *ikat* motifs. The church was first erected under the direction of the Jesuit Father Armand Lecoq d'Armandville, who later earned fame as an explorer and evangelizer of Irian Jaya.

The church replaced one that had existed from Portuguese times. But on Christmas

Opposite: *Learning windsurfing in quiet Maumere Bay, off the beach at the Sao Wisata resort. Maumere, though not the largest town in Flores, has the best facilities for tourists.*

day, a Portuguese-style play is still performed in Sikka. The play can be performed for visitors with sufficient notice and for a fee (around $50, with an *ikat* demonstration thrown in).

The play, locally called *bobu,* is a Portuguese love drama in which suitors attempt to woo a princess—beautiful, of course. The men come from all walks of life: farmer, sailor, merchant, goldsmith and gambler. But she rejects them all, as they are not wealthy enough for her tastes. She pines for a man with enough cash to satisfy her every whim. At last she finds her Mr. Right, unsurprisingly a wealthy nobleman.

Before you leave Sikka, check out the Portuguese cannon in front of the priest's residence, next to the church. The Dutch priest, a fine gentleman, speaks English and occasionally chats with visitors. He has been in Indonesia, serving the Roman Catholic Church, for 45 years and has seen plenty of changes.

Lekeba: Stations of the Cross

Back on the main road to Ende, head southwest 16 kilometers to the village of Lekeba, 35 kilometers from Maumere. We found that locals and some guides think that visitors are interested in an open area with thatch-roofed Stations of the Cross in Lekeba. It's not very interesting and best to forget it.

Just outside of town, before the downhill stretch to the village, a group of stones lie to the right. While not megaliths, these stones are an element of the megalithic culture. Offerings of betel nuts, along with the blood of animals (chickens, pigs, water buffalo) are made on the mini-dolmens and menhirs to curry favor with the ancestral spirits. A short walk leads to a sacred hilltop complex called Keuluju.

Keuluju is dedicated to the ancestors of Flores' most famous native son: Frans Seda, who has held three ministerial cabinet posts in Jakarta as well as serving as Indonesia's ambassador to Belgium (He also owns the Sao Wisata resort outside of Maumere.) The complex of traditional buildings, all built of wood imported from Kalimantan, is recent, but has been built strictly in accordance with pre-Christian architecture and decoration.

One open-sided structure shelters the bones of several Seda ancestors, currently stored in ceramic jars and awaiting their properly due ritual. A small house features new but interesting carvings of family ancestor myths, including women intertwined with dragons, an eagle and a dog-like animal suckling a baby. The third structure, open-sided, has a box dangling from it called Peti Jara. This box—which has the head of a horse protruding from one side and the tail from the other—will hold the family heirlooms when the complex is inaugurated at an undetermined future date.

LARANTUKA

A Catholic Easter in East Flores

Four figures, wearing white shrouds and hoods, and tall red hats, walked slowly in the night, carrying a coffin. The black cloth covering it was embroidered with a silver cross. This was the coffin of Christ, containing either a relic of Christ's body, or a sacred statue of the body of Christ.

Accompanied by thousands of faithful, singing and carrying candles, the sacred coffin is carried every year in a slow procession around Larantuka. The coffin is accompanied by a statue of the Virgin Mary, which, except for her face and one hand, is covered entirely in a blue cloak.

The Easter procession

The procession had started around 7 p.m. on Good Friday, led by mourning drums. The musicians were followed by the members of the religious brotherhood, Konfreria Renha Rosario—"Brotherhood of the Queen of the Rosary"—some of whom wore adornments from the Portuguese era, when Catholicism was first brought to Flores.

The shrouded bearers of the Christ coffin, called Nicodemu, originated with the Portuguese and have their contemporary European equivalent in the Easter processions in Seville, Spain. Nicodemus was one of the two men—the other was Joseph of Arimathea—who took Christ's body down from the cross.

The candle-lit procession came to a halt in front of a temporary altar, one of several, called Armida. A young girl climbed on a chair, unfurled a painting of the thorn-crowned Christ and sang, in a beautiful clear voice. She was assuming the role of Veronica, who mourned Christ when she uncovered his grave.

The girl's song was followed by prayers and a blessing by the Bishop. The procession then moved slowly on, halting at various altars. At each, the crowd would recite the rosary in Indonesian. Sometimes the procession halted in front of a house, and at others under a tree. At all of these sites there was an altar, sometimes with an old statue of a saint. Some of these are believed to have been brought to Larantuka with the Portuguese.

The last two stops were at the most important places: the Chapel of the Virgin—Kapela Maria—and the Chapel of Christ.

Larantuka town

Larantuka, the capital of the East Flores district, is an overgrown village of 25,000 with a small downtown area situated just in back of the old port. The new dock for the Kupang–Larantuka ferry is 5 kilometers away, on the road to Maumere. A volcano, Ile Mandiri, sits nearly on top of the town, squeezing it into a tiny sliver of land by the sea.

In the early 1980s, Ile Mandiri sent down a flood of mud and boulders, killing more than 200 people and destroying much of Larantuka. Miraculously, however, the Chapel of the Virgin Mary, to whom the town is dedicated, and the Chapel of Christ, where the Christ coffin is stored, were both spared. The ravaging flow bypassed the Chapel of the Virgin, then bore down straight down on the Chapel of Christ—only to divide itself at the last fraction of a second, a meter from the wall, and crash into the sea.

The Virgin herself has a miraculous origin. Some say that years ago, a man in Larantuka had several dreams in which a

beautiful woman appeared to him. In the last dream the woman told him to meet her by the sea. The next day the man went to the beach, at the spot designated in the dream, and found the statue of the Virgin, washed ashore by the waves. Others give a different account, although all agree that the statue washed ashore on a beach near Larantuka.

Each year before Easter, the statue is bathed and redressed, before being kissed by her devotees. The water from this washing is considered holy water and kept, to be used to cure sick children and help with difficult pregnancies. The relic—or statue, accounts vary—in the Christ coffin is also washed, and this water assumes curative powers.

The Konfreria and tradition

The Good Friday procession is the largest of several Holy Week events, all of which are organized and carried out by the Konfreria. This religious organization was founded by the Portuguese who arrived in Larantuka in the sixteenth century.

Over the years, especially when the town was left without clergy—from the end of the 17th to the mid-19th centuries—the Konfreria acquired paramount importance to the town's faithful. Its members taught the catechism, performed baptisms, kept up the churches and cared for the sacred statues.

There is a women's equivalent of the Konfreria, called the Mama Muji, which organizes Holy Week events as well. During Easter they keep an all-night, candlelight vigil at the chapels of the Virgin and Christ.

The Mama Muji pray in what now sounds like distorted Portuguese, although because the prayers have been passed down in a strictly oral tradition, they are likely a more-or-less exact rendition of the way the language was spoken in the 17th century. However, when the Portuguese Consul visited Larantuka several years ago, he could not understand a word of the prayers.

Some of the younger women wanted him to help them "correct" their pronunciation, but others did not. The older women were attached to their old prayers, and besides, since they serve a strictly devotional purpose, it makes little difference whether or not they can be understood by speakers of modern Portuguese.

During the many years that the Catholics of Larantuka were left to their own devices, para-liturgical elements crept into their beliefs and rituals. The Church has slowly reintroduced orthodox theology to the people of

Larantuka and has succeeded to a large extent.

Still, as the official publication of the Konfreria states, "To arrive at the Lord, to understand the Lord and the way of the faith, liturgy is not enough. Without our traditions, Holy Week is insipid."

Visiting Larantuka

The Kapela Maria and the Holy Week processions are the most interesting parts of Larantuka. Still, the old downtown dock area is worth investigation, and outside of town, there is mountain and seaside scenery, and traditional villages where *ikat* is woven.

A road leading east and then north of Larantuka leads to Tanjung Bunga ("Flower Cape"), Flores' northeastern peninsula. Visitors often go to the village of Mudakaputu, about 10 kilometers out of town on this road, which is known for its *ikat*. The road leads all the way to Waiklibang, the sub-district capital of Tanjung Bunga. About an hour's scenic walk from here is the weaving village of Riang Puho. On the coast, at Riang Koli village, is Pantai Nipa beach, favored by locals on weekends.

Opposite: *Shrouded Nicodemu bear the Christ coffin in the Good Friday procession in Larantuka. The event and some of the accouterments hark back to Portuguese days.* **Above:** *During one of the procession's many stops, a woman unfurls a portrait of Christ, and sings in a beautiful voice.*

PART VI

Introducing Lembata and Alor

A string of small islands stretches east from the far tip of Flores: the Solor archipelago, including Solor, Adonara and Lembata (in the past called Lomblen); and the Alor archipelago, including Pantar and Alor islands. These rough and jagged islands are a continuation of the northern line of the Lesser Sundas, and were formed by volcanic activity.

The modern urban world still has little relevance here, and the islanders spend their days tapping *lontar* palms, fishing, growing manioc and corn, raising livestock, weaving, and occasionally celebrating the rituals of their traditional religions.

Lembata: whalers and animists

Some 82,000 people live on the irregularly shaped, 1,200-square-kilometer island of Lembata. Most of the Lembatanese have converted to Catholicism, but there are about 8,000 Muslims and perhaps 6,000 followers of the old animist faith. Lewoleba, on the west coast, is the only real "town" on the island, and the site of one of eastern Indonesia's largest markets. Large areas of the interior are inhabited only by deer and wild pigs.

Practically nothing is known of Lembata before the Europeans arrived. The islanders offer various legends of origin, including that they simply came out of a hole in the ground. Some Lembatanese believe their ancestors sailed here from parts unknown, and on the south coast there are stones laid out to represent this craft.

The first Europeans to visit were the Portuguese, who arrived in the early 16th century on their hunt for Eastern Indonesia's precious spices. They were soon followed by Dominican friars spreading the Catholic faith.

The peninsula formed by the Ile Ape volcano is the bastion of the remaining animistic Lembatanese. The villages here maintain contact with the ancestral spirits in small temple-huts called *koker* on the volcano's slopes. Small offerings of food, cigarettes and betel nuts are left at the *koker* to gain the favor of the supernatural world, and occasionally an animal is sacrificed. The most important yearly celebration in Ile Ape is the Pesta Kacang, literally "Bean Festival."

Alor: old drums

Alor Island is the easternmost of the group. There are no international hotels here, but for the serious student of Indonesian culture Alor is a fascinating place to explore. The islanders speak some eight distinct languages. Scattered around Alor are *moko*, ritual drums patterned after the bronze creations of the 300 B.C.–A.D. 200 Dongson culture in what is now North Vietnam.

Visiting the islands

Even today, these islands seem not to belong to the 20th century. When I first visited Lembata in 1977, women and children ran from this strange, lobster-red person with his tripod and cameras. Taking photos was at times just about impossible. As soon as I pointed my Nikon at anyone, everyone else would laugh and scream, and the poor subject either hid in shame, or stared at the camera in stoic silence. "Did you ever visit the moon?" people asked. "Were there many animals there?"

In response to the missionaries and government, traditions here are changing: for example, a whaling mission that once began with a ritual cleansing of the ancestral skulls now starts on May 1 with Father Dupont saying Mass on the beach. But the old beliefs persist, as do simple pleasures like spending the afternoon chatting and drinking mild, frothy *tuak* from bamboo tubes.

Overleaf: *A whaler from Lamalera village in Lembata leaps from his boat so that the force of his weight will drive the harpoon into its victim.*
Opposite: *A boy on Alor beats a* moko, *an old bronze drum cast in the Dongson style.*

LEMBATA

Lewoleba Market, *Ikat* and Ile Ape

The people living on the peninsula formed by the Ile Ape volcano north of Lewoleba are among the most culturally traditional on Lembata. The *adat* houses of spirit worship are preserved on the volcano's slopes, celebrations such as the "Bean Festival" continue to take place, and the women here create some of the best *ikat* cloth on the island.

Further, the area is blessed with a stunningly beautiful setting. From high on Ile Ape you can look out over a large, protected bay to the east, ringed by coconut and *lontar* palms and filled with deep blue water.

Fine *ikat*

The weavers of Ile Ape spin their own thread from homegrown cotton and prepare their dyes from plant products. In all the villages along the coast road, one can see women weaving cloth on back-strap looms. The best

cloths, which consume an immense amount of labor, cost at least $100, and sometimes as much as $500. They are still an important part of a marriage exchange in which the bride's family provides fine cloths, and the groom's family an heirloom elephant tusk.

Most of the villages maintain *koker,* small huts that serve as temples to the ancestral spirits. The *koker* are kept outside the village proper, a short distance up Ile Ape's sloping sides. Although offerings—including animal sacrifices—are made to the spirits on a regular basis, the most important spiritual celebration is the yearly "Bean Festival," the Pesta Kacang.

The Bean Festival

In the 1960s, the Pesta Kacang had almost died out. But under the tolerant eyes of the Catholic Church, the government gave it some encouragement as part of a nationwide policy to encourage some regional traditions. The "new" Pesta Kacang lasts just three days whereas in the past it was a week long.

The first day is a "private" celebration involving prayers and offerings to the local village spirits—both deified ancestors and the spirits of the land. The next two days are the most fun. Hundreds—if not thousands—of guests show up and join the dances (*hamang*) and, of course, to feast and drink a bit too much palm wine. Important guests—which includes even foreigners—

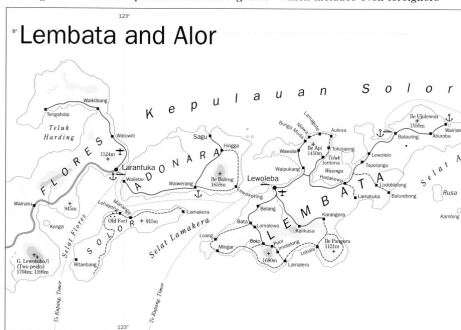

Lembata and Alor

are always provided with a place to sleep.

Lamagute village holds the celebration in July; Mawa in August; Lawotolok in September; Jontona in October. The last Pesta Kacang in the cycle takes place in Lamariang village in November.

The modern world has forced some changes on the old ways. The stick fights—wherein young men would beat each other savagely on the legs—are no longer a part of the Pesta Kacang. And married women now modestly cover their breasts.

Planning a trip north

From Lewoleba to Mawa village, along the west flank of the volcano, the road is paved. (See map below.) From Mawa to Tokojaeng village on the east coast, the surface degenerates and public transportation stops. Between Tokojaeng and Jontona village, the road can only be negotiated by motorcycle, jeep or on foot. At Jontona the road improves, and rejoins the paved road north of Lewoleba.

Passenger trucks service the peninsula's villages, particularly on Monday with all the traffic to and from Lewoleba's market. But none swings all the way around the peninsula. And they're crowded. Unless you are lucky enough to get a seat up front, all you will see are a lot of dusty faces staring at you.

If you visit the region by a combination of public transportation and walking over the rough parts, you will have to spend the night in one of the villages. This is not difficult; find the *kepala desa* (village head) and ask him to put you up for, say $3. For dinner you will get local fare (corn, manioc, vegetables, maybe fish) and you'll get coffee in the morning.

Another way to visit is to rent a motorcycle out of Lewoleba, but only with a driver, as too many foreigners rented bikes, damaged them, then refused to pay for the repairs ($10/day). The easiest way to make the trip is to charter a jeep or *bemo*. These vehicles seat five or more comfortably, and cost $40–$110 with a driver.

Visiting the peninsula

The road out of Lewoleba heads past the big landing field turnoff, goes through the neck of the Ile Ape peninsula, and then continues along the west coast. Along the roadside are small cotton fields, salt evaporation operations, and occasional stretches of *reo* trees, planted by the Dutch. The first town you reach is Wawala, dominated by a mosque, About 12 kilometers from Lewoleba.

From here the road rises along low coastal hills, and the scenery improves dramatically. All the villages here tend small plots on the steep slopes of the volcano, where the staples—manioc and corn—grow alongside beans and peanuts. There are some coconut trees here, and you can refresh yourself with the juice of a young coconut (*air kelapa muda*). The local men

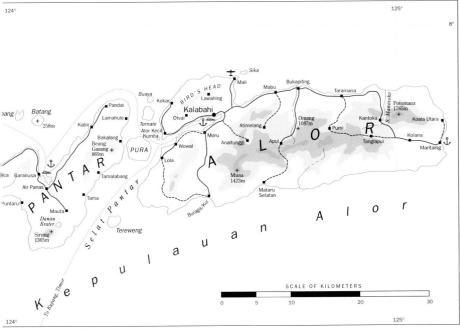

hunt wild pigs on Ile Ape's slopes, using dogs to track the game and spears and arrows to bring it down. There is little fishing here, although fish are an important part of the diet and economy of the villages on the east coast, which face a protected bay.

At Lamagute village, on the north coast, you can watch the *ikat* weaving process and have a look at a very unusual drum. A local guide can take you to the village's *koker* temples, a short but steep climb up the mountain's flanks. The most important of the *koker* shelters a bronze Dongson-style, hourglass-shaped drum. Most of these found in the area—Lembata, Solor, and especially Alor—are old copies, trade items cast during the 17th and 19th centuries in China and Java. But the Lamagute drum looks like the genuine article, perhaps even dating back to the Dongson period, before the Christian era.

Should you wish to climb the volcano, consider that it takes young, fit, local climbers two hours. Begin before dawn, so you won't still be climbing when the sun is high. A hat, sunblock and water are essential. The view from the top at dawn and dusk is beautiful, but if you plan to stay overnight, bring a sleeping bag or you will freeze.

Continuing around the peninsula, the views open into Waienga Bay. Once you pass Tokojaeng village, you can see Hadakewa village on the opposite side of the bay. At Jontona village, the worst of the road is over.

Indeed, some drivers refuse to risk their vehicles on this stretch, and backtrack from Tokojaeng, all the way around to Jontona.

At either Jontona or Lamagute village, with sufficient notice, you can arrange a traditional dance. Depending on the number of participants, figure $100-$150.

By truck, boat and foot

Lewoleba's weekly market, one of the biggest in eastern Indonesia, attracts people from as far away as Alor and Pantar to the east, Larantuka, Maumere and Ende to the west, and Savu and Raijua to the south. For the duration of the dry season, March to December, an average of 3,000 people make the Monday pilgrimage to this little port town in western Lembata.

Tough fishermen, with skin like leather, mingle with highlands women clad in bright *ikat* sarongs. Children are everywhere. Although goods of all kinds—food, plastic gizmos, spices, livestock, tools, clothes, everything— are on sale here, people come as much for the carnival atmosphere as to buy or sell. Lewoleba's market is the best show going.

The first trucks pull up around 4 a.m., and the sleepy passengers disembark. Trucks and *bemos* shuttle back and forth from dawn to 11 a.m., when the market is in full swing. By 8 p.m. everyone except the youngbloods is too tired to do anything except crowd back

into the trucks for the ride home.

Throughout the day, all manner of water craft arrive. Canoes with diamond-shaped sails gracefully glide to an anchorage. Motor launches noisily chug past the stilted houses, pull up their motors, and tie up in the shallow water. Passengers step into hip-high water, stowing their merchandise safely on their heads. The brightly wrapped women wade ashore amidst waves and giggles.

Sweating farmers arrive on foot. Some come from villages not yet served by roads, and others, with only a few handfuls of peanuts, a little bag of beans, *kemiri* nuts, or tamarind for sale, can't afford the 10¢–50¢ cent truck ride. Some of these sturdy men have walked 8–10 hours.

Seduction of the marketplace

The farmer who brings his crops into town on Mondays needs to be constantly on guard. The smell of the food stalls! The bright, wonderful plastic things! New clothes! Toys for the kids! The excitement—and the temptation to buy—is hard to resist.

For the young men and women, the food stalls at the market are the prime attraction, but this has nothing to do with food. Although flirting is rampant at the market, it is at the little *warung*s that a young man can get past shy giggles and *bon mots,* and on to serious declarations of love.

During those initial encounters, the boys are too swept up to think about the burden of marriage, not the least of which on Lembata is finding an heirloom elephant tusk. In fact, many a youthful love affair on the island has come to a halt because the young man, who left the island to find a job in order to buy a tusk, falls in love and marries elsewhere.

History of the market

Lembata was called Lomblen during Dutch colonial times, and the principal town and market then was about 20 kilometers east of Lewoleba at Hadakewa, on the south shore of Waienga Bay. After World War II, the little town of Lewoleba started to grow. In the early 1950s, the first Bajau—semi-nomadic fishermen—arrived from Adonara to build stilted huts on the tidal flats off Lewoleba.

In the late 1950s, wild pigs still roamed around Lewoleba, and Hadakewa was still the more important village. But when the Indonesian government and the Catholic Church decided to base their activities in Lewoleba, this made the little seaside town pre-eminent, and Hadakewa was relegated to

a neglected subdistrict capital.

The trade networks between the coastal and inland people date back to the dim past. The coast dwellers need the inland farmers' corn, manioc, onions and vegetables because the coast suffers from a lack of rain and poor soils. The inland people, in turn, need the protein and vitamins from the fish and shellfish available on the coast.

Ikat and gossip

Most of the marketgoers buy or trade in small amounts—a kilo of corn or rice, a handful of tobacco, one or two pineapples, a few stacked eggs, a small package of coffee. Women squat next to their friends and spread their wares on a piece of cloth. A chicken or two might be tied with string to their toes, or a grunting pig securely fastened nearby.

They spend the day talking and catching up on all the latest gossip, occasionally taking time out from this important activity to make a sale. All the while they chew betel, which stains their teeth and gums dark red.

Some women bring their weavings, usually relatively cheap ones which sell for $5–$25. Occasionally, one of the really fine heirloom *ikat* cloths—usually reserved for dowries—turns up at the market. Such an item can fetch perhaps $500, even $1,000 if it is a real gem.

Traders from Savu show up with *ikat,* which seems at first a little like bringing coal to Newcastle. But the women of Lembata appreciate good workmanship, and like the Savunese designs. They trade spools of hand-spun cotton thread for Savunese sarongs. The hand-spun cotton is much appreciated in Savu, as it holds the natural dye much better than machine-spun thread, which tends to be too smooth, and to create too tight a weave.

Opposite: The Ile Ape volcano looms in the dawn mist across the harbor at Lewoleba. **Above:** A tiny piglet at the Lewoleba market tied into a neat package of woven palm leaves.

LAMALERA'S WHALERS

Hunting the Great Sperm Whale

We were dozing under the broiling tropical sun on coils of hand-made rope. Then a startling shout, and we awoke in a hurry. The boat was seized by activity, as the men quickly took their stations—just 200 meters off our starboard bow, a sperm whale had spouted.

The sail was lowered and a dozen oarsmen grabbed their paddles. After a brief prayer, they put their backs into their work, and the craft moved swiftly towards the whale. "Hilabe Hilabe, Hela Hela," chanted the men, and the excitement became electric.

Our harpooner, a bald, muscular man in his early '50s, climbed into the pulpit, which projected a couple meters off the bow. His weapon was a barbed steel lance, fitted into the end of a three-meter bamboo shaft. Spare harpoons were laid out.

In just a few minutes, the whale surfaced again. The men paused at the sight of the 15-meter animal, and an excited discussion ensued. Eventually, a decision was reached.

"He's too big for us," one of the men told me. "If we didn't spear him just right, he would break up the boat. Perhaps if there were more boats we would try our luck, but there is only one other launch out today." Alas, we let the big "fish" go.

Lamalera village

The village of Lamalera in southern Lembata, and Lamakera on nearby Solor Island, are the last two traditional whaling villages in Eastern Indonesia. Hunting these great mammals from small boats is still the principal economic activity in Lamalera, but it is slowly dying out.

Today, most young men prefer to seek employment elsewhere. Whaling, which combines long boring periods of waiting, with brief, very dangerous periods of activity, leaves much to be desired as an occupation.

Hunting whales is a very old tradition in Lamalera. The boats and implements, as well as the techniques, are well-tested by time and experience. The whaling *prahu*s are crafted from local wood, about 10–12 meters long and 2 meters in beam. The planks are fastened together with wooden pegs, and caulked with pitch and cotton wadding. There is not a nail to be found on the vessels.

The sails are quite interesting. They are constructed of sewn-together square mats,

each mat woven from the leaves of the *gewang* palm, a fan palm similar to a lontar. For stability in the sometimes rough seas, the boats sport double outriggers.

The construction of the boat mixes craft and more spiritual matters. Planks are always aligned on the boat in the direction in which they grew on the tree, to maintain the wood's spiritual strength. (This serves a practical function as well, as wood is most dense at the base of the tree.) When the *prahu* is completed, it is rubbed down and anointed by a shaman with chicken blood.

The sperm whale

The best year for whaling in recent memory was 1969, when the men landed 56 whales. An average year brings 15–20, and during the worst year, just 9. They seek sperm whales (*Physeter catodon*), the large, toothed whale of *Moby Dick* fame.

In Herman Melville's time, the whales were hunted by Nantucketers chiefly for their valuable spermaceti, an unctuous substance that fills the beast's huge, angular head. Before the days of electricity, and even mineral oil and paraffin, " 'parm oil" was the cleanest burning substance available for oil lamps.

The whalers of Lamalera use all parts of the whale, which in Indonesian is called *ikan paus,* literally "pope fish": the meat, the rich blubber, the spermaceti and the tooth ivory.

Other whale species that wander into the territory are also fair game, as are sharks, especially the huge, but harmless 15-meter whale shark (*Rhincodon typus*), as well as manta rays, and other large fish.

The only species that is off-limits is the blue whale (*Sibbaldus musculus*), which is the totemic symbol of one of the clans, and thus cannot be caught. It is also very unlikely that the small boats would be able to catch a blue, which is both the largest creature on earth and a very fast swimmer.

The villagers trade much of the fish, whale meat and blubber to farmers for staples like corn, rice, vegetables and pork. The rich meat and blubber from the whales and other large fish is quite valuable, and fetches a premium price in the market. A few kilos of fine shark meat is worth maybe 20 kilos of rice or corn.

Many of the rites associated with whaling have been discontinued. In the past, for example, the whaling season began with the such as the ritual polishing and anointing of the ancestral skulls, which were kept in a shrine the back of the boat sheds. Today, in

Opposite: *Two girls at Lamalera village pose in front of* Pusaka, *one of the village's 15 whaling boats.* **Below:** *A whaling boat heads home after a successful day. The boats fly sails constructed of sewn together square mats woven from the leaves of the* gewang, *a local fan palm.*

this Catholic village, such throwbacks to the days of animism and head-hunting have been abandoned. But Father Dupont respects the islanders' traditions, so he performs a special Mass on the beach for the whalers before the boats set out in early May.

A visitor tags along

I went down to the beach at dawn, hoping that one of the whaling boats would be willing to take me along. Each of the village's 15 clans has its own whaling boat, which are stored in long parallel sheds just above the high tide line.

Shortly after sunrise a group of men laid out several logs in front of their boat and quickly rolled it down to the surf. I asked if I could go along, but was ignored by the men. Without a word, they pushed their boat into the surf, and paddled out to sea. I guessed that they were not particularly keen on having a useless guest along—who would probably ask a lot of questions, and certainly get in the way.

A little later another group of whalers came down to the beach. I offered them cigarettes, and helped push their boat down to the surf. Then, before I had even worked up to my question, I was hurriedly told to get in, just as the boat was shoved through the surf to the calmer waters beyond. The men quickly paddled out of the reach of the shore-bound rollers.

Two bamboo spars, lashed together at the top, were raised and fixed in place. Then one corner of a large palm leaf mat made up of plaited squares was raised, and we were sailing quietly under a diamond-shaped sail. Each man on board had a well-defined task: some were lookouts, others steersmen and sail handlers. There was a designated bailer, and a harpooner and an assistant. When a whale or fish is sighted, all but the helmsman and the harpooner become oarsmen.

Once the sail was up, the *lamafu*—the harpooner—whetted the edges of his spear heads, which were forged out of pieces of recycled car chassis. When the honing was completed, we all bowed and prayed. Then the harpoon was fixed onto its shaft. A long coil of hand-made rope, coated with resin, was attached to the barbed steel spear. This was to insure that a securely hooked whale would not get away, even if it towed the boat for days, as has occasionally happened.

One happy photographer

Most of the afternoon we napped. Our dozing was periodically cut short by several sharp blasts of the conch shell. This was required when the wind died down, and seemed most of the time to successfully call up a breeze. We sighted a manta ray and another whale, but both were too far away.

The men decided to return. But they saw how disappointed I was at not being able to

take any pictures, so they went through a dress rehearsal. The harpooner stood on the end of his pulpit and hurled his weapon into the water, jumping in after it for added thrust, just like he would if he had been spearing a real whale. The imaginary whale didn't put any food on the table, but the boat returned with at least one happy photographer.

A few more days of the same and I ran out of time and patience, and left Lembata. I stopped again, a few years later. Still no whales. Then I returned for the third time, this time committing myself to stay until the whalers caught something. I knew there would be days of floating around, waiting for a whale. But I was not prepared for the powerful combination of hot equatorial sun and a boring routine, which quickly put me into a strange state of suspended animation.

A boat with eyes

I fell into a routine. Every morning at dawn I met the crew of the whaling *prahu Pusaka* ("Heirloom"). One of the men pulled off the plaited leaf wrapper that covered a wooden stake projecting forward from the boat's prow. This allowed the boat to "see," so it wouldn't run aground on any reefs. Then we lined up on either side of the boat and bowed our heads in payer. After this, we put our shoulders into the task of shoving the craft forward and into the sea.

Then everyone except the steersman grabbed an oar, and with a song to keep rhythm, we stroked out to sea. Three or four other *prahu* set out at the same time, oar-legged water spiders skittering forward on the calm morning sea. As soon as we felt the hint of a breeze, we hoisted sail and another long day had begun. The men always trailed fishing lines, light ones for flying fish and a stronger one for medium-sized fare. Some men drifted off to sleep, while others scanned the waters for signs of game.

By this time, I had a designated space on a coil of rope back towards the stern. Here I could doze, or consider the weightier problems of life. During the first few days I conversed often with Antonius, the elder ex-chief of the village, who sat nearest to me. He asked the questions so typical of this part of the world: "How much did it cost to come to Indonesia?" "Did you ever go to the moon?" And, betraying his sailor's interest, "Is there water on the moon?"

A long way from Sulawesi

Antonius said his ancestors—indeed, those of everyone in Lamalera—came from Sulawesi (the Celebes), several hundred kilometers northwest of Lembata. During a slow migration, which lasted over 200 years, these fish-

Opposite: *A blacksmith hammers scrap steel into the barbed hook of a harpoon.* **Above:** *The harpooner applies his whole body to the task.*

ing folk travelled a wide arc in the seas, often staying for a generation or longer on islands like Seram and Ambon, before finally settling on Lembata.

Since there were already a few people living here, the immigrants struck a deal. When any whale or large fish is caught, the whalers set aside a share for the original clan, a practice that continues today. The ancestors of the present "owners" of Lembata struck a good bargain for their descendents.

The *Pusaka,* Antonius said, was built in 1968 and had so far caught more than 30 whales. Whenever a large fish is speared, the builder of the boat is given a share. In exchange, he helps renew the bindings when necessary, and perform other little repairs.

Although these days at sea seemed endless, each ended around 2 p.m., so we could take advantage of the shore breeze to sail back. The flying fish, the only thing we were assured of catching, were divided among the crew. I usually received a couple of the tasty fish, which became my evening meal. The harpooner often popped out the eyes of the fish and ate them raw, to help him see better.

We saw a big fish about once every couple days. Then we would snap out of our torpid existence, and try to get close enough for the kill. But like most fish stories, the big ones always got away. I was beginning to feel like a Jonah, but the other vessels weren't having any luck either.

A change of luck

Then one morning, just as we started rowing, a huge fish surfaced not more than 10 meters to starboard. The metal head was frantically slammed onto its shaft and our harpooner jumped on his prey. Although his efforts opened up a large gash on the fish, the barb failed to take hold—the ritual sharpening had not yet taken place.

The creature was an *ikan hiu bodoh,* literally "stupid shark." This was a whale shark, a notoriously sluggish, plankton-feeding animal. We all fell into a depression at having missed such a simple mark.

About an hour later, another large fish was sighted, a marlin. This time we were ready—nerves taut, and muscles straining. "Ikan raja," Antonius grunted, as we set our backs to the oars. The *ikan raja*—"king of fish"—was truly a regal sight as it knifed through the calm sea, seemingly unaware of us. Poised on the prow, the harpooner waited patiently until he was within range, and then hurled his spear, plunging in after it. A solid whack assured us of a clean hit. Then the work began.

Even as the harpooner was scrambling

Above: *A whale shark is hauled up to the boat for butchering. Despite its great size, this shark is a harmless plankton feeder.* **Opposite:** *A sperm whale is flensed on the beach at Lamalera.*

back on board the marlin had already taken out 50 meters of line. The orderly coils of rope suddenly made sense, as first one, then two, then three lengths were tied on before the marlin began to tire. Then the long tug of death began as he was slowly brought back to the boat.

Every now and then the *ikan raja* would find an untapped store of energy, and bolt away, forcing us to let out the rope again. After more than a half-hour, he was close enough to harpoon again. When the second harpoon took hold, the last of the fight left this magnificent fish. The crew was positively jubilant as the marlin was hauled on board—after weeks of bad luck, a prize at last!

No sooner had everyone relaxed than a whale shark surfaced nearby—and we were off again. A single, well-placed harpoon was enough, and the fish gave up without a struggle. "Too stupid to fight," Antonius said. "That's why it's called the 'stupid shark.'" The animal was too big to be hauled aboard so he was butchered in the water. Great chunks of flesh were heaved over the gunwales and slid to the bottom of the craft.

The sea around the boat was churning with blood. As the men were nonchalantly carving up their catch, I asked if they were not worried that the blood would attract dangerous predatory sharks. Everyone just laughed. We hope so, they said, then they too will be harpooned.

Feeling no pain

The day was winding down, and we headed to a designated spot on shore to make the traditional exchange—a large chunk of meat for several bamboo tubes full of *tuak,* palm wine. From here back to Lamalera, we grew increasingly exuberant on the *tuak* and tasty chunks of fresh, raw marlin. By the time we reached shore, and children scrambled on board to inspect the catch, we were feeling no pain.

Many eager hands—hoping for a handout—helped to push the *Pusaka* back to its shed. The two fish were then cut into manageable portions and divided among the crew, the builder of the boat, and the representatives of the original "owners of the land." Even I received a share—not as big as the crew members' only because, it was carefully explained to me, I did not have a family to feed. But my portion was much more than symbolic: several kilos of prime meat.

The *Pusaka* was not the only lucky boat that day. Another craft had just returned with a large sperm whale, which required all the next day to be butchered and split into shares. Because of family relationships and other ties, just about everyone in the village got some portion of our fish or the sperm whale. Also, there was now plenty of meat to trade for rice and corn. And one satisfied photographer, who sailed away the next day a happy man.

ALOR

Island of Bronze Drums and Tradition

Alor, and its sister island of Padar just to the west, offer white sand beaches, fine snorkeling and world-class scuba diving. There are scattered traditional family houses, three-tiered and thatch covered, sometimes whole villages of them. Some villages still follow the old lifestyle, depending on historical factors and how isolated they are.

Thanks to recent improvements in air and sea links, Alor is now much more accessible to visitors. Merpati flies there several times a week, although you can really only count on about two of the flights making it, and numerous boats call on the island, including Pelni Lines' *Keli Mutu.*

Alor is at the far eastern end of the Solor–Alor archipelago, about 60 kilometers from Timor Island. There are about 110,000 people on Alor, about three-quarters of whom have been absorbed into one or another of the Protestant sects since missionaries began working the area in the 1940s. Most of the rest—23 percent—are Muslim, and there is a fine old mosque at Lerabaing village.

The remaining few percentage points are conceded to "other" religions, meaning the die-hard animists who tend the remaining ancestral cult houses. But these numbers are misleading, because spiritual belief and tradition—particularly bride prices of old hourglass–shaped, bronze drums—continue even among the "Christian" populations.

On Alor Island, the Suku Abui ethnic group is the most traditional, while on Pantar it's the Suku Kaera. The latter hold harvest rituals in March or April.

Eight distinct languages are spoken on Alor, a remarkable diversity for an island of just 2,800 square kilometers. Most of the languages of Alor are non-Austronesian and are related to languages spoken in Irian Jaya. The Alorese physically resemble the Papuans of New Guinea as well. The language often referred to as "Alorese," which is spoken around Kalabahi, is the exception—it is a dialect of Lamaholot, an Austronesian language spoken from east Flores to Alor.

The linguistic isolation of the Alorese can perhaps be explained by the rugged geography of the island interior, as well as the formerly widespread practice of head-hunting. Understandably, both these features discouraged casual social visits.

Visiting Alor

As in many of the more isolated areas of Indonesia, it takes time and patience to reach the more traditional, interesting villages. Although a program of road building and paving is well along on mountainous Alor (see map), most of the inland villages and hamlets of the interior can still only be reached on foot. The majority of the settlements on the south coast of Alor, as well as all population centers on Pantar, are accessible only from the sea.

While there are fairly frequent boats from Kalabahi to Baranusa, the principal town on Pantar, and to Kabir, the second most important center, for the other places it's largely a matter of luck. You can either wait for something heading your way or charter a local boat, price varying according to distance and bargaining skills.

Kalabahi town

Kalabahi, with some 25 thousand people, is the largest—in fact, *only*—town in Alor. The island's capital lies at the inland apex of narrow Kalabahi Bay. This bay, 16 kilometers long and only 1 kilometer wide, holds a whirlpool, locally called "the goat's mouth."

The panorama overlooking the "goat's mouth" and bay is the picture most often seen in tourist brochures. And there is a nice, 3-kilometer-long beach at Mali, 18 kilometers (11 mi.) from Kalabahi, close to the landing strip. But there is a lot more to Alor.

Although not as famous for its weaving as other parts of Nusa Tenggara, Alorese craftsmen produce quite good *ikat,* as well as plaited leaf baskets and other useful objects, such as betel nut containers. And the islanders maintain traditional ways of life. With a bit of effort one can get to the old style villages, of thatch-roofed huts, where marriages and other rituals still take place. The most accessible of the villages is Tapkala, which sits atop a hill, with a nice view, about 13 kilometers from Kalabahi by paved road.

Takpala, with a population of mixed Catholics and Protestants, features a half-dozen traditional houses and is Alor's most organized tourist destination. An ancestral meeting place features a pile of stones and two posts where sacrificial animals were attached. There's also a raised platform where traditional dances are performed for tourists sitting on bamboo benches. Travelers looking for an authentic setting, might be put off, but tour groups love the ambiance.

Around the bird's head

Called "kepala burung" (bird's head), a low, flat plain connects this peninsula with rest of Alor. A paved road almost encircles the bird's head, with just a stretch missing on the north coast between Mali and Kobar. For those with limited time and finances, walking around or across this peninsula could be as satifying as treks in the interior of Alor, or long boat rides around Pantar.

Mali, on the northwest tip of the bird's head offers a nice beach for swimming and snorkeling. At low tide, a spit of sand connects the "mainland" with tiny Sika Island, a home for several bird species, more beach and clear water.

Heading out of town to the west, the road follows the north shore of Kalabahi Bay through several villages and passes a couple of massive Muslim graves. During the dry season, the village of Ampera specializes in the fabrication of simple fired earthenware pots, sold both locally and as far as Flores. At the western end of Kalabahi Bay, its road turns north at Alor Kecil.

This village is home of several lineages whose ancestors landed here from Java or Sulawesi. Each clan maintains an "adat" house here, the anchor of heir heredity. Here are their roots, holding after dispersal around Alor, Pantar and elsewhere. Every five years or so, a huge Sunat circumcision ritual takes place here, for all young Muslims between the ages of about 7 and 15. While the boys are circumcised by the *imam* (religious leader), his wife takes a drop of blood from the girls' clitorises (but does not perform the excision as practiced in parts of Africa). Just up the road, Alor Besar is proud of its hand-

Opposite: *The slaughter of a pig on Alor is always cause for celebration. Meat is usually only eaten on ritual occasions.* **Above:** *This stylized frog is a detail from the head of a Dongson-style moko.*

written Koran, claimed to be 600 years old. It can be seen and photographed for a small donation. Another short drive and you reach the end of the road at Kokar with its fishermen and small harbor. Great sunsets. If you're lucky, a sailing freighter might just glide to anchor while you watch.

Interior of the bird's head

The cool interior of the bird's head peninsula can be partially explored by jeep, and more thoroughly on foot. There's a steep but mostly decent road which you can do by jeep: Kalabahi to Kebun Kopi, Otvai and back down to Kalabahi. Passenger trucks also make this run, in either direction. Between Lawahing and Otvai a road is being built which will eventually reach Batu Putih on the north coast. The steep roads from the coast to Kebun Kopi or Otvai are lined with vegetation which part occasionally to give a panoramic view over Kalabahi and its long bay. Part of the way up to Kebun Kopi, you can stop at Monbang, a hamlet with only traditional huts, and no setups for tourists.

In the central part of the peninsula, which reaches 700 meters, stretches of forest vegetation are dominated by tall *kaneri* trees whose nuts are Alor's principal exports, followed by tamarind, a fruit used for flavoring, from a tree also found in the interior. (The third most important export, copra or dried coconut meat, comes from the coastal areas.)

Clove trees are also found in the interior, along with the areca palm. The areca nut, usually taken with gambier and lime, and wrapped in a betel pepper leaf, forms "sirih pinang," the so-called betel chew. This mildly narcotic quid produces bright red lips and blackened teeth over the years.

Should you feel like walking back to the coast, there are two options aside from returning to Kalabahi. From Otvai, a path leads to Kokar, about 2 hours. Another path, also from Otvai but longer, reaches the sea at Alor Besar or Ampera. This path forks near Bampalola, a traditional hillside village with its ancestral house ornamented with masts symbolizing the forefathers. Make sure you reach the coast before nightfall as *bemos* are few if any after dark and walking back to Kalabahi in pitch black holds few charms.

Surprised by a warrior

In the isolated villages of Alor the old lifestyle is still being followed. I headed up to Atimelang from Mabu, five thigh-straining hours over mountain ridges. Back in 1980, this was the only way to reach Atimelang. Nowadays you can hire a jeep ($75) and be driven there from the lowland village of Lelahomi. But, if you have the time and energy, we recommend trekking there. In April, near the end of the rainy season, the slopes were a beautiful green. I picked Atimelang because this village was the site of Cora

Dubois' 1932–1935 study, described in *The People of Alor.* Although I had been told the people of Atimelang maintained the old ways, I was not prepared for the greeting I got.

The first person I saw was a fully outfitted warrior, who popped out of one of the huts, scaring the bejeezus out of me. He brandished a wicked looking cutlass, and was further armed with a bow and a quiver of arrows.

The warrior began a dance that is a throwback to the days when the Alorese were head-hunters. But today he was just impressing a visitor, and his cutlass was not going to see any use. As soon as he was finished, he jumped back into the hut and emerged smiling in his civilian clothes: a dirty shirt and a ragged pair of pants.

The *moko* drums

Moko are bronze kettle-drums that display the motifs and basic design of the pre–Christian era Dongson culture of northern Vietnam. These drums have turned up in several places in Indonesia—most notably the "Moon of Pejeng" on Bali and the Selayar drum on an island off south Sulawesi—and seem to have served as trade objects. Most were cast in Java and China, long after the passing of Dongson.

It is still a mystery how so many *moko* ended up on Alor Island. It is likely that ancient trading ships called at Alor to take on food and supplies on their way to and from sandalwood-rich Timor, but there is no reference to any valuable Alorese products for which outsiders might wish to trade.

Most of the *moko,* probably from Java, were still being imported to Alor by Makassarese traders as late as the 19th century. During the late 1910s, a Dutch government census showed 200,000 of the drums on Alor. The survey noted more than 20 named categories of *moko,* each one worth twice the next lower ranking, with prices ranging from the equivalent of 50¢ to over $1,500.

The *moko* served as a great store of value, but perhaps more importantly, had ritual importance—they were a necessary part of the bride price, and were exchanged for the human heads necessary for rituals.

Although they are no longer traded for human heads (head-hunting stopped in 1941), the *moko* are still an essential part of the bride price and trade on the island. The number and quality of *moko* required for a bride varies with her social status, but it is not unusual for it to take the better part of a lifetime to settle the bride price. This system purposely encourages debt and obligation as a way of cementing social bonds.

Opposite: *Local ikat and traditional ornaments adorn the dancers of Takpale village, who put on an excellent show for Alor's slowly increasing number of visitors.* **Above:** *Stiff palm leaf spines, woven by an expert, will form a fine fish trap.*

PART VII

Introducing Sumba

The cultural life of Sumba, a hot, dry island south of Komodo and Western Flores, is distinguished by spectacular rituals, huge megalithic grave sites, unusual peaked houses and beautiful *ikat* cloths. The island is one of the most culturally interesting places to visit in East Indonesia. Some of the island's beaches are excellent, and the rocky highlands provide great panoramic views of the coastline—but the traditional culture is the best reason to come here.

The old ways remain alive on Sumba in a large part because the island was relatively unimportant to the European colonists and the archipelagic empires, such as the Majapahit, that preceded them. Sumba was a source of sandalwood, livestock and slaves, but when the Portuguese first sailed by Pulau Cendana—"Sandalwood Island"—in the early 16th century, Sumba's landscape must have looked as barren and inhospitable as it does today. This, combined with the fragmented political structure of Sumba, insured that any attempt at conquest would be a thankless and unrewarding endeavor.

A small, mountainous island

By Indonesian standards, 11,150-square-kilometer Sumba is relatively small, with a bent, irregularly oval shape. The island stretches 210 kilometers along a northeast–southeast axis, and is 40–70 kilometers wide. The southeast is the most mountainous region, crowned by the island's highest peak, Wangga Meti, 1,225 meters. Much of the interior is made up of grassy plateaus, punctuated by deep valleys and scattered hills.

The island and its approximately 350,000 inhabitants are divided into two administrative districts: East Sumba, in area about two-thirds of the island, holds just one-third of the population; West Sumba, which receives notably more rainfall and is thus more fertile, sustains the majority of the Sumbanese.

East Sumba is rocky and mountainous, and the Massu mountains here drain into the Watumbaka, the Payeti, the Kambaniru and the Kamberu basins, all reaching the Sumba Strait near Waingapu, the eastern capital.

Cattlemen and farmers

The East Sumbanese are a relatively homogeneous group, speaking a single language. Although both East and West Sumba depend on the export of water buffalo, horses and *angole* cattle, the drier East ships the lion's share of the 10,000–13,000 head a year shipped. East Sumba is also the site of the weaving cottage industry, where the *ikat* is woven that is either shipped to Bali or sold to the growing numbers of tourists to the island.

West Sumba, with its capital at Waikabubak, is much greener than the East. Here coffee and copra (dried coconut meat) are grown for export, and vegetables and fruit provide for a healthier diet. The West is self-sufficient in rice, and ships this staple to East Sumba. The West Sumbanese are more culturally diverse, and the society is less stratified. Seven different languages are spoken here.

Travel in Sumba

Visiting Sumba, especially the West, can be an experience to treasure if one has an appreciation for non-industrial culture. The women spend their days planting, harvesting and pounding the husks off rice, fetching water in bamboo tubes, and minding the little kids. The men build and repair the huts, prepare the fields by breaking up the dry soil with hoes or—in the wetter areas—driving the buffalo across the paddies to aerate the mud. Men also attend to ritual matters.

Overleaf: *Hundreds of horsemen fight with spears in Sumba's yearly Pasola ritual. Although the government forbids sharp points, occasional deaths still occur.* **Opposite:** *A high priest of Sumba's animist Marapu religion.*

In many villages—recently commercialized Tarung is a glaring exception—locals don't quite know what to make of western visitors. They stare in disbelief at camera wielding foreigners who, unfortunately, often barge right in in flagrant disregard of the first rule of Sumbanese courtesy: sharing the betel nut, and chatting with one's hosts. Well, it's probably too much to ask that tour groups, in a hurry to get through their packed schedules, are going to sit around chewing betel.

Traditional culture

Officials estimate that half the Sumbanese are practicing animists, but such classifications are impossible to make. Where do you put the people who are registered Christians, yet still follow most of the traditional practices? An inevitable result of modernization is that adherence to the old practices will fade away, and Sumba is no exception. For example, the younger women, even in the villages, now wear blouses. Still, faith in the old ritual cycles is very strong, and a visitor can still get a glimpse of this complex, pre-Christian culture. (See "Tradition," page 170.)

Tarung, with its megaliths and ancient ways, perches on a hilltop almost within Waikabubak. Primordial megalithic tombs are everywhere in Tarung, and the area holds one the district's greatest concentration of the followers of the Marapu religion—the Wanokaka/Lamboya area and the

Kodi subdistrict are the other Marapu centers. The region is the site of many rituals, particularly in the period from July to October, when the fields require little attention. Following this period, the month-long Wula Padu—literally "Bitter Month"—around the November full moon, marks the Marapu New Year.

The Pasola and funerals

The most spectacular ceremony on Sumba is the Pasola, a ritual fight with spears featuring hundreds of horsemen. It is a wild and martial event, and although the government now insists on blunted spears, serious injuries are common and there are occasional deaths. The Pasola takes place a few days after the second and third full moons of the solar year—February in Lamboya and Kodi, March in Gaura and Wanukaka—and culminates in the spring ritual cycle. (See "The Pasola," page 184.)

The funerary rituals of Sumba continue, and the huge blocks of stone are still cut and dragged to the mortuary grounds to construct mausoleums for the rich and the nobility. In 1988 these celebrations lost some of their grandeur, however, when the government restricted to five the number of animals that could be sacrificed.

In the past, particularly at the funerals of noblemen, literally hundreds of water buffalo, horses and pigs were slaughtered to accom-

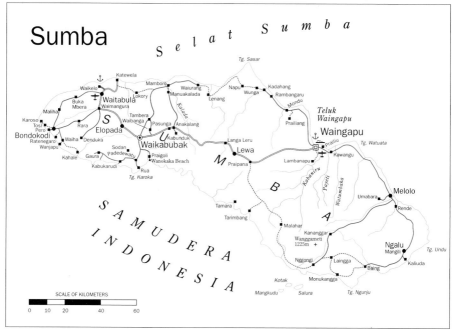

pany the departed soul to the afterlife. The number of animals dispatched was prestige-enhancing and in Sumba—where the remains of a highly stratified society of nobles, commoners and slaves still exists—it was not uncommon for a family to bankrupt itself to put on a good funereal show.

Now the government does not allow families to impoverish themselves for added status. Even the descendents of slaves can afford five animals.

Slaves and sandalwood

Little is known of the history of Sumba before the colonial period, by which time records show that the island's exports were sandalwood, horses and slaves—probably in that order of importance. Over-cutting led to the decline of the fine stands of sandalwood, and by the late 19th century Sumbanese horses were the island's most profitable product. The slave trade, always profitable, peaked in the 18th century but lasted into the second half of the 19th century.

The chronicle of the Hindu-Buddhist Majapahit empire, which lasted on East Java until the 15th century, mentions Sumba as a dependency, but the hubris of the Majapahit was such that most of the archipelago was so listed. By the 17th century, records show Sumba subordinate to Bima, in East Sumbawa. Bima was allied with the Makassarese based in Goa, in South Sulawesi.

In 1756, the Dutch East India Company (V.O.C.) signed their first trade agreement with Sumbanese leaders. At the time, the area's largest trade entrepôt for slaves was Ende, in Flores. The Endenese either purchased their slaves from Sumbanese leaders, captured them in raids, or took them as booty when they were hired as mercenaries in local wars between Sumbanese rulers.

The slaves were traded all over the archipelago, particularly to Bali and Lombok, where they were paid for in rice, and some may have made it as far as Zanzibar. Many never made it out of the region, and were traded to other kingdoms in Sumba.

The Dutch in Sumba

Presumably out of a sense of moral outrage—although at least partly because they got no profits from the deals—a Dutch fleet destroyed Ende and 50 Endenese trading ships in 1838 when it refused to end the slave trade. The moral high ground of the Dutch was somewhat eroded by the fact that the Dutch government representative had been

regularly receiving slave girls from the Raja of Mangili. Despite the destruction of Ende, the slave trade resumed.

The next year, 1839, Holland sent Sharif Abdul Rahman, a member of the Arab royal family in Pontianak, western Kalimantan, to set himself up as a horse-trading agent in Ende. Abdul Rahman was indebted to the Dutch, who had helped his family establish Pontianak, and the Dutch hoped he would offset the independent Endenese. After a horse-buying trip to Sumba, Abdul Rahman decided to base himself there, thus founding Waingapu, Sumba's principal town ever since.

Abdul Rahman, however, had no moral qualms about slavery—as long as no Muslims were taken—and did nothing to impede the traffic. But, perhaps in deference to Dutch weapons, he concentrated on horse trading—at least according to his official reports. Still, an official report in 1870 found that Sumba exported 500 slaves yearly.

The Roman Catholic church established its first base in Sumba in 1886, but it was abandoned ten years later when internecine fighting flared up on the island. In 1906 the Dutch began a "pacification" campaign on the island, installing a colonial administrator in 1912, but not until 1933 was it deemed safe enough to replace the garrison with police.

Above: *Two boys and their charges pose in front of a traditional, peaked hut from West Sumba.*

TRADITION

Old Ways Still Strong in Sumba

Like the rest of Indonesia, Sumba is modernizing. Economic development is the main subject of discussion and so-called "anti-economic behavior," like huge gift-exchanges at marriages or animal sacrifices at funerals, fall more and more under control of the administration. New beliefs are also at work, and the island is in transition between old and new patterns of life.

Still, the traditions remain and the social structure of Sumba is organized—at least according to *adat,* or customary law—around *uma,* which are both physical and genealogical "houses." The funerals and gift exchanges go on, and the Pasola, albeit with blunted spears, still crowns the *nyale* series of planting festivals. (See "The Pasola," page 184.)

Village organization

Though all the Sumbanese share common basic traditions, differences are to be found between the people of East and West Sumba. Contrary to the sharp administrative borders, however, no similar clear-cut demarcation is yet possible in cultural matters. Generally speaking, social stratification is less marked in West Sumba, and the West is generally more ethnically and linguistically diverse. Still, the boundary between the western and eastern linguistic areas remains a subject for discussion.

Traditionally, Sumba was divided in a number of named regions, *tana,* and the inhabitants organized in kin groups called *kabisu.* The *kabisu* are exogamous patrilineal clans. The leading clans of each of these regions or domains are associated with one or more ancestral villages, and these form the ritual and hegemonic centers of the so-called princedoms. These preeminent clans inherited their authority from their ancestral spirits, the *marapu.* All those who take part in the ceremonies performed in these villages belong to the same domain.

The ancestral Sumbanese village is usual-ly built on a defensive height. It has a roughly rectangular form and is surrounded by a defensive wall of stone or a cactus hedge, which today has often fallen into disrepair. Traditional houses with high peaked roofs are aligned in rows around an open space, which contains rectangular stone graves. Some villages—those that fielded war expeditions—kept a "skull tree" on which were hung the heads of the enemy victims. The village may be made up of one or several clans.

Hamlets with low-roofed houses are scattered around the countryside, near the fields. Here is where people spend much of their time, tending their fields and stock, but these hamlets are strictly practical. The inhabitants refer important matters to the village or

house which gives them their social identity.

The Sumbanese house

Like elsewhere in eastern Indonesia, a Sumbanese "house" is not just a dwelling, but also a particular kind of social unit. *Uma* means both the traditional house and the patrilineal group that claims descent from it. Ancestral houses have a proper name and must be perpetuated over time as ritual centers. Building or rebuilding *uma* demands the mobilization of a large number of people, and a great deal of wealth. Today, the necessary cooperation and expense seem more and more difficult to justify.

All traditional Sumbanese houses are built on piles and, apart from the shapes of their roofs, are similar in plan. Houses without towers are figurative extensions of the single ancestral peaked house, the *uma marapu.* This house is the meeting place and major ritual site for all the descendants of the *uma.*

The roof of the *uma* is shaped like a truncated pyramid, and encloses an interior platform divided into "male" and "female" sections. The four main supporting posts are also gendered. Sacred heirlooms, the objects through which contact is made with the ancestors, are stored inside the tall roof peak. The right front corner post of the house is where offerings are made, and where the ancestors or other spiritual beings are addressed. During a ritual, the officiant sits near this corner.

Social stratification

Rigid social hierarchy has been a prominent feature of many Sumbanese societies, especially in the East part of the island where there existed hereditary classes of nobles, commoners and slaves.

The aristocratic houses and their ancestral villages were both politically and ritually the focus of the domain over which they presided. The wealth they gained from the export of horses and cattle, and from the production of fine textiles by noblewomen, gave the noble families the means to stage impressive rituals. The splendid rituals, in turn, reinforced their authority.

Hierarchy in West Sumba is not so rigidly determined. A number of societies have not developed an overall ranking system. Houses enjoy a prominent status within the village communities because of seniority, relationship to a founder, or because of ability. In these more competitive societies, individuals who demonstrate mastery of ritual speech or the capacity to mobilize a large labour force and wealth may gain renown and a consequent elevation of status.

Ritual life

The main aim of traditional Sumbanese religion is to maintain a peaceful and fruitful relationship with the *marapu,* the ancestral spirits. The living observe the many customary rules, and during all ritual celebrations provide the ancestors with food and wealth. In exchange, the living expect increased fertility and prosperity. Special ritual speech is required to communicate with the spiritual world. Spokesmen fluent in this highly metaphorical language can be found at all ceremonial occasions.

In Sumba, as in most of eastern Indonesia, marriages are regulated by a system called an "asymmetrical alliance." The simplest model of this system has just three groups, defined by lineage, in which women from group A are married to men of group B, women from group B to group C, and those from C to A.

The essence of a Sumbanese marriage is an elaborate exchange of goods between the partners. Both a dowry and a bride price are paid, and the specific gifts making up each of these offerings are defined by tradition— water buffalo, cloths, etc.—and are characterized as either "female" or "male." (See "Sumba Textiles," page 172.)

Funeral celebrations are quite important

in the ritual life of the Sumbanese. The combined display of wealth (fabrics) and destruction of wealth (water buffaloes) ensures the safe journey of the deceased to the world of spirits. These ostentatious displays reflect the status the dead enjoyed in life, and can also influence the status of the deceased's clan. But the most important reason for the funeral is to insure the deceased makes it to the spirit world, whence he can bring prosperity to the group.

— *Brigitte Renard-Clamagirand*

Opposite: *Sumbanese priests dance at a celebration of the Marapu New Year.* **Above:** *Women pound rice to remove the outer husk. The rice will then be winnowed in flat baskets.*

TEXTILES

Stunning Decorated and *Ikat* Cloth

Sumba textiles are distinguished by their complexity—combining *ikat* and supplemental decoration like shells and beads—and the beauty of their human, animal and supernatural motifs. Sumbanese women are prolific weavers, and produce their valued textiles not just for local use, but also for an export market that has existed since at least the early part of this century. The weavers, who use traditional back-strap looms, acquired their skills at their mother's side and execute the patterns from memory.

Traditionally, fine weaving was the exclusive right of high-ranking women from the coastal districts of East Sumba. Today, there are no status requirements for weavers, but most textiles still originate from the East. At the western tip of Sumba, in the region of Kodi, *ikat* textiles are woven too, but designs are almost totally of a geometric nature, with white figures on a blue ground.

Ikat is a technique of reserve dyeing. Before weaving, yarn bundles are stretched on a frame and the pattern is produced by tying it into the threads, binding the bundles in the necessary places with dye-resistant fiber. After dipping, the bindings are removed and the design appears in reverse against a dyed background. The design can be tied into the fixed threads, the warp, or into the cross threads, the weft. In some parts of Indonesia (not Sumba) so-called double *ikat*—with both warp and weft threads pre-dyed—is produced.

Traditional garments

The *lau* and *hinggi* are the main garments for women and men, and they provide the major field for decorative work. Cotton is the only material used in the cloth, and the basic techniques of decoration are dyeing, weaving and sewing on ornaments.

The *lau* is the cylinder-skirt for women. Though bands of warp *ikat* appear in the fabric of the woman's skirt, the dominant designs are carried out with other techniques: *lau pahudu* is a ceremonial skirt with designs worked by supplementary warp; the *lau hada* is a skirt with designs outlined in beads and shells.

The *hinggi,* a mantle worn by men, is constructed from two separately woven panels that are sewed together into a large rectangular cloth. *Hinggi* are always woven in pairs. One piece is wrapped about the hips, the other draped over the shoulder. In patterned *hinggi,* the two panels are identical with a fringe on both ends.

The panels are divided into an uneven number of bands, of different size and color, each band containing a row of figures. Figures are sometimes also used in the center band, but schematic motifs are more common. The design is arranged symmetrically along the center band, with the figures standing up when the cloth is folded in the center.

The most striking men's mantle is the *hinggi kombu,* which is made of two-color *ikat*—blue and rust. The blue dye comes from the indigo plant, and is fairly strong. The rust color comes from the bark and roots of the *kombu* tree, and requires that the cloth be treated with various plant oils and and an alum-containing local plant, as well as subjected to repeated dippings in the dye, for the color to appear strongly. Deep, saturated tones are the most valued, but these require tedious dippings in the natural dyes.

Motif conventions

The sheer variety of figurative and schematic motifs in Sumba is exceptional among the *ikat* producing areas in East Indonesia. Sumbanese weavers reproduce standing human figures, skull trees (related to head-hunting), gold ornaments worn in ceremonies, plants, birds, dogs and lizards, as well as geometric shapes like coils, hooks and lozenges. Some of the designs obviously derive from foreign sources: dragons, taken

from Chinese ceramics; rampant lions, from the Dutch coat of arms; and schematic *patola ratu* patterns, from Indian silk. But most of the designs derive from the local context.

Certain formal conventions dictate the depiction of figures in Sumbanese textiles. For example, most quadrupeds appear in profile (although the head position may vary) while monkeys or felines present a rampant or a climbing posture. Standing human figures appear in a frontal view, with arms in a praying or akimbo position.

Individual figures are identified from these stereotypes by adding a specific detail. For example, all "bird" shapes, roughly like a fowl, are understood as birds, but a crest and curved beak makes the particular figure a cockatoo. The bodies of all quadrupeds are nearly alike, but if it has an open barking mouth, it is a dog. If it has whiskers, it is a lion. The generic type of the plant or the animal is easy to recognize, but the species determination is quite difficult.

Ritual use of textiles

At the same time they serve as clothing and ornaments, decorated textiles also serve in the important system of gift exchanges. (See "Tradition," page 170.) These exchanges regulate relationships between Sumbanese social groups, and between the visible and invisible worlds. In these systems, the cloths are tokens of status and ritual goods.

The cloths used in the exchange system are the men's *hinggi* and women's *lau*. Within the fixed patterns of gift-giving between social groups, the bride-givers offer symbolic "female" textiles, and receive "male" items—precious ornaments and horses—from the bride-takers.

Traditionally, the use and dispensation of fine textiles were the exclusive right of the nobility. The best cloths were worn only at great festivals. The colors and designs of *hinggi* revealed a man's station in life. Commoners wore simple blue and white fabrics, and aristocrats added red. Cloths worn by the nobility had complex patterning and displayed motifs reserved for their rank.

Fine textiles play an important role at Sumbanese funerals, not just as gifts, but also as shrouds. Traditionally the corpse was wrapped in the finest fabrics available to members of the deceased's station. Protected in this way, the corpse might wait months or even years before the final burial takes place.

Textiles buried in the grave play an essential role in the safe journey of the deceased to the next world, and in his well-being there. Chickens, for example, ensure sustenance, horses provide transport and *patola* patterns announce the deceased's rank.

An increasing demand for Sumba "market *kain* (cloth)," as well as transformations in Sumbanese society have given way to a number of new standards for textiles. Imported colored thread and synthetic dyes are now commonly used, and there is now a tendency to cut down on labor by using fewer, larger motifs, as well as the incorporation of new designs.

— *Brigitte Renard-Clamagirand*

Opposite: *The dyed warp threads for an* ikat *cloth aligned on a frame before weaving.* **Above, left:** *This cloth from Rindi in East Sumbawa has been decorated with cowrie shells.* **Above, right:** *Detail from a Sumbanese* ikat *showing human figures.*

EAST SUMBA

Fine *Ikat,* Tombs and a Hilltop Village

For the visitor, East Sumba is something of a poor sister to the western district. The only unusual tombs here are in the Melolo area (there are hundreds in the West) and the relatively fewer traditional houses in the East, less spectacular to begin with, are now mostly covered with distinctly unesthetic galvanized steel.

Even with all these caveats, it is worth a visit to East Sumba if only to see the *ikat* weaving process, which is centered here. The weavers of the East have always produced a more beautiful and intricate cloth that their counterparts in the West. Inferior quality *ikat* is beginning to surface—store-bought thread, artificial dyes and coarse motifs—but this is chiefly because tourists are unwilling to pay the high prices required for a fine piece crafted from hand-spun thread and carefully and tediously colored with natural dyes. Still, there is plenty of good *kain ikat* being woven here on backstrap looms.

Waingapu: eastern capital

Waingapu is the largest town in Sumba, the island's seaport, and the administrative capital of the East Sumba district. Some 25,000 people live in this sprawling urban area, with the greatest concentration found in the harbor area, and about a kilometer inland, around the bus terminal and adjacent shops.

A walk around the southwest shore in the old pier and harbor area provides a relaxing diversion if you have an afternoon in Waingapu. Just off Jalan Yos Sudarso, the main street leading to the pier, a small street leads along the raised shoreline, offering a good view of the area.

The old pier, usually with a fair variety of inter-island craft docked, juts out across a little bay. The Pertamina oil storage tanks are serviced by a separate pier to the left. A large stock pen near the main pier holds East Sumba's principal export: cattle and horses.

If you are lucky, you might arrive when handlers are attempting to convince the animals to board ships for the three day ride to Surabaya. There is a new harbor outside of town where larger ships, including the Pelni passenger liner *Kelimutu,* dock.

Prailiu and Kwangu: ikat

Some of the finest contemporary Sumbanese *ikat* cloths are produced within a few kilometers of Waingapu, at Prailiu (2 kilometers) and Kwangu (10 kilometers). By giving the weavers some advanced notice, you can arrange a demonstration of all the phases of making traditional Sumbanese *kain*—preparing the cotton, spinning it into thread, tying the design into the threads, dyeing, and the final weaving. These villages are perhaps the only places on Sumba where you can see all processes going on at once.

There is lots of cloth for sale in both Prailiu and Kwangu, but as both are very close to Waingapu, bargaining is essential. At Prailiu, a right-hand turn off the main road leads to Lambanapu (about 6 kilometers) another weaving village. Together, these three villages produce some of the most intricate Sumbanese *ikat* found today.

Melolo: peaked huts

At Melolo, 62 kilometers from Waingapu, a dirt road leads inland. Take this road 3 kilometers to a fork, marked by a crude stone horse, and then take the right fork to Umbara, a dusty little village. Here there are three peaked and thatched huts, displaying huge water buffalo horns. There are also four tombs here, two with recent carvings. Offerings of betel are sometimes made to the coarsely carved crocodile and turtle. Umbara is a sad looking place, and you sign the guest book and pay at the third hut down the row, where posters of Indonesia's president and vice-president compete with Rambo.

Rende: funerary sculpture

Tin-roofed—but otherwise traditional—huts in Rende village, 7 kilometers out of Melolo, enclose the finest funerary sculptures in East Sumba. Here are four massive *menhir*-supported tombs, as well as smaller sculptures. Carvings mushroom out of the top of several slabs, featuring a menagerie of animals, a graceful kneeling figure, and in one case, a man being killed by a house. (This last looks a bit like an unnatural sex act.) There is a small Wednesday market nearby, and Rende boasts some good local weaving.

The road out of Rende leads to Baing village, 55 kilometers away. The trip is dusty, but the road is scheduled for paving in 1991. Just outside of Rende, the road climbs the side of a valley, offering the only decent glimpse of scenery on the entire trip from Waingapu: a beautiful green valley, following the snaking course of a river.

Kailala: exclusive resort

Just 5 kilometers before Baing, a dirt road leads to the exclusive (over $100 a day) beach resort at Kailala, which opened in November 1990. The resort specializes in deep sea sport fishing, and is registered with the International Game Fishing Association. Large billfish, shark and tuna strike all year, but the seas are rough from December through March. The owners plan to provide scuba facilities soon, and a few years down the road, an 18-hole golf course.

The resort has been a good neighbor, providing employment for 50 people, and helping to set up a fishing cooperative. But the resort has had some problems, so better check at Waingapu before heading there.

Northwest from Waingapu

From Waingapu, the main highway cuts almost due west across the interior of the island to Waikabubak. But there is a smaller dirt road that heads northwest along the coast. At Mondu, 32 kilometers from the city, the road hits a river, which can be forded in the dry season. From the river, the road continues to Rambangaru, the subdistrict capital, and the village of Kadahang. Here the road hits a river that is waiting for a bridge. One can venture past this point only by four-wheel-drive jeep.

Because of the lack of a good road, it is very difficult to reach the traditional area of Kapundak. Wunga, at the base of the Sasar peninsula, is the ritual center of this region, and has great importance for all Sumbanese, because this is where the ancestors of all the islanders first landed. The government plans to improve this road, as well as extend it all the way to Mambora in West Sumba.

Prailiang: hilltop village

Just out of Waingapu on the road north, a DC3 by the beach marks the site of the Elim Hotel bungalows. (Yes, it's an airplane; it was wrecked when it brakes failed on landing and it hit a bulldozer.) Past the wreck, the road continues to follow the coast rising to an overview where, if the weather is clear, you can see the mountains of Flores to the north.

This road continues to Mondu, but just before, a dirt track inland leads to Prailiang village, tough to find but well worth the

Above: *The traditional huts of Prailiang village are among the few left in East Sumba with thatch roofing. Many of the traditions are observed here.*

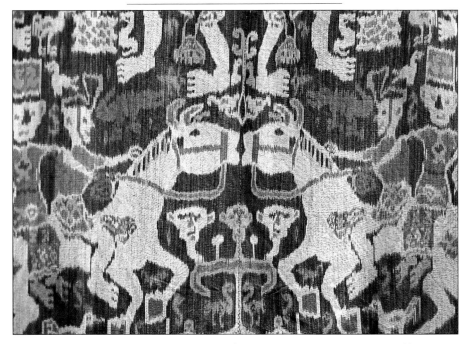

effort. The owner of the Elim Hotel "discovered" this place in 1989, but a year later the village had still received just three visitors.

After making the turnoff, you bounce on an unmarked track through desolate countryside for some 3 kilometers before you can see a river valley below, snuggled between parched hills. Your driver then stops the vehicle at the bottom of a not very promising steep peak. But the 500-meter trek up to the village is not very arduous.

Prailiang (sometimes referred to as Prainatang) is a group of 10 huts, with a number of graves positioned about the small, flat site. It is a perfect example of an old Sumbanese fortified hilltop village.

Because they were so close to the coast, the villagers had to keep out of sight of the slaving expeditions, which would arrive with 30–40 boats filled with Muslim slavers from Endes. Parts of a stone wall, now crumbling, at one time encircled the entire hilltop. The Prailiang villagers' neat rectangular rice paddies and vegetable plots decorate the valley floor below.

The village's strategic location helped to repulse an attack, but a sustained siege would have worked well: there is no water anywhere nearby. Today, as in the old days, one must negotiate the long drop to the valley for a bath or to get drinking water. The water is brought up in bamboo tubes, which hold more, are easier to carry, and less prone to spills than modern buckets.

Visiting Prailiang

Howling, mangy curs announce your arrival to the few people who remain in the village during the daylight hours, when most villagers are working in the fields below. A chat with an elderly man revealed that this was the resident village of the local ruler, whose descendants still occupy the second house from the end.

He said the people of Prailiang belong to a group called Kanatang, and follow the ancestral religion. The ritual life of the village is still strong, and various numbers and combinations of livestock are still the only acceptable bridewealth. No missionary or native preacher had yet set foot in the village.

The six largest huts stand at the very top, neatly aligned. Below them are four more, presumably less prestigious. All the huts have relatively narrow porches in front, and their walls of split bamboo enclose a large floor raised on stilts. The thatch roots are peaked, but less steep than is the style in West Sumba.

The many scattered graves in Prailiang consist of horizontal stone slabs held up by low, unworked rock pillars. In most examples the stone work is crude, but one—the largest—is constructed of several finely fitted blocks. None of the stones is carved at all.

WEST SUMBA

Peaked Roofs, Stone Tombs and Ritual

Sumba's most exciting district for the visitor is West Sumba, where stone graves, traditional houses and the rituals of the Sumbanese religion have been best preserved. In Kodi, on the island's southwestern tip, you can see the tallest, peak-roofed houses on Sumba; Anakalang has the island's best megalithic tombs, huge and well decorated; and right around the capital there are several traditional hilltop villages, encircling the tombs of the clans' forebears.

The capital of the district is Waikabubak, a little inland town of 15,000. One need not even venture out of town to reach the area's ritual center, Tarung. Here is one of the headquarters of the Marapu religion, and the site of some spectacular rituals.

The highway west

The 140 kilometer highway between the capital of East Sumba, Waingapu, and Waikabubak, is not only paved but surfaced with what's locally called "hot mix," a thick, smooth layer of asphalt and gravel which won't wash away after the first rain. This comes as sheer joy to travelers who bounced over this stretch in the '70s, choking with dust for seven or more hours. But of course, back then the drivers could not take the curves with such wild abandon, a positive point for the past.

Buses make the run—once they finally leave town, after sometimes an hour-long search for passengers—in 4 to 4 1/2 hours, about a half-hour slower than a private vehicle. The road sweeps through fairly dull countryside, dry savannah at first, then the rice fields around Lewa, and finally the wooded mountains of the interior. Buses make a *de rigeur* stop at Langa Leru, around the halfway

mark, for a rest, food and coffee. The site is just past a bridge over a clear, gurgling creek. Simple meals are 50¢–75¢, and the snacks available include bread, boiled eggs and delicious *arabica* coffee, strong and full of grounds. Back on the road, it's another couple hours to Waikabubak.

The very adventurous can take a side trip south off this highway. Twice a week a passenger-truck makes the rough trip south to Tamara (see map page 168), which takes about 4 hours. At Tamara, on the south coast, there is a weekly Wednesday market. Nearby Tarimbang is said to be blessed with a beautiful beach, with white sand and big waves.

Tarung: a ritual center of the west

Some of West Sumba's best megalithic graves are in Tarung, a hillcrest village just west of the commercial center of Waikabubak. And Tarung remains one of the island's most powerful spiritual centers. It is the high priests of Tarung who officiate one of each year's Wula Padu ceremony, which honors the deified ancestors at the beginning of the Marapu religion's new year, which coincides with the start of the rainy season.

The new year cycle consists of a series of five rites, taking place over a month, beginning on a full moon in November. The series culminates with the priests, in full ceremonial dress, escorting the spirits on horseback from a holy grave a short way outside of

Opposite: *A detail from an East Sumba ikat.*
Right: *An elderly woman chews a mixture of betel nut and tobacco. She keeps a reserve supply of the quid tucked in a hole in her earlobe.*

town. In Tarung, the visiting spirits are entertained with song and dance, and animals are sacrificed in their honor to insure abundant harvests and good health for the village. The Wula Padu celebration introduces a period of enforced quiet, during which even weeping for the dead is forbidden.

When the priests ride through Waikabubak to Tarung, accompanied by the spirits, all traffic must stop—the ancestors don't take kindly to vehicles zipping by. A few years ago, a local official—in a hurry to get on with his

business and considering the Wula Padu spiritual nonsense—passed the procession in his jeep. With no human intervention, the vehicle overturned, killing the hapless rationalist.

Despite the powerful presence of the Marapu religion, Tarung has been changing in response to the recent increase in tourism. Several 500-meter paths lead to the village, and foreigners walking along these will be greeted by shouting children—"Hello Smokey!"—and the cries of women flogging *ikat*. (Before going up, stop at the perfect little group of thatch-roofed huts at Kampung Ende, just 100 meters from the post office.)

Tarung is the highest hamlet in a complex of three little *kampung*s, with 33 huts in all. The houses on the lower slopes have modernized somewhat with corrugated steel roofs, but each of the nine main huts of Tarung retains a traditional thatch roof. These huts, each with a separate ritual function, encircle a group of plain tombs whose top slabs are used for household tasks such as drying rice. The best tomb is crowned by an obviously important ritual object, which is almost completely hidden from sight by an awful little steel roof.

Bondomaroto: *ikat* and rice terraces

To find this hamlet, go past the government offices strung out to the east—where the urban sprawl is being directed to prevent it from taking over the fertile rice paddies—

about two kilometers from downtown, and look for a house with the panel stating "Desa Teraba." Here a short dirt road leading south reaches a valley, where there are some simple graves. At the bottom of the valley, the path left (east) leads up a short, steep climb to Bondomaroto. Kampung Praijing, a beautiful five-terraced settlement, decorates a hilltop in the opposite direction.

Both villages are worth visiting, and you can see women weaving with traditional backstrap looms on the front porches of the houses. You will be asked for some money for visiting and photos, but there is one tomb—the best—that you are not to photograph.

The ancestral tomb at Bondomaroto is graced by two unusual megalithic carvings, one of which is a two-headed water buffalo. Only a priest can give permission for a snapshot, the villagers said, and he never seemed to be around. Although it may seem like an overreaction, the villagers are nervous because another sculpture was recently stolen.

West of Waikabubak: Kodi district

Leaving Waikabubak on the main road northwest (towards the airport at Tambolaka), continue about 25 kilometers to Waimangura, where there is a Saturday market. Here, turn left onto a paved road that heads west. The road ends at Kodi (officially called Bondokodi) on the coast. Just after leaving Waimangura, a road cuts off to Ombawangu village, about 15 kilometers south, where there are some irrigated rice fields, but there is not much to see on the road to Kodi.

Shortly before Kodi, a dirt road leads to the seaside hamlet of Ratenegaro, where there are seaside tombs and a magnificent view. The first dirt road you come to, just before Kodi, leads to the seaside village of Waiha. Just beyond this turnoff, but still before Kodi, is the 4-kilometer road to Ratenegaro. On the way, stop at Pronobaroro, where the traditional houses have the highest roofs in all of Sumba. The people of this village get their water from a well dug over 20 meters into the rock.

Ratenegaro: tombs and beach

Approaching Ratenegaro, you begin to pick out the local-style tombs planted into the gently sloping countryside. These are flat, rectangular slabs set on square bases, with very little carved decorations. There is one exception, and it is a prize winner in the modern art contest. Near the *kampung* entrance is a brand new tomb, topped by two figures—gaudily painted and dressed in cloth—having at each other with spears.

The tombs continue towards the beach, and there are three on the narrow spit of land that forms part of the outer shell of a splendid lagoon. The lagoon receives the Bondokodi River at one end, and the tidal influx at the other. From the slight elevation of Ratenegaro, you get a perfect view of this lagoon, with the tall roofs of Wainyapu hamlet included in the scene.

At low tide, you can splash across to the traditional hamlet, where there is a white sand beach that gets lots of waves. (The side road to Waiha, mentioned above, also passes by Wainyapu.)

Heading back to Kodi, you can follow the coast to the inlet and beach at Pero, also called Redakapal ("Ship Lookout"). This is the site of a proposed star-ranked hotel. Some Australians come here to surf, and they stay at the houses of some of the local Muslim fishermen nearby. Just north of Kodi is Tosi hamlet, the site of the yearly Pasola (See "The Pasola," page 184). Tosi, near a nice beach, is the raja's *kampung,* the oldest in the entire subdistrict.

South of Waikabubak

Wanokaka and Lamboya are two traditional areas south of the western capital. Each hosts a yearly Pasola celebration, and have stone tombs. All the roads in the district that lead to the main tourist sites are in the process of being paved.

Due south out of Waikabubak, the road forks. The left fork heads down to the Wanokaka coastal valley and—if you can look

past the garbage at the rest stops—is surrounded by pretty ricefields. Waigili hamlet is to the right of the road, just before it reaches the coastal plain. That this little town is on the usual tourist itinerary is obvious from the concrete path leading up to the local tomb, and the little woodcarvings for sale.

It is worth a stop, however, to see the large upright sculpture that stands at the head of the stone. If given the proper offerings, this carving—named Waiurang—brings on the rains for the rice. The two other tombs here display excellent stone carving along the periphery of their top slabs. The head priest living here has the responsibility of determining the day of the yearly Pasola, which takes place at nearby Wanokaka sometime in March.

Laihuruk area: the Praigoli tomb

Past Waigili, the road reaches the head of a valley and flattens out. It runs for a short stretch along the Praibakul River, and the concrete block houses of Laihuruk village, the site of a Saturday open air market. There are several traditional hilltop hamlets here, just to the left of the road, including Mamodu, Waiwuli and oft-visited Praigoli.

Praigoli is graced by a huge tomb, fronted by a fine and ornate sculpture featuring a human figure, and draws groups of tourists. This tomb definitely ranks among the island's very best. It is said that inside is a cache of

Opposite, left: *The peaked clan huts of Kadengar are on a hilltop, in the past a crucial element of village defense.* **Opposite, right:** *Detail from a carved tombstone in Praigoli village.* **Right:** *The representation of a man and his wife stare out from the large tomb they share.*

gold heirlooms, which was placed here centuries ago to keep them out of the hands of Portuguese raiders. The owner was then buried with his treasure. Although the occupant of the tomb saved his gold, his pretty wife was snatched away by the Iberians, presumably for nefarious purposes.

At the end of the valley the road turns right, and follows the beach to the sacred spot where the priests scoop up the *nyale*—the multi-hued sexual parts of local seaworms—at dawn on Pasola day.

Rua beach: planned resort

To visit the rest of the south coast, you have to backtrack most of the way to Waikabubak, and take the other fork. Instead of leading southeast to the Wanokaka valley, this one leads due south to Rua. A bit more than halfway from the fork to the beach is the crossroad town of Padedewatu, where a road heads off to the west. Usually deserted, this crossroads comes alive during the area's Wednesday market.

From here, the road drops steeply to a long, curved white sand beach. This is the planned site of a government run hotel. The roadside offers a fine panoramic view of the area. The ricefields extend all the way up to where the sand begins. While waiting for the hotel to be built, you can sleep at a complex of huts owned by a local ethnic Chinese man, whose small boat provides fish for the markets in Waikabubak.

The Rua beach hotel is still only in the dreaming stage, but the basic construction is finished for the five-star, Sumba Reef Lodge a bit to the south on Karoka Cape. A 7-kilometer dirt road, beginning just past Padedewatu on the road to Rua, leads to a fantastic beach. This site was picked by an American investor after months of prospecting for a location. A gate bars the way to casual visitors.

Sodan: high priests

Backtrack out of Rua, head west at the Padedewatu crossroads, and you soon reach modern Kabukarudi village. Here a gaudily painted, very modern tomb features a carving of the occupant. He gazes out proudly, a posture befitting a deified ancestor. His was a recent funeral, although it took place before the 1988 government-imposed 5-animal limit on sacrifices, and hundreds of water buffalo, horses, dogs and pigs were slain.

The current raja, who lives in the traditional house next to the tomb, recoups part of the investment in his father's funeral. by

charging 60¢ for a visit—with photos—of the tomb. His house is decorated with the horns of some of the water buffalo sacrificed in the ceremony. Try Pak Hogabora's house nearby for a homestay. This is handy if you plan to attend the yearly Pasola in nearby Lombaya.

Eastof Kabukarudi is the hilltop village of Sodan, home of the area's *ratu,* the high priests of the Marapu religion. Unfortunately, a fire consumed the fine traditional huts here in 1988, and took with it the sacred humanskin drum. But the deities continue to respond to the new drum of water buffalo hide, which is, however, fringed with human hair.

Past Sodan, the road drops past Bondundata, a striking traditional village. Unfortunately, two of the houses have been roofed in that practical, but distinctly unesthetic modern wonder: corrugated steel. Kadengar hamlet, further on, has many large, conical huts. A rice plain follows, split by the Kadengar River, spanned by a new bridge. Just beyond the river, a side road leads to Marosi beach, the usual limit of tour groups.

Marosi beach: *nyale* site

A really rough looking, stone-studded track

Opposite: *Bura Gela, a rich landowner in West Sumba, had a reputation for sorcery. Accused of killing a little girl with black magic, he was abducted by vigilantes and hacked into tiny pieces.* **Above:** *A Marapu priest in West Sumba.*

leads off to the east of the dirt road to Marosi and ends at Lemandonga, the site where the *nyale* worms are gathered for the Lamboya Pasola. (It is possible to make this in a jeep.) Here two great blocks of coral, each with arched caves worn in their sides, sit at one end of a gray sand beach. To the west, just over a low hill, is a pretty white sand beach, in splendid isolation.

Continuing west on the road from Sodan past the turnoff to Marosi, another little road leads down to the water. This is Patiala beach, said to provide good surfing, with beautiful turquoise water and white sand. Cliffs cut off the beach to the west, and there is also a little high-tide-only island here. Back inland, these same cliffs force the road to climb upward to a magnificent overlook.

Just 10 kilometers past the beach turnoff is Gaura village, where there is a Saturday market. Just before Gaura, a 3 kilometer side road leads to Dasang Beach, which has brilliantly white sand. The road ends here. But by jeep, you can continue 5 kilometers west to where there is supposed to be a great snorkeling spot, with lots of untouched coral and reef fish. All forms of fishing are taboo here, but snorkelers do not, it is said, provoke the spirits' wrath.

From Gaura, it's currently a 2—3-day trek to Waiha village. Even a jeep won't make this. But road construction is planned between Guara and Waiha—which as of this writing could only be reached from Kodi.

East of Waikabubak: Anakalang

The wonderful tombs of the Anakalang area, on or just off the main road to Waingapu, are a fast 22 kilometers from Waikabubak. Sumba's most photographed tomb—60¢ charge—is just on the roadside. Opposite the famous tomb is a paved road that runs south to Kabunduk.

At Kabunduk, check in with the *kepala desa,* the village head. His house is the first on your left as you enter the hamlet. Sign the guest book, and pay a fee which allows you to visit this village and several nearby graves. At the back of Kabunduk's wide central pathway, there are two graves: a huge but plain one called Resi Moni (at one time the largest on the island) and an interesting smaller one, with carvings on the slab, which is topped by two horsemen. The traditional house facing the altars is open for homestays.

To the back of the *kampung,* a path leads up a hill and then follows a ridge through scattered huts and old graves. Keep going to Lai Tarung, where a very ordinary thatch roof sits on 10 carved stone columns, holding up a floor. Here is where the corpses used to lie in state. The structure's name—Uma Dapa Daungu—means, roughly, "Not Built by Mortals." The structure is built right above an inconspicuous round stone, which covers what informants told us were black and white *watu kabala*—"lightning stones." The stones, they said, come out by themselves to bring rain or to kill anyone foolish enough to try to steal the harvest.

Kabunduk: rituals and heirlooms

After coming down the hill from Lai Tarung, ask the *kepala desa* or someone from his family to show you a set of photos he keeps. These were taken in 1949 by a Swiss anthropologist, and copies were finally sent here in 1982. Some of the shots show the Purong Takadonga ritual, which has not been performed for decades.

The Purong Takadonga, lasting several weeks, demanded the participation of the entire clan, and honored the ancestors' arrival to these lands. The event itself looked spectacular enough, as the men wielded gigantic, 7-meter spears, two of which are still preserved.

Approximately two-thirds of the people in the Anakalang area have become Christians, and the Purong Takadonga is one of the victims of this conversion. They still perform the Kataga war dance, but for tourist dollars rather than for building up adrenalin prior to head-hunting raids.

Most of the ancient religious paraphernalia has been sold following Christianization, but the village chief at Kabunduk has kept several items of crucial spiritual importance. These include gold heirloom decorations and the *lejungabang,* an ancient bronze gong which, unlike the usual brass instruments, is said to have been fashioned by spirits.

The most fascinating object in the collection, called *tugu keamanan*—"safety tower"— is a 40-centimeter-long iron rod. The village chief, a member of the royal family, assembled the device by placing ten crude little golden heads on fixtures branching out from the iron rod. The topmost head, with the highest gold content, represents the raja's clan. The others, of gold-copper alloy, represent the other principal clans.

Opposite: *A rousing war dance in West Sumba recalls the days of head-hunting and warfare, finally stopped by the Dutch in the 1920s.*

Until recently, only the highest priests could view this object. But now it has been cleared for the public, who pay $1.40 per viewer to see it. The money goes to buy sacrificial chickens.

Gulabakul: the largest tomb

About two kilometers south of Kabunduk the road stops at Gulabakul (formerly called Prai Bakul), the site of Sumba's largest tomb. The huge slab is said to weigh 70 tons. It took three months and 2,000 men to drag it from the quarry to its present position. The tomb is the final resting place of Umbu Sawola and his wife, and was constructed in 1971.

Pavement was scheduled for one more *kampung* past Gulabakul, just 1 kilometer away. From here, locals say that it takes an easy 5–6 hours to walk to the Wanokaka area.

Along the way, a total of 7 kilometers from Anakalang, is the Omata Yangu waterfall. This falls cascades down 75 meters, and the pool at its bottom was a favorite spot of the local Dutch residents. Four-wheel-drive jeeps are supposed to be able to reach within two kilometers of the falls.

North to Mamboro

After visiting the Anakalang area, you might want to take the "long way" back to Waikabubak. Mamboro, with a Saturday market, is a Muslim fishing village on Sumba's north coast. There is almost no public transportation this way.

The road north turns off the main Waikabubak–Waingapu road just east of Anakalang. It is 36 kilometers of monotonous scenery along the way. There is so little traffic on this road, however, that horses might throw their young riders in panic at the sight of your vehicle. Just before Mamboro, a dirt track—only jeeps only can make this— leads to Manuakalada, an interesting hilltop village of traditional huts.

The people here are unregenerate animists. The dolmen and *menhir* tombs are not particularly noteworthy, but the tomb of Raja Umbu Saramani, the first ruler of this area, is unique. The bottom part of the tomb ends in peaked corners and supports a pyramid-shaped top ending in twin, oval bumps. The grave's general configuration resembles—in a scaled-down version—that of one of the sultans of Bima, Sumbawa.

No connection between this tomb and Bima has been made, as far as we know, but the people of nearby Mamboro are descendents chiefly of Endenese settlers, but also of Muslims from Sulawesi, Komodo and Bima.

This area, along with much of the northwest coast, was effectively depopulated of native Sumbanese by slave raids. Mamboro was the center of the export trade in slaves, and nowhere on Sumba was there greater wealth than among the rajas here.

THE PASOLA

Fighting Horsemen of Sumba

The air was charged with tension and taunts were hurled as the black-clad horseman spurred his mount for yet another charge. At full gallop, he survived a shower of lances, and reached his target. His spear was flung, and landed squarely and strongly on the back of one of his opponents.

The blunt-pointed spear bounced off with an audible thud. Had this been a real battle, the victim would have been dead. Out of weapons, the man in black dropped his reins and fended off spears with both hands while he used only his legs to guide his horse, at full gallop, back to the sidelines. The son of Bura Gela had struck again. The women went wild, shrieking and ululating for the triumphant warrior. It was the Pasola.

The *nyale* cycle

The Pasola is the culmination of a series of fertility rituals called *nyale*. Hundreds of warriors riding bareback on their agile ponies whirl, and charge, and hurl spears at each other. It is dangerous mayhem. Although the government now requires that the spears be blunted, serious injuries are common, and deaths are occasional. In the past the event was deadly.

The spear fight allows accounts to be squared with the ancestral spirits, as anyone who dies during the Pasola does so because they have offended the supernatural guardians of the village. The wounded are *de facto* guilty as well, though of a more minor infraction than the outright casualties. With offerings of chickens and pigs, anyone wounded in the melee can atone. In this way, the Pasola allows the new year to begin without any lingering offenses against the ancestors that might compromise the coming crop and the health of the village.

The event has a strange beginning. A long time ago, it is told, the King of the Moon had a beautiful daughter called Nyale. She took pity on the sufferings of mankind and sacrificed herself to insure that there would be abundant food on earth. The strange, multi-colored worms represent the body of the princess, coming to shore each year to give fertility to the land. The number and behavior of these mysterious worms, called *nyale*, augur the success of the upcoming rice crop.

Science offers a no less strange explanation. The "worms" are a result of the bizarre reproductive process of a segmented marine worm (*Eunice* sp.). The worms live in the waters year-round but are nocturnal and thus not seen. The moon triggers a once-a-year reproductive phase, in which the worms shed their tail ends. These, filled with sperm or eggs, wriggle to the surface. The sexual parts of these worms are considered a delicacy in many parts of the archipelago.

Blood and fertility

I briefly met Bura Gela and his son, the black-suited warrior, on my first trip to Sumba in the late 1970s—it was he who first told me about the Pasola. People warned me that he was a black magician, but I didn't think much of their warning. Others, however, evidently did. Early the next year, a band of 25 men sneaked up to Bura Gela's house one night, and hacked the old man to bits. The murder was apparently a result of vague accusations of his having killed children with his magic, although many envied his wealth.

The *nyale* cycle I witnessed began with the ritual ploughing of a sacred plot of rice paddy. Then, the night before the *nyale* worms were due to arrive, young men and women gathered at a sacred beach. Around midnight, just as the moon rose, the men began a ritual boxing match to draw blood, the best offering one can make to the spirits.

The fertility aspect of the ritual was also strong that night, and some of the young champions, together with their admirers, wandered after the boxing to some secluded spot nearby.

The next day, the focus of the ceremony shifted to the village of Sodan, which crowns the peak of a steep hillock. Most of the high priests of the *nyale* live in Sodan and the area is charged with mysticism. (See "West Sumba," page 177.) There are many taboos here—sacred paths that must not be crossed—as well as dangers, including ghost dogs whose bite brings insanity. At sunset,

Opposite: *The dramatic black and red of the son of Bura Gela, one of the best Pasola fighters, doubtless strikes fear and rage in his opponents.*

the priests beat the sacred drums, the most important of which was made of human skin. (This rare drum was destroyed recently in a fire.) The high priests then walked to the beach, some 5 kilometers away.

Augury of the worms

Shortly before dawn, two of the priests waded out and peered intently into the water. They scooped up a handful of the multi-colored *nyale* and brought them back to their associates for examination and auguries. On this date, by mysterious means, the experts cautiously predicted a good harvest—provided the upcoming Pasola was performed well.

Two priests initiated the fighting, right there on the beach. But the sand prevented the horses from hitting their stride, and the warriors were overall a bit cautious. The opposing teams, about 150 on each side, moved to firmer ground, the sacred Pasola field nearby.

Groups of horsemen sallied forth in quick charges, often led by a brave individual. Spears rained down. Warriors left the fray to allow their foam-flecked horses to cool down, and others, with fresh mounts, took their place. Some of the young men simply changed mounts when their horses tired, themselves seemingly immune to fatigue.

At first the fighting looked just like a free-for-all, a mad riot of spears and charging horses. But after a while, I could see how controlled and skilled the horsemanship was. The most appreciated feat was for a single warrior to charge in, alone, and brave a storm of spears to single out an opponent for a "simulated" kill.

A warrior falls

As the morning wore into afternoon, the sun grew increasing hot and tempers began to fray. The young men glistened with sweat, and even the horses seemed to taste blood. Then, escaping after a particularly fast charge, a man was thrown from his horse, and trampled under the horses of his pursuers. He was carried off the field, dead.

Rather than casting a pall over the ritual, this dark event spurred everyone to a higher pitch of excitement. The men's eyes narrowed, and they grew reckless. The field shrank as the reserves edged closer. The spears were raising nasty looking welts. The mood of the event grew ugly.

Suddenly, men began to shout for their long knives and throwing rocks! The elders, with cooler heads, moved in to try to break things up, and several horsemen were pulled from their mounts by groups of elders. Gradually the arena cleared, and everyone breathed a bit easier. Had this been the old days, the even would have degenerated into a massacre for sure. As it was, enough blood has been spilled that the ancestral spirits would be happy, and a good harvest ensue.

PART VIII

Introducing Savu and Roti

The small islands of Savu and Raijua and Roti and Ndao, offer much to the visitor interested in traditional culture, but only if he or she is a seasoned traveler. Except for surfers who have discovered the waves off south Roti, very few outsiders come to these islands. These are not islands for a casual visit, and it helps to speak at least some Indonesian. Allow yourself at least a week to visit either Roti or Savu, and more if you plan to go to Ndao from Roti, or Raijua from Savu.

Palms and tradition

These relatively isolated islands are unusual for their inhabitants' extensive use of the *lontar* palm tree. This tall palm allows the arid soil to support a much higher population than would otherwise be possible. The nutritious sap is gathered in the morning and late afternoon, and is sweet and refreshing. Fermented, the *lontar* sap yields a mildly alcoholic "toddy," and boiled down, rich palm sugar. Even the leftovers are used as pig feed.

On Roti, one group retains the old religion, and the *lontar* economy is still going strong. The island of Ndao is famous for its itinerant jewelers, who travel all over eastern Indonesia plying their craft.

On Savu, the traditional religion and ritual cycle is maintained in spite of professed Christianity. Adherence to the old customs is even stronger on Raijua Island, which is considered the source island of much of the Savunese animist religion. If you visit, keep your schedule flexible, to take advantage of any upcoming ritual events.

Islanders in Kupang

There are many Rotinese and Savunese living in and around Kupang, Timor, the provincial capital. The people of Roti caught on early to the value of the education offered by the Dutch Reformed Church, and even in the days of the Dutch East India company insisted on schoolteachers. Because of their education and good relations with the Dutch, the Rotinese were invited to settle around Kupang to provide a sort of *cordon sanitaire* to keep the "unruly" Timorese away from the city.

The Savunese were not at first receptive to any outside influences on their culture, but by the end of the 19th century they accepted the presence of missionaries and schools. Warriors from Savu were famous for their skill and bravery, and many were hired by the Dutch. Their descendants now live around Kupang.

Thanks to their energy and high level of education, both groups are disproportionately well represented in the civil service and other prestigious jobs. Try to meet some of the Rotinese and Savunese in Kupang before traveling to their "home" islands.

Visiting Roti and Savu

Roti is easy to reach from Timor on one of the frequent ferries or occasional flights. From there to Ndao is more difficult, unless you are patient or charter a boat. There is a ferry to Savu as well, and a plane, but cancellations are frequent and the trip is long. Reaching Raijua is more difficult; like Ndao, it depends on your patience, willingness to charter, or good luck.

Ba'a, the capital of Roti, boasts a single decent—but far from fancy—place to stay, and there are a couple of cheap places as well. On Savu, there are some commercial homestays. The best way to get a feel for the culture, of course, is to find someone who will put you up, which should not be difficult.

The islands have fine beaches, but again, don't come here to lie around on one. There are other beaches much easier to reach.

Overleaf: *On Roti and Savu, dry and barren land supports large populations thanks to the* lontar *palm.* **Opposite:** *High up in the crown of a* lontar, *a tapper crushes the tip of a bud to insure the smooth flow of sweet and nutritious sap.*

SAVU

Island of Ritual and Palm Wine

Savu, a small island about halfway between Timor and Sumba, is one of the most interesting destinations in Nusa Tenggara. Like nearby Roti, and unlike most of Indonesia, the Savunese derive their staple nutrition from the *lontar* palm, and the nutritious juice of this drought-immune tree makes possible a relatively high population concentration on Savu's 461 square kilometers.

The cultural and religious life of the 55,000 Savunese, despite that most are now entered on the census as (nominal) Christians, is rich and varied, including rites of passage, seaworm festivals, harvest festivals, and violent battles with stones. The Savunese are tough and industrious, and sizeable migrant communities have grown up along the east coast of Sumba and in Kupang.

The only difficulty in visiting Savu is getting there and back in less than a week, as ferry and plane schedules (from Kupang) are less than well coordinated. One of the more adventurous ways to get there is to hop an unscheduled passenger boat, as I did a few years ago.

'All Eyes' to Savu

It was night, and the motorized schooner *Paramata*—"All Eyes"—purred quietly somewhere in the Savu Sea. There were 80 passengers on board, human passengers that is, as well as pigs—tied up, and none too happy about it—fighting cocks, and an amazing assortment of cargo: plastic cans full of petrol, bicycles, sewing machines, bags of rice and furniture. *Paramata* was a typical Indonesian inter-island boat, with every square centimeter of space taken up by bodies and goods.

In my half-sleep I tried to stretch a cramped leg. It touched a head of hair and was impatiently pushed back. Another body snuggled against my twisted back. I tried another direction with my aching foot and felt some soft flesh—was it the pretty girl I saw on board before we left the harbor at Kupang, or was it the fat old lady with her? I tried not to think about who it was or what part of his or her anatomy my foot was resting on—at least one leg was comfortable.

Dawn arrived, none too soon, and I extricated myself from the tangled mass of humanity. The island of Savu lay dead ahead, but was still a couple of hours away. Agile crew members served up breakfast, paying no heed to the squeals of the pigs accidentally stepped on or the sight of ladies vomiting over their luggage. I was hungry and ate heartily of my octopus and rice, and washed it down with a cup of good Indonesian coffee. Life was not so bad after all.

Soon we were off the shore of Savu. Small boats crowded up to us in the clear, turquoise water, vying for the disembarkation business. Pigs, roped to stretchers, squealed their protests through tied snouts. Sewing machines were wrestled overboard into the little boats. We popped down into a small boat and were rowed through the surf line to the beach. Today there is a dock, which makes things easier, if less romantic.

The lontar economy

The "palm wine" economy of the Savunese sets them (and the Rotinese) apart from the

Left: *The grandson of the raja of Seba, Savu's largest and most important district.*

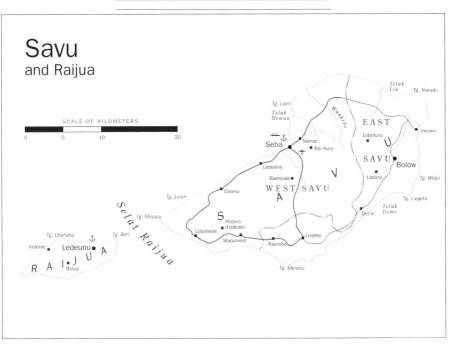

Savu
and Raijua

SCALE OF KILOMETERS

0   5   10   20

Teluk Liu   Tg. Niwudu

Tg. Laini
Teluk Hewau

Seba   Namat   ■ Rai Koro

EAST

Loboturu   ■   Jiwuwu

Ledeana

Raenyale ■

SAVU

Bolow

Tg. Leloh   Daieko

WEST SAVU

Ladara ■   *Tg. Waiju*

Tg. Mesara

Pedero
(Ledeae)

Lobohede ■

Wadumedi

Ledeke

Deme   *Teluk Deme*

Tg. Liegeta

Tg. Ubahaba   *Tg. Beh*

Kolorae   Ledeunu ●

Raerobo

Bolua

R A I J U A

Tg. Merebu

Selat Raijua

rest of the Lesser Sundas islanders. The *lontar* palm (*Borassus sundaicus*) is a common fan palm found throughout the archipelago, preferring dry climates and growing up to 30 meters high. This one tree provides the people of Savu with almost complete nutrition, as well as a variety of construction materials. Because of the extensive use of the *lontar* on the island, Savu supports more than 100 people per square kilometer, a far greater density than Timor, which receives considerably more rainfall than Savu.

What is the secret of the lontar palm? Although my informants were happy to explain the tapping and juice-gathering process, I decided to climb one of the *lontar* palms to find out for myself.

Up the tree

Although the Savunese scamper up the trees effortlessly, it is not nearly as easy as it looks, let me tell you. With an audience of several dozen delighted children and a few apprehensive adults, I stripped to my bathing suit, spit in my hands like they do in the movies and glanced up at the tree. It suddenly looked a lot higher. But there was no turning back. A man was already up there, urging me to start—"It's easy," he said. Maybe it is—for someone who's been doing it twice a day from the age of twelve.

The bottom part wasn't so bad, as there were some closely spaced notches cut into the trunk. Then the tough part began. Fortunately there were some stepping stones—literally—although for high steppers. Stones about two centimeters wide were lashed to the trunk at about 1-meter intervals. Just about when I reached the third stone, I encountered the bane of the *lontar* tapper—some vicious red ants had found a soft place to sink their strong jaws: the back of my knee.

To the apparent delight of my audience below, I attempted an acrobatic act, hanging with one hand while trying to swat at my tormentors with the other. It didn't work. I doubled up my leg, crushing a few of the beasts, but there were plenty of others to avenge their mates. Nothing to do but keep going up. I wasn't about to come down in disgrace. The man ahead of me kept asking what was the matter, but at the time I couldn't think of the word for ants in Indonesian. I ignored him and sweated my way up.

I received plenty of unneeded advice from below: "Up with your left leg"…"Hang on, you'll fall"…"Pull yourself up," etc. My arms were shaking from the strain and my style was far from smooth, but after about 5 minutes I made it to the crown of leaves. The trip takes the Savunese tappers about 15 seconds. Getting to the tangle of leaves at top didn't solve all the problems. I had to squeeze through, and the leaves have sharp edges. My hands and back were bleeding, but all I wanted was to stand on the stems of the first tough leaves and deal with my tormenting ants—finally, sweet revenge was mine.

Then I got a first-hand view of the *tuak*—palm juice—gathering technique. Between April and October, the male *lontar* palm begins to put out inflorescences; the female begins to produce fruit. The male inflorescences will eventually produce a spray of flowers, but just before they are about to form blossoms, when the inflorescence is about 40 centimeters long, the tapper squeezes it several times with a set of long wooden tongs, and then cuts off the tip. The female *lontar* must be squeezed in the same way, but earlier, before the fruit stalk can form. This squeezing produces a stunted

fruit stalk that can be cut at its tip, releasing a flow of juice. In each case, the tip is bent down and a leaf basket placed beneath it to collect the now dripping juice. Twice a day—early morning and late afternoon—the baskets have to be collected, and each time the inflorescence is cut a bit more to keep the *tuak* flowing.

Uses of the lontar

Tuak is the staple food on Savu. Some crops are grown, but the arid climate—sometimes less than 20 days of rain in the three-month rainy season—is certainly not ideal for agriculture. Mung beans and drought-resistant sorghum are cultivated on the island, but if their crops fail, a family on Savu can survive on the *tuak* from two or three trees, which are impervious to drought. In contrast, the people of Timor rely heavily on corn, and if the rains are late, or if there is a bit less rain than usual, there is famine.

During the juice producing season, all the Savunese drink several liters of fresh *tuak* every day. The surplus is boiled down to a carmel-flavored syrup in clay ovens. These are partially buried, and constructed so as to make efficient use of firewood. The froth from the boiling *tuak,* as well as some of the syrup, is fed to the pigs.

A *lontar* palm can begin to produce at 10–15 years of age, and can be tapped for up to 30 more years. Each inflorescence of a mature tree can produce 3 liters of juice each day—perhaps 500–700 liters a year, over the 5-month season, for each tree.

But *tuak* isn't all that the *lontar* palm provides. If the inflorescence is not tapped, it will blossom and, on a female tree, produce a dark-colored fruit that looks like a large eggplant. The gelatinous white interior of these palm fruits is relished.

The utility of the *lontar* does not stop when the tree quits being productive. The strong trunks are shaped into house beams. Leaves that fall off the trees are burned for fertilizer, and the fan-like leaves, perhaps a meter across, are used for roof thatch. Leaf ribs are used for house walls and partitions, as well as fences and firewood.

The Savunese used to make clothing from the tree, and their dead are still buried under mats plaited from *lontar* leaves. A variety of containers, including garden sprinklers, are fashioned from the leaves. The tree also yields the raw material for musical instruments, fans, knife sheaths, rope, and even cigarette paper.

Religion and ritual

Despite that more than 80 percent of the Savunese are officially Protestant (only some 30 percent were Christians in 1955), most Savunese participate in a traditional ritual cycle based on the lunar calendar. For administrative purposes, Savu has two subdistricts, east and west, but for religious purposes there are four: Seba (north), Mesara (west), Liae (center-south) and Timu (east).

These four spiritual domains are complemented by a fifth: tiny Raijua Island. Raijua is considered the "source" of Savu's religion, and it is believed that all customs concerning supernatural matters originated on the little island. Each of the five religious districts has a similar priestly hierarchy and ritual cycle, although the same ceremony might be performed at different times in the island's different districts.

Because of Savu's isolation, few foreign visitors ever witness the island's ritual life. When you arrive in Savu, inquire as to upcoming ritual events. There are "life cycle" ceremonies for births, marriages and deaths. There are events celebrating seasonal agricultural events.

One ritual cycle begins with the yearly appearance of the *nyale* seaworms in March, and culminates in April harvest ceremonies. The *nyale* is the same species of worm that triggers Sumba's Pasola (See "The Pasola" page 184.) This cycle includes the *hole* ritual, in which a miniature boat is pushed out to sea, with live dogs, goats, pigs and chickens—wrapped in *ikat*—as offerings.

Try to witness the *petuku hobo,* a ritual—but bloody—battle in which opposing teams hurl stones at each other. Brave men get up close, unprotected, while the cowards slink around behind shields or at the back of the pack. The event takes place in July at Loboae in the Mesara area; in November—December at Namata in the Seba district.

Even if you miss this spectacular ritual, take a look at Namata, a power spot of the traditional religion. (Get permission from the priests first.) When I arrived, priests were sitting on oval granite boulders, hilltop altars called *nada ae,* forming a circle of black megaliths outlined against the sea and sky. (See photograph page 195.)

Colonial Savu

At Namata, there is a stone with a sailing ship carved into it. The message below is worn and unreadable. Is it Captain Cook's ship? The great navigator visited Savu in 1770 and in fact came to this sacred spot, which he compared to Stonehenge. While Captain Cook—diplomatic and peaceful—was well received on Savu, the first Dutch ship, which called 122 years earlier, received a different greeting: a battalion of sword and spear wielding warriors.

Some of them brandished Savu's human meat cleavers, very effective for close-range carving. After this initial contact between Holland and Savu, relations went downhill: in 1674 a Dutch sloop went aground and all of its crew were massacred. The retaliatory Dutch expedition was unable to breach Timu's defenses, in spite of its firepower. But, to save face in the no-win situation, Holland agreed to withdraw upon receiving 240 slaves plus a payment of gold.

Soldiers and statesmen

Savunese mercenaries hired by the Dutch were key to Holland's 1749 victory at Penfui, which put a halt to the Portuguese mestizo superiority in West Timor. (See "Introducing Timor," page 205.) Among all the native auxiliary forces, the Savunese were the only ones not to run away from the adversary. Recognizing their valor, the Dutch requested armed Savunese to help them fight their battles, with a tacit agreement not to interfere in the island's internal affairs.

Left alone, they showed no interest in Christianity or education throughout most of

the 19th century. But when they did accept the outsiders' education, they did very well. Savunese have worked their way into leadership positions in the Nusa Tenggara Timor administration in Kupang in proportions far surpassing their percentage of the province's total population. Savu's most famous native son, El Tari, fought the Dutch on Java in the Indonesian independence struggle and later served as one of the province's most popular and effective governors.

Opposite: *Just a few* lontar *trees can support an entire family. The basket the tapper carries is woven from one of the palm's leafy fans.* **Above:** Lontar *juice not drunk fresh, or left to ferment, is boiled down into syrup or sugar.*

COOK'S ACCOUNT

Endeavour Calls at Savu Island

Sailing north from Australia and west from New Guinea in September 1770, Captain James Cook came upon the small island of Savu, which appeared on none of his sailing charts. He imagined that he was on the verge of a new discovery. The voyage from Botany Bay had been a difficult one; the *Endeavour* was in great need of fresh supplies. The captain and his crew, many of whom were sick and discontent, hoped that they had found another paradise like Tahiti, which they left more than a year before.

"We were upon the coast at the later end of the dry season, when there had been no rain for seven months…yet nothing can be imagined so beautiful as the prospect of the country from the ship," Cook writes.

The hills were covered with fan palms and coconut trees lined the seaside. As the *Endeavour* sailed along the north coast, it was possible to see people, houses, and great flocks of sheep. To Cook, the island offered "a temptation not to be resisted," and he resolved to send a landing party ashore.

To their surprise, the men that Cook put ashore at Seba were met by a guard of 20–30 Savunese, armed with muskets, who conducted the Englishmen to the Raja of Seba, Ama Doko Lomi Djara. There they were also introduced to Johan Christopher Lange, a European from Saxony who had lived on Savu for 10 years. Lange, Cook writes, was "distinguished from the natives only by his colour and his dress," for in every other respect he had "adopted their character and manners."

An obstacle

Lange was the representative on Savu of the Dutch East India Company, for the Dutch had already established contact with the island 122 years before Cook's arrival. And in 1756, the V.O.C. had signed formal treaties of trade with each of the island's five local rulers that specifically forbade trade with foreign vessels.

These restrictions posed a major obstacle to Cook, as his "chief business," according to his account, was "to purchase such refreshments as the island afforded," especially the water buffalo, sheep, pigs and fowl that abounded on the island. He set about this delicate business with characteristic diplomacy.

The Raja and Mr. Lange, with several attendants, were invited aboard the *Endeavour* and asked to dinner. As liquor circulated freely, "the greatest good humour and festivity" prevailed during their meal of mutton. Raja Ama Doko was presented with an English sheep, the last onboard the *Endeavour,* and one of Mr. Banks' greyhounds. Mr Lange, in turn, was given a spy-glass. As they came on deck, the visitors were escorted by "marines under arms." When the Raja asked to see them exercise, Cook ordered his men to fire three rounds. This exercise delighted Ama Doko and, as he departed for shore, Cook ordered a nine-gun salute.

The next day the captain and his men were feasted by the Savunese. The Englishmen sat down on mats and were offered a dinner served in 36 dishes "or rather baskets, containing alternatively, rice and pork; and three bowls of earthen ware, filled with the liquor in which the pork had been boiled." Cook, who had brought his own wine, reports: "We made a most luxurious meal: we thought the pork and rice excellent, and the broth not to be despised." When the captain and his officers had finished, they made way for the seamen and servants. They, too, could not finish all that was set before them.

Securing the supplies

After two days of feasting, Cook was still no nearer than before in obtaining the animals he requested. It was obvious to him that the company representative, Mr. Lange, was doing everything in his power to prevent trade with the Savunese who, Cook surmised, were anxious to provide what he required.

On the following day, Cook went ashore alone to trade with the Savunese. He recognized Manu Djami, an old man who was a kind of "Prime Minister" to the raja. Cook made him a present of a spy-glass. He then began to negotiate the price of a small water buffalo. He offered three guineas, which the owner was willing to accept, provided the raja

Opposite: *An animist priest sits on a stone* nada ae, *which is a kind of altar. Cook described these megaliths, still an integral part of Savu's religion.*

gave his approval. As the messengers were sent off, all of a sudden a hundred or more Savunese appeared, armed with muskets and lances. They bore a message from Mr. Lange—there was to be no trading that day.

Cook sensed that Manu Djami "did not heartily approve of what was doing." He grasped the old man's hand and presented him with a broadsword. Instantly, the scale tipped in the captain's favor. Flourishing his new sword, Manu Djami ordered the hostile-looking Savunese to sit down, and commanded the others to begin trading.

Cook paid 10 guineas for the first two buffalo he bought. Then he discovered that he could buy as many as he wanted for a musket each. In the end, he managed to procure "nine buffaloes, six sheep, three hogs, thirty dozen of fowl, a few limes, and some cocoanuts; many dozen of eggs, half of which however proved to be rotten; a little garlic, and several hundred gallons of palm-syrup."

A marvelous palm

Cook's mention of "several hundred gallons of palm-syrup" provides a clue to a remarkable feature of Savunese life—one that Cook described with admirable detail. From his first view of the island, Cook noted that Savu's hills "were richly clothed, quite to the summit, with plantations of the fan palm, forming an almost impenetrable grove."

And very soon after his men had gone ashore, they were offered palm wine to drink—the fresh, unfermented juice of the most abundant tree on the island. They found that "it had a sweet, but not disagreeable taste," and they even conceived the hope that this juice might help to cure sick crewmen of scurvy. The syrup that resulted from boiling down this juice, they agreed, was "infinitely superior to molasses or treacle."

This palm which so fascinated Cook is still a major source of life and sustenance for the people of Savu. Thus Cook's description of the tree and its many uses is as accurate as any that might be written today.

"The sugar is prepared by boiling the liquor down in pots of earthen ware…it is not unlike treacle in appearance, but it is somewhat thicker, and has a much more agreeable taste; the sugar is of a reddish brown…and it was more agreeable to our palates than any cane sugar, unrefined, that we ever tasted."

Cook further noted that the syrup was mixed with rice hulls, and fed to the hogs: "they grow enormously fat without taking any other food." The syrup is used to feed other animals as well, and, Cook writes, "the inhabitants themselves have subsisted upon this alone for several months, when other crops have failed, and animal food has been scarce." Finally he notes the uses to which the leaves are put: to thatch houses, and make baskets, umbrellas—even tobacco pipes.

—James J. Fox

ROTI

Lontar Palms, Surfing and a Pretty Harbor

Roti island, which is the furthest south you can go in Indonesia—11°S—is almost unknown to travelers other than a few diehard Australian surfers. The island is beautiful, with transparent water, rugged rock formations, and offshore islands fringed with white beaches.

The approximately 100,000 Rotinese live in little hamlets of thatched cottages, with neat palm rib or coral block fences around the fields and yards. Bright bougainvillea decorates the yards, and horses graze nearby. In some areas the setting is further graced by the sweeping roofs of traditional houses.

Farming and lontar palms

The great majority of the Rotinese—83 percent—are farmers. A few rivers allow continuous cropping of rice in *sawah,* or irrigated paddies, even during the dry season. Roti is now self-sufficient in rice, most of which is grown in the east. The Rotinese also raise corn, millet, sorghum and mung beans.

Water buffalo, used for bridewealth and to prepare the paddies for the rice seedlings, are now Roti's most valuable export. Cattle are also shipped out and pigs are raised for local consumption.

Agriculture on Roti depends on the life-giving, December–March rainy season, which each year brings an average of only 1,000 millimeters of rain. The limited vegetation allowed by this dry climate is dominated by the *lontar* palm.

The *lontar* palm (*Borassus sundaicus*) serves a great range of human needs, from food and drink to building materials, clothing and household articles. The tops of the *lontar* palms are tapped, and the sweet juice is drunk fresh, fermented into mild toddy (locally called *laru*), or boiled down to a rich, nourishing syrup called *gula air,* literally, "sugar water." *Gula air* is a local specialty, but jerrycans full leave on every ferry for

Kupang, destined for "expat" Rotinese. The sweet *laru* is sometimes distilled into a more potent drink, called *sopi.*

These trees are so productive that it has been estimated that just two adult trees can support an entire family. The *lontar* trees are tapped through most of the dry season, but the peak periods are in April and May, then again in September and October.

Geography and wildlife

There are no craggy mountains on Roti, and the highest elevations do not exceed 350 meters. But the island's 1,280 square kilometers offer a diversity of landscape surprising for such a small area. The soil varies from rich black to rust to chalky white. And the island has several small, shallow lakes.

Macaques, sulfur-crested cockatoos and parrots are indigenous to Roti. Crocodiles still prowl a few isolated areas. A remarkable number of deer inhabit Dana Island, in the southeast, where the spirits of the former inhabitants, massacred a few centuries back, strongly discourage human settlement.

History of Roti

Before the colonial period, many chieftains ruled over small sections of Roti. The Dutch East India company never tried to unify the island, and thus until independence little Roti was divided into 17 districts. The petty leaders of these little districts held the rather grandiloquent title of "raja," and Roti held the dubious distinction of having the highest density of rajas in the East Indies.

In 1662, the Dutch initiated treaties with the rajas, and for a while considered moving their main base in the area from Kupang to Roti. But when southwest Timor was secured, after Holland's victory over the so-called "black" Portuguese in 1749, the Dutch lost most of their interest in Roti.

Relations between the colonial power and the Rotinese were generally good (in contrast to the Timorese), but in 1756, the Dutch Commissar in Kupang sent his troops in to end a succession dispute in the Landu area. The soldiers rounded up 1,000 of the leaders and chief followers of the various factions and sold them as slaves. This discouraged, but did not put and end to, the famous Rotinese talent for intrigue and fractiousness. In fact, the Rotinese are today some of Indonesia's best lawyers.

In the 18th century, the Rotinese accepted—in part—the Dutch Reformed Church, but did not take kindly to missionary interference with their religious affairs. Teachers, however, were much in demand, even with an initial "price" of either two slaves or a ton and a half of mung beans.

Traditions today

The Rotinese possess a common language, although there are considerable regional variations in dialect. An overwhelming majority is Protestant, but no one on the island would dream of having a church wedding until after the traditional wedding.

In the past, brides had to be chosen from a particular clan of wife-givers, while the maidens of one's own clan went to a different group. The wife-giving, wife-taking circle reinforced alliances. Both bride prices and dowries were paid, in an excruciatingly complicated system. Wife-givers received a bride price of "male" goods—swords, spears, gold, water buffalos and raw meat. In turn, wife-takers received dowries of "female" items—cloth, antique beads, pigs and cooked food.

Life is far simpler today. But the bride price can still involve water buffalo, along with a substantial wad of cash. The family of a commoner might require $1,500 to $3,000 if their son wished to marry a noble girl.

Full adherence to the ancestral religion of animist practices survives only in the Boni area, but rituals to honor spirits and to ask for rain are still occasionally held elsewhere on the island. Especially along the northeast

coastal villages, men wear the unusual and distinctive *tilangga,* a plaited leaf hat sprouting an appendage like the horn of a unicorn. The hats are individually decorated with spiked fringes and even plastic flowers.

In several areas traditional houses survive. These have a thatched roof that sweeps down almost to the ground, protecting a raised living space. The ridge pole extends beyond the thatch, and is carved and occasionally painted. There are modern versions as well. The new houses have low walls of plaster or palm-leaf ribs, and thatch roofs of less imposing dimensions.

The traditional Rotinese musical instrument, the *sasando,* survives in various old and new styles. The traditional design uses nine strings and an accordion-like, palm leaf resonator. Today, some of the *sasando* are strung with up to 40 strings, and one instrument-maker in Kupang has mounted a pickup and hooked up his *sasando* to an amplifier. Unfortunately, today most of Roti's young men prefer to play ordinary guitars.

Visiting Roti

The island capital is Ba'a—the reverse apostrophe represents a glottal stop—a town of 3,000 on the west coast. The little town is a rather nondescript strip of tin-roofed buildings along a coastal road. The government administration is here, and the island's cash economy is run out of the shops here by local

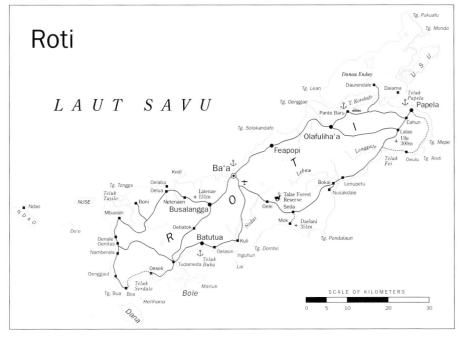

ethnic Chinese merchants. When groups come by, wealthy foreign tourists are entertained with song and dance, and souvenirs of *ikat, sasandos* and *tilanggas* are brought out.

Ba'a's inhabitants live on slightly higher ground away from the downtown, and a few local Muslims live in the eastern part of town, close to the beach. Namodale, a suburb to the west, is inhabited by weavers and jewelry makers from the island of Ndao. Ba'a's soccer field faces the most important buildings: the fading colonial style house of the area's

former rajas, the district head's offices, a church and a brand new mosque (the mosque is seldom filled, as the Muslim residents prefer their fine old one on the beach). The only decent *losmen* on the island is Ricky's, next to the church, and foreigners group here prior to exploratory jaunts.

Boni: traditional religion

A one-day swing out of Ba'a leads past some beautiful beaches and coastal scenery, and to the island's most traditional area.

Head first for Busalangga (Wednesday and Saturday markets) and continue to Oelaba (Thursday market), 25 kilometers from Ba'a (See map page 197). Oelaba is a Muslim coastal village raised above a mangrove fringed tidal zone. Along the narrow opening through the trees to the sea, the fishermen park their boats on blocks, waiting for the tide.

From Oelaba, it's some 22 kilometers to Mbueain, on Cape Tongga. Before reaching the village, a rough side road on the way leads to the Boni, the only viable remaining center of Roti's traditional religion. Some 1,000 unregenerate animists live here, and the area hosts many rituals and festivals, including a big harvest festival.

Mbueain: white pelicans

Back on the main road, the next stop is Mbueain, close to the entrance of Tasilo Bay

and near the tip of Tongga Cape. The bay opens to sandy, 200-meter-wide tidal flats with lots of coconut trees. Just west of Tasilo Bay, locals fill giant clam shells with seawater, and then collect the crust of salt.

Small Nuse Island, just offshore, is home to a few fishermen. To its south is even tinier Do'o Island, little more than a raised sandbar, where during the past few years, a flock of large white pelicans has taken up residence. Visible in the distance, between Nuse and Do'o, is Ndao Island, a historical center of itinerant gold and silver craftsmen.

Back on the main road, the next village is Oenale. Here the ubiquitous baskets of plaited leaves and red clay pots are produced. These are used all over the island gathering *lontar* sap and boiling it down into either *gula air* (syrup) or *gula merah* (red sugar). During the morning and late afternoon, you can see the clay pots steaming away, concentrating the sap.

Down the road a bit, Oenitas village sits near a crossroad with the track to the left leading inland to Tudameda, whence to Ba'a. Straight ahead is the surfer's heaven: Namberala village, also known as Dela (and Delha), the name of its former mini-kingdom. There are homestays here for young men tired of fighting for space on Bali's waves. The reef edge, where the breakers are, is a ways out—close to 200 meters from the beach. Here the waves break from April through October.

Oesili: traditional houses

Just past Boa, the truck road ends, with a view of 12 square kilometer Dana Island, just

Above, left: *Detail of a carved roof beam on a traditional Rotinese house.* **Above, right:** *The waves have sculpted these limestone formations off the west coast of Roti.* **Opposite:** *Papela harbor is the home port of tiny fishing boats that hunt* trepang, *mother-of-pearl and trochus shells.*

offshore. Only in a four-wheel-drive vehicle, on a motorcycle, or on foot can you follow the rough road along Serdale Bay that leads to Oesili village, 6 kilometers away.

The walk or rough ride is worth it, however, as between Tudameda and Oesili, almost all the houses are of the traditional type, with thatched roofs enclosing a raised shelter. The ridge poles of many of the huts sprout lateral extensions, carved to represent fish, birds and water buffalo.

Oesili village, which lies at the base of a narrow peninsula marking the end of Serdale Bay, is home to Muslim Bugis sailors and fishermen and Christian farmers. East of this peninsula, a narrow bay holds tranquil, turquoise waters.

East from Ba'a

The eastern swing out of Ba'a starts by climbing to the plateau just in back of town, past the landing field and across the central highlands. This route sees very little traffic, so you will likely have to hire a car.

A *sawah* area leads to Oele village, 20 kilometers from the capital. From there, the road continues through the Talae Forest Reserve. Here white cockatoos flock, and deer, monkeys, wild pigs and jungle fowl roam the forest floor.

The area's main village, Seda, has only a betel nut market but provides the coolest climate in Roti, thanks to its elevation. The main road out of Seda stays inland a few kilometers as it winds down to the coastal plain, a copra-producing center. Close to the coast, around Bokai village (Saturday market), men frequently wear *tilangga* hats of different styles and shapes.

A couple of kilometers from Bokai, near Nusakdale, there is a yellow sand beach at the end of a bay. The sides of the bay are lined with raised coral, full of tide pools. Here, as well as Fei Bay to the north, waves crash in during the May–September, southeast monsoon.

From Fei Bay, the road cuts inland to Lalao village, and then joins the main Ba'a–Eahun/Papela public transportation axis. A couple of kilometers past the crossroad, a massive ancient grave holds the remains of a raja of Bilba, one of east Roti's most important domains. There are two massive traditional clan houses here.

Papela: beautiful bay

The harbor of Papela village in the far east is pretty as a postcard: the blue water is crowded with graceful wooden sailing ships, waiting to make the 450-kilometer run south to the Australian coast to gather sea cucumbers (*trepang*) and trochus shells.

This beautiful harbor is itself worth the trip to Roti. The fishing village is inhabited by Muslim Bugis descended from immigrants from South Sulawesi.

NDAO

Tiny Island of Goldsmiths and Weavers

Before he is allowed to marry, a young man on the island of Ndao must master the art of working gold and silver. He must also have accumulated at least some of the gold he needs to pay the bride price. When he marries, his father-in-law gives him a polished black stone, on which to rub gold to test its carat. In this way, the young man takes his place in adult Ndao society, where every man is a gold- and silversmith.

Sailing the short distance between Roti and Ndao, just off Roti's western tip, can be extremely dangerous, as the way is marked by reefs and strong currents. Ndao's single anchorage, on the eastern side of the island, is safe only part of the year. When the southeast monsoon winds come, the harbor provides no protection and Ndao is cut off.

It takes only an hour to walk across Ndao. The island is poor and, for most of the year, dry. There are *lontar* palms to be tapped for sugary juice, but there is little land for fields or gardens and even less for grazing. On its own, Ndao seems to offer few possibilities for making a livelihood. And yet, the island is densely populated, thanks to the unusual occupation of the Ndaonese.

Expert jewelers

At the outset of the dry season, when the winds are favorable, men leave Ndao to ply their craft on other islands. Some go to Roti, others to Timor, Sumba, Flores or Savu. There they make jewelry for which they are paid in rice and small animals.

The tools of the Ndaonese are simple. An assortment of tongs, nippers and pliers, a hammer, a miniature anvil, a blowing pipe, a black assay-stone and a small scale make up a basic kit that can be carried anywhere. Most of the raw gold and silver comes from old coins that still circulate in eastern Indonesia—Dutch guilders and rijksdaalders, old Mexican gold coins, and counterfeit sovereigns from Hong Kong.

There is no single Ndaonese style; they produce for their market. On one island they may make bracelets, on another earrings, on yet another necklaces. On Roti, for example, Ndaonese produce an unusual kind of chain-like ornament called a *habas*. They draw gold into long, thin threads and then braid numerous threads to make what is literally a golden rope. Silver tobacco boxes and lime containers, decorated with geometrical or floral designs and joined by a silver chain, are another Ndaonese specialty on Roti. These are part of the equipment wealthy Rotinese use to store their betel quid ingredients.

Tradition and legend

While the men are absent, the women of Ndao spend much of their time weaving *ikat* cloth. A generation ago, the women used vegetable dyes, producing their designs in muted natural colors. Now they use commercial dyes to produce a more bold and brilliantly colored cloth. A generation ago, Ndaonese cloths resembled traditional cloths from the island of Savu. Today, they bear imitations of patterns from the neighboring island of Roti.

In legend and oral history, the Ndaonese claim ancestry from Savu. Their language is indeed close to that spoken in Savu. In time, the descendants of these ancestors divided into two groups, one called Loasana, the other Apu Lungi. Marriages take place between these two groups. For centuries, despite gradual changes in their social life, the Ndaonese preserved a religious and ceremonial life related to their homeland of Savu.

Although Ndao is only a short distance from Roti, the languages and cultures of the two islands remained distinct. The Indonesian government made Ndao an administrative part of Roti, but the Ndaonese maintained their distinctive culture. In their travels, most Ndaonese men learned a dialect of Rotinese, and some settled permanently on Roti. But those who stayed kept to the old ways.

The past two decades have brought major changes. Most Ndaonese have become Christians, and the last of the communal ceremonies that followed the ancient lunar calendar has been abandoned. Without religious differences standing between them, the Ndaonese have more and more adopted the culture of their neighbors the Rotinese.

— *James J. Fox*

Opposite: *Palm hats are traditional headgear on Roti. The T-shirt is a more contemporary touch.*

PART IX

Introducing Timor

Timor, the largest of the islands east of Bali, is a rugged, dry land that once was best-known for its valuable sandalwood. Politically, the island is divided in two. West Timor, Timor Barat, is part of the province of Nusa Tenggara Timur (NTT). East Timor, Timor Timur, made up of the northeastern half of the island and the Ambeno district (Oecussi) on the north coast of West Timor, is a separate province, annexed by Indonesia in 1976.

Timor Barat, covering about 19,000 square kilometers, had a population of 1.4 million in 1990. Its capital, Kupang, is also the capital of NTT province and the largest city in the southeastern islands. Timor Timur, or Tim-Tim, is somewhat smaller (14,600 sq. km.) and less populous, with 700,000 people in 1980. Its capital is Dili, on the north coast.

Timor island stretches along a southwest–northeast axis, and the 33,615-square-kilometer island is about 500 kilometers long and 80 kilometers wide. The southwestern tip of Timor is just 500 kilometers from Australia.

A rugged land

The central highlands concentrate much of Timor's population in what has become an eroded, almost treeless landscape. The highest point on the island is 2,963-meter Tata Mai Lau ("Highest Old Man") which is due south of Dili in East Timor. Rainfall patterns are unevenly distributed and the amount of precipitation in the same area varies considerably from year to year. Some areas along the northwest coast receive an average of less than 600 millimeters a year; towards the southeast, especially in the mountains, as much as 3,000 millimeters can pour down.

Unlike many other Indonesian islands, the soils of Timor are unenriched by volcanic ash. The poor, eroded soils, combined with the erratic rainfall, have always made agriculture a risky proposition. And the problem has increased lately, as the end of tribal warfare, and the better medical facilities and transportation services of the 20th century have produced overpopulation in some areas, putting great pressure on weak soils.

The traditional method of agriculture used here is slash-and-burn, wherein the burnt scrub temporarily enriches the soil. The field is farmed for a season or two, and then abandoned to the weeds and shrubs for several years. It is then burned, and put into use again. Population pressures have led farmers to shorten this crucial fallow period, to the detriment of the soil and its fertility.

Prehistory and languages

Material evidence shows that the first inhabitants of Timor, of the Australoid race, practiced hunting and gathering at least 14,000 years ago. Giant rats were their main prey, becoming extinct around the birth of Christ. About 5,000 years ago, the Austronesians, of the Mongoloid race, started arriving in Timor. Oral histories tell of migrations from western Indonesia as well as from Seram (in Central Maluku) to the north. Over the next several centuries, these migrants brought with them pottery-making techniques, millet and perhaps rice cultivation, pig husbandry, goats, dogs and monkeys. The expanding agriculture led to the cutting of large tracts of forest, especially after the introduction of metal during the first millennium B.C.

Today, there are some 18 distinct languages spoken on Timor (with the majority in East Timor), several of which are non-Austronesian. The Atoni and the Tétun are the two numerically most important ethnic groups. The Atoni (sometimes just called Timorese) live in the mountains and make up close to half of west Timor's population. The

Overleaf: *Leaf raincoats protect these highland Timorese. During the brief wet period, the brown countryside dons a thin green coat of vegetation.*
Opposite: *Dancers in ritual garb strike heroic poses with ancient heirloom swords.*

400,000-odd Tétun are split by the border dividing the two provinces.

The Tétun are East Timor's most numerous single ethnic group, and a grammatically simplified version of their language has become the province's lingua franca, understood by about 70 percent of the population.

The Indonesian language is used exclusively in schools and administration. Although some middle-aged and many older people in relatively isolated areas do not understand Indonesian, almost all the younger Timorese speak it well and it has gained wide acceptance everywhere.

The sandalwood trade

Timor's sandalwood may have been traded directly by the Chinese from the seventh century A.D. onward. Much of the commerce in the fragrant, valuable wood was concentrated in the hands of Arab and Chinese merchants. The first written reference to Timor's sandalwood comes in traveler Fei Hsin's 1436 *General Account of Peregrinations at Sea.* Fei notes in his account that the mountains of Timor were thickly covered with the trees. The fragrant white sandalwood (*Santalum album*) was used by the Chinese for joss sticks, perfume, fans, boxes and coffins.

Today, most of the sandalwood is crushed, boiled and distilled to extract its oil, used for fixing perfumes. Locally, a small amount of the sandalwood is processed into crude carvings and fans. The oil is exported to France and the United States, while the waste powder is sold to Hong Kong, Taiwan and Singapore for joss sticks.

Sandalwood first drew the Portuguese to Timor in 1515, only three years after their conquest of Malacca. Just seven years later, in January of 1522 the remnants of Ferdinand Magellan's crew anchored the *Victoria* off the island. In a brief note, Antonio Pigafetta, Magellan's chronicler, reported that the hot-blooded Portuguese had already contaminated the Timorese with syphilis.

At first the Portuguese were not allowed by local rulers to set up any permanent posts on Timor. Not least among the deterrents was the Timorese penchant and talent for head-hunting. But later in the century, Antonio Taveira, a Dominican Friar, arrived on nearby Flores, where he began proselytizing in Larantuka on Flores and built a fortress on Solor to keep out Muslim attackers.

Portuguese trade in the region grew after the fort was built in 1566. Most of this commerce soon came to be concentrated in the hands of the locally powerful mestizo—mixed Portuguese and Timorese—families, called Topasses, perhaps from the Dravidian/Tamil word for "interpreter." The Dutch used the derogatory "Black Portuguese." Timor's sandalwood brought extremely high prices in Canton. By 1640, the Topasses—based in the region of Larantuka in eastern Flores—had a virtual monopoly on the market.

The Bugis Muslims who had participated in the sandalwood trade until the Portuguese showed up tried to force the Iberians from the region. However, superior ships (and the chance arrival of a Portuguese fleet during a 1602 siege) kept the Portuguese ensconced in the region.

But the Dutch were not so easily repelled, and in 1613 captured the fort at Solor, but could not take Larantuka. (See "Introducing Flores," page 119.) The Dutch set up their first post on Timor in 1653, at Kupang, getting rid of the few Portuguese there. The town grew slowly around Fort Concordia.

Meanwhile, through local alliances and marriages, as well as brute force, the Topasses maintained their monopoly on Timor's sandalwood. Their base was at Lifao, in Ambeno (formerly Oecussi). For a long time no fort or permanent settlement was established there, and only very gradually did Lifao become a small fixed settlement.

Europeans, Topasses and Timorese

Over the next two centuries, power in the region was determined by four factions: the Topasses, the Portuguese, the Dutch, and the Timorese. Alliances shifted frequently, especially among the 60 or so Timorese rajas or *liurai,* who usually supported one or another of the European groups rather than banding together. While conflicts over the trade went on, Timorese society—a strict hierarchy of nobles, commoners and slaves—went on more or less undisturbed.

The Dutch East India Company or V.O.C. (Vereenigde Oostindische Compagnie) was busy in Batavia (now Jakarta) establishing its monopoly on cloves, and had little energy for Timor. In 1656 the Dutch sent a force to Timor under commander Arnold de Valming, but his soldiers were soundly thrashed at Amarasi by the Topasses and their Timorese allies. The Dutch didn't bother to seek revenge. For the next century they maintained their presence in Kupang and engaged only in some mild scheming with disaffected Timorese.

Timor was claimed as a Portuguese colony, ruled out of Goa, India. But the Iberians had little real control in the region, and the Topasses reaped the profits from the sandalwood trade. Thus, in 1701, the Viceroy of Goa appointed the first governor to Timor, Antonio Coelho Guerreiro. With a small force from Portuguese Macao, he succeeded in somewhat undermining Topass control.

The Dutch step in

In 1749, the Dutch took advantage of the rivalries and defeated their competitors at Penfui near Kupang. They were helped in this effort by native mercenaries from Ambon, Timor itself, and especially some tough warriors from Savu Island.

After the trouncing by the Dutch, the Topasses concentrated on their Iberian rivals at Lifao, in Ambeno (then Oecussi), setting up a blockade so efficient that, in 1769, the governor was forced to move—taking the entire colony of 1,200. The Iberians were allowed to leave by sea, and they travelled to Dili, where the new "White Portuguese" capital was established in the malaria-ridden swamps. Worst of all, Dili was far from the center of the sandalwood trade.

In 1869, when naturalist Sir Alfred Russel Wallace stopped in Timor, he noted: "The Portuguese government of Timor is a most miserable one … after 300 years of occupation, there has not been a mile of road made beyond the town." The Portuguese who served in the colonial administration had their own name for the island: Ante-camara do Inferno, or "Gateway to Hell."

By the latter half of the 18th century, the situation was thus: the Dutch controlled a bit of southwestern Timor, the Portuguese controlled portions of the northeast, and the Topasses controlled Oecussi and west-central Timor between them. Much of the sandalwood trade was still in Topass hands, and the Topasses also controlled the export of slaves, Timor's other main commodity.

The 19th century brought drastic changes to Timor. Over-cutting just about destroyed all the sandalwood trees. Then the Portuguese, in 1851, sold their claims to (and nonexistent control of) Flores and the islands to its east—Solor, Adonara, Pantar and Alor—to the Dutch, keeping only the areas of Timor that were under their sphere of influence. This led to an initial border agreement in 1858, which created the Portuguese and Dutch Timor division. The 1913 Hague Round Table Conference finally fixed these boundaries, which existed until Indonesia annexed East Timor in 1976.

World War II and Independence

The Japanese landed on Timor in 1942. While they quickly overcame the Aussies and a few Dutch, in East Timor it was a very different story. There, 400 Australian commandos who had been stationed there since Christmas did not spread out any welcome mats. The commandos, with a great deal of support from the Timorese, fought a protracted guerilla war against the Japanese outposts.

Amazingly enough, in three years of fighting, only 40 of the tough Australians died. Unfortunately the Timorese, who were shocked and angered by the brutality of the Japanese soldiers, suffered greatly from starvation and retribution from the occupying force: some 70,000 died during the war.

The post-war winds of change brought independence to Indonesia, and the new nation inherited West Timor along with the rest of the Dutch colonies. The Salazar dictatorship in Portugal retained East Timor, at least until the "Carnation Revolution" in 1974 replaced the right-wing regime with an anti-colonial, left-leaning one. In December of 1975, fearing a left-wing government in East Timor, the Indonesian government invaded and later annexed the territory.

Right: *An Atoni hut in the Ambeno district.*

WETAR

Laliki

Ilwaki

Lirang

Selat Wetar

Kisar

MALUKU
TIMOR TIMUR

Atuaro

Maumela

MALUKU
TIMOR TIMUR

Ombai

Tg. Banduro

Baucau

Buihomau

Irara

Tg. Hero

Tutuala

Tg.
Fatukama

Metinaro

Manatuto

Vemasse

Lautem

Desa Rasa

P. Jaco

Dili

Hera

Lamsana

Laleia

Military
airport

Ili Haumau

Los Palos

*Danau
Surubel*

Aileu

Venilak

Laga

Quelicai

Lekumau
1236m

Luro

nera

Lacluba

Laclubar

Mundo
Perdido +
1790 m

Ossu

Matedia +
2315m

efoho

EAST TIMOR

Lacluta

Uatocarbau

Hiomar

abe

Tata
Mai Lau
2963m
+

Maubesi

Viqueque

Uatolari

Hatabuilico

Tg. Beako

ana

Ainaro

Same

Tg. Lalete

i

LAUT TIMOR

Timor

SCALE OF KILOMETERS

0   20   40   80   120

KUPANG

A Bustling Provincial Capital

Kupang, the capital of Nusa Tenggara Timur province, is a lively town of 200,000 people, easily the largest in the region. The city stretches along the sea and climbs a low hill before spreading inland near Timor Island's southwest extremity.

The heart and soul of Kupang is the area around the *bemo*/bus terminal and the main one-way thoroughfare, Jalan Siliwangi (which becomes Jalan Garuda). Here the road heads along the coast to the fish market and beyond.

Mornings and afternoons you will see men walking around with two large leaf buckets, each pleated like an accordion, balanced across their shoulders. The containers hold *tuak,* or "toddy," the mildly fermented juice of the *lontar* palm. The new *tuak,* 5¢ for a drink out of a *lontar* leaf cup, tastes sweet and refreshing. (Unfortunately it is sometimes diluted with unboiled water, which can give you a nasty case of the runs.) As the day rolls on, the juice continues to ferment, and eventually turns into an alcoholic beverage that can pack a sneaky wallop.

Charging around the downtown area, Kupang's irrepressible *bemo* drivers propose to every pretty girl they see. The *bemos* of Kupang had enjoyed some fame for their elaborate custom paint jobs: portraits of movie stars, beauty queens and in one case, a grinning, camel-aviator. Unfortunately, a recent tax got rid of these bright paintings, although some of the *bemos* now sport scale models on their roofs—one had a 747 jet sprouting out of its roof, another a tank.

The *bemos* advertise their territories in a complex code that involves numbers on the roof panel. It's more complicated than the New York subway, so it's better to ask a local which number *bemo* to take to your destination, or the closest point to it.

Before moving out of Kupang to explore the nearby islands or the interior of Timor, spend some time looking over the city and its immediate vicinity. This can be done in a day with a rented car or taxi ($4/hr., 2 hrs minimum) or— more hassle but far cheaper—by *bemo.*

Old Kupang

There is almost nothing left of historical Kupang. Perhaps the oldest physical remains are the graves of the raja of Taebenu and his family, located on an in-town hilltop called Mautasi. At the site, which is only accessible by a dirt road, Raja Tanof rests in a long, semi-circular grave. The grave has been replastered, and has a faded plaque.

The seal of the Dutch East India Company, the V.O.C., is still visible on the plaque, which is dated 1736 and 1737, probably the dates of the deaths of the raja and his wife. The graves of the family, unadorned, are nearby. The hilltop gravesite offers a good view of Kupang city.

Only a large, flat carved stone remains of Fort Concordia, built by the Dutch in 1653, but it still serves as the site of a garrison, now for the Indonesian army. Depending on the mood of the young soldiers on guard duty, you can take a look at the stone, just to the right of the barracks. The stone carries its original seal. To photograph the stone, however, might require your passport and an interrogation by a superior.

On the town side of Fort Concordia the Air Mata creek flows into the sea. This is where, in 1789, Captain Bligh's 41-day, 3,816-nautical-mile open boat voyage from the Tonga Islands ended, when he was kicked off H.M.S. *Bounty* by mutineers. In World War II, Japanese submarines entered the mouth of Air Mata during cleanup operations.

The oldest church in town is Gereja Kota Kupang, near the downtown bus terminal. Originally built in 1873, the church was reconstructed in 1987, at which time it got a new front porch and a fresh coat of paint. Next to the church is an old grave marker, with the same seal and design as the one at the fort. You don't need to pass an interview with the commander to photograph this one.

An old Dongson drum

Don't miss Kupang's provincial museum. Here you will see an excellent display of *ikat* cloths from the region, scale models of the traditional houses of East Nusa Tenggara, and weapons, musical instruments, and

Opposite: *Kupang's old seaside houses sit on solid outcroppings of uplifted coral limestone.*

carved wooden and stone ancestor figures. Perhaps the highlight of the museum is an excellent Dongson-style drum found on Alor Island. These brass drums, which are still something of a puzzle to archeologists, have been found in a few scattered locations throughout the archipelago. They are styled after and present the motifs of the Dongson period—circa 300 B.C.–200A.D.—in North Vietnam. (See "Alor," page 160.)

The museum also has some interesting seashell fossils and a small collection of Chinese porcelain. Best of all, there is usually a knowledgeable, English-speaking guide around to explain things. The NTT Museum, on Jalan Perintis Kemerdekaan, is open from 8 a.m. to 4 p.m. Monday through Thursday, and Saturday. It is closed on Fridays, Sundays and holidays.

The museum is located in an area convenient to reach as several *bemos* work the area. The eastern part of the city is developing, with some government offices and the Sasando Hotel. The new Walikota out-of-town bus terminal is also located to the east, near the museum, so *bemos* are plentiful.

Ikat and dance

The Loka Binkra Crafts Center, just outside of Kupang heading east towards the airport, is also a must-see. The large shop in front of the center sells *ikat* from all over the province, good quality cloth at reasonable prices. Some work is done on the premises, using traditional backstrap looms and a foot-operated horizontal loom that has been brought from Java.

The pavilion in back serves as the venue for traditional dances, which can be commissioned to suit your schedule. The cost depends on the number of performers—usually 5–10—and runs in the $30 range. You can get soft drinks here and the souvenir shop sells local specialties like dried and shredded meat, coconut and palm sugar wafers, and the famous local honey.

The Loka Binkra Crafts Center is east of Kupang on the main road; the center is at the 8 kilometer marker, just before the turnoff to El Tari Airport. Loka Binkra is open every day from 8 a.m. to 2 p.m., and 4 p.m. to 8 p.m.

Visiting a fishing platform

On the way into Kupang from the airport, few visitors miss the sight of the strange contraptions that dot the sea along the coastal road into town. These are fishing platforms called *bagan*s. Although found elsewhere in the Lesser Sundas, none are as gigantic as those off Kupang. Fishing off a *bagan* takes place at night, and involves dropping a net straight down under the structure, and using up to 50 lanterns to attract fish and squid, and then hauling the net straight up again.

The platform rests on two long, narrow rails, perhaps 15 meters long, reach down 3-5

meters below the surface. Above water, the hulls are connected by a platform, with a little cabin amidships. Two or three masts, and a profusion of guy ropes, turn the *bagan* into a circus tent lacking only the canvas. The net is connected to a complicated series of pulleys, capstans and winches, which are required when the 15–25 man crew needs to raise or lower the net. These nets are remarkable, with a mesh so fine you can't even poke a match through it.

Get a canoe to take you to one of the *bagans,* some of which are operated by Bajau, former sea nomads, and spend part of the night on one to see the hauling up of the net. On a night when the moon is full or near full, activity ceases because the lanterns are then not strong enough to attract the catch.

After the *bagan,* if you're up early, start with the morning fish market, beachside, just off the main road going east from the bemo terminal (see map). Lots of activity and for the best view of the boats coming in with the catch, get down to the waterline around 6:30 a.m. Just past the market area, a seaside temple serves as the religious center for the 5,000-odd Balinese community in Kupang.

Lasiana Beach

While Semau island has some nice beaches and snorkeling, it is a bit far for just a swim. Locals prefer Lasiana Beach, just 11 kilometers east of town. Past the airport turnoff and

a kilometer off the paved road to Atambua is a wide, 2-kilometer-long sandy beach. Lasiana is deserted on weekdays, and crowded on weekends. But even on weekends there are almost no bathers, as most people come to the site for a family picnic, and stalls and venders offer snacks like coconuts, grilled corn and soft drinks.

A bit past the Lasiana Beach turnoff, fruit and vegetable stalls line the Atambua roadside. One set of stalls is at kilometer 13, another a half kilometer further. Here all the fresh produce is gathered into bundles worth 1,000 rupiahs, hence the market's name, Pasar Seribu (*seribu* means one thousand).

Eight kilometers past the market, almost exactly opposite the 21-kilometer marker, a dirt road leads off to the huts of Oebelo's traditional salt-makers. Here seawater is hauled ashore in push-carts, filtered and boiled over a wood fire to yield sea-salt, worth 16¢ a kilo.

Sandalwood factories

Just 7 kilometers out of Kupang, at Batuplat, are two modern sandalwood factories. Unfortunately, however, these are not open to visitors. The unprotected saw blades and the high-pressure steam used to process the wood present too much of a hazard. The oil distilled here is shipped to Jakarta, and then to France and the United States, where it is used to fix volatile scents.

There is a less mechanized sandalwood factory north of town, C.V. Horas, which you can visit. The shop sells knick-knacks—rosaries, fans, and small carvings ($4-6)—as well as incense ($4 for ten coils) and joss sticks ($4 a kilo). The little factory is on the airport road, just beyond the Atambua turnoff.

World War II relics

Nostalgia tours have been organized in Timor for Australian and Japanese veterans of World War II, but for visitors curious to see old wrecks and bunkers, there are few around Kupang. There is a shore battery 200 meters off the main road to Atambua, about 4.5 kilometers out of town. A dirt road leads to the old gunner's station. A little paved road heading inland from the new Ausindo Hotel leads to two more bunkers, which were built into caves. 23,000 tank-backed Japanese landed near Kupang in February 1942 and quickly finished off the mostly Aussie defenders.

The ferry terminal

Heading southwest from Fort Concordia and the downtown on Jalan. Pahlawan, you pass

the New Ausindo Hotel where a rooftop restaurant-bar offers the best sunset views. Continuing on, you pass a small boat anchorage, a large cement factory and finally reach Tenau harbor, the main shipping port for West Timor, 8 kilometers from downtown.

A bit further along, the road branches to the right. Here is the Bolok terminal, where large ferry boats make regularly scheduled runs to Kalabahi on Alor, Larantuka on the far eastern tip of Flores, Ende, on the coast of south-central Flores, and Roti and Savu islands west of Timor. A *bemo* to the terminal costs 30¢ from downtown, and the ride is 13 kilometers.

The Bolok Caves

About 3 kilometers past the ferry landing are the four Gua Bolok, the Bolok caves. These are really weathered sinkholes, and a swim in one of the clear, spring-fed pools is a refreshing diversion. At the height of the rainy season, late January through March, a myriad of fireflies appears at the caves at night.

The four caves are similar, having been formed from the extensive uplifted coral rock of the area. The first two caves, Uihani ("Sleeping Water" in Helong) and Uiklaus ("Cactus Water") are within a half kilometer of the turnoff to the ferry terminal; just continue straight ahead on the dirt road instead of taking a right to the terminal. The cave of Uiamnisi (named after a local bloke) requires a short walk, but it has the largest of the pools and is the best for swimming. Uilabahang ("Clear Water") is a bit further yet.

The descent routes through the sinkhole openings are very slippery during the rainy season, and as the water level lies some 50 meters below ground level, caution is recommended. A flashlight is essential to the descent, and even better is a strong underwater light, which is the only way the cave formations, which lie in the clear depths of the pools, can be revealed.

At Uihani, we got a bit of a shock as we played the light through a small passage and saw a tangle of bras, panties and other clothes. According to our guide, we stumbled upon the place where many local folks do their washing.

Further afield: weaving, snorkeling

The center of the Amarasi weaving district is 30 kilometers from Kupang at Baun, which also has a Saturday market. Don't expect much traditional cloth here, however, as the

artisans now use machine-spun thread and synthetic dyes. Here, the days of hand-spun cotton and vegetable dyes are over. But the venerable backstrap loom is still in use. Past Baun and near Burain, an easily accessible cave contains traces of World War II Japanese use. Also on the south coast, but reached by a different (paved) road from Kupang, Tablolong offers wide beaches—especially a bit to the east, at a spot called Air Cina (Chinese water).

Pulau Semau is a 45 square kilometer island that serves to shelter the port of Tenau. About 10,000 people live on Semau, in 9 villages. The dry, rugged island offers some good snorkeling, diving and there are a couple of rustic, but comfortable, bungalow-style hotels. Paths along the shoreline provide for nice walks, but bring a hat and plenty of water. A clear pool on the island, surrounded by trees is a fine place for a cool dip.

The main economic activities here are fishing, growing corn and raising cattle. There is also a small-scale salt-making operation here. Giant *Tridacna* clam shells are filled with seawater and set out to evaporate to provide salt for seasoning.

Opposite: *A small sailboat slowly tacks toward shore in Kupang bay.* **Above, left:** *A Japanese shore battery built during World War II.* **Above, right:** *Elvis Presley croons from a bemo shuttling passengers along Kupang's seafront.*

COLONIAL KUPANG

Debauchery and Grace in the Dutch Port

On June 14, 1789, Captain Bligh, exhausted and half-starved after a voyage of nearly 4,000 miles in an open boat, reached his intended destination. The captain was hailed by the firing of two cannon, and welcomed ashore. "[We] arrived safe in an hospitable port," he later wrote in his account of the voyage, "where every necessary and comfort were administered to us with a most liberal hand."

Bligh and his ragged crew had reached Kupang, then a Dutch East India Company settlement nestled within a wide bay at the western end of Timor. Bligh was not the first, nor was he to be the last European navigator to seek refuge in Kupang. As one of the most hospitable outposts in the eastern islands, for centuries Kupang served as a port of call for famous explorers: Captains Bligh, Nicholas Baudin, William Dampier, Apollonius Scotte and many others.

Fort Concordia

The indomitable Apollonius Scotte, sailing the Dutch East India Company ship *Half Moon,* explored the bay of Kupang, and in 1613 signed the first Dutch treaty with a local Timorese ruler. Henry Hudson sailed the same ship in 1609 when he first entered the sheltered harbor of New York.

All early Dutch claims to Timor date from this treaty, but it was decades before the company—Vereeningde Oostindische Compagnie, or V.O.C.—decided to erect a fort and establish a small garrison there. In the meantime, Portuguese Dominicans appear to have begun building, and then abandoned a small fortification at Kupang. On this embryonic foundation the Dutch built the fort that they named "Concordia."

Despite its optimistic name, however, Concordia was certainly not peaceful. Hostile Timorese, allied with the Portuguese, surrounded the fort and Concordia continually faced the threat of attack. An expeditionary force led by Arnoldus de Vlaming van

Oudshoorn went into the interior to subdue the Timorese, but returned in disarray, routed by the enemy. At this point, the company ordered that Concordia be abandoned, and the garrison moved to nearby Roti island. The order, however, was never carried out.

On September 21, 1699, William Dampier attempted to put his *Roebuck* in at Kupang, but was turned away. From the safety of a sloop with 40 armed soldiers, the governor of the fort explained his caution to Dampier. It seems that hospitality had been offered two years before to French sailors, who then turned out to be pirates and attacked the Dutch, seizing Fort Concordia and plundering the town of Kupang.

In the end, the Dutch provided Dampier with water, on the condition he kept his ship at a good distance from the fort. Only after lying at anchor at the far end of the bay for some weeks, performing repairs to his ship, was Dampier invited ashore to dine with the governor.

"[T]here was plenty of very good Victuals," the captain writes, "and well drest; and the Linnen was white and clean; and all the Dishes and Plates, of Silver or fine China. I did not meet any where with a better Entertainment, while I was aboard; nor with so much Decency and Order. Our Liquor was Wine, Beer, Toddy, or Water, which we liked best after Dinner."

'Drinking and fornication'

Much seems to have had changed in Kupang in the preceding decades. In 1665, V.O.C. merchant Anthony Hurt described Dutch conduct in Kupang as "foul, slovenly and unregulated...with drunken drinking and fornication."

Even more than a century later, passing along the coast of Timor in September 1770, Cook turned his *Endeavour* away from Kupang, because of its reputation, and instead put in at the nearby island of Savu. Here Cook discovered that the rulers of the island were allied with the Dutch, who had successfully turned back the last effort to drive them from Kupang and were now expanding their influence in the area. (See "Cook's Account,"

Opposite: *A French etching of a "Slave Market" in Kupang. It must have taken quite a bit of imagination to represent a slave market in such an idyllic way, but traffic in bodies was a fact of life in eastern Indonesia. Even the Dutch authorities in Kupang required a payment of two slaves for every school teacher they sent to Roti.*

page 194.)

After Bligh's return to England, the *Pandora* was sent out under the command of Captain Edward Edwards to comb the Polynesian islands in search of the mutineers. Two loyal members of Bligh's original crew, Hayward and Hallett, were appointed to the ship.

After capturing the mutineers on Tahiti, Edwards attempted to return via the Endeavour Straits, but on August 29, 1791, the *Pandora* broke up on a reef. Once again the nearest port of refuge was Kupang.

On September 17, for the second time in just over two years, Hayward and Hallett arrived in Kupang, ragged and starved, in an open boat, with the *Pandora*'s crew and at least some of the *Bounty* mutineers. They were greeted by Timotheus Wanjon, the very same officer who had welcomed Captain Bligh in 1789.

A remarkable escape

By now the Dutch in Kupang were becoming accustomed to the arrival of English castaways, and had standing orders to provide for their needs and to assist them in their return passage.

Kupang was the nearest European port to the convict colony founded at Port Jackson in New South Wales in 1788. On March 28, 1791, a man named Bryant with his wife Mary, two children and seven other convicts escaped from the colony and made their way in a small boat along the coast of Australia and then across the Timor sea to Kupang—a voyage almost as long and as arduous as that of Bligh.

Bryant introduced himself as Captain Martin, and the occupants of the boats as the only survivors of a ship wrecked on a reef to the southeast of Timor. The Dutch accepted his story and advanced Bryant money for himself and his party.

Unfortunately, Bryant's boatswain—out of drunkenness, spite or both—revealed the true story of their escape, and the Dutch locked the party up.

"[W]hen all the circumstances of this boat and its crew are considered, they will be thought as wonderful as those of Bligh or Edwards," writes Captain Amasa Delano, a Yankee skipper who visited Kupang in the *Massachusetts* just after the convicts had been taken away by Captain Edwards.

According to Captain Delano, Kupang in the 1790s was just this side of paradise:

"A beautiful river runs through the town, coming down from the country and passing over picturesque falls. A short distance from the mouth of the river is one of these falls, where we used to resort in the afternoon to bathe.

"Ladies and gentlemen were collected; male and female servants prepared the tea, the smoking apparatus, bottles and glasses,

and the bathing clothes; and thus we set out for the place of the bath, while some of the servants played on instruments of music, and others sang.

"The bank of the river was covered with beautiful rows of fragrant trees, under which small houses were placed to afford convenient shelter for throwing off, or putting on clothes.... Half an hour, or three quarters, we often spent in the water.... After dressing in the small houses the company assembled at tables which were spread under the trees, with a charming prospect before them, aromatic gales around them, and luxuries for their repast.

"The tables were furnished with fruits and liquors of exquisite flavor. The Dutch have the merit of adapting everything to their taste in their East India settlements. A visit to them in succession is a perpetual feast."

The Napoleonic years

Towards the end of the eighteenth century, Kupang was rocked by a succession of political changes. The V.O.C. was going broke, and with the formation of the French-dominated Batavian Republic back home, local Dutch outposts came to depend increasingly on their own resources. During the Napoleonic Wars, the British and Dutch were on opposite sides.

In 1797 the British seized Fort Concordia, but were forced to relinquish it to a native force loyal to the Dutch. Some reports state that a similar failed attempt took place in 1810 as well. Only in 1811 were the British able to gain full control of Kupang, and they didn't return it to the Dutch until after 1815.

At the turn of the century a French expedition under Napoleonic orders was instructed to visit Timor on its expedition of exploration. The *Géographe* and the *Naturaliste,* commanded by Captain Nicholas Baudin, arranged to rendezvous in Kupang in 1801—the *Géographe* arriving first with Péron and Freycinet on August 18, and the *Naturaliste* a month later on September 21.

Péron, who had time to explore the town of Kupang and meet its inhabitants, describes his reception by the wife of the former governor of Timor, Madame van Este. He was no less rapturous of the town than was Captain Delano.

"The mistress of the house, a Malay, and a native of Amboyna, waited to receive us, standing under the gallery: she was dressed in a rich and beautiful *pagne* or wrapper. On her left hand stood about thirty young

The tables were furnished with fruits and liquors of exquisite flavor. A visit to [the Dutch settlements] is a perpetual feast.

— Captain Delano, 1791

women, elegantly clothed in cotton wrappers and white corsets, with their long black hair platted and folded round the head. On her right, stood several male slaves in jackets and white pantaloons: in the lower gallery were other male slaves in long red cloaks.

"This regular order, these singular uniform costumes, the young girls dressed with so much neatness, and who appeared like so many young nymphs surrounding their goddess, the beauty of the scene, the coolness of the adjoining forest, the soft murmur of the stream, the view of the ocean, on the shore of which this delightful habitation was situated; in short, all united to present at once every thing we could conceive of noble, grand, beautiful and picturesque, in a manner that perfectly enchanted us."

"All helped to remind us Frenchmen," he writes, "of the beautiful scene of the toilet of Venus in the ballet of Paris."

The decline of Kupang

Voyagers continued to visit Kupang regularly throughout the 19th century, but with the demise of the V.O.C. and the establishment of Dutch colonial rule, descriptions of Kupang reveal dramatic changes. The old style of living came to an abrupt end in 1816. Captain Freycinet, who was as charmed by Kupang as Péron on their first visit, is almost bitter in his 1818 account.

"The Dutch government, probably, never thinks of this colony except when it has a governor to appoint, which must occupy attention but a few moments. The town has two quarters. The first is the Chinese quarter. This is the richest; yet one of our shops, of the second rank, contains twenty times as much wealth. The second is the Malay quarter, and consists of hovels.

"It is protected by a fort called Concordia, studded with cannon, nailed up, and defended by ten men, a couple of muskets and some rocks. At our arrival, the governor's secretary, M. Thilmann, requested us not to salute the fort, as he should have to regret being unable to return our civility, the keys of the powder magazine not having been entrusted to him. At present a single brig would make itself master of the town."

Philip King, who visited in the same year, presents a similar picture:

"The principal street, as is common in most Dutch towns, is shaded by an avenue of trees, which forms an agreeable walk, and, is a great ornament to the place: at the upper end of this street is the Company's garden, but its ruinous state shews that it has long since ceased to be cultivated for the purpose for which it was originally intended."

By the time Captain Stokes visited Kupang in the *Beagle* in 1840, he was surprised to see so great a deterioration of Fort Concordia. Traces of the old V.O.C. buildings were few; and eventually even the walls of Concordia tumbled in an earthquake.

A polyglot town

But the company did more than build buildings. It laid the foundation for the polyglot town that Kupang has remained to this day. Not just the European navigators stopped here—Solorese, Rotinese and Savunese also came, by the hundreds, in small sailing ships. Chinese came to trade in Kupang, many of them moving to the town from older settlements on Timor.

Others came from Sulawesi— Butonese, Buginese and Macassarese. The Bajau Laut, the wandering fishing folk of eastern Indonesia, were also attracted to the vicinity of the town. Even a contingent of Philippine soldiers—the Papangers—transferred to Kupang. In addition, various groups of Timorese descended from the mountains to settle in and around the town.

It was V.O.C. policy to assign each ethnic group a portion of land to serve as its own community. Loyal allies of the Company were particularly favored. The Rotinese were granted the beach to the west of Fort Concordia, the Savunese the beach to the east, and the Solorese the beach directly beside the Savunese.

Until recently, each of these groups jealously guarded their rights to these V.O.C. entitlements. Today, however, Pantai Solor— the Solorese Beach—has become the site of Kupang's fish market, and a harbor for sailing *prahu* has been established in front of the Rotinese beach of Namosain.

Today, *bemos* race through town with pop

> *The Dutch government, probably, never thinks of this colony except when it has a governor to appoint. A single brig would make itself master of the town.*
> — Freycinet, 1818

music blaring from their stereos. But the routes they take traverse the sites of the old settlements. From Air Nona, where the Savunese settled, to Mardeka, where the Company's free-soldiery—the Mardijkers— were once located, to Benteng, the old fort, is a short lesson in the history of Old Kupang.

A bustling melting-pot

Since the days of the V.O.C., the language of Kupang has been a dialect of Malay. This dialect, which truncates Indonesian words by the omission of final syllables, is now saturated with local loanwords. It is so distinctive that it is simply called "Bahasa Kupang"—the language of Kupang. Anyone who settles in Kupang quickly adopts this lively and direct form of local speech.

Some sights have not changed at all since the time of the V.O.C. We know this from the many superb drawings done of the town by the artists who accompanied early expeditions. In 1818 Kung, for example, refers to the crowds in the street and the sight of women carrying water in vessels made out of the broad part of the fan palm leaf.

Petit, who accompanied the 1801 Baudin expedition, drew a portrait of a woman carrying two leaf buckets; Arago, who accompanied Freycinet in 1818, created a similar drawing. A visitor to Kupang today can see the same sight: young girls carrying leaf buckets filled with fresh palm juice, which they sell to early morning shoppers in town.

Although traditional costume is no longer as important as a means of social identification as it used to be, nevertheless one can still recognize Savunese, Rotenese, and Timorese from different parts of the island by the telltale elements of their dress. These simple hints from a sarong, or a *slendang,* or perhaps a palm-leaf hat, are reminders of Kupang's rich past and of the company that founded a town on a bay in Timor.

— *James J. Fox*

VISITING WEST TIMOR

Lively Markets, Weaving and Great Vistas

Somebody in a hurry to cross West Timor to East Timor could cover the 280 kilometers from Kupang to Atambua in a night bus and reach Dili, East Timor a few hours later. But why rush? A leisurely ride across West Timor leads through ruggedly beautiful mountain scenery and takes you to centers of traditional weaving. In addition, we suggest two side-trips off the main trans-Timor highway: to Pante Macassar in the Ambeno district of East Timor (formerly Oecussi), and to the Betun district on the south coast.

The best time of the year to take the paved highway is around April or May, when the heaviest of the seasonal rains are over but the countryside is still green. Within a month or so the vegetation dries to a dull brown. Unfortunately, April–May is still a little early for many of the region's dirt roads, which are easier to navigate when they dry out further, so some compromise is in order.

The main trans-Timor road follows the coast for just 15 kilometers out of Kupang before heading inland to cross plateaus and mountains. Just before the East Timor border, 315 kilometers from Kupang, it drops to the sea again and stays a coastal road almost to the very eastern tip of Tim-Tim (see map page 208–209). At present, this is the only road covering the island, there are two other paved thoroughfares under construction: one will follow the north coast through Ambeno to Atapupu; another branches off the central highway just past the Mina River and heads south to the coast, and then eventually to Betun. Both are scheduled for completion in before 2000.

Leaving Kupang

The road rises gently for the first 40 kilometers out of Kupang, until it reaches Camplong, where there is a recreational park with an artificial lake and a nearby cave. Rising more steeply, the road passes through Takari, the site of a weekly (Monday) market

where Bali cattle are sold on the hoof. Just before crossing the Mina River, the largest in West Timor, the highway passes a side road that heads north to Kauniki. This village, with its royal graves, was once the center of the Sonbai dynasty.

Just past the Mina River, a side road heads south. This road, which leads to Panite, is the first leg of the south coast trunk road now under construction. Continuing on the main road, the highway heads for Soe town, a district capital 110 kilometers from Kupang.

Molo village: traditional houses

Just before reaching Soe, you begin to see the traditional houses of the region, called *lopo*. These have steeply pitched thatch roofs that continue all the way down to the ground, forming a perfect circle. The conical arrangement is pierced only by a very small, crawl-through door. The thatch provides quite effective insulation, and retains smoke, which helps preserve the corn and tubers stored inside. With the door closed, it's dark enough inside the *lopo* to serve as a photographic dark room.

The government considers these huts unhygienic, however, and has exerted varying degrees of pressure on the people of Soe to get them to move into "normal" rectangular houses. Those who have done so, however, still retain a *lopo* in back to serve as a

kitchen and food storage area. There are other traditional structures in which the roof stops a meter or so from the ground, allowing air to circulate inside. These serve in the area as day-houses for meetings and weaving.

A couple of kilometers before Soe, a road heads north towards the mountain range topped by 2,427-meter Gunung Mutis. Some 20 kilometers down this road at Molo, next to Kapan village, a women's cooperative keeps alive the old *ikat* weaving traditions as well as other ancient and modern crafts.

While most of the women now use machine-spun thread and commercial dyes, some cloths are woven with thread hand-spun from local cotton and dyed with natural colors from leaves, barks and roots. The finished items are offered for sale, but since there are few visitors to Molo, most of the production is sent to Kupang.

The ride to Kapan village offers some splendid views of Timor's mountain scenery, including towering Gunung Mutis. Even better for lovers of mountainous terrain is Fatumnasi village, further on. The road here is rough, and the village can only be reached by jeep or truck on Thursdays, Kapan's weekly market day.

Soe: bustling market

The large, sprawling market at Soe is active every day, but busiest during the early morning hours. Soe is the largest town in the region, and the people who live in the surrounding mountains, small, tough-looking men with betel-stained teeth and home-woven sarongs, bring their produce to the market here. They take home simple manufactured household items or cheap, western-style clothing.

Soe is an administrative town with wide streets and government buildings, but there is little to see here other than the market. The Mahkota Plaza Hotel, the largest in town, and the bus terminal in front of it serve as the downtown. There are several Padang-style restaurants close by. If you spend the night in Soe, make sure you have plenty of blankets—it can get damn cold!

There is a sandalwood carving establishment called Mutis Jaya/APIKC (open from 7:30 a.m. to 4 p.m.), just down the road from the Bank Rakyat Indonesia. Here large pieces of this very expensive wood are crudely carved by lots of young men.

Although we were told the items were for sale in Kupang, it looked suspiciously like the pieces were meant for export. Since exporting raw sandalwood (and other precious hardwoods) is prohibited in Indonesia, some

Opposite: *A shaman in West Timor examines the liver of a dog for signs of the upcoming harvest.*
Above: *Ambeno, like much of the western part of the island, was covered by forests until unchecked logging denuded the landscape.*

entrepreneurs will take large chunks of wood, decorate them with just a bit of carving, and then export them as "craft."

Niki Niki: fine *ikat*

Kefamenanu, the next large town along the road from Soe, lies at the end of an uninteresting 85-kilometer ride across a high plateau. The little town of Niki Niki, some 30 kilometers out of Soe, has a large Wednesday market. This market is a good place to buy the island's best and most traditional *ikat* weavings.

From Niki Niki, the adventurous can find a ride to the traditional villages of Ayotupas or Kolbanu, way off the beaten track. Another road from Niki Niki leads to Oenlasi, which on Tuesdays hosts one of the biggest market in all of West Timor.

A lot of coriander is grown in this area, and the market is full of its fragrance after the post–rainy season harvest. Just northeast of Niki Niki, in the Amanuban and Amanatun subdistricts, there are huge, exposed rock faces, laden with fossils.

Niki Niki has no *losmen,* and we were warned not to try the overpriced Chinese restaurant here. Just off the main road is a more or less "modern" raja's house, with a couple of unusual *lopo* raised on stilts and sitting on stone platforms. You can see similar structures by the main road. The royal graves are behind the raja's house, but you

need to find the *camat*—the district "mayor"—to get permission to see them and we doubt it is worth it.

Boti: traditional village

A better excursion is to head for Boti village, about 7 kilometers south of Niki Niki. Boti is perhaps the most traditional village in the Atoni region of West Timor. The people of Boti live in thatch-roofed huts, and many wear traditional clothes on a daily basis. Their weaving uses hand-spun thread and natural dyes. Everyone was quite friendly, and refused to let this thirsty traveler pay for his *air kelapa muda,* the sweet water from a young coconut.

Boti is in fact about the same distance from both Soe and Niki Niki, and the 7-kilometer trek from Soe, which follows a dry river bed littered with huge boulders, is more scenic. Not long ago, if you wanted a ride to the village, you had to be patient: only one truck a month made the trip.

Kefa: exploring the area

The district capital of Kefamenanu, usually called just "Kefa," offers simple accommodations and can serve as a base for exploring

Above: A woman, wearing hand-woven ikat, *beats a drum to accompany a traditional dance near Atambua.* **Opposite:** In the past, this dance greeted successful warriors returning from battle.

the district. Tourists are sometimes taken to Maslete, 4 kilometers south of Kefa on a paved road, then Nimasi, a traditional village, and Nilulat, the site of a colonial resthouse. From Nilulat, 1,300 meters, you can see Alor Island. The road out of Nilulat heads to Miomafo, and eventually to Eban. Buses and *bemos* cover all this stretch—or you can hike.

The best *ikat* in the region comes from the Oelolok/Kuafeu village district. To get there, continue on the main road out of Kefa some 32 kilometers to Numafo village in the *kecamatan* (subdistrict) of Insana. Turn right at Numafo and continue on 3 kilometers to Oelolok. Along the way, 27 kilometers out of Kefa, there is a partially open cave, which can be reached by stairs, that holds a statue of the Virgin Mary.

The raja of Oelolok village, obviously much better off than his counterpart in Niki Niki, lives in a very nice big colonial house, along with several traditional buildings. One of these holds the family heirlooms, and the other—capped by an unfortunate tin roof—serves as the venue for local dances. These can be arranged for a fee.

Although there is some weaving in Oelolok, the best in the region comes from Kuafeu, about 6 kilometers further on the same road. But even here, factory made thread has mostly replaced traditional handspun thread, and the cloth does not hold color as well as the old handspun variety.

Side trip to Pante Macassar

The turnoff for the most rewarding side trip from the Kupang–Atambua trunk highway is at Kefa. Here a road cuts north across a coastal mountain range to reach Ambeno, part of the East Timor province that is surrounded by West Timor.

The capital of the Ambeno district pop, about 50,000) (Oecussi) is Pante Makassar, 65 kilometers from Kefa. Every day, at least a couple buses and passenger trucks make the run from Kefa and Pante Macassar, and even more on Tuesdays, the regional market day. Parts of this road are paved, and the rest is being upgraded.

This road crosses the most traditional area we have seen in all of Timor: almost all the huts are of thatch, with conical roofs reaching right down to the ground, and most of the men and women wear colorful, homewoven *ikat* cloths. The men are tough and wiry—nice chaps really, they were always ready to return a visitor's smile—and amble about on horseback, usually without a saddle.

The huts are erected in small groups, often the home of an extended family. There are no decorations, and the elder's hut is only marginally better than the rest. With little maintenance—except for the thatch, which has to be replaced about every three years—these huts last 30 years. By this time, little of the original basic structure remains.

Tono: wonderful market

The big market in the area is held along the main road just outside of Tono village, about 40 kilometers from Kefa. The market area is shaded by a huge banyan tree, which grows next to a wide riverbed. The Tono river dwindles to a mere trickle in the dry season, turns into a proper river after a heavy rain in the mountains and carries water to irrigate *sawah*s—rice paddies— many kilometers downstream.

The Tono market is one of the best in eastern Indonesia, both because of the locale and the great mix of traditional people who come here to buy and sell. Homemade pottery, neatly stacked, is offered, along with *tuak* and its distilled counterpart, occasionally still referred to by its Portuguese name, *aguardiente*—literally, "firewater."

Locally grown vegetables, tubers and grain are bought by wives and servants of local officials and businessmen and among the often cashless locals, some of the transactions are bartered.

Wide-awake young Bugis and a few Mingangkabau staff the ubiquitous clothing stalls, and local ethnic Chinese sell household items. Try to get to the market early in the morning, say 6 or 7 a.m., so you can watch the people arrive: on foot, on horseback, and by truck, *bemo* and bus.

Ambeno: East Timor enclave

Ambeno makes up about one-eighth of East Timor's total area. During the time Tim-Tim was a Portuguese colony, Ambeno, then called Oecussi, was the territory's least populated and most backward region. In 1960, when some 500,000 people lived in all of East Timor, only 20,000 lived in Oecussi.

Today, about 45,000 people live in the district, which is still part of the province of East Timor. The East Timor independence party Fretilin (See "East Timor" page 225), was

never active in Oecussi, and the enclave was integrated into Indonesia in 1975, six months before the the rest of Portuguese Timor.

The district capital is Pante Macassar, some 25 kilometers from Tono by paved road. The city spreads over a wide area and does not have a recognizable center. This "urban" area holds perhaps 3,000 people, many of them recent arrivals seeking economic opportunities.

Three kilometers west of Pante Macassar is a new monument—defended by ancient cannon—that commemorates the arrival of the Portuguese. The monument now stands in a deserted spot, but this was once a settlement called Lifao. Lifao, according to oral histories, was the landing place of several migrations during the centuries before the arrival of the Iberians.

According to Portuguese sources, the Atoni ethnic group (locally called Baiqueno) predominates in Ambeno. The huts here resemble those of the Atoni in the mountainous interior, in contrast to the usual Tétun villages of the coast.

In the 1960s, Ambeno held some of the largest remaining stands of primary forest on Timor, mostly eucalyptus. Little of this remains today, since grasslands have been opened for cattle grazing. Cattle ranching has become a big business here, and the animals are trucked along the new coastal road through West Timor and shipped to Surabaya, Java at the port of Atapupu near the border with East Timor.

Transmigrants from Java have been settled in Ambeno, and they have begun irrigated rice cultivation, supplementing the millet,

*Above, left: The pleasures of rainy season travel in Timor are many and various. **Above, right:** Two roosters and a piglet bundled up for the trip to market. **Opposite:** The weekly market at Tono. Some people living in remote hamlets have to walk for hours to reach this market.*

tubers and corn that have traditionally been grown in the region.

Back to the main road

From the memorial at Lifao, a dirt road of sorts follows the coast, supposedly going all the way back to Kupang. We have been told that, in the dry season at least, a jeep can make this trip. This would have to be quite an adventure. Let us know if you try it.

The easiest way back from Pante Macassar is to return to Kefa the way you came: past Tono, along the road south. Another option is to take one of the daily buses straight to Dili ($6), which is supposed to take just 6 hours. Or you can take the coast road that heads northeast toward the port town of Atapupu.

We went northeast. In the area of Pante Macassar, and for the first 30 kilometers or so, the mountain scenery is splendid. Just inland from the coast, steep, folded slopes rear up from the coastal plain. The dark patches of bare rock contrast with the thin covering of light brown dry-season vegetation—Magnificent!

About 20 kilometers out of Pante Macassar, at Wini village, the road divides. One branch heads back south across the mountains and reaches the main trans-Timor road near Maubesi, 20 kilometers out of Kefa. Off this road, starting from Manufui, it's 8 km to Tamkesi, probably the most tradi-tional village in all of West Timor. The other branch of the road continues along the coast, a bouncy, very tiring ride along a dirt road. The scenery is mostly dull.

After five tough and dry hours, you emerge at at the main trans-Timor road near the village of Atapupu. At this point on the road, you are between the 292 kilometer and 293 kilometer road markers from Kupang, and just 13 kilometers north of Atambua. The rough coast road from Pante Macassar, which has some bridges, is scheduled for upgrading.

Atambua is the biggest town in central Timor island. From here, there are frequent buses to Kupang as well as to Dili. Three hours east of Atambua, on a 60 kilometer roller coaster of a road, are the traditional villages of Weluli and Lamaknen, close to the border with East Timor. Lamaknen is considered one of the most traditional areas of central Timor.

Side trip to the south

Between Atambua and Kefa—21 kilometers southwest of Atambua and 64 kilometers northeast of Kefa—a paved road joins the main trans-Timor highway.

At the junction, a heroically large monument of an Indonesian soldier, rifle raised, marks the road heading south. This is the road to the Wehali area, which in the past had been the religious and mystical center of

Timor. The area still holds a great deal of spiritual power today.

The first village past the turnoff is Halilulik, then a mountain passage takes you to Boas village, and finally, 40 kilometers from the main road, reaches Betun, the subdistrict capital.

About 5 kilometers before Betun, a road branches off to the east to Suai, the capital of East Timor's southwest district. From the turnoff, the 50 kilometer trip takes about three hours (there is a daily bus from Betun). This road connects the Tétun-speaking area around Betun with the Tétun speaking area of Viqueque, East Timor.

The two groups are separated in the area around the border by Mambai speakers. The road is partially paved, and the rough sections are scheduled for improvement.

Keltek: flying foxes

Just a bit further, almost at Betun, another road leads off to the seaside village of Kletek. Here you can hire a local canoe to take you the 5 kilometers to a grove of seaside trees that are swarming with large fruit bats called flying foxes.The nocturnal animals fly off each dusk to feed, and return at dawn to spend the day sleeping in the trees.

If you make too much noise, the bats will be spooked and fly off in a magnificent swarm, only to circle right back and settle again in their trees, perhaps a little irked. The local government plans to build cottages at a scenic beach in nearby Besikama—if it can find a partner to invest.

Betun: large market

Betun, which lies on a rich coastal plain, hosts one of Timor's largest markets, with some people walking 30 kilometers from the mountains to attend. The market is a permanent fixture, but sees most of its action on Mondays or Wednesdays.

The people are not as traditionally dressed as those at the Tono market in Oecussi, but on some days groups of sarong-clad horsemen joyfully gallop into town. Although some cash changes hands, much of the business transacted here is barter, with coastal products such as grain, tobacco and thatch being traded for highland game, tubers and wood. Betun has accommodations and restaurants, and makes a good base.

Laran: magic paraphernalia

Laran, the center of the realm of Wehali, is just south of Betun, continuing on the paved road leading in from the main highway. (The road eventually ends up, 15 kilometers away, at the coastal village of Besikama.) Laran is a little hamlet, recognizable by the thatch huts lining both sides of the road.

There is still a raja around, and the sacred ritual paraphernalia is kept safe in an ordinary-looking hut, shut tight except during ceremonies. Most of the traditional rites take place towards the end of the dry season, around September–October. Nearby is a spring with magical properties. This spring, which is called Maromaon, was until recently hidden by a thicket of rattan.

The raja of Wehali and the chief of traditions still hold a measure of authority in matters of *adat*—customary law—over a wide area of Timor, and they are consulted on this subject by people living far from Laran.

Wehali: the 'Mother Kingdom'

Today, the realm of Wehali covers 85,000 square kilometers and is populated by 11,000 people. In the past, Wehali had been isolated, but also the most fertile area in all of Timor.

According to anthropologist James Fox, Wehali was a "matrilineal enclave," where rule devolved through female heirs. Wehali never directly ruled any other area of Timor, but served indirectly to legitimate the rule of the other kindoms.

Men from Wehali were "exported" to give moral authority to the patrilineal leaders of other realms—even across linguistic and ethnic boundaries. Wehali was, Fox writes, the "mother kingdom…of the whole world."

In 1642, the kingdom of Wehali was destroyed by a Portuguese-led force of 90 musketeers (and three Dominican friars) under Solor-born Francisco Fernandez. To forestall Dutch encroachments on the sandalwood trade, the invaders burned everything.

Wehali gradually recovered, and it was more than 250 years later, in the early 20th century, that the Dutch themselves conquered the area after finally defeating the great warrior, Maroe Rai.

The Wehali/Betun area received a large influx of Tétun-speaking refugees who fled the Portuguese in East Timor when the border was officially marked off in 1911. This took place just after the time of the great 18-month long rebellion against the colonial rule in Portuguese Timor.

Opposite: *Indonesian military landing craft, drawn up on the beach at Dili, rust quietly under the cover of dusk.*

EAST TIMOR

Indonesia's Newest Province

East Timor, a province most famous as the site of a long-running guerrilla war, was opened to tourism in 1989 for the first time in almost 14 years. Timor Timur, or Tim-Tim, is a spectacular land of craggy mountains, high forests and panoramic views of the sea. It is not as parched as West Timor, and a few monuments from the Portuguese era are still standing, including statues of the Virgin, some fine old churches, and crumbling forts.

Centuries of Portuguese rule have left their mark on East Timor. The capital, Dili, has an Iberian feel in the architecture of its seafront and governor's offices. Almost all—95 percent—of the 800,000 East Timorese are Roman Catholics. Portuguese spelling of town and place names is only very slowly giving way to Indonesian orthography. (We have followed the former, as most signs still display the old spelling.) The new spelling, more logical and phonetic, substitutes *k* for hard *c* and *qu*; and *s* for soft *c*. Thus Becora in the old spelling becomes Bekora in the new; Viqueque becomes Vikeke; Liquica, Likisa.

A decade and a half of Indonesian rule has left its mark as well: a greatly improved infrastructure of roads and services, better farming methods, and a better educated population. Unfortunately, however, East Timor's induction into the republic was accompanied by a long civil war, bringing painful memories which are only slowly healing.

The Carnation Revolution

From 1932 to 1974, Portugal was a dictatorship, ruled by Antonio de Oliveira Salazar until 1968, when he retired due to illness, and from then on by Marcello Caetano. Then, suddenly, the dictatorship of more than 40 years was overthrown on April 25, 1974, by a junta led by Gen. Antonio de Spinola in a bloodless coup called the Revoluçao dos Cravos, the "Carnation Revolution."

The new government granted independence to the Portuguese colonies of Angola, Guinea-Bissau and Mozambique, where protracted, communist-backed guerrilla wars had been going on for more than a decade, as well as the Cape Verde islands, Sâo Tomé and Principe. East Timor, where there had been no anti-Portuguese fighting, was included in this decolonization sweep as well.

In East Timor, the result was sudden inde-

pendence from a colonial power that had long offered neglect. In 1970, four years before the Portuguese pulled out, there were only 1,463 "Europeans" in Tim-Tim. This number includes soldiers and administrators on temporary duty as well as Indians from Goa. Fewer than 5 percent of the Timorese spoke Portuguese, and of these only about 1,500 were given the same rights and privileges as their colonial masters. The region's 15,000 ethnic Chinese businessmen controlled 98 percent of the trade.

When the news came from Lisbon that Timor would soon be independent, local intellectuals and business elites gathered to form political parties. A half-century of intolerant, fascist rule—under the dreaded PIDE, the state security police—had left Timor with no politicians of experience, and ill-prepared for self-rule. Nevertheless, three political parties quickly formed in the spring and summer of 1974.

Fretilin is founded

The first to form was the União Democratica Timorense (UDT), a fairly conservative group of establishment figures who sought a slow, controlled break from the Portuguese. One of the founders of this party was Mario Vegas Carrascalao, former governor of Indonesian East Timor.

The group destined to win the most support in Timor, formed by people who were more anti-colonial and populist than the UDT members, was the Frente Revolusionario Timor Leste Independente (Fretilin) which translates as "Revolutionary Front of Independent East Timor." Although later Fretilin would be called a "revolutionary Marxist" organization, they were basically a mixed bag of leftists running on a populist platform. The group dubbed its ideology "Mauberism," from a Mambai word meaning "poor and ignorant." Fretilin's teaching campaigns and clinic-building in the interior made the party very popular.

Both UDT and Fretilin were opposed to integration with Indonesia, but the Associação Popular Democratica Timorese (Apodeti) was formed by José Osorio Soares with the express platform of merger with Indonesia. Apodeti was headed by Arnaldo dos Reis Aranjo, who had the dubious distinction of being the only Timorese to serve time for war crimes (he worked for the Japanese during the war, leading rebel Timorese against their fellow countrymen and the Australians.) Apodeti was corrupt, and had no popular support in Timor.

The initial elections during the decolonization process gave UDT and Fretilin the most delegates; Apodeti received only one. In January of 1975, Fretilin and UDT formed a coalition, which broke down a few months later. On August 11, 1975 João Carrascalao—Mario's younger brother—led a UDT coup. It

took three weeks for Fretilin, the more popular and better armed force, to retake the capital, and 2,000–3,000 people died in the fighting. By mid September, 1975, Fretilin had complete control of the territory.

Indonesia steps in

In the mid-sixties Indonesia had experienced a harrowing crisis with an internal Communist movement, and it was not about to tolerate a new neighbor of a leftist cast. Fretilin's name alone—"Revolutionary Front of Independent East Timor"—was enough to make Indonesian leaders nervous.

The Indonesian government had been trying to influence matters in East Timor through its counsel in Dili and through various contacts, but corruption and the overwhelming popularity of Fretilin made such efforts futile. After UDT failed in its coup attempt, Indonesia sent soldiers to its border. On November 28, 1975, Fretilin declared an independent East Timor. Little more than a week later, on December 7, 1975, the Indonesian army invaded.

Fretilin put up a surprisingly good fight, but Indonesia's overwhelming superiority in weapons and manpower soon prevailed, as Dili and key points throughout the territory fell to the Indonesian army. Several thousand Fretilin fighters, some with their families, took to the rugged mountains in the interior. On July 17, 1976, Indonesia incorporated East Timor as her 27th province.

A controversial rule

No one can argue that Indonesia has neglected this poor province. Since 1976, Jakarta has built 570 primary schools, 85 middle schools, and 29 high schools for the 700,000 East Timorese. There is also a private university and a $7.6 million polytechnic institute. By contrast, after centuries of Portuguese rule, only 10 East Timorese had graduated from college. Under Jakarta, roads were built,

electrical lines strung, hospitals constructed and harbors dredged.

But Indonesia was also ruthless in its pursuit of Fretilin and its sympathizers, employing aerial strafing of villages and dropping napalm and fragmentation bombs. Crops were burned and Fretilin guerrillas and their supporters were pursued into the arid mountains by thousands of soldiers.

A 6-month amnesty in 1977 split the guerilla's leadership, and with U.S.-supplied helicopters, the army conducted a fierce, 2-

year "pacification" program that broke most of the Fretilin resistance. In 1980, Operation Security led to a large-scale relocation of Timorese farmers, including entire villages, cutting off Fretilin guerrillas from their food supplies. By the early 1980s, the military operation against Fretilin had wound down considerably.

From 1975 to 1980, an estimated 100,000 East Timorese died in fighting, or from starvation and disease brought on by the disruptions of the war. This is at least 1/6 of the population, a staggering figure. Although the United States, Australia and most of the Islamic world have now recognized Indonesian East Timor, the Indonesian government continues to be criticized by Amnesty International, the Red Cross and other international human rights organizations.

Fighting winds down

Although there are still a few Fretilin guerrillas in the mountains, clashes with the army are rare. The 12,000 Indonesian troops in East Timor maintain a visible presence, and

Opposite: *An old Portuguese fort crumbles near Los Palos. The fort's arched entrance now bears the emblems of the Indonesian Armed Forces.***Above, left:** *A statue honors the integration of East Timor into Indonesia as its 27th province.* **Above, right:** *The Catholic faith is the most lasting legacy of Portuguese rule.*

frequently patrol the main roads. The army has increasingly turned to social work, with some helping in the mountain regions to build roads and bridges, and to demonstrate improved agricultural technologies.

The army judged East Timor safe enough to accede to former Governor Mario Carrascalao's request to open the province to tourism. You are free to circulate in Tim-Tim, without harassment from the police.

Traditions in East Timor

The fighting destroyed most of the fine traditional East Timorese houses in the Los Palos district, some of which were said to be centuries old. These were fashioned of stout pillars and heavy, carved planks. The traditional design has a high pitched roof set over a small, raised room. The two best remaining examples, complete with carvings and decorations, stand proudly in the village of Rasa, near the Los Palos district center, a couple of hundred kilometers east of Dili.

These served as models for a traditional house built to shelter Pope John Paul II during the mass he celebrated here for 300,000 people in 1989, as well as for several government and privately built showpieces in Dili.

Weaving is only occasionally practiced today with cheap Javanese batiks and western clothes having replaced traditional garb, although the Ambeno district still produces traditional cloth, woven tais of vegetable fibers and dies.

A slowly growing economy

In centuries past, some of Timor island's petty rulers thrived on the sale of sandalwood and slaves. (See "Introducing Timor," page 205.) But over-cutting led to the end of sandalwood exports by the early 19th century, and moral indignation in Holland stopped the slave trade by the end of the century.

At first, Timor found no ready replacements for these export items. In 1910, however, after the Portuguese quashed an 18-month rebellion, the Iberians concentrated on coffee exports from plantations that had been started in 1815. The area under cultivation increased steadily until today, some 20,000 hectares are planted in coffee.

Coffee is Tim-Tim's most valuable export, but sandalwood plantations are being expanded in several areas. A factory outside Dili processes the wood into an oil, which is sold to perfume makers.

While there was scattered gold panning in Portuguese times, the known deposits of chromite, manganese, copper and petroleum were not deemed extensive or rich enough for exploiting. These resources, particularly the oil, are being reassessed today. And quarrying marble has begun near Manatuto, which is rich in the valuable stone.

The Indonesian government has concentrated on agricultural programs, especially in the mountain areas where people settled to escape the fighting and hardships of their home territories. There are perhaps 150 of these resettlement areas, once holding as many as 200,000 people. Although some have settled there permanently, many families have now moved back to their ancestral lands, others are waiting to return.

World War II in East Timor

In 1942, during the initial phase of World War II, Timor was the scene of the heaviest fighting in Indonesia. After the fall of Singapore, the Japanese quickly blitzed their way through the Dutch East Indies on their way east, to be stopped only in New Guinea, just outside of Port Moresby. Thanks to the Japanese military's extensive intelligence network, superb panning, superior forces and overwhelming firepower, the Dutch colonial army (which, like everyone else, had grossly underestimated the Japanese) melted away.

Just prior to the Japanese invasion, as part of their forward defense, the Australian army landed several hundred soldiers in two locations: the Gull Force on Ambon, and the Sparrow Force on Timor. The latter group was split into two, with one guarding Kupang and the other stationed at Dili. While the Aussies put up a heroic resistance in Ambon, they were quickly forced to surrender. The scenario was repeated in Kupang, where a tank-backed assault force of 23,000 Japanese overwhelmed the under-armed Australians.

Sparrow Force

East Timor was a far different story. Initially, the Australians and a small Dutch detachment were concentrated around Dili and its airport. But after realizing that they could not oppose the superior Japanese forces in any set battles, the Sparrow force decided to rely on hit-and-run tactics, guerrilla fashion. They were successful in this for almost a year, tying up about 12,000 Japanese troops which the Imperial Army could have effectively used elsewhere.

The East Timor section of the Sparrow Force, a 350-man unit called the 2/2 Independent Company, had been trained to

fight commando fashion. Small groups of just a few men ambushed Japanese units, then melted into the mountainous terrain before their opponents' superior firepower could be brought in retaliation. The Independent company even succeeded in a daring night raid on Dili, causing considerable damage and Japanese casualties with no losses to themselves. Indeed, the final tally after the East Timor detachment of Sparrow Force was withdrawn amounted to only 40 Australian fatalities against some 1,500 Japanese.

It was not just bravery and skill that allowed the Australians to do so well against the Japanese. At least during the initial phases of the campaign, the Japanese alienated the Timorese by forcibly taking food and whatever else they wanted, including women for sex. The Aussies behaved themselves, and paid for everything with silver coins especially brought for this purpose. And of course the initial success of the Australians impressed the Timorese, who gave them invaluable information as to enemy defenses and troop movements.

All the Australians acquired a "criado," a personal servant and porter who lugged all the soldier's essential gear to the battles, then showed escape routes afterwards over the unmapped, mountainous trails. A special affection developed between the white soldiers and their "criados," who saved many Aussie lives. After the Australians were evac-

uated after a year's fighting, some of the "criados" were killed, while others suffered brutalities from the Japanese. An estimated 40,000–70,000 Timorese died in the war.

Towards the end of 1942, relations between the Timorese and the Australians grew strained. Japanese propaganda against white oppressors had begun having some effect, as did a military drive which forced the Australians to retreat into a relatively small area of the south coast. Inexplicably, the Japanese offensive stopped short of annihilating the Aussies, probably because troops were needed elsewhere in the war zone. After this offensive, the Australians were never again able to range freely over most of East Timor, although they could still help plan and assess Allied air raids on Dili and elsewhere.

Towards the end of 1942, fighting erupted between rival groups of Timorese, some who sided of the Japanese, others with the Australians. Because of these troubles, the Sparrow Force lost its ability to obtain information about enemy troop movements, food became scarce, and even tough blokes began to feel the effects of poor diet, malaria and chronic dysentery. The Japanese also switched tactics, using small groups of their Timorese allies, led by a few Japanese soldiers, to keep the Australians on the run.

Australians pull out

After emotional farewells to their loyal "criados," the Australians were forced to withdraw. Some 150 Portuguese, including officials—many of whom had quietly helped the Australians—were also evacuated with the main body of the 2/2 Independent Company. They were joined by a small detachment of the Dutch colonial army.

One of the evacuation ships, the corvette *Armidale,* was sunk by Japanese airplanes killing, along with the Australian officers, two Dutch officers and 61 Timorese soldiers.The Aussie men of the rear guard made their getaway at night, by an American submarine.

The fighting in East Timor had an important, if secondary, role in World War II. But the help of the East Timorese to the Australians was to take on unexpected importance after the end of Portugal's colonial rule there. The affection of the Australian fighting men for the Timorese was partially responsible for the initial strong objections made by Australia to the 1975 Indonesian invasion and takeover of East Timor.

Above: *A weaver in Desa Rasa.*

DILI

A Slowly Awakening Capital City

Dili is a strange town, beautiful in some ways, super-clean, and yet soul-less. Mediterranean-style colonial buildings face a tree-lined seafront. Rusting military landing craft are tied haphazardly along the beach. There are a couple rows of shops, but few people wander the streets. Perhaps Dili is too well-planned. It seems only the shell of a Mediterranean seafront, slowly coming to life. An adjustment process to Indonesian ways is still taking place, but slowly.

Sights in Dili town

There are two markets in Dili which bring some vitality to the morning hours, but they are located in the suburbs, Compang and Becora, each several kilometers from the center of town. There is a crafts center, in a beautifully constructed traditional house, but it seems uninspired. Next to the crafts center is an aesthetically awful monument to the integration of East Timor into Indonesia. There is also a monument to de Santos Resende, an architect whose works unfortunately dominate East Timor.

A more appropriate monument stands in front of the governor's offices. It commemorates the 500th anniversary of the death of the death of the "Infante Enrique" (Prince Henry the Navigator (1460–1960) who launched Portugal to its century of glory by encouraging navigational exploration.

A quick drive around Dili, which has a population of 125,000, reveals the results of planning and efficiency. There is a brand-new, gleaming white cathedral, inaugurated by President Suharto and blessed by the Pope in 1989. The city is full of ruler-straight, one-way streets. But the drive is quick, thanks to the irrepressible taxi drivers, who careen about in ancient blue station wagons spewing clouds of smoke.

Distance presents the most flattering view of Dili. From the road winding south up through the Dare hills towards Aileu you see a more charming Dili. The road ends at the church in Balibar village. On the way, about 9 kilometers out of town at Fatu Saba, a simple pool of water overlooking Dili serves as a World War II memorial. It was offered by the Australian Commandos who served here in 1942 and dedicated to "all the Portuguese peoples from Minho to Timor."

Another World War II memorial, dedicated to the "Portuguese victims of the occupation of Timor," is located at Taibesi, a suburb of Dili, which can be reached by turning left on the Aileu road just before the government palace, formerly the residence of the Portuguese governor.

A town on the sea

Dili's long seafront offers a pleasant two hours' stroll, especially if you set out in the early morning or late afternoon. Atauro Island, 20 kilometers offshore, looms in the haze. Start at the Pertamina storage tanks at the westernmost end of the city and head east, past small outriggered fishing canoes with a kaleidoscope of sails. A bit further on is the lighthouse, which is often open, and those unafraid of ladders and trap-doors can clamber to the top for a great sunset view.

Just past the lighthouse, Timor's oldest church, the Motael, presents its graceful facade to the sea. Continuing around the bay, you pass the integration monument on the landward side, the busy port, then the long-arched offices of the governor, a marble statue of the Virgin Mary and a handsome building, now Navy headquarters, formerly the Taiwanese consulate.

Just past the governor's offices on the seaward side, four ancient cannon with the Portuguese royal seal point to sea, and rusted landing craft used by the Indonesian Army are parked along the beach.

The end of the bay presents a lovely curve of beach a kilometer or so east of town. Pasir Putih or Branca, 4 km out of town, is equipped with dozens of pastel-colored concrete cabins for changing or resting under a wide thatch roof. A road from the beach climbs into the hills, affording a superb view onto the small bay.

Beautiful churches

Roman Catholicism was first brought to Timor by Dominican friars in the 16th century. But the evangelization process only began

Opposite: *Dili's seafront drive follows the coast from the Pertamina oil tanks to Pasir Putih beach.*

in earnest—on both sides of the border—after the Dutch and Portuguese had stopped head-hunting and pacified their respective regions. Today, more than 95 percent of East Timor's native population professes the Roman Catholic faith.

Dili's beautiful white cathedral, dedicated to the Imaculada Conceicao (the Immaculate Conception) is the largest church in all of Southeast Asia. When the Pope visited in 1989, 300,000 of Timor's faithful, almost half the province's population, gathered to hear his Holiness celebrate mass outside of town. The altar was placed under a high, sweeping roof topping a traditional house.

Motael, which faces the open harbor in front of the city, is East Timor's oldest church. Close to the seafront, an Italian marble statue of the Virgin Mary stands tall atop a white column. She also occupies a small cave a half kilometer opposite the airport turnoff.

The unique Timorese cult of the Virgin manifests itself once a century in a special procession, when a statue of Nossa Senhora Peregrina kept in the church in Ermera is carried to all 13 of the province's districts. It's worth seeing, so take it in the next time: A.D. 2088. But annual processions, albeit on a smaller scale, take place for the Virgin Mary on May 13 and October 13, and there is a three-day carnival before Lent begins.

In the past, the only way to Dili was a tough, mountainous road. But a new coastal road has been opened. All the Atambua–Dili buses follow the new route, which cuts travel time from 8–9 hours down to 4–5 hours.

The coast road

You reach the coast 24 kilometers from Atambua, at the port village of Atapupu, where cattle are shipped to Surabaya in Java. From here, it's 11 kilometers to the East Timor border at Motaain village. The police post here was where foreigners had to stop in the past, but now they just wave you through.

Four kilometers into Tim-Tim, the first village, Batugede, is announced by a beach-side fort, built in 1655. You are welcome to enter and look over the few rusting cannon and walls, all in fairly good shape. In front of the fort, a not very appealing dirt road starts the way to Dili, which from here is 125 kilometers away. The road is a nice, paved coastal drive leading to a long bridge over the Lois River. Then the road rises and skirts coastal hills before dropping down to Maubara village. From here, it's all paved, 49 kilometers to Dili, past Liquica.

The alternate route from Batugede begins with a very promising paved section which climbs into the hills to Balibo and its fort. Soon thereafter the pavement stops for a 14-kilometer stretch as you cross the wide Lois river bed before reaching the district capital of Maliana. A big harvest festival is supposedly held here sometime in August.

VISITING EAST TIMOR

A Trip to the Island's Eastern Tip

One of the easier jaunts out of Dili is the two- to three-day trip to Los Palos, a district capital in the far eastern end of Tim-Tim. Here you can visit Desa Rasa, perhaps the most traditional town in the province. The road passes hillside towns, a mountain of marble, and some beautiful stretches of coastline. At least four buses leave Dili for Los Palos daily, and the 227-kilometer road is paved for most of the way. A *losmen* awaits in Los Palos.

East from Dili

As you cross the hills east of Dili, you will pass by the brand new $7.6 million Polytechnic Institute. Check out the morning fish market at HERA, then, past Metinaro, a great stretch of coastal scenery begins, as the road rises to Manatuto along a right of way hacked out of the steep mountainsides. Here you skirt a mountain where marble is quarried.

Just before reaching Manatuto, a great new bridge spans the junction of the Laklo and Sumasse Rivers. On clear days, Wetar island is visible across the strait to the north.

The next little town is Laleia, which sits on a river by the same name. Laleia boasts a fine old church, and at Vemasse, just a bit further, there is an old fort. To your right is 1,790-meter Mundo Perdido, and its name—"Lost World"—is an appropriate description of the surrounding countryside.

A large military airport announces Baucau, 15 kilometers away. Until 1975, civilian flights landed here from Darwin, Australia. Baucau, a hillside town with tin-roofed houses and new government buildings, is Tim-Tim's second-most important city. A fine Portuguese-style market, the "Mercado Municipal," is built on a raised semi-circle that looks out to sea.

The market is the center of activity, and next to it are the local bus terminal, food stalls and restaurants serving Padang food. Accommodations of sorts can also be found here, at the Wisma Goya Lida (ask for Pak Yose, $3/night), hidden behind the Ja-Tim restaurant. Baucau's great old Flamboyant Hotel has been opened for tourists.

Once out of Baucau the road continues to Laga, where there is a fort and a salt lake, whose mineral is harvested once a year, at one time in accord with an elaborate ritual. Here a group of mountains rears up from the

plain, topped by 2,315-meter Mt. Matedia. Along the road here are several villages of resettled families from the interior. The cattle look very healthy and seem to thrive in the dry countryside. A 40 odd–kilometer stretch, from past Laga to Lautem, was still unpaved in late 1990 but was scheduled for upgrading.

Crossroads at Lautem

The tiny crossroads settlement of Lautem sits under an imposing set of ancient fortifications, the best we have seen in Tim-Tim. There are two paved roads out of Lautem.

One follows the sea 20 kilometers to Com, the site of a new dock meant to receive supplies for the troops stationed inland. The village of Irara, on the way to Com, is centered around a beautiful spring-fed pool. Most of the houses are palm rib and thatch, but there are a few concrete block houses and a school.

The other road out of Lautem swings inland to the district capital of Los Palos, 30 kilometers away. Just outside Lautem, the road climbs up to Maina, then Desa Rasa.

Desa Rasa: traditional village

Despite the electric poles and Western and Javanese clothes, the 44 families living in Desa Rasa have maintained the old ways of life. The most obvious sign of this are the many granaries and huts that display the elements of the region's traditional architecture: steeply pitched roofs set over a small, raised square room.

Even just 15 years ago there were many such houses here, but Fretilin guerrillas burned down all but two of the best examples. They also tried to burn down the two that remain, which sit right next to each other a stone's throw off the main road. But the ancestral spirits drove the arsonists away before the houses caught fire.

Two fine houses

The two remaining houses are by far the finest traditional structures in all of Timor. Each of the houses was built, by special carpenters paid with horses and water buffalo, for a noble family. One is occupied, while the other, whose last occupant had recently died, was empty during our visit. The basic frames of these houses are said to be centuries old, although 50–100 years seems more likely.

The one-room unit is raised on pillars, some two meters off a stone base. The carved supporting planks for the floor are handsome, curved items. The top of the roof soars to almost 12 meters, covered by thick sugar palm thatch. Some of the carvings of flowers and curvilinear shapes still show traces of the original natural pigment paints.

A ladder is needed to reach the entrance,

Opposite: *The market at Bacau, East Timor's second largest town.* **Below:** *Pak Silveira, Desa Rasa's chief of traditions, dances for a visitor.*

a trap-door on the floor of the raised single room. One corner of the room is reserved for cooking, and beds line one side. Food reserves—sacks of millet, rice and sweet potatoes—were kept in this living space, safe from rodents. The pillars have circular metal "squirrel" guards to keep animals from crawling up. Heirlooms were kept above the room, just under the roof. Ancestral spirits temporarily reside here, upon the invitation of their descendants.

The thick roof is festooned with decorative strings of large cowrie shells, and shells of the chambered nautilus are hung from the eaves. These ocean creatures are said to symbolize the ancestors' arrival from the sea. Atop the roof, carved birds communicate with the ancestral spirits who live to the west.

Until the 1960s there were many fine houses in the Los Palos district (then called Lautem). Although most of the decorations were traditional—snakes, the sun and moon—there were also carvings of modern power symbols: cars, steamships and even the Portuguese administrator on horseback with his family. Unfortunately, all these have now been lost. But Rasa's two remaining huts are an excellent reminder of splendors past.

Most of Rasa's inhabitants are officially Catholics. Although the steeple of the Catholic church in Los Palos has Desa Rasa–style decorations, Rasa's own church is a very simple affair, with an inaugural plaque signed by Benny Murdani, Indonesia's former chief of staff.

The ritual life of Rasa

In a short visit to Rasa, you will see women making simple but handsome pottery, waving *ikat* patterns—using, however, store bought thread and analine dyes—and men cooking palm toddy (*tuak*) in crude stills to produce potent, clear *arak*.

Despite these signs of traditional life, unless your visit coincides with a ritual, your impression of Rasa will be that it is more or less "modern," except for the few remaining examples of regional architecture. Everyone wears Western clothing or cheap Javanese *batik* sarongs. Electricity has reached the village, and many huts now have light bulbs.

But to understand the continuing strength of the ancient lifestyle, talk to Alesandre Silveira, the *kepala adat* or chief of traditions of Desa Rasa. Silveira, a fine looking old man with a handsome white mustache, speaks very little Indonesian. He communicates in Fataluku (a non-Austronesian language of the Makassae family), but there are young men around who can translate into Indonesian. And the local catechist and primary school teacher speaks quite passable basic English.

Pak Silveira told me that he continues to maintain respectful contact with the ancestral spirits to avert potential disasters, primarily failed harvests or outbreaks of disease. When

problems arise, he must walk to a sacred spot, a couple of hours away. At this site are two large stones, one upright (representing the male ancestors) and the other rounded (the female ancestors). Here Pak Silveira sacrifices animals, begging for supernatural intervention.

The chief of traditions

The stones can also bring individual strength. Village members with a problem, such as sickness or difficulties conceiving a child, come to "kiss" the stones. Only Pak Silveira has the spiritual strength to kiss these stones directly, however, and the others must kiss his hand while he simultaneously places his lips to the stones.

The story is told of a Fretilin member who kissed the stones directly. The result? "He died straight away," said Pak Silveira. Even the Catholic priests are afraid to come near the place.

Pak Silveira directs all the rituals in Rasa village. These include a week-long harvest festival in July, wherein the first rice grains harvested are offered to the ancestors. Before this event, nobody can eat the new rice. The old man also officiates at the traditional wedding (there is also a church wedding over which a priest presides) which is necessary for the proper consummation of the union. A bride price is paid by the groom, which consists of gold objects, woven cloth, horses, pigs and at least a dozen water buffalo. This is quite a sum, particularly since water buffalo, which are used to prepare the rice fields, are worth $250–$300 a head.

Pak Silveira is the scion of a long line of *adat* chiefs, and the job remains in the family. Much of the mystical knowledge is imparted directly from father to son, although some comes directly from the ancestors in the form of dreams.

Just outside of Desa Rasa, a fort at a curve marks the road to Tutuala, a little port town at Tim-Tim's easternmost point. From here to Tutuala is only 40 kilometers over a hillside road. A minibus makes the trip.

Los Palos town

The little port is just south of Kisar Island, and motorboats occasionally make the trip. There is an old fort at Tutuala and informants say there is a cave there with rock paintings: hands, canoes, humans. The old woodcarvings are said to have been smashed by Fretilin guerrillas.

The bus skips the turnoff at Rasa and heads up to Los Palos, which sits on the 500-meter Fui-Loro plateau, on a rich rice plain. A large Indonesian army garrison is stationed next to the district capital.

Los Palos is quite a "modern" little town, with a large daily market and numerous ethnic Chinese-run general stores. A Rasa-style traditional house has been recently built next to the market, alongside another larger structure, both meant to host traditional events. Take a close look at the steeple of the Catholic church, which is decorated in the style of Desa Rasa's traditional houses. In this case, however, the decoration is topped by a small cross.

The Wisma Raja Agung, close to the market and bus terminal, receives travelers. There is no sign outside, but the good sized house is easily recognizable by its handsome, blue-arched front porch. There are two rooms available in this family run losmen, with a total of 7 beds, at $3 per person. They will prepare meals for you (cost depending on how much meat you require) or you can eat at the *warung*-type food stalls in the nearby market.

Opposite: The two finest surviving traditional houses in East Timor, in Desa Rasa. **Above, left:** The Catholic church in Los Palos has incorporated elements of traditional architecture. **Above, right:** Detail from one of the Desa Rasa houses.

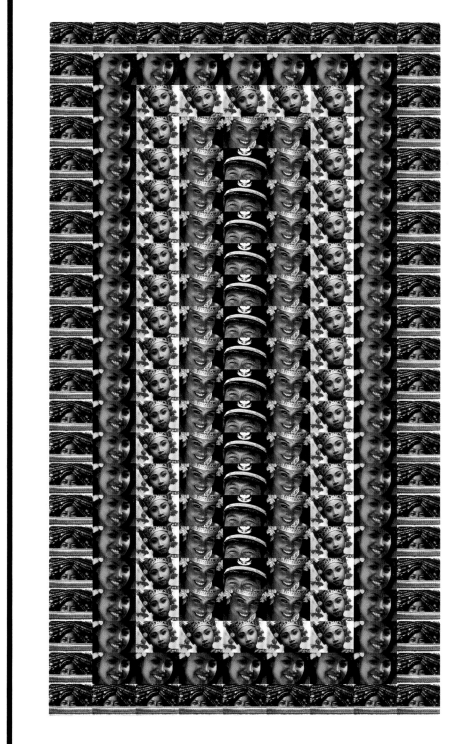

YOU COULD ENCOUNTER THEM in Paris or Vienna, Ambon or Biak. The faces that come from a melting pot of over 300 ethnic groups and 17,508 scattered islands.

OUR FACES NOW SPAN FOUR CONTINENTS AND 300 CULTURES.

The smiles and eyes that light up 38 far-flung cities across four continents and spread to 45 cities in the Indonesian Archipelago.

These are the people that have been hand-picked and trained as our cabin crew. And as they go across the world, they know no foreigners. Because the word 'foreigner' does not exist in our language. The nearest word that we have is 'tamu'. It means very simply, guest.

Garuda Indonesia
THE AIRLINE OF INDONESIA

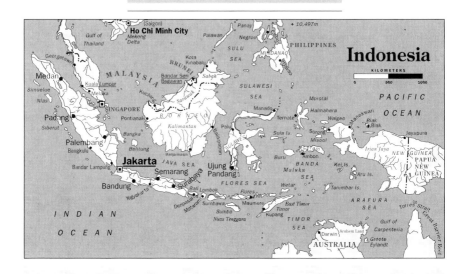

Indonesia at a Glance

The Republic of Indonesia is the world's fourth largest country, with 190 million people. The vast majority (88%) are Muslims, making this the world's largest Islamic country. More than 400 languages are spoken, but Bahasa Indonesia, a variant of Malay, is the national language.

The nation is a republic, headed by a strong President, with a 500-member legislature and a 1,500-member People's Consultative Assembly. There are 27 provinces and special territories. The capital is Jakarta, with 9 million people. The archipelago comprises just over 2 million square km of land. Of 18,508 islands, about 6,000 are named, and 1,000 permanently inhabited.

Indonesia's $120 billion gross national product (1993) comes from oil, textiles, lumber, mining, agriculture and manufacturing, and the country's largest trading partner is Japan. Per capita income is $605 (1993). Much of the population still makes a living through agriculture, chiefly rice. The unit of currency is the rupiah, which trades at approximately 2,150 to $1 (1994).

Historical overview The Buddhist Sriwijaya empire, based in southeastern Sumatra, controlled parts of Western Indonesia from the 7th to the 13th centuries. The Hindu Majapahit kingdom, based in eastern Java, controlled even more from the 13th to the 16th centuries. Beginning in the mid-13th century, local rulers began converting to Islam.

In the early 17th century the Dutch East India Company (VOC) founded trading settlements and quickly wrested control of the Indies spice trade. The VOC was declared bankrupt in 1799, and a Dutch colonial government was established.

Anti-colonial uprisings began in the the early 20th century, when nationalism movements were founded by various Muslim, communist and student groups. Sukarno, a Dutch-educated nationalist, was jailed by the Dutch in 1930.

Early in 1942, the Dutch Indies were overrun by the Japanese army. Treatment by the occupiers was harsh. When Japan saw her fortunes waning toward the end of the war, Indonesian nationalists were encouraged to organize. On August 17, 1945, Sukarno proclaimed Indonesia's independence.

The Dutch sought a return to colonial rule after the war. Several years of fighting ensued between nationalists and the Dutch, and full independence was achieved in 1949.

During the 1950s and early 1960s, President Sukarno's government moved steadily to the left, alienating western governments and capital. In 1963, Indonesia took control of Irian Jaya, and began a period of confrontation with Malaysia.

On September 30, 1965 the army put down an attempted coup attributed to the communist PKI. Several hundred thousand people were killed as suspected communists.

In the following year, Sukarno drifted from power, and General Suharto became president in 1968. His administration has been friendly to western and Japanese investment, and the nation has enjoyed several decades of solid economic growth.

No One Knows Indonesia Better

Indonesia... an archipelago of tropical islands : historic Java, fascinating Bali, scenic Sumatra, rugged Kalimantan, mysterious Sulawesi, primitive Irian Jaya and thousands of other virtually untouched isles.

The arts and crafts of Indonesia are as diverse as its people and culture. Modern hotels provide a range of accommodations. Transportation and communications are up to date and efficient.

Satriavi Tours & Travel have a tradition of arranging holiday packages throughout the islands. As part of the Garuda Indonesia Group and Aerowisata Hotels, it is perhaps the best connected travel company in Indonesia.

No one knows Indonesia better, and no one can take better care of you than Satriavi Tours & Travel.

SATRIAVI

Jalan Prapatan 32 Jakarta 10410 Indonesia (P.O.Box 2536)
Phone : (021) 231 0005 Fax : (021) 231 0006
Cable : RYATUR JAKARTA Telex : 45745 RYATUR IA SITA : JKTHSGA

Practicalities

TRAVEL ADVISORY, TRANSPORTATION, AREA PRACTICALITIES

The following Practicalities sections contain all the practical information you need for your journey. **Travel Advisory** provides background about traveling in Indonesia, from the economy and health precautions to bathroom etiquette. It is followed by a handy language primer. **Transportation** is concerned exclusively with transportation: getting to Indonesia and traveling around Nusa Tenggara.

The **Area Practicalities** sections focus on each destination and contain details on transport, accommodations, dining, the arts, trekking, shopping and services. Most include local street maps. These sections are organized by area and correspond to Parts II to IX in the first half of the guide.

Lombok 1

Sumbawa 2

Komodo 3

Flores 4

Lembata & Alor 5

Sumba 6

Sawu & Roti 7

Timor 8

1 Lombok
2 Sumbawa
3 Komodo
4 Flores
5 Lembata & Alor
6 Sumba
7 Savu & Roti
8 Timor

Travel Advisory

WHAT YOU SHOULD KNOW BEFORE YOU GO

WHAT TO BRING ALONG

When packing, keep in mind that you will be in the tropics, but that it gets chilly in the higher elevations, and sometimes over the water. Generally, you will want to dress light and wear natural fibers that absorb perspiration. A heavy sweater is also a must, as are sturdy shoes.

Don't bring too much, as you'll be tempted by the great variety of inexpensive clothes available here. Most tourists find a cotton *ikat* or batik shirt more comfortable than what they brought along. If you visit a government office, men should wear long trousers, shoes and a shirt with collar. Women should wear a neat dress, covering knees and shoulders, and shoes.

For those wanting to travel light, a *sarong* bought on arrival in Indonesia ($5–$10) is one of the most versatile items you could hope for. It serves as a wrap to get to the *mandi*, a beach towel, required dress for Balinese temples, pajamas, bed sheet, fast drying towel, etc.

Indonesians are renowned for their ability to sleep anytime, anywhere; so they are not likely to understand your desire for peace and quiet at night. Sponge rubber **earplugs**, available from pharmacies in the West, are great for aiding sleep on noisy journeys.

Tiny **padlocks** for use on luggage zippers are a handy deterrent to pilfering hands.

Also bring along some **pre-packaged alcohol towelettes** (swabs). These are handy for disinfecting your hands before eating, or after a trip to the *kamar kecil* (lavatory).

In most Indonesian department stores and supermarkets you can find western **toiletries**. **Contact lens** supplies for hard and soft lenses are available in major cities. Gas permeable lens wearers should come well-stocked.

Dental floss and **tampons** are available in western style grocery stores like Gelael that are fast becoming common in Indonesian cities. **Sanitary napkins** are widely available. *Kondom* (**condoms**) are available at all *apotik* (pharmacies).

On your travels you will meet people who are kind and helpful, yet you may feel too embarrassed to give money. In this kind of situation a small gift (*oleh-oleh*) is appropriate. Fake designer watches from Singapore or Hongkong selling for $5–$10 are a good idea (do tell them it's fake!). Chocolates, cookies and pens or stationery from your hotel are also appreciated.

CLIMATE

The climate in this archipelago on the equator is tropical. In the lowlands, temperatures average between 21°C and 33°C, but in the mountains it can go as low as 5°C. Humidity varies but is always high, hovering between 60% and 100%.

In general, Indonesia experiences two yearly seasons of monsoon winds: the southeast monsoon, bringing dry weather (*musim panas*—dry season), and the northwest monsoon, bringing rain (*musim hujan*—rainy season). Often the changing seasons can bring the time of high waves (*musim ombak*).

The **rainy season** is normally November to April, with a peak around January/February, when it rains for several hours each day. The rain is predictable, however, and always stops for a time, when the sun may come out. Before it rains, the air gets very sticky. Afterwards it is refreshingly cool.

The **dry season**, May to September, is a better time to come, and especially June to August. This is the time to climb mountains or visit nature reserves.

This nice, neat picture is interrupted in Maluku province, where local effects alter weather patterns, and in areas where the rain shadow of mountains changes seasonal patterns. We have tried to give the best local times for diving in each relevant section.

Tides in Indonesia average between one and three meters. The only place in the country with really big tidal fluctuations is the south coast of Irian Jaya, where the shallow Arafura Sea rises and falls from 5 meters or more.

TIME ZONES

Nusa Tenggara is on Central Indonesian Standard Time, the middle of Indonesia's three time zones, which is Greenwich mean time + 8 hours. This puts Nusa Tenggara on the same time zone as Singapore.

MONEY AND BANKING

Prices quoted in this book are intended as a general indication. They are quoted in US dollars because the rupiah is being allowed to devalue slowly, so prices stated in US dollars are more likely to remain accurate.

Standard **currency** is the Indonesian rupiah: Notes come in 50,000, 20,000, 10,000, 5,000, 1,000, 500 and 100 denominations. Coins come in denominations of 1,000, 500, 100, 50, 25, 10 and 5 rupiah. Unfortunately, the new coins are very similar in size, so look carefully.

Money changers and banks accepting foreign currency are found in most cities and towns. Banks are generally open 8:30 am to 1 pm, Monday to Friday and 8:30 am to 11 am on Saturdays. Some banks however, open until 2 pm on weekdays and close on Saturdays. Gold shops usually bunch together in a specific area of town and change money at competitive rates during hours when banks are closed.

Money changers offer very similar rates and are open longer hours. The bank counters at major airports offer competitive rates. Bank lines in town can be long and slow; the best way around it is to arrive promptly at opening time.

Get a supply of Rp 1,000 and Rp 500 notes when you change money, as taxi drivers and vendors often claim to have no change for big bills. When traveling in the countryside, Rp 100 notes are also useful.

Carrying **cash** (US$) can be a handy safety precaution as it is still exchangeable should you lose your passport, but it must be carefully stored and not crumpled: Indonesian banks only accept foreign currency that is crisp and clean.

Major **credit cards** are accepted in a wide variety of shops and hotels. But they often add a 3% surcharge for the privilege. Most cities have at least one bank at which cash advances can be made — look for Bank Duta, BCA and Danamon. Visa and MasterCard are the most frequently accepted foreign credit cards in Java.

There are no exchange controls and excess rupiahs can be freely reconverted at the airport on departure.

TAX, SERVICE AND TIPPING

Most larger hotels charge 21% tax and service on top of your bill. The same applies in big restaurants. Tipping is not a custom here, but it is of course appreciated for special services. Rp 500 per bag is considered a good tip for room-boys and porters. Taxi drivers will want to round up to the nearest Rp 500 or Rp 1,000.

When tipping the driver of your rental car or a *pembantu* (housekeeper) of the house in which you've been a guest, fold the money and give it with the right hand only.

OFFICE HOURS

Government offices are officially open 8 am to 3 pm, but if you want to get anything done, be there by 11 am. On Fridays they close at 11:30 am and on Saturdays at 2 pm. In large cities most offices are open 9 am to 5 pm, and

shops from 9 am to 9 pm. In smaller towns shops close for a siesta at 1 pm and re-open at 6 pm.

MAIL

Indonesia's postal service is reliable, if not terribly fast. Post Offices (*kantor pos*) are usually busy and it is tedious lining up at one window for weighing, another window for stamps, etc. Hotels normally sell stamps and can post letters for you, or you can use private postal agents (*warpostel*), or freelancers set up outside the bigger offices, to avoid the aggravation.

Kilat express service is only slightly more expensive and much faster than normal mail. International *kilat* service gets postcards and letters to North America or Europe in 7 to 14 days from most cities. *Kilat khusus* (domestic special delivery) will get there overnight.

TELEPHONE AND FAX

Long distance phone calls, both within Indonesia and international, are handled by satellite. Domestic long distance calls can be dialed from most phones. To dial your own international calls, find an IDD phone, otherwise you must go via the operator which is far more expensive.

Smaller hotels often don't allow you to make long distance calls, so you have to go to the main telephone office (*kantor telepon*) or use a private postal and telephone service (*warpostel*). It can be difficult to get through during peak hours but the service in Indonesia now is quite good.

International calls via MCI, Sprint, ATT, and the like can be made from IDD phones using the code for your calling card company. Recently, special telephones have been installed in airports with pre-programmed buttons to connect you via these companies to various countries.

Faxes have become common, and can also be sent (or received) at *warpostel* offices.

ELECTRICITY

Most of Indonesia has converted to 220 volts and 50 cycles, though a few places are still on the old 110 lines. Ask before you plug in if your are uncertain. Power failures are common in smaller cities and towns. Voltage can fluctuate considerably so use a stabilizer for computers and similar equipment. Plugs are of the European two-pronged variety.

TOURIST INFORMATION

The **Directorate General of Tourism** in Jakarta has brochures and maps on all Indonesian provinces: Jl Kramat Raya 81, Jakarta 10450. ☎ (21) 310 3117; Fax: (21) 310 1146.

Local government tourism offices, Dinas

LOMBOK

Unspoiled

Unhurried

Unbelievable

Sheraton
Senggigi Beach
R E S O R T
LOMBOK, INDONESIA

Sheraton

CALL: 0364-93333
FAX : 0364-93140

Telephone Codes

From outside Indonesia, the following cities may be reached by dialing 62 (the country code for Indonesia) then the city code, then the number. Within Indonesia, the city code must be preceded by a 0 (zero).

City	Code	City	Code
Ambon	911	Mataram	364
Balikpapan	542	Maumere	382
Bajawa	384	Medan	61
Bandar		Merauke	971
Lampung	721	Metro	725
Bandung	22	Mojokerto	321
Banjarmasin	511	Nusa Dua	361
Banyuwangi	333	Padang	751
Batam	778	Palangkaraya	514
Belawan	61	Palembang	711
Bengkulu	736	Palu	451
Biak	961	Parapat	625
Bima	374	Pare-Pare	421
Blitar	342	Pasuruan	343
Bogor	251	Pati	295
Bojonegoro	353	Pekalongan	285
Bondowoso	332	Pekanbaru	761
Bukittinggi	752	Pematang-	
Cianjur	263	siantar	622
Cilacap	282	Ponorogo	352
Cipanas	255	Pontianak	561
Cirebon	231	Probolinggo	335
Cisarua	251	Purwakarta	264
Denpasar	361	Ruteng	385
Dili	390	Sabang	652
Ende	381	Salatiga	298
Gresik	31	Samarinda	541
Jakarta	21	Semarang	24
Jambi	741	Serang	254
Jember	331	Sibolga	631
Jombang	321	Sidoarjo	31
Kabanjahe	628	Sigli	653
Kalabahi	397	Situbondo	338
Kebumen	287	Solo	271
Kediri	354	Sorong	951
Kendal	294	Sukabumi	266
Kendari	401	Sumbawa	
Klaten	272	Besar	371
Kota Pinang	624	Sumedang	261
Kotabaru	518	Surabaya	31
Kutacane	629	Tangerang	21
Kuala Simpang	641	Tapak Tuan	656
Kudus	291	Tarakan	551
Kupang	391	Tasikmalaya	265
Lahat	731	Tebingtinggi-	
Larantuka	383	deli	621
Lumajang	334	Ternate	921
Madiun	351	Tulung Agung	355
Magelang	293	Ujung Pandang	411
Malang	341	Waikabubak	387
Manado	431	Waingapu	386
Manokwari	962	Yogyakarta	274

Pariwisata, are generally only good for basic information. More useful assistance is often available from privately run (but government approved) Tourist Information Services. Be aware that many offices calling themselves "Tourist Information" are simply travel agents.

Overseas, you can contact the Indonesian embassy or consulate, or one of the following Indonesia Tourist Promotion Board offices:

North America 3457 Wilshire Boulevard, Los Angeles, CA 90010-2203. ☎ (213) 3872078; Fax: (213) 3804876.

Australia Garuda Indonesia Office, Level 4, 4 Bligh Street, Sydney, NSW 2000. ☎ (61) 2 232-6044; Fax: (61) 2 2332828.

UK, Ireland, Benelux and Scandinavia Indonesia Tourist Office, 3–4 Hanover Street, London W1R 9HH, UK. ☎ (44) 71 4930030; Fax: (44) 71 4931747.

The rest of Europe Indonesia Tourist Office, Wiesenhuttenstrasse 17, D-6000 Frankfurt/Main, Germany. ☎ (069) 233677; Fax: (069) 230840.

Southeast Asia 10 Collyer Quay #15–07, Ocean Building, Singapore 0104. ☎ (65) 5342837, 5341795; Fax: (65) 5334287.

ETIQUETTE

In the areas of Indonesia most frequented by Europeans, many are familiar with the strange ways of westerners. But it is best to be aware of how certain aspects of your behavior will be viewed. You will not be able to count on an Indonesian to set you straight when you commit a *faux pas*. They are much too polite. They will stay silent or even reply *tidak apa apa* (no problem) if you ask if you did something wrong. So here are some points to keep in mind:

☛ The left hand is considered unclean as it is used for cleaning oneself in the bathroom. It is inappropriate in Java to use the left hand to pass food into your mouth, or to give or receive anything with it. When you do accidentally use your left hand it is appropriate to say *"ma'af, tangan kiri"* (please excuse my left hand).

☛ Don't cross your legs exposing the bottom of your foot to anyone.

☛ Don't pat people on the back or head. Go for the elbow instead.

☛ Pointing with the index finger is impolite. Indonesians use their thumbs instead.

☛ If you are having a cigarette, offer one to all the men around you.

☛ Alcohol is frowned upon in Islam, so take a look around you and consider taking it easy.

☛ Hands on hips is a sign of superiority or anger.

☛ It is appropriate to drop your right hand and shoulder when passing closely in front of others.

☛ Blowing your nose in public is likely to disgust everyone within hearing distance.

☛ Take off your shoes when you enter someone's house. Often the host will stop you, but you should go through the motions until he does.

☞ Don't drink or eat until invited to, even after food and drinks have been placed in front of you. Sip your drink and don't finish it completely. Never take the last morsels from a common plate.

☞ You will often be invited to eat with the words *makan, makan* ("eat, eat") if you pass somebody who is eating. This is not really an invitation, but simply means "Excuse me as I eat."

☞ If someone prepares a meal or drink for you it is most impolite to refuse.

Some things from the west filter through to Indonesia more effectively than others and stories of "*free sek*" (free sex) made a deep and lasting impression in Indonesia. Expect this topic to appear in lists of questions you will be asked in your cultural exchanges. It is best to explain how things have changed since the 1960s and how we now are stuck with "*saf sek*."

Also remember that Indonesia is predominantly Muslim and it can be startling for Indonesians to see women dress immodestly. Depending on where you are, exposed backs, thighs and shoulders can cause quite a stir.

SECURITY

Indonesia is a relatively safe place to travel and violent crime is almost unheard of, but pay close attention to your belongings, especially in big cities. Be sure that the door and windows of your hotel room are locked at night.

Use a small backpack or moneybelt for valuables: shoulderbags can be snatched. In Kuta, bags have been snatched from tourists by thieves on motorbikes, so be vigilant.

Big hotels have **safety boxes** for valuables. If your hotel does not have such a facility, it is better to carry all the documents along with you. Make sure you have a photocopy of your passport, return plane ticket and travelers' check numbers and keep them separate from the originals.

Be especially wary on crowded buses and trains; this is where **pick-pockets** lurk and they are very clever at slitting bags and extracting valuables without your noticing anything.

HEALTH

Before You Go

Check with your physician for the latest news on the need for malaria prophylaxis and recommended **vaccinations** before leaving home. Frequently considered vaccines are: Diptheria, Pertusis and Tetanus (DPT); Measles, Mumps and Rubella (MMR); and oral Polio vaccine. Gamma Globulin every four months for Hepatitis A is recommended. For longer stays many doctors recommend vaccination to protect against Hepatitis B requiring a series of shots over the course of 7 months. Vaccinations for smallpox and cholera are no longer required, except for visitors coming from infected areas. A cholera vaccination may be recommended but it is only 50% effective. **Malaria** is a problem in parts of Indonesia (see below) and you should take prophylactic pills.

Find out the generic names for whatever prescription medications you are likely to need as most are available in Indonesia but not under the same brand names as they are known at home. Get copies of doctors' prescriptions for the medications you bring into Indonesia to avoid questions at the customs desk. Those who wear spectacles should bring along prescriptions.

Check your health insurance before coming, to make sure you are covered. Travel agents should be able to direct you to sources of travel insurance. These typically include coverage of a medical evacuation, if necessary, and a 24-hour worldwide phone number as well as some extras like luggage loss and trip cancellation.

Hygiene

This can be a problem. Very few places have running water or sewerage. Most water comes from wells, and raw sewerage goes right into the ground or into the rivers. Even treated tap water in the big cities is not potable and must be boiled.

Most cases of stomach complaints are attributable to your system not being used to the strange foods and stray bacteria. To make sure you do not get something more serious, take the following precautions:

☞ Don't drink unboiled water from a well, tap or *mandi* (bath tub). Brush your teeth with boiled or bottled water, not water from a tap or *mandi*.

☞ Plates, glasses and silverware are washed in unboiled water and need to be completely dry before use.

☞ Ice is not made from boiled water. It comes from water frozen in government regulated factories. Locals who are adamant about drinking only boiled water are, in general, not fearful of the purity of ice. However we advise against it.

☞ Fruits and vegetables without skins pose a higher risk of contamination. To avoid contamination by food handlers, buy fruits in the market and peel them yourself.

☞ To *mandi* (bathe) two to three times a day is a great way to stay cool and fresh. But be sure to dry yourself off well and you may wish to apply a medicated body powder such as Purol to avoid the nastiness of skin fungus, especially during the rainy season from October to March.

Diarrhea

A likely traveling companion. In addition to the strange food and unfamiliar micro-fauna, diarrhea is often the result of attempting to accomplish too much in one day. Taking it easy can be an effective prevention. Ask around before leaving about what the latest and greatest of the many remedies are and bring some along. Imodium is locally available as are activated carbon tablets that will absorb the toxins giving you grief.

When it hits, it is usually self-limiting to two or three days. Relax, take it easy and drink lots of fluids, perhaps accompanied by rehydration salts such as Servidrat. Especially helpful is young coconut milk (*air kelapa mudah*) or tea. The former is especially pure and full of nutrients to keep up your strength until you can get back to a regular diet. Get it straight from the coconut without sugar, ice and color added. When you are ready, plain rice or *bubur* (rice porridge) is a good way to start. Avoid fried, spicy or heavy foods and dairy products for a while. After three days without relief, see a doctor.

Intestinal Parasites

It is estimated that 80 to 90 percent of Indonesians have intestinal parasites and these are easily passed on by food handlers. Prevention is difficult, short of fasting, when away from luxury hotel restaurants and even these are no guarantee. It's best to take care of parasites sooner rather than later, by routinely taking a dose of anti-parasite medicine such as Kombatrin (available at all *apotik*) once a month during your stay and again when you get on the plane home.

If you still have problems when you get back, even if only sporadically, have stool and blood tests. Left untreated, parasites can cause serious damage.

Cuts and Scrapes

Your skin will come into contact with more dirt and bacteria than it did back home, so wash your face and hands more often. Untreated bites or cuts can fester very quickly in the tropics, and staph infection is common. Cuts should be taken seriously and cleaned with an antiseptic such as Betadine solution available from any pharmacy (*apotik*). Once clean, antibiotic ointment (also available locally) should be applied and the cut kept covered. Repeat this ritual often. Areas of redness around the cut indicate infection and a doctor should be consulted. At the first sign of swelling it is advisable to take broad spectrum antibiotics to prevent a really nasty infection.

Malaria

Malaria is a problem in parts of Indonesia. This is nothing to be irresponsible about. If you will be in Komodo–Labuhanbajo, Maumere, Kupang and Roti, pay particular attention to this section.

Malaria is caused by a protozoan, Plasmodium, which affects the blood and liver. The vector for the Plasmodium parasite is the Anopheles mosquito. After you contract malaria, it takes a minimum of six days—and up to several weeks—before symptoms appear.

If you are visiting any of the above sites you must take malaria pills. Do not think that pills offer complete protection, however, as they don't. A virulent strain of malaria has recently become dominant particularly in Nusa Tenggara, and malaria is a real risk to be weighed before traveling there. If you are pregnant, have had a splenectomy or have a weak immune system, or suffer from chronic disease, you should probably not go to Nusa Tenggara.

Chloroquine phosphate is the traditional malaria prophylactic, but in the past 10–15 years, the effectiveness of the drug has deteriorated. Deciding on an appropriate anti-malarial is now more complicated. There are actually two forms of malaria: *Plasmodium vivax,* which is unpleasant, but rarely fatal to healthy adults; and *P. falciparum,* which can be quickly fatal. *P. falciparum* is dominant in parts of Indonesia.

Malaria pills As a prophylactic for travel in the malarial areas of Indonesia, take two tablets of Chloroquine (both on the same day) once a week, and one tablet of Maloprim (pyrimethamine) once a week. Maloprim is a strong drug, and not everybody can tolerate it. If you are planning on taking Maloprim for more than two months, it is recommended that you take a folic acid supplement, 6 mg a day, to guard against anemia. Note: The anti-malarial drugs only work once the protozoan has emerged from the liver, which can be weeks after your return. You should continue on the above regimen for one month after returning.

Another recent drug that has been shown effective against both forms of the parasite is Mefloquine (Larium), although unpleasant side effects have been demonstrated for it as well. Mefloquine is also very expensive, about $3 a tablet. However, it can be a lifesaver in cases of resistant falciparum infection.

These drugs are not available over-the-counter in most western countries (nor, indeed, do most pharmacists stock them), and if you visit a doctor, you may have trouble convincing him of what you need. Doctors in the temperate zones are not usually familiar with tropical diseases, and may even downplay the need to guard against them. Do not be persuaded. Try to find a doctor who has had experience in these matters.

You can also buy Chloroquine and Maloprim over-the-counter in Indonesia, for very little (a few dollars for a month's supply). Maloprim, however, may still be difficult to find. [Note: there is a non–chloroquine based drug sold in Indonesia called Fansidar. This drug is not effective against resistant strains of *P. falciparum.*]

Treatment Malaria in the early stages is very hard to distinguish from a common cold or flu. A person infected may just suffer from headache and nausea, perhaps accompanied by a slight fever and achiness, for as long as a week until the disease takes hold. When it does, the classic symptoms begin:

1) Feeling of intense cold, sometimes accompanied by shaking. This stage lasts from 30 minutes to two hours.

2) High fever begins, and victim feels hot and dry, and may vomit or even become delirious. This lasts 4–5 hours.

3) Sweating stage begins, during which the victim perspires very heavily, and his body temperature begins to drop.

If you think you have malaria, you should immediately call on professional medical help. A good medical professional is your best first aid. Only if you cannot get help, initiate the following treatment:

1) Take 4 Chloroquine tablets immediately.

2) Six hours later, take 2 more Chloroquine tablets.

3) The next day, take 2 more.

4) The following day, take 2 more.

Note: If the Chloroquine treatment does not make the fever break within 24 hours, assume the infection is the very dangerous *P. falciparum* and begin the following treatment immediately:

1) Take 3 tablets (750 mg) of Mefloquine (Larium)

2) Six hours later, take 2 more tablets (500 mg) of Mefloquine.

3) After 12 hours—and only if you weigh 60 kg (130 lbs) or more—take one more tablet (250 mg) of Mefloquine.

Prevention Malaria is carried by the *Anopheles* mosquito, and if you don't get bit, you don't get the disease.

☞ While walking around, use a good quality mosquito repellent, and be very generous with it, particularly around your ankles. Wear light-colored, long-sleeved shirts or blouses and long pants.

☞ While eating or relaxing in one spot, burn mosquito coils. These are those green, slightly brittle coils of incense doped with pyrethrin that were banned in the United States some years ago. They are quite effective and you will get used to the smell. (If you are worried about inhaling some of the poison they contain, re-read the classic symptoms of malaria above.) In Indonesia, the ubiquitous coils are called *obat nyamuk bakar*. In places where there is electricity, a repellent with a similar ingredient is inserted into a unit plugged into the wall.

☞ While sleeping, burn *obat nyamuk* and use a mosquito net. Some hotels in affected areas have nets, but not many, and you should bring your own. The *obat nyamuk* coils last 6–8 hours and if you set a couple going when you go to sleep you will be protected. Remember that mosquitos like damp bathrooms—where few people bother to light a mosquito coil.

Other Mosquito-borne Diseases

The other mosquito concern is **dengue fever**, spread by the afternoon-biting *Aedes aegypti*, especially at the beginning of the rainy season in November. The most effective prevention is not getting bitten (there is no prophylaxis for dengue). Dengue fever symptoms are headache, pain behind the eyes, high fever, muscle and joint pains and rash.

AIDS & Hepatitis B

Surprise! **Safe sex** is also a good idea in Indonesia. AIDS is just beginning to surface with a number of documented HIV positive cases recently. Another consideration is Hepatitis B virus which affects liver function, and is only sometimes curable and can be deadly. The prevalence of Hepatitis B in Indonesia is the basis for international concern over the ominous possibilities for the spread of HIV virus, which is passed on in the same ways.

Medical Treatment

The Indonesian name for pharmacy is *apotik*; and a hospital is called *rumah sakit*. In smaller villages they only have government clinics, called *Puskesmas*, which are not equipped to deal with anything serious.

Fancier hotels often have doctors on call or can recommend one. Misuse of antibiotics is still a concern in Indonesia. They should only be used for bacterial diseases and then for at least 10 to 14 days to prevent developing antibiotic resistant strains of your affliction. Indonesians don't feel they've had their money's worth from a doctor ($5) without getting an injection or antibiotics. Be sure it's necessary. Ensure syringes have never been used before.

Even in the big cities outside of Jakarta, emergency care leaves much to be desired. Your best bet in the event of a life-threatening emergency or accident is to get on the first plane to Jakarta or Singapore. Contact your embassy or consulate by phone for assistance (see below). Medevac airlifts are very expensive ($26,000) and most embassies will recommend that you buy insurance to cover the cost of this when traveling extensively in Indonesia.

Emergency Medical Assistance

AEA International 331 North Bridge Road, 17th Floor, Odeon Towers, Singapore 0718. ☎ (65) 338 2311, Fax: (65) 338 7611, Telex: RS23535 ASIAAS. Asia Emergency Assistance offers insurance packages for expatriates living in Indonesia and elsewhere in Asia, and individual travelers. This is a well-respected outfit, and they are considered to have the best response time and operation in Indonesia. In addition to Jakarta, AEA maintains alarm centers in Singapore, Hong Kong, Seoul, Beijing, and Ho Chi Minh City. Yearly premiums vary, depending individual conditions, but generally range from $115–$275/year, for a package covering emergency care and Medevac.

International SOS Assistance Asia Pacific Regional Head Office: 10 Anson Road, #21-08/A International Plaza, Singapore 0207. ☎ (65) 221 3981, Fax: (65) 226 3937, Telex: 24422 SOSAFE. Offers a range of emergency services worldwide. Numerous large corporate clients. Contact them for rates and types of coverage

ACCOMMODATION

Indonesia has an extraordinary range of accommodation, much of it good value for money. Most cities have a number of hotels offering air-conditioned rooms with TV, minibar, hot water, swimming pool and the like costing $100 a night and up. While at the other end of the scale, you can stay in a $2-a-night *losmen* room with communal squat toilet (buy your own toilet paper), a tub of water with ladle for a bath, and a bunk with no towel or clean linen (bring your own). And there's just about everything in between: from decrepit colonial hill stations to luxurious new thatched-roof huts in the rice fields.

A whole hierarchy of lodgings and official terminology have been established by government decree. Theoretically, a "hotel" is an upmarket establishment catering for businessmen, middle to upper class travelers and tourists. A star-rating (one to five stars) is applied according to the range of facilities. Smaller places with no stars and basic facilities are not referred to as hotels but as "*losmen*" (from the French "*logement*"), "*wisma*" ("guesthouse") or "*penginapan*" ("accommodation") and cater to the masses or to budget tourists.

Prices and quality vary enormously. In the major cities that don't have many tourists, such as Jakarta, Surabaya and Medan, there is little choice in the middle ranges and you have to either pay a lot or settle for a room in a *losmen*.

In areas where there are a lot of tourists, such as Bali and Yogya, you can get very comfortable and clean rooms with fan or air-conditioning for less than $20 a night. In small towns and remote areas, you don't have much choice and all accommodation tends to be very basic.

It's common to ask to see the room before checking in. Shop around before deciding, particularly if the hotel offers different rooms at different rates. Avoid carpeted rooms, especially without air-conditioning, as usually they are damp and this makes the room smell.

Advance bookings are necessary during peak tourist seasons (July to August and around Christmas and New Year). Popular resorts near big cities (like Puncak or Tretes) are always packed on weekends, and prices often double, so go during the week when it's cheaper and quieter.

In many hotels, discounts of 10%–30% from published rates are to be had for the asking, particularly if you have a business card. Booking in advance through travel agencies can also result in a much lower rate. Larger hotels always add 21% tax and service to the bill.

Bathroom Etiquette

When staying in *losmen*, particularly when using communal facilities, don't climb in or drop your soap into the tub of water (*bak mandi*). This is for storing clean water. Scoop water over yourself with the ladle in your right hand and clean with your left.

If you wish to use the native paper-free cleaning method, after using the toilet, scoop water with your right hand and clean with the left.

This is the reason one only eats with the right hand—the left is regarded as unclean, for obvious reasons. Use soap and a fingernail brush (locals use a rock) for cleaning hands. Pre-packaged alcohol towelettes from home may make you feel happier about opting for this method.

Bring along your own towel and soap (although some places provide these if you ask).

Staying in Villages

Officially, the Indonesian government requires that foreign visitors spending the night report to the local police. This is routinely handled by *losmen* and hotels, who send in a copy of the registration form you fill out when you check in.

Where there are no commercial lodgings, you can often rely on local hospitality. But when staying in a private home, keep in mind the need to inform the local authorities. One popular solution is to stay in the *home* of the local authority, the village head or *kepala desa*.

Carry photocopies of your passport, visa stamp and embarkation card to give to officials when venturing beyond conventional tourist areas. This saves time, and potential hassles, for you and your host.

Villagers in rural Indonesia do not routinely maintain guest rooms. If a cash arrangement has not been prearranged, you should leave a gift appropriate to local needs—tinned food, clothing, cigarettes or D-cell batteries for radios in remote villages. Note down their address and send prints of the photos you took of them.

FINDING YOUR WAY

Westerners are used to finding things using telephone directories, addresses, maps, etc. But in Indonesia, phone books are out-of-date and incomplete, addresses can be confusing and maps little understood. The way to find something, whether you have a specific destination in mind, or want to try to find a good place for *nasi goreng*, is to ask.

To ask for directions, it's better to have the name of a person and the name of the *kampung*. Thus "Bu Herlan, Mertadranan" is a better address for asking directions even though "Jalan

Kaliwidas 14" is the mailing address. Knowing the language helps here but is not essential. Immediately clear answers are not common and you should be patient. You are likely to get a simple indication of direction without distance or specific instructions. The assumption is that you will be asking lots of people along the way.

Maps are useful tools for you, but introducing them into discussions with Indonesians will often confuse rather than clarify. Nevertheless, Indonesians seem to have built-in compasses and can always tell you where north is. If you introduce a map into your discussion, they are likely to insist that the north arrow on the map be oriented to the north before beginning.

FOOD AND DRINK

Pay attention to the quantity of fluids you consume in a day (drinks with alcohol or caffeine count as a minus). Tap water in Indonesia is not potable and it should be brought to a full boil for ten minutes before being considered safe. Use boiled or bottled water to brush your teeth.

Indonesians are themselves fussy about drinking water, so if you're offered a drink it is almost certainly safe.

Most Indonesians do not feel they have eaten until they have eaten rice. This is accompanied by side dishes, often just a little piece of meat and some vegetables with a spicy sauce. Other common items include tofu (*tahu*), *tempe* and salted fish. Crispy fried tapioca crackers flavored with prawns and spices (*krupuk*) usually accompany a meal.

No meal is complete without *sambal*—a fiery paste of ground chili peppers with garlic, shallots, sugar, and various other ingredients.

Cooking styles vary greatly from one region to another. The Sundanese of West Java are fond of raw vegetables, eaten with chili and fermented prawn paste (*lalab/sambal trasi*). Minihasan food in North Sulawesi is very spicy, and includes some interesting specialties: fruit bat wings in coconut milk, *sambal* rat, and dog. In the more isolated parts of the archipelago, the food can be quite plain, and frankly, quite dull.

By western standards, food in Indonesia is cheap. For $1, in most places, you can get a meal with bottled drink. On the other hand, Indonesia does not have a banquet tradition and people normally eat in restaurants only out of necessity (when they cannot eat at home). The major exception to this is the Indonesian Chinese, who are fond of restaurant banquets. Most Indonesians eat better at home than outside, and the range of dishes in restaurants is not great.

In most Indonesian restaurants you will find a standard menu consisting of *sate* (skewered barbequed meat), *gado-gado* or *pecel* (boiled vegetables with spicy peanut sauce) and *soto* (vegetable soup with or without meat). Also found are some Chinese dishes like *bakmie goreng* (fried noodles), *bakmie kuah* (noodle soup) and *cap cay* (stir-fried vegetables).

In most larger towns you can also find a number of Chinese restaurants on the main street. Some have menus with Chinese writing, but usually the cuisine is very much assimilated to local tastes. Standard dishes, in addition to the *bakmie* and *cap cay* mentioned above, are sweet and sour whole fish (*gurame asem manis*), beef with Chinese greens (*kailan/caisim ca sapi*), and prawns sauteed in butter (*udang goreng mentega*). Any one of these with a plate of vegetables (*cap cay*) and rice makes a delightful meal.

Indonesian fried chicken (*ayam goreng*) is common and usually very tasty—although the chicken can be a bit more stringy than westerners are used to. Then there is the ubiquitous *nasi goreng* (fried rice), which is often eaten for breakfast with an egg on top.

There are restaurants everywhere in Indonesia that specialize in Padang food, from this region of West Sumatra. This spicy, and very tasty cuisine has a distinctive way of being served. The glass case in front of the restaurant displays as many as 15–20 different dishes, all on little plates. You tell the waiter what you want, and he brings a whole stack of the little things and sets it in front of you. At the end of the meal, you are charged for what you have eaten, and any untouched plates are put back in the case.

The beers available in Indonesia are Bintang and Anker, both brewed under Dutch supervision and rather light (perhaps appropriately for the tropics). With electricity such a precious commodity, however, in out-of-the-way places the only way to quaff it cold is to pour it over ice.

Warung (Street Stalls)

Restaurant kitchens do not necessarily have healthier food preparation procedures than roadside *warung*. The important thing at a *warung* is to see what's going on and make a judgement as to whether or not the cooks inspire confidence. *Warung* rarely have a running water supply, so always beware.

The food is laid out on the table and you point to what you want to eat. Your first portion probably won't fill you up, so a second portion is ordered by saying *"Tambah separuh"* (I'll have another half portion, please). But only the price is halved. The amount of food is more like three-quarters. Finish off with a banana and say *"Sudah"* (I've had plenty and would like to pay now please). At this point the seller will total up the prices of what she served you and ask you how many *krupuk* and *tempe*, etc. you added; so keep track. The total will come to between Rp500 and Rp2,500 (30¢ to $1.25).

Vegetarianism

Say "*saya tidak makan daging*" (I don't eat meat) or alter menu items by saying something like *tidak pakai ayam* (without chicken) or *tidak pakai daging* (without meat). Dietary restrictions are very acceptable and common here due to the various religious and spiritual practices involving food. However, finding food that truly has no animal products is a problem. Often meals which appear to be made exclusively of vegetables will have a chunk of beef in them to add that certain oomph.

POLITICAL ORGANIZATION

The area we call Nusa Tenggara in this book includes three of Indonesia's 27 *propinsi*, or provinces:

1. Nusa Tenggara Barat (NTB) literally "Western Southeast Islands." The capital of this province is Mataram in Lombok. It includes Lombok and Sumbawa.

2. Nusa Tenggara Timur (NTT) literally "Eastern Southeast Islands." Its capital is Kupang in West Timor. It includes Komodo, Flores, Lembata, Alor, Sumba, Savu, Roti and most of the western half of Timor.

3. Timor Timur (TT) literally "East Timor." Usually called Tim Tim, its capital is Dili, on the north coast of Timor island. This province includes the eastern half of Timor island and the small coastal enclave of Ambeno (previously known as Oecussi) on the north shore of west Timor.

Each of these *propinsi*, headed by a *gubernur* ("governor") is further divided into *kabupaten* (districts), headed by a *bupati* (district head); *kecamatan* (subdistricts), headed by a *camat*; villages (*desa*) headed by a *kepala desa* (mayor); and *kampung* (hamlets).

It is not quite this simple, of course, as in parts of Indonesia where there are large cities (*kota*), there are also *kotamadya*, ("municipalities"), whose "mayor" has the status of a *bupati*, and *kota administrasi* ("administrative cities") whose "mayor" falls somewhere between a *bupati* and a *camat*. But the basic progression is: *propinsi*, *kabupaten*, *kecamatan*, *desa*, *kampung*.

As an example, take Kampung Tarung, a small hamlet in West Sumba, where the high priests of the Marapu religion live:

Kampung Tarung

Propinsi	Nusa Tenggara Timur
Kabupaten	Sumba Barat
Kecamatan	Loli
Desa	Waikabubak
Kampung	Tarung

SPELLING

The Indonesian spelling of geographical features and villages varies considerably as there is no form of standardization that meets with both popular and official approval. We have seen village names spelled three different ways, all on signboards in front of various government offices. In this guide, we have tried to use the most common spellings.

CALENDAR

The Indonesian government sets a certain number of legal holidays every year, both fixed and moveable dates. Most of these holidays are for the major religions practiced in Indonesia. Both the Christian Easter and all the Muslim holidays are based on the moon, so confusion results in attempting to extrapolate several years ahead.

The fixed national holidays on the Gregorian calendar are the Christian New Year, Jan. 1; Independence Day, Aug. 17; and Christmas, Dec. 25. Easter Day, Good Friday and Ascension Day are honored in Indonesia. The Balinese new year, Nyepi, and the Buddhist Waisak New Year are also legal holidays.

Official Muslim holidays in Indonesia (the dates are for 1995):

Idul Fitri. March 3 and 4. The end of the Muslim fasting month of Ramadan; this holiday is also called Lebaran. It is very difficult to travel just before and just after Idul Fitri as just about everyone wants to return to his or her home village to celebrate, then get back to their places of work in the cities.

Idul Adha. May 10. The day of Abraham's sacrifice and the day that the haji pilgrims circle the Kaaba in Mecca.

Hijryah. May 31. The Islamic New Year, beginning the month of Muharram, when Muhammad traveled from Mecca to Medina.

Maulud Nabi Muhammad SAW. August 9. Muhammad's birthday.

Isra Mi'raj Nabi Muhammad SAW. December. 20. When Muhammad ascended on his steed Bouraq.

The 12 lunar months of the Muslim calendar are, in order:

Muharram
Safar
Rabiul Awal
Rabiul Ahir
Jumadil Awal
Jumadil Ahir
Rajab
Sa'ban
Ramadan (the fasting month)
Sawal
Kaidah
Zulhijja

Note: The Muslim calendar begins with the Hejira, Muhammad's flight to Medina, in A.D. 622 according to the Gregorian calendar. Early A.D. 1995 corresponds to A.H. 1415. The Muslim calendar is a lunar calendar, and gains 10 or

11 days on the Gregorian calendar each year. Islamic holidays will thus regress 10–11 days a year against to the Gregorian calendar.

SHOPPING

Be extremely cautious when buying antiques, works of art or other expensive objects, especially in the tourist areas. Most are reproductions, though very good ones and cheap to boot!

Handicrafts are produced all over Indonesia, and even if a good selection is available in hotels and tourist areas, it can be fun to seek out craftsmen in the villages (though often it's not cheaper unless you are very good at bargaining).

Bargaining

The secret here is not to care, or at least appear not to care. Some merchants are very upfront about giving prices that are about the minimum of what they want to sell an item for (*harga pas:* fixed price), but the trader who expects the buyer to bargain is more commonplace. A general rule of thumb is to aim for half the asking price by opening with an offer lower than that. The 50 % rule is by no means universal and many sellers will only come down by 20 %. On the other hand, in tourist areas, vendors will often ask 10 times or more the reasonable selling price, so don't feel shy about offering them 10% of the asking price.

More often than not the deal is closed in a ritual in which you cheerfully thank the purveyor for their time and take steps towards the next stall or the door as the case may be. At this point keep your ears pricked for the *real* final offer of the seller and either thank them again and move on or return and claim your prize. If your final price is accepted it is a major breach of etiquette not to consummate the purchase.

In any event, staying cheerful and good humored will not only be more fun but can make a huge difference in the price you finally pay (and the success of any important interaction with an Indonesian). This isn't just about money and, yes, you should pay a bit more than an Indonesian would. That's the way it works.

Souvenirs

The best places for souvenir-shopping are Lombok, Sumba, Flores and Timor. The traveler's problem is how to lug around what is brought for the rest of the trip. While the most common souvenir items, hand-woven traditional cloths, are relatively light, they take up a great deal of space.

Prices of cloths vary tremendously, from $2 for a simple shawl to over $2,000 for a fine, large, east Sumba cloth with intricate designs. You can buy these *ikat*-cloths directly in the villages where they are woven on backstrap looms,

but prices won't necessarily be lower than the shops in town. Worldwide demand, especially by the Japanese, have pushed up prices for fine ikat from the Lesser Sundas during the past decade. But you can still obtain good buys, if you know what you are doing.

If you are serious about buying *ikat*, you should first check the good shops in Bali for prices on fine pieces from the various districts in Nusa Tenggara. Then check the stores in Ende, Maumere, Waingapu and Kupang. Only after this experience will you have a base for judging and bargaining in the villages.

If you are looking for new weavings, we suggest buying at the government store in Kupang: the prices are most reasonable, and the quality is excellent. But you won't find old cloths there, nor will you find the more intricate cloths from East Sumba. For genuine antique cloths, try the Chinese-owned shops in Maumere and Kupang. In Lombok you can also buy antique wood carvings, but the supply of old cloth is just about exhausted.

PHOTOGRAPHY

Some 35mm Fuji and Kodak film is available in Indonesia, including color print film from ASA 100 to 400 and Ektachrome and Fujichrome 100 ASA daylight transparency film. In larger towns you can buy Fuji Neopan 100 ASA black-and-white negative film as well. You can't buy Kodachrome in Indonesia, although Fuji Velvia is available in the larger towns. Medium- and large-format emulsions are basically unavailable. Avoid local processing if you value your negatives or transparencies.

TREKKING

A well-organized, expensive Swiss travel agency sets up trekking expeditions to Lombok, Flores, Lembata, Solor, Adonara, Alor and Sumba. Their one-month Lesser Sundas tour, all-inclusive out of Zurich, costs 10,000 Swiss Francs but less if you meet the group in Bali.

Intertrek Switzerland. Mollisweid, CH-9050, Appenzell, Switzerland.

Indonesian Language Primer

Personal pronouns
I *saya*
we *kita* (inclusive), *kami* (exclusive)
you *anda* (formal), *saudara* (brother, sister),
kamu (for friends and children only)
he/she *dia*   they *mereka*

Forms of address
Father/Mr *Bapak* ("*Pak*")
Mother/Mrs *Ibu* ("*Bu*")
Elder brother *Abang* ("*Bang*" or "*Bung*")
            Mas (in Java only)
Elder sister *Mbak*
Younger brother/sister *Adik* ("*Dik*")
Note: These terms are used not just within the
family, but generally in polite speech.

Basic questions
How? *Bagaimana?*
How much/many? *Berapa?*
What? *Apa?*
What's this? *Apa ini?*
Who? *Siapa?*
Who's that? *Siapa itu?*
What is your name? *Siapa namanya ?*
(Literally: Who is your name?)
When? *Kapan?*
Where? *Mana?*
Which? *Yang mana?*
Why? *Kenapa?*

Useful words
yes *ya*   no, not *tidak, bukan*
Note: *Tidak* is used with verbs or adverbs;
bukan with nouns.

and *dan*
with *dengan*
for *untuk*
good *bagus*
fine *baik*
more *lebih*
less *kurang*

better *lebih baik*
worse *kurang baik*
this/these *ini*
that/those *itu*
same *sama*
different *lain*
here *di sini*
there *di sana*

Civilities
Welcome *Selamat datang*
Good morning (7–11am) *Selamat pagi*
Good midday (11am–3pm) *Selamat siang*
Good afternoon (3–7pm) *Selamat sore*
Goodnight (after dark) *Selamat malam*
Goodbye (to one leaving) *Selamat jalan*
Goodbye (to one staying) *Selamat tinggal*
Note: *Selamat* is a word from Arabic meaning
"May your time (or action) be blessed."
How are you? *Apa kabar?*
I am fine. *Kabar baik.*
Thank you. *Terima kasih.*
You're welcome. *Kembali.*
Same to you. *Sama sama.*
Pardon me *Ma'af*
Excuse me *Permisi*
(when leaving a conversation, etc).

Numbers
1	*satu*	6	*enam*
2	*dua*	7	*tujuh*
3	*tiga*	8	*delapan*
4	*empat*	9	*sembilan*
5	*lima*	10	*sepuluh*

Pronunciation and Grammar

Vowels
a As in f**a**ther
e Three forms:
  1) Schwa, like th**e**
  2) Like **é** in touch**é**
  3) Short **è**; as in b**e**t
i Usually like long **e** (as
  in Bal**i**); when bounded
  by consonants, like
  short **i** (h**i**t).
o Long **o**, like g**o**
u Long **u**, like yo**u**
ai Long **i**, like cr**i**me
au Like **ow** in **ow**l

Consonants
c Always like **ch** in **ch**urch
g Always hard, like **g**uard
h Usually soft, almost un-
  pronounced. It is hard
  between like vowels,
  e.g. ma**h**al (expensive).
k Like **k** in **k**ind; at end of
  word, unvoiced stop.
kh Like **k**ind, but harder
r Rolled, like Spanish **r**
ng Soft, like fli**ng**
ngg Hard, like ti**ng**le
ny Like **ny** in So**ny**a

Grammar
Grammatically, Indonesian is
in many ways far simpler than
English. There are no articles
(a, an, the).
The verb form "to be" is usually not used. There is no ending for plurals; sometimes the
word is doubled, but often
number comes from context.
And Indonesian verbs are not
conjugated. Tense is com-
municated by context or with
specific words for time.

Personal pronouns

I   *saya*
we   *kita* (inclusive), *kami* (exclusive)
you   *anda* (formal), *saudara* (brother, sister),
kamu (for friends and children only)
he/she   *dia*   they   *mereka*

Forms of address

Father/Mr   *Bapak* ("*Pak*")
Mother/Mrs   *Ibu* ("*Bu*")
Elder brother   *Abang* ("*Bang*" or "*Bung*")
             Mas (in Java only)
Elder sister   *Mbak*
Younger brother/sister   *Adik* ("*Dik*")
Note: These terms are used not just within the family, but generally in polite speech.

Basic questions

How?   *Bagaimana?*
How much/many?   *Berapa?*
What?   *Apa?*
What's this?   *Apa ini?*
Who?   *Siapa?*
Who's that?   *Siapa itu?*
What is your name?   *Siapa namanya ?*
(Literally: Who is your name?)
When?   *Kapan?*
Where?   *Mana?*
Which?   *Yang mana?*
Why?   *Kenapa?*

Useful words

yes   *ya*   no, not   *tidak, bukan*
Note: *Tidak* is used with verbs or adverbs; *bukan* with nouns.

and	*dan*	better	*lebih baik*
with	*dengan*	worse	*kurang baik*
for	*untuk*	this/these	*ini*
good	*bagus*	that/those	*itu*
fine	*baik*	same	*sama*
more	*lebih*	different	*lain*
less	*kurang*	here	*di sini*
		there	*di sana*

Civilities

Welcome   *Selamat datang*
Good morning (7–11am)   *Selamat pagi*
Good midday (11am–3pm)   *Selamat siang*
Good afternoon (3–7pm)   *Selamat sore*
Goodnight (after dark)   *Selamat malam*
Goodbye (to one leaving)   *Selamat jalan*
Goodbye (to one staying)   *Selamat tinggal*
Note: *Selamat* is a word from Arabic meaning "May your time (or action) be blessed."
How are you?   *Apa kabar?*
I am fine.   *Kabar baik.*
Thank you.   *Terima kasih.*
You're welcome.   *Kembali.*
Same to you.   *Sama sama.*
Pardon me   *Ma'af*
Excuse me   *Permisi*
(when leaving a conversation, etc).

Numbers

1	*satu*	6	*enam*
2	*dua*	7	*tujuh*
3	*tiga*	8	*delapan*
4	*empat*	9	*sembilan*
5	*lima*	10	*sepuluh*
11	*seblas*	100	*seratus*
12	*dua belas*	600	*enam ratus*
13	*tiga belas*	1,000	*seribu*
20	*dua puluh*	3,000	*tiga ribu*
50	*lima puluh*	10,000	*sepuluh ribu*
73	*tujuh puluh tiga*		

1,000,000   *satu juta*
2,000,000   *dua juta*
half   *setengah*

first	*pertama*	third	*ketiga*
second	*kedua*	fourth	*ke'empat*

Time

minute	*menit*	Sunday	*Hari Minggu*
hour	*jam*	Monday	*Hari Senin*
(also clock/watch)		Tuesday	*Hari Selasa*
day	*hari*	Wednesday	*Hari Rabu*
week	*minggu*	Thursday	*Hari Kamis*
month	*bulan*	Friday	*Hari Jum'at*
year	*tahun*	Saturday	*Hari Sabtu*
today	*hari ini*	later	*nanti*
tomorrow	*besok*	yesterday	*kemarin*

What time is it?   *Jam berapa?*
(It is) eight thirty.   *Jam setengah sembilan*
               (Literally: "half nine")
How many hours?   *Berapa jam?*
When did you arrive?   *Kapan datang?*
Four days ago.   *Empat hari yang lalu.*
When are you leaving?
      Kapan berangkat?
In a short while.   *Sebentar lagi.*

Basic vocabulary

to be, have	*ada*		
to be able, can	*bisa*		
to buy	*beli*	correct	*betul*
to know	*tahu*	wrong	*salah*
to get	*dapat*	big	*besar*
to need	*perlu*	small	*kecil*
to want	*mau*	pretty	*cantik*
to go	*pergi*	slow	*pelan*
to wait	*tunggu*	fast	*cepat*
at	*di*	stop	*berhenti*
to	*ke*	old	*tua, lama*
if	*kalau*	new	*baru*
near	*dekat*	then	*lalu, kemudian*
far	*jauh*	only	*hanya, saja*
empty	*kosong*	crowded, noisy	*ramai*

Small talk

Where are you from?   *Dari mana?*
I'm from the US.   *Saya dari Amerika.*
How old are you?   *Umurnya berapa?*
I'm 31 years old.
      Umur saya tiga pulu satu tahun.
Are you married?   *Sudah kawin belum?*
Yes, I am.   *Yah, sudah.*   Not yet.   *Belum.*
Do you have children?   *Sudah punya anak?*
What is your religion?   *Agama apa?*
Where are you going?   *Mau ke mana?*

Transportation

GETTING AROUND IN INDONESIA

This advisory gives you an overview of the wide range of travel options available during your stay in Indonesia. A comprehensive run-down of travel services enables you to plan your way around the island according to time and budget. More specific details for each area you will be visiting can be found in the relevant Practicalities sections.

Prices are in US dollars, unless otherwise stated. Prices and schedules are given as an indication only as they change frequently according to the season. Check with a travel agent prior to departure for the most up-to-date information.

In many ways, Indonesia is an easy place to get around. Indonesians are as a rule hospitable and good-humored, and will always help a lost or confused traveler. The weather is warm, the pace of life relaxed, and the air is rich with the smells of clove cigarettes, the blessed durian fruit and countless other wonders.

On the other hand, the nation's transportation infrastructure does not move with the kind of speed and efficiency that western travelers expect, which often leads to frustration. It is best to adjust your pace to local conditions. There is nothing more pathetic than a tourist who has traveled halfway around the world just to shout at some poor clerk at the airport counter.

The golden rule is: things will sort themselves out. Eventually. Be persistent, of course, but relax and keep your sense of humor. Before you explode, have a *kretek* cigarette, a cup of sweet coffee, or a cool glass of *kelapa muda* (young coconut water). Things might look different.

GETTING TO INDONESIA

You can fly to Indonesia from just about anywhere. Most people traveling from Europe and the US arrive on direct flights to Jakarta, while those coming from Australia generally first go to Bali. The main international entry points are Sukarno-Hatta airport in Jakarta, Ngurah Rai airport in Bali, and Polonia airport in Medan, North Sumatra. There are now also flights between Singapore and Surabaya, in East Java, on Singapore Airlines (direct) and Garuda (via Jakarta). SilkAir, also based in Singapore, flies direct from Singapore to Manado, in North Sulawesi.

Sukarno-Hatta airport is served by many international airlines, with over a dozen flights a day from Singapore alone. A cut-price alternative from Europe or the US may be to get a cheap flight to Singapore, and buy an onward discount ticket to Jakarta from there: the cost of these can be as low as $90 single, $155 return. A return ticket from Singapore to Bali with stops in Jakarta and Yogyakarta, good for a month, is available in Singapore for around $450. Buy through travel agents—check the *Straits Times* for details. Note: you need return or onward ticket to get a tourist visa on arrival.

Direct flights also connect Jakarta with many major cities in Asia and Europe. Air fares vary depending on the carrier, the season and the type of ticket purchased. A discount RT fare from the US or Europe costs from $850: about half that from Australia or East Asian capitals.

Air tickets from **Batam** and **Bintan** are less expensive, and these Indonesian islands just off the coast of Singapore can be reached via short ferry hops from Singapore's World Trade Centre. Tickets to Batam cost $12 single, $18 return, and to Bintan $35 single, $55 return.

There are several daily jet flights from Batam as well as Tanjung Pinang, Bintan, to Jakarta via Merpati/Garuda and Sempati: $130 single and $180 return. **Merpati/Garuda** office in Batam ☎ (778) 45820. **Sempati** in Batam ☎ (778) 411612/453050. **Sempati** in Tanjung Pinang, Bintan ☎ (771) 21612/25283.

Airport tax for departing passengers is Rp17,000 for international routes and between Rp1,500 and Rp6,000 for domestic flights.

Having arrived in Indonesia, your choices for onward travel depend, as always, on time and money. Possibilities on Java range from boats, trains, hire cars, and chauffeur driven, to both slow and fast buses. Hiring a car or minibus with or without driver, is one of the most rewarding ways of getting around, if you can afford it.

Visas

Nationals of the following 36 countries do not need visas, and are granted visa-free entry for 60 days upon arrival (this is non-renewable). For other nationals, visas are required and must be obtained in advance from an Indonesian embassy or consulate.

Argentina	Iceland	Norway

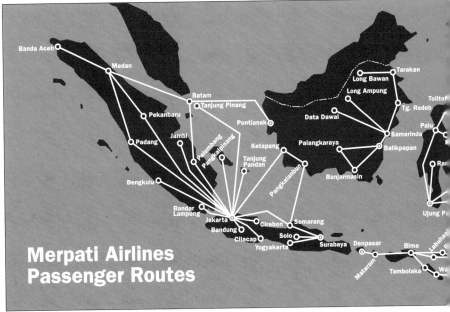

Merpati Airlines Passenger Routes

Australia	Ireland	Philippines
Austria	Italy	Singapore
Belgium	Japan	South Korea
Brazil	Liechtenstein	Spain
Canada	Luxemburg	Sweden
Chile	Malaysia	Switzerland
Denmark	Malta	Thailand
Finland	Mexico	United Kingdom
France	Morocco	United States
Germany	Netherlands	Venezuela
Greece	New Zealand	Yugoslavia

Be sure to check your passport before leaving for Indonesia. You must have at least one empty page to be stamped on arrival, and the passport must be valid for at least six months after the date of arrival. For visa-free entry, you must also have proof of onward journey, either a return or through ticket. Employment is strictly forbidden on tourist visas or visa-free entry.

Visa-free entry to Indonesia cannot be extended beyond two months (60 days) and is only given to passengers arriving at the following airports: Ambon, Bali, Batam, Biak, Jakarta, Manado, Medan, Padang, Pontianak, Surabaya. Or at the following seaports: Bali, Balikpapan, Batam, Tanjung Pinang (Bintan), Jakarta, Kupang, Pontianak, Semarang.

OTHER VISAS

The 2-month, non-extendable **tourist pass** is the only entry permit that comes without a great deal of paperwork.

A **visitor's visa**, usually valid for 4–5 weeks, can be extended for up to 6 months, but is difficult to get. You must have a good reason for spending time in Indonesia (research, relatives, religious study) and you must have a sponsor

and lots of supporting letters. Even with a sponsor and the best of reasons, however, you might still be denied. The process can take days or even weeks, and extensions are at the discretion of the immigration office where you apply.

A **business visa**, valid for 30 days and extendable to 3 months requires a letter from a company stating that you are performing a needed service for a company in Indonesia. This is not intended as an employment visa, but is for investors, consultants, or other business purposes.

Two other types of passes are available: the temporary residence pass (KIM-S) and permanent residence pass (KIM). Both are hard to get.

Customs

Narcotics, firearms and ammunition are strictly prohibited. The standard duty-free allowance is: 2 liters of alcoholic beverages, 200 cigarettes, 50 cigars or 100 grams of tobacco. There is no restriction on import and export of foreign currencies in cash or travelers checks, but there is an export limit of 50,000 Indonesian rupiah.

All narcotics are illegal in Indonesia. The use, sale or purchase of narcotics results in long prison terms and huge fines. Once caught, you are immediately placed in detention until trial, and the sentences are stiff, as demonstrated by westerners currently serving sentences as long as 30 years for possession of marijuana.

Keeping Your Cool

At government offices like immigration or police, talking loudly and forcefully doesn't make things easier. Patience and politeness are virtues that

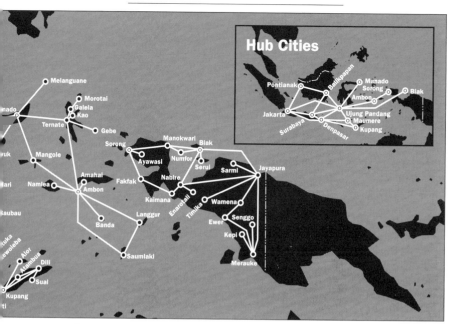

open many doors in Indonesia. Good manners and dress are also to your advantage.

TRAVELING IN INDONESIA

Getting around in Indonesia is not—to those used to efficient and punctual transportation—effortless. Bookings are often difficult to make; flights and reservations are sometimes mysteriously canceled.

What seems like nerve-wracking inefficiency is really so only if one is in a hurry. If you have to be somewhere at a particular time, allow plenty of time to get there. Check and double-check your bookings. Otherwise just go with the flow. You can't just turn off the archipelago's famous *jam karet*—"rubber time"—when it's time to take an airplane and turn it on again when you want to relax. You will get there eventually.

Peak periods around holidays and during the August tourist season are the most difficult. It is imperative to book well in advance and reconfirm your bookings at every step along the way. Travel anywhere in Indonesia during the week of the Islamic Lebaran (Ramadan) holiday (usually around 14 or 15 March) is practically impossible. Find a nice spot and sit it out.

Getting around Nusa Tenggara

Bali, just a short hop from Lombok at the western end of Nusa Tenggara, has the best air connections in the region (in fact, in all of Indonesia, except for Jakarta). Kupang, in the east, has twice weekly flights to Darwin, Australia and several daily flights to Bali.

In Nusa Tenggara, the axis of air communication is Bali–Kupang. There are two paths: one hops through Sumba, and the other hops through Lombok, Sumbawa and Flores—basically a milk run. You more or less have to follow one or the other of these tracks: there are no flights, for example, from Flores to Sumba. (Although the Kelimutu connects these islands, it stops only every two weeks.) There are two flights a week between Tambolaka airport (West Sumba) and Bima (East Sumbawa) but the plane is a 16-passenger Twin Otter and it is awfully hard to book a seat.

This is not a problem, of course, if you have the time and energy to island-hop and overland both ways—say Bali to Kupang, through Sumbawa and Flores, and then Kupang to Bali, stopping in Sumba. The two months on your tourist visa will just about cover this round-trip. Otherwise, keep in mind the limitations presented by these separate east–west routes when planning your itinerary.

While air travel is recommended for long hops, for short hops in Nusa Tenggara, airplanes are not necessarily the fastest way to travel. Flight delays, schedule changes, overbookings and cancelled flights are common. You must wait until you arrive, and there you might find that your onward flight is woefully overcommitted (or broken down).

In many cases, bus travel is much easier (and even faster!) than air travel, particularly as major roads in the region have improved tremendously over the past few years. Buses are frequent, cheap and fast— albeit crowded. You can usually get your hotel or *losmen* to arrange for

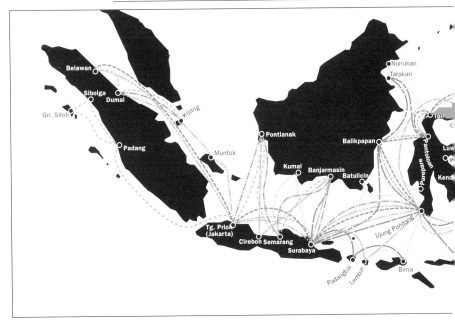

your tickets, and alert the driver to pick you up. But be prepared—once you board, there could still as much as another hour used up rounding up passengers in town. Use your judgement: if you get on early, when the bus is still almost empty, you get a good seat, but have to drive around town for an hour; if you get on late, when the bus is crowded, you get a lousy seat, but it cuts an hour off your travel time.

There are ferry connections between Bali, Lombok, Sumbawa and Flores (via Komodo) which are not too long or painful. Out of Kupang, there is a short ferry ride to Roti, and much longer ones to Savu, Larantuka and Alor. On these, space is at a premium and the overnight rides are no fun at all.

Aside from the scheduled *Kelimutu* (see Pelni below), you have to take unscheduled ships to move around Nusa Tenggara by sea. This is easy from Larantuka, Flores to Lembata Island (average of twice a day), but gets difficult elsewhere—say from Lembata to Pantar or Alor islands. But for those with a time, native boat travel around the islands can be a great experience. Bring food, drinks, a hat and enjoy the sea.

Air Travel

The cardinal rule is book early, confirm and reconfirm often. If you are told a flight is fully booked, go to the airport anyway and stand in line. While Garuda's booking system is computerized, the other airlines' are not, and bookings evaporate at the last minute all the time. However it is rare that flights are completely full.

Always keep the following points in mind:

✈ It's practically impossible to get a confirmed booking out of a city other than the one you're in. You can buy a ticket and it may say you have a booking, but don't believe it until you reconfirm with the airline in the city of departure.

✈ Reconfirm bookings directly with the airline office in the city of departure between 24 and 72 hours before your flight, particularly during peak tourist seasons and Indonesian holidays. Your seat may be given away if you reconfirm either too early or too late (or not at all).

✈ Make bookings in person, not by phone. (Reconfirmations only can be done by phone.)

✈ Get written evidence of bookings. Note the name of the person who gives it to you so you can hold them responsible if you're later told you don't have one.

✈ Note the computer booking code. Names have a tendency to go astray or be misspelled. Concrete proof of your booking is essential.

✈ If your name isn't on the computer try looking under your first or middle names as these are frequently mistaken for surnames.

✈ If you are told a flight is full, go to the airport about two hours before departure and ask that your name be put on the waiting list. See that it is. Hang around the desk and be friendly to the staff and you will probably get on the flight. A tip will sometimes, but not always, help.

✈ There are usually alternate ways of getting from point A to B. For example, from Yogyakarta to Bali, if there is no space left on the flights, take a bus to Surakarta (Solo) and fly from there.

Garuda Indonesia's flagship airline has been in business for 45 years. It serves all major cities in Indonesia and at least 28 international des-

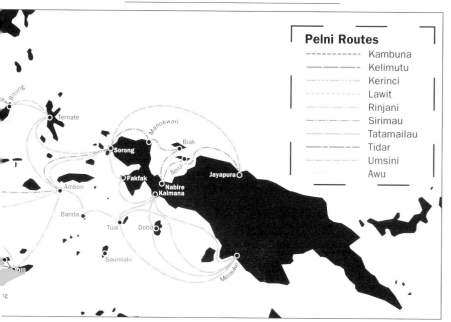

Pelni Routes

-----------	Kambuna
-----------	Kelimutu
-----------	Kerinci
-----------	Lawit
-----------	Rinjani
-----------	Sirimau
-----------	Tatamailau
-----------	Tidar
-----------	Umsini
	Awu

tinations. They fly only jets, mainly wide-bodies, and the service is reasonably good. Head office is at Jl Merdeka Selatan 13 ☎ (021) 2311801; fax: (021) 365986 with convenient sales counters in Hotel Indonesia, Hotel Borobudur and BDN Bldg., Jl Thamrin 5. After normal office hours, tickets can be purchased in a small Garuda office on the 3rd floor of Wisma Dharmala Sakti, Jl Sudirman 32 (open 24 hours).

Merpati A Garuda subsidiary, with a huge network of domestic flights serving more than 160 airports throughout Indonesia. Merpati (literally "pigeon") flies smaller jets (DC-9s and F-28s) as well as turbo-props (F-27s, Twin-Otters and locally-made Cassa CN 212s and 235s).

Merpati is not known for its punctuality or its service, but the airline does at least connect towns and villages all across Indonesia, in some cases landing on a grass airstrip in a highland village of only 100 people that would take days to reach by any other means. Consider yourself lucky that you can even fly to these places.

Merpati's standard baggage allowance is 20 kilos for economy class, but some of the smaller aircraft permit only 10 kilos (after which excess baggage charges of $1 per kilo apply).

Students (10–26 years old) receive a discount of 25% (show an international student ID card), and children between the ages of 2 and 10 pay 50% of the regular fare. Infants not occupying a seat pay 10% of the regular fare.

Main office: Jl Angkasa 2, Jakarta. ☎ (21) 424 3608; Fax: (21) 424 6616.

Sempati A new, privately-owned competitor on the scene, with quality service and a growing network inside and outside of Indonesia. Sempati

flies new F-100s to several cities in Asia, such as Singapore, Kuala Lumpur, Bangkok, Hong Kong and Taipei. Domestically they fly between major cities such as Jakarta, Yogya, Surabaya and Denpasar. Head office: Ground floor terminal building, Halim Perdana Kusuma Airport, Jakarta. ☎ (21) 809 4407; Fax: (21) 809 4420.

Bouraq A small, private company, flying mainly older planes linking secondary cities in Java, as well as Bali, Kalimantan, Nusa Tenggara, Sulawesi, and other destinations. Main office: Jl Angkasa 1–3, Jakarta. ☎ (21) 659 5364; Fax: 600 8729.

Mandala Operates a few prop planes to out-of-the-way airstrips in Kalimantan, Sumatra and Sulawesi. Main office: Jl Garuda 76, Jakarta. ☎ (21) 424 9360; Fax: 424 9491.

NOTE: Travel agents often give cheaper fares than airline offices and are easily found. The best for ticketing are **Pacto** Jl Surabaya 8, Menteng, Jakarta ☎ (21) 348 7447 and **Vayatour** Chase Plaza, Jl Sudirman, Jakarta ☎ (21) 570 4119.

Sea Travel

There is four times as much sea in Indonesia as land, and for many centuries transportation among the islands has been principally by boat. Tiny ports are scattered all over the archipelago, and the only way to reach many areas is by sea.

To travel by boat, you need plenty of time. Most ships are small, and are at the mercy of the sea and the seasons. Think of it as a romantic journey, and don't be in a hurry.

Pelni (Pelayaran Nasional Indonesia) the national passenger line, has 10 large ships (some 70 ships total) criss-crossing the archipelago carrying up to 1,500 passengers each. These boats travel on fixed schedules and the first and second class cabins are comfortable.

Many of the older vessels look like floating trash cans, but the new German-built passenger ships are modern and comfortable. (See route map previous page for destinations served.) Fares are fixed, and there are up to 5 classes, with different numbers of people sharing each cabin, and different service. Head office: 5th floor, Jl Gajah Mada 14, Jakarta 10130. ☎ (21) 384 4342, 384 4366; Fax: (21) 385 4130. Main ticket office: Jl Angkasa 18, Kemayoran ☎ 421 1921. Open in the mornings.

There are a myriad of other options. Rusty old **coastal steamers** ply the eastern islands, stopping at tiny ports to pick up copra, seaweed and other cash crops and deliver commodities like metal wares, fuel and the occasional outboard motor. You can book deck passage on one of these ships in just about any harbor, for very little money. If you do, stock up on food—you will quickly tire of the rice and salt fish that the crew eat. Bring a waterproof tarpaulin and a bag to protect your gear. You can often rent bunks from the crew, to get a comfortable night's sleep.

Crowded **overnight ferries** connect smaller islands. Use your luggage to stake out a spot early, and bring a straw mat to lie on. It is usually best to stay on deck, where the fresh sea breezes keep your spirits up. Below deck tends to be noisy, verminous and smelly.

Small **perahu** can be rented in many areas for day trips upriver, around the coast, or to neighboring islands. These can be hired by the hour or by the trip, to take you snorkeling, sightseeing or birdwatching. Outboard motors are expensive in Indonesia, and tend to be small. Inspect any boat carefully before hiring it, as some craft are only marginally seaworthy. See if the boatman can rig up a canopy to block the blazing sun or the occasional cloudburst.

You could even book passage on a **luxury catamaran**. P&O Travel runs the 37 m, 42-passenger *Spice Islander*, through Nusa Tenggara. It begins in Bali and calls at Lombok, Gili Suda and Sekotong, and then proceeds to Sumbawa, Komodo, Flores, Lembata, Roti, Sawu, and then returns to Benoa. There are either one- or two-week packages. Sample fares: 7 days. 6 nights: $1,983 based on double occupancy. 14 days, 13 nights, $3,655. Add 30% for suite. Add 50% for single occupancy. P&O representatives in the United States:
Abercrombie and Kent International Inc. 1420 Kensington Road, Oak Brook, Illinois 60521-2106. ☎ (708) 954-2944, (800) 323-7308; fax: (708) 954-3324. Representative in UK: **Swan Hellenic Ltd.** 77 New Oxford Street, London WC1A 1PP. ☎ (071) 8311234; fax: (071) 8311280. Representative in Singapore: **P&O Travel(S) Pte. Ltd.** 80 Anson Road, IBM Towers Suite 31-01, Singapore 0207. ☎ 2247433; Fax: 2227925.

TRAVEL OVERLAND

Road conditions in Indonesia have improved dramatically over the past years, but traffic has also increased and driving is a slow and hazardous affair.

Trucks and buses, minivans, swarms of motorcycles piled with goods or carrying a family of four, ox-drawn carts, bicycles and pedicabs (*becak*) and pedestrians of all ages, compete in what is at times a crazy battle for tarmac, where the biggest and fastest rule.

Rental cars and motorcycles are available in many major cities, and a number of different types of buses run cheap and regular services.

Planning an Itinerary

The first thing to realize is that you can never cover the entire island even if you were to spend months here. Don't give yourself an impossibly tight schedule. Be aware that things happen slowly here, and adjust yourself to the pace. Better to spend more time in a few places and see them in a leisurely way, than to end up hot and bothered. You'll see *more* this way, not less.

Wherever you are, keep in mind that the tropical heat takes its toll and you should avoid the midday sun. Get an early start, before the rays become punishing (the tropical light is beautiful at dawn). Retreat to a cool place after lunch and go out again in the afternoon and early evening, when it's much more pleasant.

Night Express Buses—*bis malam*

The preferred mode of transportation for Indonesians, these buses operate only at night. Available in a wide variety of classes: from the public *patas* air-conditioned with reclining seats (crowded, run by the army) to the ultra-luxurious "Big Top" buses that run from Jakarta (these have seats like business class airline seats).

The better buses have a bathroom and arctic air-conditioning: the other reason you brought a sweater. The key to successful *bis malam* trips is sleep. Choose the best bus available as the price difference is usually not very great, and justifiable in that a good sleep is saving you a night's accommodation.

Most buses are fitted with televisions and show movies whether you want them or not, often followed by music. You are likely to be the only one who is annoyed by the volume, but a cheerful suggestion that the music be turned off (*dimatikan*) will at least get it turned down to the point where earplugs can block out the rest. The seats to avoid are in the very front and the very back. The back seats are raised up over the engine and don't recline, while front row seats give you too intimate a view of what the driver is doing.

There are also karaoke "sing-along" buses—

for masochists and anthropologists only.

These buses leave in late afternoon and go all night, and often well into the next day. When *bis malam* cross from island to island, they go on the ferry. Tickets are sold at the bus terminal, or by agents, and there are usually a number of different buses going your way. Shop around, to see what you are getting.

You can also buy two seats, which will make sure you don't get squashed. The price is cheap enough that most budgets can handle two fares. If possible, get the two front seats next to the driver, as you get the best view from there. Or at least get a window seat. On many buses, you can reserve one day ahead. Always see if your hotel or *losmen* can make the bookings for you; this is a common practice, particularly in Sumbawa and Flores.

Local Buses

The major advantages of these rattling buses is that they are extremely cheap, run every few minutes between major towns, and can be picked up at the terminals or any point along their routes. This is also their biggest disadvantage: they stop constantly.

If you depart from a terminal, find a seat near a window that opens. Try not to share this breeze with passengers behind you; they are likely to have a strong aversion to wind for fear of *masuk angin* (the wind which enters the body and causes a cold).

The seats are very small, both in terms of leg room and width. You and your bag may take up (and be charged for) two seats. This is fair. But be sure you're not being overcharged for not knowing any better. The key is to know better. Ask someone what the proper fare is to your destination before getting on. A few words of Indonesian are indispensable to be able to ask for directions. People are generally very eager to help you.

Larger towns have city buses charging nominal fares, usually Rp300 (15¢). Flag them down wherever you see them. The catch is knowing which one to take as there are no maps or guides.

Express Minibuses—"travel" or "colt"

These come in two varieties: old and hot (sit by a window and keep it open) and the newer, much revered, L300 van with air-conditioning. Even the L300 gets a lot of engine heat, and at midday can still be sauna-like: especially if the air-conditioning is broken and the windows shut.

These 8 to 11 passenger vans connect major cities and deliver you right to your destination. They sometimes also pick you up. They usually travel during the day, though on longer routes they travel at night like the *bis malam*. Express minibuses are slightly more expensive than *bis malam* but more convenient.

Local Minibuses—*bemo*

These non air-conditioned vans ("colt" or "*bemo*") are the real workhorses of the transport network, going up and down even relatively impassable mountain tracks to deliver villagers and produce all over the island. Regular seats are supplemented by wooden benches, boosting the capacity of these sardine cans to 25. And there is *always* room for more. Take a seat up front with the driver whenever possible.

There are standard fares but these are flexible to account for how much room you and your bag are taking up. Ask someone before flagging one down if you are concerned by the potential Rp100 price gouging. Flag one down on any roadside. You can also charter one to most destinations. Just say "charter" and where you want to go, then bargain for the fare in advance.

Car Rentals

At first glance the unwritten driving rules of Indonesia seem like a maniacal free-for-all. It is only later that the subtle hierarchy (truck vs. car: you lose) and finesse (2-centimeter tolerances) become evident. This is as good a reason as any that self-drive car rentals are rare. Sedans or taxis with drivers are available in Jakarta but are very expensive; they don't really like to go long distances, and you have to return them to your starting point. In Bali, various companies offer self-drive cars, for reasonable rates. To drive in Indonesia you need a valid international license. Traffic here moves on the left, British style.

Chartering a Car or Minibus

This can be the best way to handle a land tour as you have the freedom to stop whenever things look interesting and the flexibility to try out some less traveled routes. This can also be an economical alternative if you can fill up a van. The minibus can take up to 7, but you need extra space if you are to be in it for a few days, so 5 passengers is generally maximum.

Some asking around will quickly give you an idea of where to hire a driver and what the local going rates are for a specific excursion or longer itinerary. A full day of driving one-way will cost from $50 to $80 and a five-day trip around $300. Much of this is for fuel, so distance is a major factor. Most of the rest goes to the owner of the vehicle, and only a tiny percentage left for the driver. It is understood that you will pay for the driver's meals and accommodation both while he is with you and on his journey back home. A tip of Rp5,000 per day is also appreciated if the driver is good.

The quality of both the driver and the vehicle will figure heavily in the enjoyability of your trip so don't be shy about checking both out before striking a deal.

Lombok PRACTICALITIES

Lombok is becoming a second Bali. Only a few years ago, accommodation was scarce, and transportation limited. But now that tourists have started to venture beyond the shores of Bali, the island is following the tremendous development of its neighbor, though at a slower pace. New hotels open every month and a whole range of options are now offered to visitors, from trekking trips to five-star luxury.

Prices in US dollars. S = Single; D = Double; T = Triple; AC = Air-conditioning. Telephone code for Mataram is 364.

GETTING THERE

By Air

Currently three airlines (Merpati Nusantara Airlines, Sempati Air, and Bouraq) fly to Lombok's Selaparang airport, conveniently located in Rembiga, 4 km north of Mataram. Flights from Denpasar, Bali, take 25 minutes and cost $27.

A new airport, which will enable larger aircraft to land on the island, is planned to be built in Central Lombok as part of a national infrastructure development program.

Merpati operates a daily service between Bali and Lombok: Fokker F-27 planes leave from both islands almost every two hours. These flights can now be booked in advance, which was not the case in the past. For booking, contact any Merpati or Garuda office.

DEPARTURE TIMES

Merpati Bali to Lombok: 7 am, 8:50 am, 9 am, 9:30 am, 10 am, 11 am, 1 pm, 2 pm, 3 pm. Lombok to Bali: 8 am, 10 am, 11 am, 12 noon, 12:30 pm, 2 pm, 3 pm, 4 pm.

Some services don't run daily, (such as Denpasar–Mataram–Sumbawa Besar flight on Mon, Wed and Fri), so don't leave it until the last minute.

In Denpasar, Bali contact Merpati at: Jl Melati 57, ☎ (361) 235 358, 225 841, 222 864.

In Mataram, Lombok, try either: Jl Langko, ☎ 21757; Jl Pejanggik, Mataram; or Jl Selaparang 40, Cakranegara, ☎ 22670.

Sempati has two daily flights from Bali departing at 1:30 pm and 3:35 pm; and from Mataram at 12:40 pm and 2:45 pm. Contact: Bali Beach Hotel, ☎ (361) 288824, 289640, 289641, Fax: 287917; or the office at Ngurah Rai airport, ☎ (361) 754219, 755619, 755620; Fax: 754218. In Lombok, ☎ 27416.

Bouraq now also has one flight a day to Lombok, leaving Bali at 3:55 pm, and from Lombok at 3:30 pm. Contact Bouraq in Bali at: Jl Sudirman 7A, ☎ 223564, 63978; (Lombok) Jl A.A. Gde Ngurah G3, Cakra, ☎ 31640, 35651.

Garuda. In Denpasar, Bali. Jl Melati 61, ☎ (361) 225291, 225245. In Kuta, Bali: Natour Kuta Beach Hotel, ☎ (361) 751179, 751361–2 ext. 158-9. In Sanur, Bali: Bali Beach Hotel, ☎ (0361) 288243, 287920, or 288511 ext. 130, and Sanur Beach Hotel, ☎ (361) 287915 or 288011–15 ext. 178–9. In Nusa Dua, Bali: Sheraton Nusa Indah Resort, ☎ (0361) 71572 ext. 560-1-2, 71864, 71906, or Galleria Nusa Dua, ☎ 71444, 72231. In Mataram, Lombok try Jl Yos Sudarso 6, ☎ 23762. General flight information: ☎ (361) 751174. Reservations & reconfirmations: ☎ (361) 235169, 227825, 751178.

By Sea

FERRIES

If you are prone to sea-sickness be warned; the seas in the strait can be very rough, especially between Nusa Penida and the south peninsula of Lombok. The waves are particularly fierce during the rainy season which begins in October. Seas are generally calmer in the morning.

The traditional way to reach Lombok from Bali is the 3.5-hr ferry crossing from Padangbai to Lembar. Boats now leave both harbors every two hours starting from 2 am, and usually run on time. Facilities aboard have been upgraded recently, especially in VIP class: AC, TV, video, music and karaoke. The newest vessel, the *Dharma Kosala*, has air-conditioned economy class. Snacks and drinks are available (prices higher than ashore).

Fares are still very low: $2.50 (economy); $4 (VIP). If you bring your bicycle, motorbike or car, it will cost you an additional fee: 40¢, $2.50, and $17 respectively.

The **Mabua Express** is the newest, fastest and most comfortable way to make the crossing. This luxury jet-propelled catamaran, accommodating 248 passengers, crosses the strait twice a day between Benoa, Bali and Lembar, Lombok in barely two hours, at an average speed of 32 knots.

It leaves Benoa at 8:30 am and 2:30 pm; and Lembar, at 11:30 am and 5 pm. This is most convenient for those staying in Sanur, Kuta or Nusa Dua, or those leaving from Denpasar, and it saves time and energy—but certainly not money. Facilities include AC (no smoking), reclining chairs, TV, bar, and facilities for handicapped people. The crew is very helpful.

Fares: Emerald class (economy) on the lower deck: $17.50, including a drink; Diamond class (VIP) on the upper deck: $25, with snack, welcome drink, and free transfer from port to next destination (Benoa, Kuta, Sanur, Nusa Dua; Mataram or Senggigi). Children aged 2–12 pay 50% of adult fare. You can book in advance, but tickets are also available at the harbor and boats are seldom full. Try to be there 15–30 min before departure, as the ship leaves on time.

Package deals are available including a return ticket on the Mabua Express (Emerald class), a full day tour with lunch, and hotel transfer. Price: $75 (adult); $37.50 (child). Ask your travel agent for details. **Natrabu** (☎ 288447 or 288660) also offers a similar package, including two nights at Lombok Intan Laguna Hotel, Senggigi. Price: $182 S, $150 D.

Contact: Benoa, Bali ☎ (361) 72370, 72521; Fax: 72370. Mataram, Lombok, ☎ 25895, 37224; Fax: 37224.

Pelni lines Two Pelni passenger ships, the *Awu* and the *Kelimutu*, now sail eastwards from Bali. Both call at Benoa harbor, Bali, but only the *Kelimutu* calls in at Lembar, Lombok: once a month. on its way back to Surabaya, Java from Bima, Sumbawa. This may be useful if you happen to be there on the right day. Contact them in Benoa, Bali ☎ 228962; or Ampenan, Lombok at Jl Industri 1, ☎ 21604. You can call them anyway for information on further destinations (*Awu* for Sulawesi and *Kelimutu* for East Nusa Tenggara). See Pelni route map pages 254–255.

By Land

There are a host of bus companies operating throughout Nusa Tenggara Barat, linking Mataram and Bima, via Sumbawa Besar. Most travel direct from Mataram to Surabaya. Others operate along the Surabaya–Denpasar–Mataram route. Because of fierce competition the vehicles are increasingly new and comfortable: many have AC, reclining chairs, music, video or karaoke, and meals included. The drivers are usually reliable, and Lombok's roads are nothing near as crowded as those on Java or Bali.

Reliable companies are, among others: **Puspasari**, **Surabaya Indah**, **Damri**, **Bali Cepat**, **Bali Indah**, **Karya Jaya**. Tickets can be bought from the respective offices in Denpasar and Mataram, or from the various ticket agencies scattered everywhere in both towns. In Mataram, most of them can be found along Jl Pejanggik and Jl Selaparang. You can also jump on board at the Sweta terminal in Mataram, if they are not full. Again, if you're lucky and there's room, you can also get on buses at Padang Bai harbor (east of Klungkung in Bali) before they make the crossing to Lombok. Oddly, most buses traveling from Surabaya to Mataram don't go via

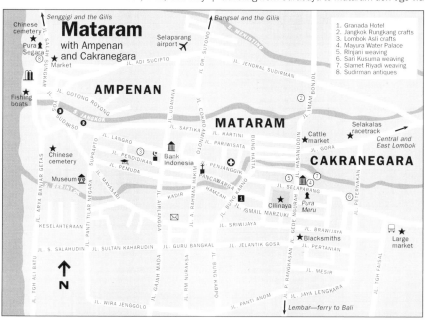

Mataram
with Ampenan
and Cakranegara

1. Granada Hotel
2. Jangkok Rungkang crafts
3. Lombok Asli crafts
4. Mayura Water Palace
5. Rinjani weaving
6. Sari Kusuma weaving
7. Slamet Riyadi weaving
8. Sudirman antiques

Denpasar, except for Karya Jaya, which leaves from Ubung Terminal (north of Denpasar) at 2:30 pm every day. Fare: $8.50.

LOCAL TRANSPORTATION

As a whole, the island's road network is excellent, except for some stretches in the South and on the southern peninsula. However, several of the more interesting sites off the main road are difficult to reach without a jeep, such as the waterfalls on the northern slopes of Mount Rinjani or Tiu Pupus waterfall in the north west, only 5 km away from Gondang but with an access track that is in a dreadful condition.

Public Transportation

On arrival at Lembar ferry terminal, you can take a bemo to Mataram ($1), Praya or Senggigi, among other destinations. Minibus tickets are also sold on board the ferry at the cafeteria; they will enable you to avoid troublesome hassling when you get ashore. Look firm and resolved when disembarking, and if you hold tickets do not allow your luggage to be grabbed by competing conductors!

If you intend to go straight to Labuhan Lombok on the east coast and cross to Sumbawa, you can find special buses at Lembar (max. $1.50); but they sometimes force you to change to another vehicle at Sweta terminal in Mataram, where they stop to pick up passengers. Buses can be quicker than bemos, but there's no general rule for this.

If you travel on the Mabua express in Emerald class (not including free transfer to Mataram or Senggigi) and do not want to use the minibus service available (booking can be made during the crossing), you run the risk of not finding bemos waiting for you outside, or if you do, you will be charged more than the normal fare unless you are a tough bargainer. Mabua charter fare is $3–$6 to Mataram; $3.50–$7.50 to Senggigi; $13.50–$35 (to Labuhan Lombok) depending on the number of passengers.

In Mataram itself bemos follow two parallel routes: west to east from Ampenan to Cakranegara along Jl Langko, Jl Pejanggik and Jl Selaparang, and returning east to west along Jl Pancawarga, Jl Pendidikan, Jl Majapahit and Jl Yos Sudarso on the way back. Fare: Rp250.

Traditional cidomo (horse and cart) are a pleasant way to get around, but they are now banned from many of the main streets inside the city, especially along bemo routes. They are nevertheless still very common in other district towns and villages.

Outside the city, fares vary somewhat. From Sweta terminal east of Cakra(negara), the rates are approximately: Tanjung Rp1,200; Praya Rp1,000; Bayan Rp2,800.

Bemos to Senggigi can be found in Ampenan,

along Saleh Sungkar road, which leads north out of town. Fare: Rp400.

Charter and Rental

To tour around the island, you can always charter a bemo with driver—or rent a taxi, which is always much more expensive. However, the car rental business is growing in Lombok. A number of rental companies have sprung up in Mataram and further north in Senggigi. Prices are a little lower in town, but rental conditions are also more strict. You will usually be asked to leave your passport and/or a photocopy of your driving license as a deposit. The price per day is about $25 (no insurance), and you will be charged an extra $2.50 for each hour of delay on returning the vehicle.

In Mataram, try **Rinjani** in Jl Bung Karno, opposite Granada Hotel (they have a lot of cars); **Dewata** in the northerly Monjok area, on the road to Rembiga; **Yoga** inside the Pacific supermarket on the centrally-located Jl Pejanggik (possible discounts); **Chans** at Jl Pejanggik 7A (in the Haccandra Tours & Travel office), and also **Parameswara Tourist Service** at Jl Pejanggik 66, which offers car, motorbike and bicycle rental as well as a variety of other services.

A number of travel agents rent cars with drivers for trips around town, including **Vistawisata** close to the Pacific supermarket (4 hrs for about $5–$8).

In Senggigi, many car rental offices and/or counters are available, such as **Surya Rental** in Batu Layar (☎ 93076) and others scattered along the road near the Marine Sports Centre, and further north opposite Rinjani Cottages and Hero photo center. The price per day for a car is $30 minimum. Many companies also rent motorbikes ($7.50–$8.50 depending on engine size), and bicycles ($3 a day). Also ask your hotel, they will usually be able to help.

To the Gilis

These three islands of the northwest coast— Gili Air, Gili Meno and Gili Trawangan—are Lombok's most popular tourist destination along with Senggigi beach. Consequently, a whole range of transport alternatives are available.

The best way to save money is to take a public minibus from Mataram or Sweta some 20 km northwards to Pemenang (around Rp300). From here it's a Rp400 cidomo ride to Bangsal harbor. If you charter a bemo straight from Mataram or Senggigi to Bangsal, you will be charged at least $15–$20.

At Bangsal, you will have to book passage aboard one of the regular passenger boats which head out in the early morning and late afternoon, or in between when one fills up. Approximate fares: to Gili Air, Rp1,000; Gili Meno, Rp800; and Gili Trawangan, Rp1,200. You can also arrange a one-way charter: to Gili Air (20 min, $6); to Gili Meno (30 min, $7) and to Gili Trawangan (45 min, $9). You also have these two alternatives for the return trip.

Most travel agencies and diving centers organize all-in day tours to the Gilis, including transport by boat (a snorkeling round-trip to Gili Air or Gili Trawangan should cost you around $15).

SERVICES

Regional Tourism Office (DIPARDA), Jl Langko 70, Ampenan. ☎ 21730, 21866. They offer several maps and leaflets (not always up-to-date) and general information. The local Tourism Office for the West Lombok Regency is in Jl Cokroaminoto, Mataram.

Police station Jl Langko 17, Ampenan. ☎ 23524 (provincial office). ☎ 23773 (West Lombok regency).

Immigration office Jl Udayana, Mataram. ☎ 22520.

Post Office Jl Langko, opposite DIPARDA. There are others in Jl Majapahit, and in Jl Selaparang, near Cakra.

Telephone Office Jl Langko, near the Post Office. You can also use the services of the new *wartel* near Pacific supermarket for overseas calls. The new cardphone system is available at several places, including the airport. Cards are now much easier to find than previously. Minimum price (60 units): $2.50. In Senggigi, there's a cardphone outside the Pacific supermarket.

Money changing As well as banks, there are plenty of money-changers in Mataram and in the Senggigi area. There you can also change money at most of the big hotels. There are several moneychangers in Ampenan, on the road to Senggigi. Many look tiny and unconvincing, but they are trustworthy. In Mataram, you can also go to Bank Dagang Negara, Jl Langko 46. You can also change foreign currency and travelers' checks in the Gilis.

ACCOMMODATION

A decade ago, the only resorts on Lombok were Ampenan and Meninting beaches, barely 5 km north of Mataram. During the last four or five years, there has been a real boom, focused on Senggigi and the nearby Krandangan area and hotels of all categories have begun to pop up along the west coast. It is also rumored that the still virgin white sand beaches of Kuta, Tanjung Aan and Sira down south may soon become a luxury tourist complex similar to the Nusa Dua resort in Bali.

For years, the Gilis have been the trendiest spot on Lombok. Visitors head there en masse in search of good diving and snorkeling and a relaxed atmosphere. It is currently difficult to forecast what will happen as far as accommodation in the Gilis is concerned, especially on Gili Trawangan. Many of the homestays and restaurants were built without permits, and have been served with demolition orders, which had not been carried out at the time of writing. What can certainly be predicted is that the general standard of accommodation will go up in future, along with prices.

Ampenan, Mataram, Cakranegara

Most *losmen, wisma* (guesthouses) and hotels in the three cities area are patronized by Indonesian travelers, as foreign tourists usually head straight for Senggigi and the Gilis.

LOSMEN

The most famous among travelers are the low-budget *losmen* in Ampenan, although many are crowded and noisy.

Triguna Jl Adi Sucipto 76, Ampenan (a little street near the harbour, also known as Jl Koperasi). The restaurant offers good, cheap meals. Triguna rents cars and motorcycles, and can make bus arrangements to either the ferry landing or all the way to Bima and Sape in Sumbawa. The owner, Pak Eddy, specializes in Rinjani climbing tours, and rents camping equipment.

Latimojong, 24 rms, and the **Zahir**, 19 rms, are also in Jl Adi Sucipto. There is also the **Pabean** in Jl Yos Sudarso, 18 rms.

Travelers can find a variety of other inexpensive digs in Mataram and Cakra, all for about the same price ($2.50–$6) a night:
Ayu Jl Nursiwan 20 (in Cakra, near Sweta). ☎ 21761. Car/motorcycle rental.
Cakrajaya Jl Tenun, Cakra. 10 rms.
Kamboja Jl Supratman 10, Mataram. ☎ 22211. 12 rms, car rental.
Madia Jl Angkasa 16A, Mataram. ☎ 22677.
Srikandi Jl Gelatik, Cakra. 25 rms.
Tenang Jl Pancawarga, Mataram. ☎ 23345. 22 rooms, inside a quiet (*tenang*) lane.

WISMA

These are quiet guesthouses in Mataram, usually patronized by local businessmen and civil servants, where you can spend one or two nights if you are stuck in town on your way to Senggigi, the Gilis, or back to Bali. Prices at the following establishments range from $5.50 to $20 a night.
Astiti Jl Panca Usaha (in Cakra), ☎ 23676. 18 rms.
Handika Jl Panca Usaha, ☎ 23578. 20 rms w/fan or AC, bar.
Kertayoga Jl Pejanggik 64, ☎ 21775. 14 rms w/AC and fan.
Mareje Jl Pariwisata 3 & 9, ☎ 21711. 11 rms. Housed in two buildings on opposite sides of the street.
Ratih Jl Pejanggik 127, near Cakra, ☎ 21096. 50 rms w/fan and AC, convention hall. Restau-

Senggigi Beach

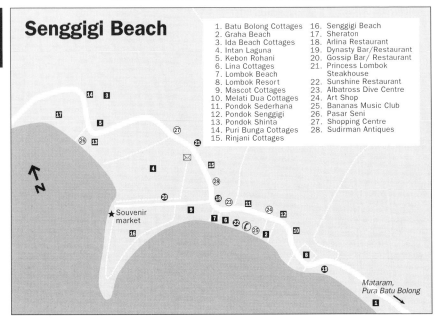

1. Batu Bolong Cottages
2. Graha Beach
3. Ida Beach Cottages
4. Intan Laguna
5. Kebon Rohani
6. Lina Cottages
7. Lombok Beach
8. Lombok Resort
9. Mascot Cottages
10. Melati Dua Cottages
11. Pondok Sederhana
12. Pondok Senggigi
13. Pondok Shinta
14. Puri Bunga Cottages
15. Rinjani Cottages
16. Senggigi Beach
17. Sheraton
18. Arlina Restaurant
19. Dynasty Bar/Restaurant
20. Gossip Bar/ Restaurant
21. Princess Lombok Steakhouse
22. Sunshine Restaurant
23. Albatross Dive Centre
24. Art Shop
25. Bananas Music Club
26. Pasar Seni
27. Shopping Centre
28. Sudirman Antiques

Mataram, Pura Batu Bolong

rant serves Indonesian food and packs lunches. Car, motorcycle rental available.

Rinjani Jl Pancawarga 18, ☎ 21633. 13 rms.

Wisma Chandra Jl Pancawarga 55, ☎ 23979. 22 rms, a restaurant and shops.

Wisma Eka Sari Guna Jl Pariwisata 26, ☎ 21963, 23 rms.

Wisma Giri Putri Jl Catur Warga 9, ☎ 23222. 11 rms w/bath.

Wisma Nusantara Jl Suprapto 28, near the crossroads to the museum, ☎ 23492. 36 rms w/AC, TV and restaurant.

Wisma Paradiso Jl Angkasa 3, Mataram.

HOTELS

Granada Hotel Jl Bung Karno, ☎ 22275, 23138, 23856, Fax: 23856. 100 "Spanish style" rms. One of the few luxury accommodations in the area. Rooms have AC, video, radio, fridge, telephone, laundry service. There's a 150-seat restaurant (Indonesian, European, Chinese food). The swimming pool is surrounded by lush tropical gardens and an arcade. $20–$33 S, $25–$40 D.

Wisma Melati Jl Langko 80, ☎23780. 24 cottages and rms. Old and cosy, said to be one of the best in its class. The cottages are quieter. Restaurant serves Indonesian, Chinese and European food. Conveniently located near the Garuda office, the post and telephone offices, and Ampenan shopping area. $17–$28 w/breakfast; some rooms w/AC.

Selaparang, Jl Selaparang 40, in front of Pacific supermarket, ☎ 22670. 18 rms w/fan or AC. $9.50 standard to $22 VIP.

Mataram, Jl Pejanggik 105, opposite the Selaparang (this is one street with two different

names depending on the side!). ☎ 23411, 23415. 28 rms w/fan or AC. $8.50 (economy) to $20 (VIP).

Ayung Near the Granada Hotel on Jl Bung Karno. 25 cottages. A newcomer that should be recommended. AC, TV, in a pleasant garden. $25.

Senggigi Beach

BUDGET AND INTERMEDIATE

In Senggigi, simple accommodations now mingle with the luxury resorts. Prices are getting higher and higher in tune with the growing prestige of the area, but facilities are not always what you would expect for the price. Accommodations in the center of Senggigi area are always crowded, especially those that have been patronized for years. The newer ones further north are more pleasant and peaceful—at least for the time being. The following are listed in order of appearance from south to north.

Meninting

Asri Beach Cottages Several rms and bungalows. $7.50 (rooms), $10 (bungalows).

Attiti Sanggraha Guesthouse ☎ 21140. Several rms w/fan and bath. $11.

These two are very simple and away from the heart of Senggigi area. Seldom is either full.

Batu Bolong

Batu Bolong Cottages & Restaurant Jl Raya Senggigi, Km 12. ☎ 93065, Fax: 93198. 20 beach and garden view cottages, located on either side of the road and patronized mainly by German tourists. Restaurant and bar, serving

Chinese and Western food. Beach: $17.50 D; $20 T. Garden: $15 S & D.

Senggigi

Melati Dua At the km 13 marker. 9 pleasant little bamboo cottages. Restaurant and bar. An old classic with a friendly atmosphere. Fancooled $16 and $20; w/AC $35.

Pondok Senggigi Jl Raya Senggigi, ☎ 93273, 93275. Another favorite, just next door to Melati Dua. Always crowded. It has recently been upgraded, and offers now a whole range of room standards. Restaurant serving Indonesian, Chinese and Western food, live music four times a week (not for those who seek peace!). Class C, w/shared bath: $5 S; $ 6.50 D. Class B, w/fan and bath: $7.50 S; $10 D. Class A, w/fan and bath: $12 S; $15 D. Deluxe, w/AC and hot water: $35 S; $40 D.

Lina Cottages On the beachfront. 15 small brick cottages w/AC and bath. Good value for the price. Restaurant opens rather late, and closes very early. Breakfast not included. Transportation service, watersports equipment for rent. $20.

Pondok Rinjani Located opposite Intan Laguna, at the end of a small lane. 15 pleasant bamboo cottages and a restaurant. $12.50 (including tea).

Pondok Sinta A very simple accommodation located on the beachfront, a veteran on the scene. Simple bamboo huts and more comfortable rooms. Rates are very competitive. Bamboo hut: $3 S; $3.75 D; $5 T. Brick rooms: $5 S; $6 D; $7.50 T including breakfast.

Kebun Rohani. A cluster of very simple bamboo huts on the hill opposite Pondok Sinta. Not recommended for people who are afraid of a climb every time they forget something in their rooms. A bit overpriced considering facilities: $10, without breakfast.

Pondok Sederhana. A very simple single-story, located across the street from Kebun Rohani. Downstairs: $4. Upstairs: $5.

Mascot Berugaq Elen Cottages. Jl Raya Senggigi, ☎ 93365. A cluster of standard and VIP cottages, designed in the traditional Sassak style. The 2-room VIP cottage is fitted w/AC. Restaurant open from 7 am to 11 pm. Canoe rental.

Mangsit

These two hotels are highly recommended, because of their out-of-the way location, beautiful and quiet surroundings, friendly service, and excellent value for the money.

Santai Beach Inn, Bungalows & Special Bungalows. P.O. Box 1123, Mangsit. ☎ /Fax: 93023. A cluster of bungalows and villas of various standards, cosily hidden under thick coconut groves. All are designed in the Sasak style, with an "antique" flavour. You can choose between rooms of various standards. All are without AC, but you won't need it. Has a nice, restaurant furnished with antiques. Friendly service. Santai Beach Inn: $7.50 S; $9.50 D (w/breakfast). Bungalows: (Class A) $7 S; $9 D. (Class B) $12.50 S; $15 D. House: $22.50. Special bungalows: (room) $15 S; $17.50 D. Bungalow: $22.50 S; $25 D. House: $50. Villa w/pool: $100.

Windy Beach Cottages. P.O. Box 1116, Mangsit. ☎ 93191, 93192, Fax: 93193. Very nice bamboo bungalows on stilts scattered in a garden. Romantically windy—at night it's like *Wuthering Heights* with coconut trees. Has a restaurant. $10 (w/AC), $17.50 (larger, w/AC & hot water), including breakfast.

LUXURY CLASS HOTELS

Lombok's fanciest hotels are all found in Senggigi. The Senggigi Beach hotel is the oldest, and five star-rated hotels have emerged in Senggigi and further south in Meninting (with the brand new Senggigi Palace Hotel). Further north towards Krandangan and Mangsit plans are afoot for a Park Royal Hotel, a Holiday Inn, a Patra Jasa hotel, and other huge hotel resorts. The west coast, now still dramatically beautiful with its bays surrounded by hills covered with coconut trees, seems in danger of becoming engulfed in hotels. Listed from south to north.

Senggigi Palace Hotel Jl Raya Senggigi, Ampenan. P.O. Box 1112. ☎ 93045–9; Fax: 93043. 76 rooms. A hotel belonging to the same group as the Kuta Palace Hotel in Bali and the Yogya Palace Hotel in Yogyakarta. Located on Meninting beach, just 10-min drive from the airport. Two-story cottage-style with all modern facilities. Each room has private balcony, AC, minibar, IDD telephone, TV, video & radio. Set in a large tropical garden with bar, restaurant (24-hr service), conference facilities, laundry and fitness center. Garden view: $60 S, $70 D. Ocean view: $75 S; $85 D. Suite: $200.

Graha Beach Jl Raya Senggigi. ☎ 23782, 93101, 93401, Fax : 93400. 29 rms and bungalows fully equipped w/AC, minibar, TV, private balcony. Open restaurant & bar opened from 6 am to midnight (European, Chinese, Indonesian, seafood). Laundry, moneychanger. Ocean view: $45 S; $50 D. Garden view: $40 S; $45 D. Also has a marine sports center offering various watersports facilities and tour packages, including diving tours to Gili Trawangan, Meno and Air.

Senggigi Beach Hotel P.O. Box 1001. ☎ 93210 through 93219. Fax: 93200. 150 thatched-roof bungalow rooms, and 2 deluxe private beach bungalows. Owned by the Aerowisata/Garuda group. This 3-star resort is located among 12 hectares of tropical gardens. Swimming pool, drugstore, money-changer, laundry, beauty salon, tour service (Satriavi), 120-person conference room, tennis courts and other recreation facilities, such as badminton, table tennis, and windsurfing. It has 2 restaurants. Standard: $60 S; $75 D. Moderate: $70 S;

$80 D. Standard bungalow: $100 S; $110 D. Deluxe bungalow: $150 S; $160 D. Grand bungalow: $500 S; $600 D. The **Baruna** diving center is located in this hotel.

Lombok Intan Laguna Spa & Club P.O. Box 50. ☎ 93090 (10 lines), Fax: 93185. 209 rooms. Owned by the Intan group, located on the beachfront. The rooms (all w/AC, minibar, TV, IDD, radio and private balcony) include 82 bungalows, 121 Garden Wing rooms, and 6 suites, including a presidential suite w/ private pool. Also has 24-hr restaurant, two bars, lagoon-shaped swimming pool, 24-hr room service, laundry, shopping arcade, baby-sitting, tour/taxi desk, money-changer, doctor, conference & banquet facilities (10 to 50 persons), 2 floodlit tennis courts, squash court, fitness center and watersports operated by **Rinjani Diving Club** (waterskiing, scuba, fishing, snorkeling, canoeing). There's a 9-hole golf course nearby. Garden wing: $80 S; $85 D. Bungalow: $90 S; $95 D. Suites: $200 and $350. Reservations can also be made at Jakarta Intan Reservations office ☎ (21) 3908178, fax: (21) 3908177.

Puri Bunga Beach (formerly Ida Beach Cottages), P.O. Box 51. ☎ 91013–93353. Fax: 93286. 50 rms. Cosily nestled on the hill slopes. 20 standard rooms, 20 deluxe and 10 suites all decorated in typical Sasak style. 24-hr restaurant, bar, 24-hr room service, laundry, drugstore, money-changer, tour & travel service, swimming pool. Deluxe $60 S; $65 D. Suite $110.

Sheraton Senggigi Beach Resort Jl Raya Senggigi, Km 8, P.O. Box 155, ☎ 93333. Fax: 93140. 156 rooms, including 10 suites and 2 beachfront villas. The only international standard (4-star) resort on the island. Located in a 4 ha park, rooms are decorated with timberwork and traditional Sasak handicrafts, and have spacious balconies or patios. All have IDD phone, individually-controlled AC, TV/video and minibar. Has a great swimming pool. The suites include a living/dining room and the deluxe ones also have a kitchen. The villas each have their own swimming pool, garden and covered sitting/dining area. Facilities include: indoor & outdoor 200-seat restaurant, serving Indonesian and international cuisine, barbeque seafood restaurant and pizzeria near the pool, sunken pool bar, karaoke & games room, lobby lounge, 24-hr room service, 2 floodlit tennis courts, fitness center, golf, watersports facilities (sailing, snorkeling, scuba diving), children's playground, open stage for traditional performances, gift shop, business center, transport desk, laundry, PACTO travel desk. Poolside: $105. Ocean: $115. Patio: $125. Executive suite: $275 Deluxe suite: $325. Beachfront villa: $800.

Pacific Beach Cottages Kerandangan, Senggigi. P.O. Box 1035. ☎ 93006, 93068, 93069. Fax: 93027. Located at the northernmost end of the Senggigi area. 26 rms decorated in the traditional

Sasak style w/AC, TV and seaview terrace. Facilities include: 24-hr restaurant, coffee-shop and bar, room service, swimming pool, water sports center, laundry, drugstore, karaoke. Standard: $25 S; $30 D. Deluxe bungalow: $30 S; $35 D. Executive deluxe bungalow: $45 S; $50 D.

Several other international resorts are planned to be built in this area: namely Lombok Resort Hotel, at the south end of Senggigi, Lombok Beach Hotel, opposite Albatross Diving Center, and Park Royal Hotel in Krandangan.

A new area further north, in Mangsit and Klui, is also soon to be developed. Here you can still escape the maddening crowds of Senggigi and enjoy the sea-breeze whispering through coconut groves while gazing at the glittering sea. But time is fast running out. Two huge resorts are under way: a Holiday Inn resort in Mangsit, and Klui Beach Cottages in Klui, plus the Lombok Dame Indah. It even seems that the gungho development may reach as far north as Tanjung, but at the time of writing only one hotel offers high standard facilities in this area: **Bunga Beach Cottages** Jl Senggigi-Pemenang (Klui). P.O. Box 1118. ☎ 93035. Fax: 93036. A new hotel tucked away in a secluded bay 5 km north of Senggigi, near a traditional village. The thatch-roofed, air-conditioned cottages, made of traditional local material, are surrounded by a beautiful garden. Rms include standard, deluxe and family room—with 3 bedrooms, 3 bathrooms and 1 living-room. Restaurant near the pool, garden restaurant (European, Indonesian, seafood), bar and room service. The managing director, Mrs Anja, is very helpful. Standard: $42 S; $45 D. Deluxe: $52 S; $55 D. Family room: $150.

The Gilis

Homestays and bungalows have been springing up for years on these three islands. At the height of the tourist season (July and August) they now become so crowded that it is almost impossible to get a room after 10 am. This sudden growth of tourist interest has put a strain on the local infrastructure and the islands still have no fresh water supply or waste disposal facilities. Disputes have also arisen (especially on Gili Trawangan), because many accommodations were more or less illegally built, and have been threatened with demolition. Check locally as details are subject to change.

With the exception of **Indra Cemara** on Gili Meno, the accommodations mostly comprise *losmen*-type twin bed bungalows on stilts, fitted with simple bamboo furniture. Prices usually include three meals, and range from $10 upwards.

GILI AIR

The best accommodation is **Hans Bungalows**, in the extreme north. Its 29 rms are being upgraded. 10 of them will soon be VIP standard (AC, hot & cold water), and facilities should in-

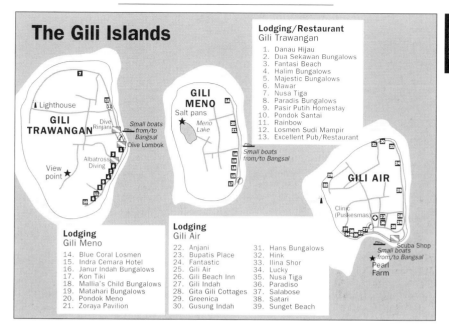

The Gili Islands

Lodging/Restaurant
Gili Trawangan

1. Danau Hijau
2. Dua Sekawan Bungalows
3. Fantasi Beach
4. Halim Bungalows
5. Majestic Bungalows
6. Mawar
7. Nusa Tiga
8. Paradis Bungalows
9. Pasir Putih Homestay
10. Pondok Santai
11. Rainbow
12. Losmen Sudi Mampir
13. Excellent Pub/Restaurant

Lodging
Gili Meno

14. Blue Coral Losmen
15. Indra Cemara Hotel
16. Janur Indah Bungalows
17. Kon Tiki
18. Mallia's Child Bungalows
19. Matahari Bungalows
20. Pondok Meno
21. Zoraya Pavilion

Lodging
Gili Air

22. Anjani
23. Bupatis Place
24. Fantastic
25. Gili Air
26. Gili Beach Inn
27. Gili Indah
28. Gita Gili Cottages
29. Greenica
30. Gusung Indah
31. Hans Bungalows
32. Hink
33. Ilina Shor
34. Lucky
35. Nusa Tiga
36. Paradiso
37. Salabose
38. Satari
39. Sunget Beach

clude swimming-pool, tennis and disco. You can also sleep at **Gili Indah** on the southernmost tip, which includes 35 bungalows. Prices range between $15–$25 per night for both, but these may be subject to change. Other accommodations available at **Nusa Tiga, Gili Beach Inn** and **Gita Gili Beach**.

GILI MENO

Stay at the **Blue Coral** if you plan to do a lot of snorkeling, or at the **Kon Tiki**, which has nice bungalows and bathrooms, or at the **Casablanca**. The **Indra Cemara** is still the only *real* hotel on the island. Other places to check out: **Matahari Bungalows** and **Janur Indah Bungalows**.

GILI TRAWANGAN

The situation was in flux at the time of writing so check before visiting this island. To date, the most well-known place has been **Paradisia**: 11 bungalows, 3 shared baths, and a cheap restaurant. Albatross diving center is located on its premises. $4.50 S; $6 D. Other places to try out include: **Trawangan** (noisy), **Karin Homestay**, **Coral Beach Homestay** (quieter, on the northeast coast), as well as **Pak Majid's** (good food) and **Makmur**. The best snorkeling is off the northeast, between **Karin** and Coral Beach Homestay, the latter perfect for those looking for quiet nights.

Other Areas

KUTA BEACH

Although it's predicted that the virgin sands of the south coast will sooner or later be deflowered by the development of huge resorts, at the time of this writing all remained unspoiled. A num-

ber places to stay which have been around for a while are still there: **Mascot Cottages, Penginapan Anda, Sekar Kuning** among others. Enjoy this area while you can.

GILI NANGGU

The barren and hilly area around Sekotong in southwest Lombok has wonderful beaches and diving spots. As yet, there is only one set of bungalows, **Istana Cempaka**, on Gili Nanggu, one of the many off-shore islands. It is run by a Balinese, and has 10 double cottages. Fishermen occasionally stop by, and the manager will help you bargain for a fish or lobster if you want a special meal. Reservations by letter or phone, Jl Tumpang Sari, Cakra, ☎ 22898. $12.50 (seafront), $7.50 (rooms), including meals. Although, as elsewhere, development projects are slated for this area there is nothing new yet. So, apart from Istana Cempaka, your only real option is camping under the stars—which can, after all, be fun.

NARMADA (WEST LOMBOK)

Suranadi Hotel P.O. Box 10, Narmada. ☎ 23686. 24 bungalows w/bath & fan. This is an old guesthouse built by the Dutch near a holy spring (now a swimming pool) and the Suranadi temple. Perfect for those who prefer the coolness of the mountains and a traditional setting. There is a nature reserve and park nearby. Taman Hutan Suranadi. Pool, tennis courts, poolside restaurant (Chinese food). $22 (cottage); $10 (room).

TETEBATU (CENTRAL LOMBOK)

Wisma Soedjono. 13 rms and bungalows. More bungalows are being built. All rooms have color

TV w/parabolic antennae. The restaurant serves Indonesian and western food. Minivan and motorcycle rental, and English-speaking guides available for hire. Write ahead for reservations: Wisma Soedjono, Tetebatu, Lombok Timur, NTB. $15 for bungalows.

A little before Tete Batu, there is another small *wisma* with a restaurant, **Dewi Anjani**.

LABUHAN LOMBOK (EAST LOMBOK)

Two *losmen*, the 20-room **Munawar**, and the **Dian Dutaku** can accommodate you in an emergency if you happen to be stuck there before crossing to Sumbawa, as the last ferry leaves at 5 pm.

EKAS (EAST LOMBOK)

This fishing village north of Kaliantan, on the west coast of Lombok's southernmost peninsula, some 60 km from Mataram, is a great spot for escaping to. Here, you can enjoy unspoiled nature and wonderful surfing, and spend the night at **Laut Surga Cottages & Restaurant**, (Fax: 93122) a cluster of thatched bungalows. There's also diving, horse-riding to Seriwe and Kaliantan, or fishing from a boat. $12.50 for a bungalow, plus $3.50 for extra bed (incl. breakfast).

Another group of traditional cottages is due to be built at Serewe, near Kaliantan, in the near future, as a starting-point for horse-back riding, boating, diving and trekking tours around this beautiful area. Inquire locally for an update on progress.

DINING

Those with no fear of red hot chilies should certainly try the local Sasak style of cooking. *Ayam Taliwang*, a spicy dish "imported" long ago from the Taliwang district of west Sumbawa is the most famous dish: whole chicken (*ayam*) is fried or grilled—it is better grilled—and eaten with hot chili sauce. The chicken is served with side dishes such as *pelecing kangkung*, a spinach-like vegetable prepared with grated coconut and more chilies, and *beberuk*, a mixture of eggplant, tomato and other spices usually accompanying raw vegetables or salad.

Three Cities Area

There are restaurants of all kinds in Mataram, ranging from small foodstalls (*warung*) to simple "eating houses" (*rumah makan*) and luxury restaurants; yet they are not always easy to spot.

The restaurants and foodstalls beside the Pacific Supermarket and along Jl Erlangga usually open at dusk. They sell *ayam Taliwang* and other delicacies. Sasak food can also be found at the locally renowned **Deny Bersaudara**, Jl Pelikan 6. ☎ 23619, as well as *gurami* freshwater fish and *saté*. The restaurant is located in a quiet side street and has a pleasant atmosphere. We also recommend **Al Azhar** in Pusat

Pertokoan Mataram shopping center opposite the hospital in Jl Pejanggik. This simple *rumah makan* serves *ayam Taliwang* at roughly the same prices as **Deny Bersaudara** (around $2). Another *Taliwang* restaurant is on Jl A.A. Gde Ngurah 26, in the market area of Cakra. *Taliwang* can also be sampled at **Madya I**, Jl Hasanuddin 7, and **Muksin Taliwang**, Jl Cilinaya.

For less fiery food, try the following good restaurants: the well-known **Garden House Restaurant**, facing Pusat Pertokoan, serves Chinese and European food. **Pattaya** in the Pacific Supermarket complex (Indonesian, Chinese, seafood); **Shanti Puri**, Jl Maktal 15, in a side street nearby; **Flamboyant**, Jl Pejanggik 101, near the petrol station (tasty seafood, fairly cheap); **Dirgahayu**, Jl Cilinaya 10; **Empat Lima**, Jl Pariwisata and **Friendship**, Jl Panca Usaha.

In the commercial area, you will find many *rumah makan* serving simple food, such as **Sekawan**, Jl Pejanggik 59, Cakra (Chinese, seafood); **Remaja**, Jl A.A. Gde Ngurah, Cakra; **Manalagi**, Jl Meninting in Ampenan, and some more along Jl Yos Sudarso in Ampenan. In Sweta terminal, if you are in a hurry to take a bus to another destination, we recommend **Sumbawa** just outside the station: it's small and crowded, but has good *nasi campur*. It's worthwhile eating before you leave, as good places to eat outside the Mataram area are very hard to find (the only treat is **Ria** in Praya, the central Lombok district town, serving Indonesian standards).

Balinese food—such as spicy minced *lawar*—can be tasted at several places in Cakra, where most people of Balinese descent live and do business. There are also fewer *Padang* restaurants in Lombok than elsewhere in Indonesia—look out for signs saying "*rumah makan Padang*" to sample the west Sumatran style so popular throughout the archipelago. In short, when outside the three cities area, be prepared to walk a few miles before you can find the place of your choice!

Caution: remember that during the fasting month of Ramadan it is even more difficult to find food. Restaurants do not open until after twilight.

Senggigi

Finding places to eat is not as easy as you might think outside expensive hotel restaurants. Intermediate accommodations often have restaurants, but these tend to close quite early (sometimes around 9 pm), and in many cases, room rates do not include breakfast. **Batu Bolong** restaurant, overlooking the sea, **Dynasty** and **Sunshine** are old classics. **Sunshine** is very popular and crowded, prices are not too high, but the food is not outstanding. **Dynasty** has karaoke. Other fashionable and expensive restaurants have sprung up, such as **Flam-**

boyant in Meninting, **Sassak Garden restaurant & Sea Sports** in Batu Bolong, **Princess of Senggigi Steak House** and **Princess of Lombok** in the center of the area, near the supermarket. The **Ocean Bar**, next door, opens every night.

Those who like Italian food as well as seafood barbeque, should contact Giuseppe and Rahmi on Meninting road. They also breed horses and organize diving and horseback treks in East Lombok (see below). Look out for the "Lombok Adventure on Horseback" sign. At the time of writing, they were about to open **Caffe Alberto**. Set menu to include Indonesian and Italian specialties and drinks for lunch/dinner ($10). They will pick you up from your hotel when asked. They also organize beach parties on request—for lunch or at sunset—including barbequed *sate*, drinks and transfer from/to hotel for the same price ($20 with lobster). Extra entertainment (traditional dance and music for groups) on request. ☎ 36781, Fax: 34342.

Budget travelers can still find cheap food in several small *warung* along the main road.

Markets

Lombok has entered the era of the supermarket. **Pacific** (formerly Cilinaya), in Jl Pejanggik, shelters a bakery and a supermarket, as well as a cassette shop, a bookshop, a money-changer, Pattaya restaurant, a batik shop, and a small *wartel* telephone center. **Ruby**, opposite the Mataram Hotel, has a good bakery and a small supermarket. **Mataram Supermarket** is in Jl Pejanggik 129B in the Kompleks Pertokoan Mataram Plaza.

The main shopping streets in Ampenan are Jl Yos Sudarso and Jl Niaga. There are plenty of food shops in Cakranegara, along Jl A. A. Gde Ngurah and Selaparang. Mostly Chinese-owned, these sell bread and flour or rice cakes at the front, and other goods at the back including *dodol nangka*—a local delicacy made of palm sugar and jackfruit. Try, for example, **Jembatan Baru**, Jl Pejanggik 41. For fruit, **Cakra market** is a paradise, but beware of the beggars swarming around the place.

There's a Pacific supermarket in the center of Senggigi, flanked by the **Ocean** restaurant & bar, and a steak house.

SHOPPING AND SOUVENIRS

Sudirman is one of the most famous art shops and antique merchants in Lombok. His shop was formerly located in Jl Yos Sudarso 88, in the heart of Ampenan, flanked by other smaller art shops, in Jl Saleh Sungkar. His business improved steadily, and he has now moved to Senggigi, into a brand new white store. ☎ 93025, 26315. Fax: 22553. Packing and shipping services available.

Sudirman, and the shops along Jl Yos Sudarso, sell all kinds of old and "new" antiques (including amazing imitations); traditional bamboo containers, agricultural tools, tobacco and betel-chewing accessories (prices from $5 to $50), palm-leaf wedding trunks ($50 up), bone, wood and bamboo jewels ($10 up), and wooden statues (usually expensive). Some shops also sell silverware from Bali and Yogya. Remember that real antiques are rare and most are sent to Bali, where they fetch even higher prices.

Sassakagung at Jl Pejanggik 63, Mataram, is a nice little shop run by friendly owners. They sell earthenware from Penujak, rattan and *ata* root basketry, as well as textiles. Also for pottery, go to the **Lombok Pottery Center** in Jl Majapahit 7, Ampenan.

If you are particularly looking for textiles, go to **CV Rinjani**, in Jl Selaparang, opposite Pacific supermarket. They have a nicely decorated, cosy showroom: local weavings, including *endek* (a type of *ikat*), and Sasak style creations, as well as scarves, sarongs and bags.

There are more weavings at **Balimurti** and **Slamet Riyadi**, Jl Tenun, near the Mayura water palace in Cakranegara. **Sari Kusuma**, an old business founded as early as 1956, in Jl Selaparang 45—on the east towards Sweta bus terminal—sells weavings (you can watch the weavers at work), but also wood-carvings (☎ 23338, Fax: 93122).

In Senggigi, souvenirs can be found in the arcades of most of the big hotels, and small souvenir shops have sprung up everywhere.

Beyond the three cities area, you can visit the villages specializing in Sasak handicrafts, and buy the goods on the spot. Prices may be cheaper than in the art shops, but they are just as likely to be more expensive, particularly if you are not accomplished at bargaining.

Try the **Sukarara Cooperative** (some 30 km southeast of Mataram), for *ragigenep* fabrics, men's *dodot*, brightly striped sashes or scarves, and a complete bride costume. Also in Sukarara, check out **Widasih's Taufik**—Lombok's most well-known weaving company. Weavings are also produced in **Sengkol** and **Sade** (north of Kuta in southern Central Lombok), and in **Pringgasela** (some 45 km southwest of Labuhan Lombok, in the east).

For wooden statues, bamboo baskets and ceramic pots, go to **Loyok** and **Kotaraja** (almost in the center of the island). For palm-leaf boxes and hats head for **Suradadi** (west of Labuhan Haji in East Lombok). Look in **Beleka** (some 15 km east of Praya, as the crow flies) for various woodcarvings and handicrafts made of rattan. **Banyumulek** (some 10 km south of Mataram), **Penujak** (8 km south of Praya) and **Masbagik** (6 km west of Selong, East Lombok) specialize in clay earthenware pottery. Head to and **Sukaraja** (near the southern peninsula, east of Praya) for carved wooden statues.

To visit the craftsmen of Gunung Sari, contact Eko Suryono or Azhari at Kelompok Empat, Jl Halmahera in Rembiga, close to the junction between Mataram and the airport.

TRAVEL AGENCIES

Many travel agents have sprung up in Lombok in response to the recent tourism boom, and numerous agencies outside Lombok—especially in Bali—have included Lombok packages in their tour programmes.

In Lombok

Most local agencies (and airline offices) are located close to one another along the Langko-Pejanggik tp Selaparang axis, or in its immediate vicinity. The following have been found to be reliable:

Anthea Wisata Jl Cokroaminoto 3. ☎ 21281, 21517.

Bidytours Jl Ragigenep 17, Ampenan. ☎ 22127, 21281. We highly recommend this local agent, which offers a wide ranges of services. The place is a little difficult to find, as it is on a side street concealed behind the bridge to Ampenan.

Natrabu Pusat Pertokoan 6–8.

Perameswara Jl Pejanggik 66, Mataram, ☎ 22764, 23368, Fax: 23368; and Jl Raya Senggigi, at Deny Restaurant. ☎ 93007–9. Offers a whole range of services, including tours, car, motorcycle and bike rental, taxi service, bus tickets to Bali, Java and Sumbawa, and Bali-Lombok shuttle bus services to and from any destinations on the two islands. Open until 10 pm. It also has a counter at Segara Anak Inn in Kuta, and in Warung Pak Mitro in Bangsal.

Sassak Jl Yos Sudarso 22B, owned by Merpati.

Satriavi Jl Pejanggik 17. ☎ 21788, 23423. Fax: 21707. Good services and lots of alternatives.

Other agencies that organize city tours, handicraft and diving tours, trekking trips to Mt. Rinjani, as well as excursions to other islands, including tours to Komodo and East Nusa Tenggara:

Haccandra Tours and Travel In the Pacific supermarket complex. ☎ 23253.

Mataram Vistawisata In the same location. ☎ 22314, 25817, Fax: 22314. Tours and car rental for half-day city tours ($5–$8).

Paloma Tours Jl Caturwarga 11, ☎ 21388.

Putri Mandalika Jl Pejanggik 49, ☎ 22240.

Sakatours Jl Langko 48, P.O. Box 47. ☎ /Fax: 23114.

Surya Orient Indotours ☎ 21272, 23837.

In Bali

You can also organize a tour to Lombok from Bali. Among others, try the following reliable agents:

Golden Kris Tours Jl By Pass Ngurah Rai. ☎ (361) 289225–6, Fax: 289228.

Natrabu Tours & Travel ☎ (361) 223452, 232362, 232371, 231449; Fax: 25448.

Satriavi Tours & Travel Jl Danau Tamblingan, Sanur. ☎ (361) 87074, Fax: 87019.

Suar Nusa Jaya Tours Jl By Pass Ngurah Rai. ☎ (361) 235037, 234636; Fax: 34636.

Sunda Duta Jl By Pass Ngurah Rai 28X, P.O. Box 282. ☎ (361) 288658, 288764, Fax: 288658.

Tunas Indonesia Bali Beach Hotel arcade, Sanur. ☎ (361) 284015.

Tunjung Petak Tours & Travel Jl Teuku Umar 88X. ☎ (361) 225849, Fax: 234785.

Vayatours Jl Hayam Wuruk. ☎ (361) 223757, 234780, 224449; Fax: 231741.

Tours

Most travel agencies offer the following range of tours:

•**City** tour including Puri Mayura, Pura Meru Lingsar, Getap blacksmiths village, and Batu Bolong (3 hrs).

•**South countryside** tour: Sukarare weavings, Penujak pottery, Sengkol & Rambitan native villages, Kuta Beach (7 hrs).

•**Narmada summer palace,** Suranadi, Lingsar and Batu Bolong temples (4 hrs).

•**Gili Air diving** tour (7 hrs).

•**North countryside** tour: Sendanggile waterfall, and Senaru village (7 hrs).

There are also a number of 2 night/3-day or 3-night/4-day package tours to numerous destinations.

MEDICAL SERVICES

The General Hospital is in Jl Pejanggik, near the bridge, ☎ 22254. The Muslim Hospital is in Jl Rumah Sakit Islam. There are already a few good specialists in Mataram, but if you feel really ill, go to Denpasar. There are several drugstores (*apotik*) in town.

ENTERTAINMENT

Museum In Jl Panji Tilaar (near where it meets Jl Majapahit) Ampenan. The ethnographic collections are very clearly and pleasantly displayed. Open Tues–Thurs 8 am–2 pm; Fri until 11 am; Sat until 1 pm. Closed Mon and holidays.

Library On Jl Majapahit, near the museum. A beautiful modern building where reading is a pleasure.

Nightlife Due to the strict traditionalism still prevailing in the area, "discotheque" is still a dirty word in Lombok, although a few have opened up on Gili Trawangan. However, Lombok has not escaped the wildfire epidemic sweeping Indonesia: karaoke is rife on the island. There's a karaoke restaurant in Batu Bolong, and the affliction is also endemic in many star-rated hotels in the Senggigi area. Some hotels also have discos, such as the Senggigi Beach Hotel. You can also swing the night away to the live band at Pondok Senggigi four times a week.

Cultural events Many dance performances are held for the HUT Propinsi NTB (West Nusa Tenggara Province Anniversary), on Dec 16–17, as well as for PORSENI NTB (West Nusa Tenggara Sports and Arts Week), an annual event held alternately in Lombok and in Sumbawa.

Also, if there is a Pekan Pariwisata ("Tourism Week"), you will have an opportunity to watch quality performances. A marching parade in traditional dress is also usually held around Aug 17, Indonesia's Independence Day. Many of the big hotels in Senggigi have open stages where traditional dances are performed for guests. Most are new creations performed by young dancers.

Do not miss the *Bau Nyale* (seaworm catching) ceremony at Kuta during the full moon of February every year, nor the *Pekelem* ritual held at the Segara Anak crater lake around the end of October or the beginning of November.

Horse racing Horse racing (*pacuan kuda*) takes place at the Selakalas field, off Jl Gora, near the intersection with Jl Peternakan. The races, jockeyed by young boys, are often held on Sundays, and during various celebrations: Apr 17 (anniversary of West Lombok); Aug 17 (Indonesia's Independence Day); from Aug 28 well into September (the anniversary of Mataram); Oct 5 (war memorial); Dec 16–17 (anniversary of the NTB province).

ALTERNATIVE TOURISM

More adventurous travelers can avoid both the crowds of camera-wielding day-trippers and the tan-at-all-costs sect on Senggigi and the Gilis by gettig off the beaten track. Renting a jeep is the best way to reach villages where few, if any, tourists go. This is an excellent way to meet local people and gain a deeper understanding of their culture and way of life.

Obviously, this kind of travel is not for everyone. You should be able to speak some Indonesian, or bring along somebody to act as an interpreter. In many remote places, people cannot speak Indonesian well, and it would even be better if your interpreter speaks some Sasak (a language related to Balinese and Javanese). People are sometimes very shy, but they are nevertheless as curious about you as you are about them!

You may wish to experience life in a village first hand. If you do so, keep in mind that while people in Lombok are as welcoming and hospitable as they are everywhere else in Indonesia, they are also often very poor. Their sense of hospitality commands that they cater to guests as well as possible, but you will be something of a nuisance anyway. You will have to be content with what you get as far as food

and accommodation, both of which can be extremely basic. They may either accept, or refuse offers of money, just saying "*Terserah*" ("up to you"). It's always a good idea to give food, especially what they usually lack—that is if any is available for sale.

If you go out in a local boat, we suggest paying $3 for a half-day to the boatman, plus the cost of his fuel if he uses an outboard. Of course, in places where tourists go, the prices are higher.

Remember too that local etiquette would request you to stay preferably at the village chief's house. Anyway, wherever you spend the night, the head of the village (*kepala desa*) is supposed to know—as is the case with any other visitor from outside—so that he may report your presence to the nearest police station. This is only a formality.

LOMBOK ON HORSEBACK

Nusa Tenggara province is famous for horse breeding (particularly in Sumbawa and Bima), and as many roads and paths are not accessible by vehicles, horse-riding expeditions can be an exciting alternative way to discover Lombok. Giuseppe, an Italian horse lover, and his wife Rahmi run an excellent outfit. You will find them on Jl Meninting 1G, Komp. Presok. ☎ 36781, Fax: 34342.

They have a dozen beautiful Sumbanese sandalwood horses, bearing the names of Mozart, Vivaldi and other famous composers. At feeding time, the animals are played classical music to make them calmer (these are former race-horses!). Giuseppe can organize half-day or full-day rides along the beach and in the countryside (lunch included), evening treks along the beach. and weekends of trekking and camping, with a seafood barbeque on the beach. The weekend trip goes to Serewe, near Kaliantan (southeast Lombok). Accommodation is either in tents, in Laut Surga Cottages at Ekas, or in Giuseppe's own cottages, when building is completed (10 bungalows w/bath planned).

Rates: $15/hr; $55/day; $120 for 2 days, including 3 daily meals and drinks, accommodation and transport by jeep from Mataram.

For those who are not keen on horse-riding, Giuseppe offers two alternatives: boat trips or mountain bike treks. one-day treks can also be organized, proceeding the following day to Selong Belanak further west by jeep. Prices are around $100.

You can also contact **Sunda Duta Tours & Travel** in Bali, as Giuseppe is their local representative. ☎ (361) 288658.

SCUBA DIVING AND WATERSPORTS

There are now three established diving centers

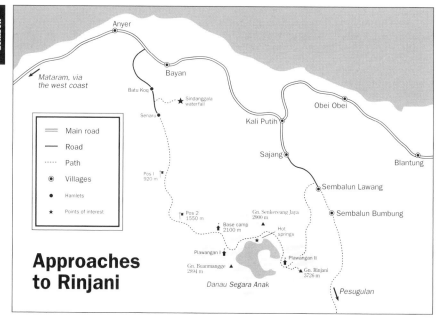

Approaches to Rinjani

in the map: Anyer, Bayan, Batu Koq, Senaru, Sindanggala waterfall, Obei Obei, Kali Putih, Sajang, Blantung, Pos I 920 m, Pos 2 1550 m, Gn. Senkereang Jaya 2900 m, Sembalun Lawang, Sembalun Bumbung, Base camp 2100 m, Hot springs, Plawangan I, Plawangan II, Gn. Buanmangge 2894 m, Gn. Rinjani 3726 m, Danau Segara Anak, Pesugulan, Mataram, via the west coast

Legend: Main road, Road, Path, Villages, Hamlets, Points of interest

in the Mataram area, a number in Senggigi and two in the Gilis. However, qualified diving instructors and divemasters are still scarce. Only experienced divers should consider diving on Lombok. Snorkeling is a safer option. The best season for diving and snorkeling visibility is from May to November. You can rent a range of watersports equipment at reasonable prices in numerous places.

Expect to pay around $3 for mask & fins; and $3 for a paddle-boat.

In Mataram

Satriavi Diving Center Jl Pejanggik 17, Mataram (part of Satriavi Tours). ☎ 21788. Also, has a poolside branch at the Senggigi Beach Hotel. Satriavi offers a training package, including a 3-hr lesson in the pool, one open water dive, with all equipment included for $45. All-inclusive packages: Single dive off Senggigi, $35/person; two dives off Senggigi, $45/person, two-dive trip to Gilis, $75/person for two clients, $50/person for four clients. Equipment available for rent: mask, snorkel and fins, regulator, buoyancy compensator (BC), tank and weight belt.

Rinjani Diving Club Jl Banteng 9, Mataram. ☎ 21402. Has a branch at the Intan Laguna Hotel. Single day of diving off Gili Trawangan or Tanjung Bonita, $60. Includes tanks, weight and lunch. Add $3/day for BC, two dives, 2 clients minimum. Same to Gili Petangan (east coast), $65. Diving off Senggigi $35/person, min.two. Pool training for beginners, $35; pool plus one open water dive, $60.

Corona Diving Club Jl Dr. Wahidin, Rembiga. A branch of the Bandung club in West Java.

In Senggigi

Albatross. Jl Raya Senggigi, P.O. Box 1066. ☎ 93399, Fax: 93388. Operates chiefly on Gili Meno and Gili Trawangan. Dive trips are rated as follows: two tanks dive, $55. Two introductory dives, $60 (min. two persons). One night dive, $35. Four-day PADI scuba dive course, $300. Snorkeling trip, $20. Joint dive trip, $15. Five-day NAUI scuba dive course, $325. Prices include transport by car and boat, tank and weight belt, diving guide and equipment, plus lunch. Payment must be made before the trips. All-inclusive 3-day, 2-night package, $175 (extra $10/day for BC/regulator rental). Min. two clients. Includes 5 boat dives, one night dive and unlimited beach dives. Airport pickup and drop off. Accompanying non-divers, $75, incl. snorkeling. Extra days (2 divers), $60. Simple accommodations in beachside cottages, plus three meals. Can also be booked from **Bidytours** in Mataram, ☎ 22127, Fax: 21821.

Baruna A branch of this large, Bali-based diving operator is located at the Senggigi Beach Hotel. For 2 boat dives to the Gilis, $65 (add $10 for BC/regulator). Min. 2 clients. Single dive off Senggigi Beach (strictly for beginners), all equipment provided, $35. "Fun dive" for beginners off dive boat, $50. Introduction to diving (in pool, plus one open-water dive), $75.

Marine Sports Center Inside Graha Beach Hotel. Water scooter: $10/15 min. Waterskiing: $10/15 min for 2 persons. Fishing, $10/hr for 2 persons plus equipment. Snorkeling, $15 for min. 3 persons. Scuba diving off Senggigi reef, $25 for one dive. Canoe hire $2. Glass-bottom boat (max. 18 persons); transportation to the Gilis, $10 (min.4 persons). They also have a sail boat, parasailing facilities and paddle boards.

Also try the **Sassak Garden Restaurant & Sea Sports**, in Batu Bolong, as well as at most of the big hotels (see above).

Snorkeling you can rent snorkeling equipment in many places in Senggigi. Snorkeling trips to Gili Air cost around $15/person from places such as Sunshine Restaurant.

In The Gilis

GILI AIR

Baronang Divers Pak Sjahrul Nasution. P.O. Box 24, Mataram. This operator caters only to walk-in clients on Gili Air. For 2 boat dives (min. 2 clients), $48. Price drops to $43 for groups of 3–6 clients. Take off 20% if you bring your own BC/regulator. Beach night dive, $28 with rental gear, $20 with your equipment.

GILI TRAWANGAN

The local representative of **Sunda Duta Tours & Travel**, Giuseppe Marchesi, organizes snorkeling trips to the Gilis ($40 up to 4 persons, $10 each extra person), as well as trips to the less-visited Gili Nanggu off southwest Lombok, 1.5 hr from Senggigi ($60, $10 for each extra), and surfing trips to Bangko-Bangko, at the southwestern tip of Lombok ($80, $15 for each extra person). For the most adventurous, he offers camping trips to a dazzling white coral atoll, known only to turtles, which come to lay their eggs at full moon. There are two kinds of packages: 2-day/1 night, $100; 3-day/2-night, $150, all-inclusive with seafood barbeque on the beach (3 meals), snorkeling equipment and lifejackets provided.

CLIMBING GUNUNG RINJANI

You can get to Senaru, the northern gateway to Rinjani, by taking public transportation to Bayan, and then walking up to the village. You can also make arrangements with a driver to drop you off in Senaru in the evening, and then pick you up three days later around noon to take you back to Mataram.

You may wish to go up from Senaru and come back down the mountain on the Sembalun side in the east, but this makes for difficult arrangements, because your driver cannot reach Swela without a jeep, and even if you meet him in Sembalun, he has to take your porters back to the Bayan area. This is not very efficient, and they are reluctant to do so. If you return by the eastern route, you had better count on taking public transportation.

The trail from Batu Koq, a few kilometers from Bayan, is well marked, and many people trek up the mountain with their own gear, without hiring a guide or porter. If you need a guide and porters (which we recommend), check at any of the three *losmen* in Senaru, where you will have to stay overnight anyway (Check in at the Conservation Service Office while you're there).

Recommended Accommodations

The Rinjani Owned by the Balinese conservation service ranger, this *losmen* has four double rooms, which are often full. $4 /person, including dinner and breakfast. They can rent sleeping bags or mats, tents and cooking pots.

Homestay Guru Bakti 7 rms, 9 beds w/outside bath. Guru Bakti rents sleeping bags ($3) and tents for two persons ($7.50). They will also pack lunchboxes for the climb, and find guides ($12.50/day) and porters ($7.50/day). You will get all information you need about Rinjani climbing here, including knowledge from other climbers from all over the world. Spend the night here, and start at dawn for Segara Anak and the Rinjani top. $5/person for the rooms, including dinner and breakfast. During the trek, you are supposed to supply food for porters and guides at your own cost, and provide for their return *bemo* trip. Pak Suma can arrange everything for you. You can give him advance notice by letter: Pak Suma, Pondok Guru Bakti, Senaru, Bayan Lombok Barat 83354, NTB.

Pondok Senaru. 6 rms, up to 4 persons per room. The highest of them all, near a nice, open-sided coffee-house. Rents tents and makes other arrangements for the climb.

On the east side, at Sembalun Lawang, there is a *losmen* that accommodates climbers, **Wisma Cemarasu**, 3 rooms w/double bed in each. Meals available with prior notice, $1. Can make arrangements for porters. $3 S, $4.25 D.

Travel Agencies

Wisma Triguna Jl Adi Sucipto 76, Ampenan. ☎ 21705. Pak Eddy has set up climbs for hundreds of foreigners. His all-inclusive prices for the 3-day/2-night round trip to the lake are: $125 for one person, dropping by $15 per person, until a maximum party of five is reached. For the climb to the very top, which takes one day extra, prices start at $175 for one person, then drop as above. Pak Eddy has an excellent map of the Rinjani routes, and a three-dimensional model of the mountain at his *losmen*. He offers tours either directly, or through Nazaret Tours based in Senggigi.

Satriavi (see "Travel Agencies" above). Offers a 3-day, 2-night Rinjani tour for $185 /person, minimum 2 clients, from Mataram.

Perameswara (see "Travel Agencies" above) also organizes a 3-night /4-day trekking to Rinjani for $175, including transport, camping equipment, porter/guide, and full board.

—*Agnès Korb*

2 Sumbawa PRACTICALITIES

INCLUDES MOYO ISLAND, HU'U AND MT. TAMBORA

Sumbawa has not changed much in the last few years, and tourism is only timidly stepping into this scarcely populated and traditional area. Here you will find basic facilities suitable for the experienced traveler, at prices which remain low. People here are always ready to help, usually at no cost—which is becoming very rare. As long as you dress and behave decently, so as not to offend traditional ways, you will be welcome. Prices in US dollars. S = Single; D = Double; T = Triple; AC = Air-conditioning. Telephone code for Sumbawa Besar is 371; for Bima, 374.

GETTING THERE

By Air

Merpati schedules a number of flights on Fokker F-27 aircraft from Denpasar to Sumbawa, most of via Mataram, Lombok. It is not possible to make guaranteed return bookings. If you book ahead, you will have to re-confirm on the day of departure. Flights:
Denpasar–Mataram–Sumbawa Besar: 9 am (Tues, Thurs, Sat).
Denpasar–Bima (non-stop): 12:25 am (Mon, Wed, Fri, Sun) and 9:25 am (Tues, Thurs, Sat).
Bima–Denpasar (non-stop): 10:25 am (Mon, Wed, Fri); 8:55 am (Tues, Thurs, Sat) and 10:50 am (Mon, Thurs, Sat).
Denpasar–Mataram–Bima: 8:50 am daily.
Bima–Mataram–Denpasar: 11:30 am daily.
   Fares from Bali, each way: Sumbawa Besar ($47.50), Bima ($72).
   Brang Biji airport is only 5 min from the center of Sumbawa Besar. Pale Belo airport in Bima is 20 min south of town, but the road along the blue waters of Bima deep bay offers fabulous views, past salt ponds and barren hills. Taxis ($4) or buses that pass along the main road will take you to the heart of the city.
Merpati Sumbawa Besar: Jl Hasanuddin, ☎ 21206, 21991 (also Jl Kebayan near the Tambora Hotel). In Bima: Jl Sukarno Hatta 30, ☎ 2197, 2382.

By Sea

FERRIES

The ferry crossing from Kahyangan in Labuhan Lombok to Labuhan Tano on the west coast of Sumbawa takes 1.5 hrs. This tiny fishing village is 10 km from the main road to Taliwang, and 30 min by bus from Alas. The sea is rarely rough, except in the middle of the strait, and then only at night from August–December. Ferries leave Lombok at 8 am, 9:30 am, 12 noon, 3 pm and 5 pm. The last is the choice for those coming over to Lombok on the morning ferry from Padang Bai (Bali)—a non-stop double crossing that is not as exhausting as it may seem.
   From Sumbawa back to Lombok, the ferry leaves at 7:30 am, 8:30 am and 1:30 pm. The ships often go into dry dock for repairs, however, and the schedules are often modified so check locally. Fare: $1 (economy); $1.50 (VIP).
   All the ferries are fine, but the *Nusa Wangi* offers a VIP class for $2. The ships now have karaoke, which is probably something you could do without: there is enough to see during the crossing, as you will sail past scores of little islands, and the sea is very calm.
To Komodo A ferry runs from Sape, on the east coast, to Komodo ($4, 7 hrs) and then to Labuhanbajo, west Flores ($2, 4 hrs) and back. It runs every day except Fri, leaving Sape at 8 am.

PELNI

Two Pelni ships call at Bima every two weeks, *Kelimutu* and *Awu*. The *Kelimutu* serves East Nusa Tenggara as far as Dili, East Timor. It calls at Lembar, Lombok from Bima on its twice monthly trip to Surabaya, Java and Banjarmasin, Kalimantan. From Surabaya to Bima it stops in Benoa, Bali. Benoa to Bima departs Thurs 12 noon, arrives Fri 6 am. Bima to Lembar departs Sat 8 pm, arrives Sun 11 am.
   The *Awu* serves most ports in Sulawesi as well as many on the east coast of Kalimantan. It is often used by transmigrants heading to Central Sulawesi, and the decks are usually full. It stops at Benoa from/to Bima every two weeks. Bima to Benoa departs Fri 12 noon, arrives Sat 7 am. Benoa to Bima departs Mon 12 noon, arrives Tues 4 am. The next port of call after Bima is Ujung Pandang (South Sulawesi), and the crossing usually takes around 18 hrs.
   Pelni boats are actually quite an exciting way to visit Indonesia, especially since most passengers are Indonesians coming from and going

to all parts of the archipelago. The ship offers 1st class cabins (for 2 persons), 2nd class cabins (for 4 persons), and three economy decks, all w/full AC and video, and bathrooms w/hot & cold water showers. Economy passengers get 3 meals a day at the pantry (canteen-type trays, simple food). 1st and 2nd class passengers are entitled to special service: luxury cabins w/ private bath and lockers, access to the restaurant for meals, bar with singers every night. The ship also has a meeting-room, a prayer-room for Muslims, a cafeteria on the upper deck, and over-priced shops.

Prices are as follows (Benoa–Bima): Class I: $42 (adult) ; $31.50 (1–11 yrs) ; $4.50 (baby). Class II: $28 (adult) ; $21 (1–11 yrs) ; $3 (baby). Deck: $10 (adult) ; $7.5 (1–11 yrs) ; $1 (baby).

Cabins are usually quite difficult to obtain and cannot be booked in advance. In Benoa, you have to wait until the ship is moored to find out if there are any left. The deck is fine unless the ship is overcrowded in which case it could turn into a nightmare. Try to get Class II if possible.

Pelni Offices In Bima: Jl Martadinata 103 (the road to the harbor); ☎ 2046, 2203. In Benoa, Bali: ☎ (0361) 228962. In Mataram, Lombok: Jl Industri 1, ☎ 21604. Main office in Jakarta: Pelayaran Nasional Indonesia, Jl Angkasa 18, Jakarta. ☎ (21) 416262, 417136, 417137, 417139.

SAILBOATS AND YACHTS

Sailboat charter The schooner **Sri Noa-Noa**, based at Benoa, Bali, can accommodate 2–5 passsengers, and is available for 3–15 day package trips and charter. There are single and double cabins w/ locker bath and hot water. Food and water, soft drinks, and water sports equipment (snorkeling and fishing) is included. Rates: $350/day (under 15 days), $400/day (over 15 days). You can embark or disembark at another port, with an additional charge of $200/day per day of travel. The routine 12–day itinerary is: Benoa–Alas–Moyo–Bima–Komodo–Sumbawa–Lombok. The ship can also be chartered for any destination in Indonesia. In Bali contact Mr and Mrs Petiniaud, ☎/Fax: 233555; or PT Alfatours, 288020 or 289046.

P&O Travel P&O runs a luxury yacht, the 37 m, 42-passenger *Spice Islander*, through Nusa Tenggara. It begins in Bali and calls at Lombok, Gili Suda and Sekotong, and then proceeds to Sumbawa, Komodo, Flores, Lembata, Roti, Sawu, and then returns to Benoa. (See "Transportation" page 254 for details.)

By Land

BUSES FROM LOMBOK TO BIMA

Buses usually leave Mataram around 2 pm to catch the evening ferry (for the return, buses leave Bima at around 8:30 pm to catch the morning ferry). Average fares: Mataram–Bima $18.50. Some companies (Rasa Sayang, Pe-

muda, Fajar Indah) only go as far as Dompu, west of Bima. These usually leave Mataram at dawn.

Due to the fierce competition between various bus companies, most of them have upgraded their vehicles, which are now as sophisticated as those running along the Java–Bali route. Most are full AC, w/ reclining seats. Fares include snacks and meals, often in quite decent restaurants, usually serving Javanese cuisine.

Most of the bus companies are located along Most bus companies are found along Jl Pejanggik in Mataram, and Jl St. Kaharuddin, the street leading to the terminal, in Bima. Most are Bima-based operations.

The best operators are **Langsung Indah**, **Surabaya Indah**, **DAMRI** (safe, good food), **Jawa Baru**, **Jakarta Indah** and **Rasa Sayang** (caring towards its passengers, as its name, "Love Bus" implies!). Baruna Arta, Merpati, Damai Indah and Bima Indah continue to run more obsolete vehicles.

Langsung Indah Jl St. Kaharuddin, Bima. ☎ 2547.
Jawa Baru Jl Hasanuddin 34, Bima. ☎ 2451.
DAMRI Jl St. Kaharuddin 7, Bima; Jl Imam Bonjol 1, Sumbawa. ☎ 22146, 21426.

Jawa Baru and DAMRI also run morning buses between Surabaya, Java and Bima.

BUSES TO SUMBAWA BESAR

If you want to go just from Mataram to Sumbawa Besar, you are probably better off on public transportation. Langsung Jaya (AC/non AC), Tirtasari (AC/non AC), DAMRI (AC/non AC), and Mawar Indah (AC) all claim to ensure "express direct service" between the two cities for $5 (AC) and $4.50 (non AC), but are not necessarily reliable. They will pick you up at 5:30 am in Mataram for the morning ferry (going the other way, 9:30 am in Sumbawa Besar for the afternoon ferry). You may nevertheless have to change from bus to ferry to bus again by yourself to make sure that you catch the boat. See what you get at the Sweta (public bus) terminal before opting for an "express" package.

ACCOMMODATIONS

Both in West Sumbawa and Bima, facilities are still rather limited, but you can find friendly little hotels at reasonable prices. Bima is slightly better off in this respect, as a new hotel resort, Lawata Beach Hotel, has just been developed just 5 km outside the town center.

The once virgin Moyo Island, just off the coast of Sumbawa Besar, has recently been converted into a retreat for millionaires. Access conditions to the island have changed altogether (see "Moyo Island" below).

Sumbawa Besar

Avoid spending the night in Alas, which only has three *losmen*, **Losmen Selamat**, **Losmen Anda**

Sumbawa Besar

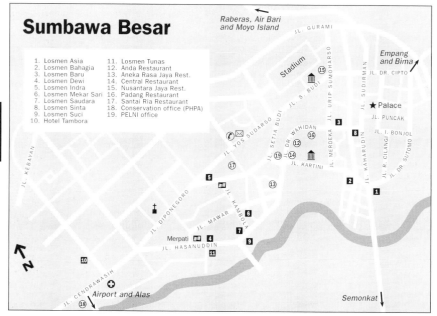

Raberas, Air Bari and Moyo Island

1. Losmen Asia
2. Losmen Bahagia
3. Losmen Baru
4. Losmen Dewi
5. Losmen Indra
6. Losmen Mekar Sari
7. Losmen Saudara
8. Losmen Sinta
9. Losmen Suci
10. Hotel Tambora
11. Losmen Tunas
12. Anda Restaurant
13. Aneka Rasa Jaya Rest.
14. Central Restaurant
15. Nusantara Jaya Rest.
16. Padang Restaurant
17. Santai Ria Restaurant
18. Conservation office (PHPA)
19. PELNI office

Empang and Bima

★ Palace

Airport and Alas

Semonkat

and **Losmen Telaga**. The first two are in Jl Pahlawan 7 and 14 (8 and 17 rms, $2–$5). Head straight to Sumbawa Besar from Poto Tano harbor, even if you arrive on the evening ferry. The best choice in town remains Hotel Tambora, owned by a friendly Balinese family, which promotes art, culture and handicrafts, although there are also more inexpensive places to stay.

Tambora Jl Kebayan 2, ☎ 21555, 22111, 22444, Fax: 21624. 55 rms. In front of the hospital and 5 min from the airport. Restaurant serves Indonesian, Chinese and European food. Hotel can provide you with traditional massage service, car rental w/driver, bus ticket reservations. They can arrange dances and cater to meetings of all sorts (they have a meeting-room with stage). They can also arrange tours via their agency, Tambora Duta Wisata Tours & Travel. This is especially useful if you wish to visit Pulau Moyo National Reserve, as it is becoming increasingly difficult to go there on your own now (see below). Next door is the regency's first mini-supermarket: a real novelty. Economy: $4.25 S, $5.50 D. Standard w/ fan $8.25 S, $11 D. Standard AC: $14 S, $17.50 D. VIP: $19.50 S, $22 D. Deluxe suite: $38.50 S, $47 D.

Suci Jl Hasanuddin 57 ☎ 21589. 24 rms. This is probably the best of the town's *losmen*. Their restaurant should be completed by mid-1994. Fan-cooled, $2–$8.

Saudara (11 rooms) Jl Hasanuddin 50 ☎ 21528. Also recommended. $1.75–$4.

Also: **Dewi**, Jl Hasanuddin 60, 11 rms, $1.75–$3 (under renovation); **Indra**, Jl Diponegoro 44, $1.50–$3 ; **Mekarsari**, Jl Hasanuddin,

12 rms, $2.50–$4.50; **Sumbawa** Jl Gurami, on the road to Bima, $2–$4; **Tunas** Jl Hasanuddin 37, 10 rms, $1.50.

BEACH RESORTS

Tirtasari About 6 km on the main road west towards Alas. 30 rms. Swimming-pool, dining-room with inexpensive Chinese food. Crowded with locals on weekends, especially the pool. Perama Travel Information desk. $4.50–$30.

Kencana Beach Inn Jl Raya Tano Km 11 (Badas). ☎ 22555. West of Sumbawa Besar, a little beyond the junction to Badas harbor. A beautiful, huge wooden house on stilts in the style of Alas mansions comprises 5 simple rooms upstairs and shelters a restaurant below (large range of simple dishes available, open all day). Nearby, 15 pleasant little bamboo cottages line the beach, each fitted with simple furniture and including a bathroom w/shower and toilet (private access to the beach). Facilities available: horseback riding and snorkeling equipment for rent. Speedboat or *sampan* available (their boat can take up to 20 passengers). Dances can also be arranged on the beach, including dinner for groups. Fishing or diving parties to nearby Tanjung Menangis ("the cape of tears"), or boat expeditions to Pulau Moyo and Medang, and even as far as Pulau Saelus, half-way to Sulawesi (12 hrs one-way) can be arranged on request. Prices should be discussed on the spot. Santoana House: $7.50 (standard), $10 (family room). Sumbawa Village: $20 for a "village room" and $40 for a "chief of the village room". Recommended for honeymooners because of its quietness and beauty.

Taliwang

Water buffalo races across flooded rice paddies sometimes take place in this area. This used to happen only around October, but with more extensive irrigation and new 3-month rice crops, it could happen at any time of the year.

Tubalong In front of the movie house. 15 rms. Noisy up front till 11pm–12pm, but the back rooms are quieter. Restaurant up front, inexpensive Indonesian food, cold beer or soft drinks. $1.50–$6/night.

Ashar Next to the market. 12 very simple double rms. $3 per night for one or two.

Bima

Sanghyang Jl Hasanuddin 6. ☎ 2788, 2017. 60 rms. Owned by members of the Sultan's family. Its building, inspired from Bimanese architecture, is conveniently situated beside the bank and the newly-built supermarket, close to the shopping area. Restaurant serves Indonesian food. The Sanghyang also runs a travel agency and can provide car rental service w/driver. For travelers wishing to go to Komodo, its sailing company, Peltasa, can take you there: 3 ships run everyday from Sape. Standard: $15S, $17.50D. VIP: $20S, $22.50D. All rooms w/AC and TV. Prices include breakfast.

Lila Graha Jl Lombok 20, a small street near the market, ☎ 2645, 2740. 25 rms. The friendly, but noisy, Lila Graha is owned by a Balinese couple, Ibu Sarini and her husband. The restaurant serves Chinese and Javanese food. They are ready to help with any tourist information and

car rental (rates depend on the destination, e.g.: Donggo $30/day, Wawo $20/day). They can organize tours to Komodo, including transportation and two nights at a hotel ($200). Economy, fan $3.50S, $5D. Standard, fan $5S, $6D. VIP with AC & TV $19D, $30T.

Parewa Jl Sukarno Hatta 40, on the road to Raba, in front of the horse-racing track ☎ 2652. 24 rms. Restaurant serving Chinese and Indonesian food, and a small shop. The main Merpati office for Bima is next door, and the people who own the Parewa can get you a seat easily. The hotel rents minibuses for tours in and around town, including trips to the weaving areas and the museum ($4–$5/hr), as well as exploration tours to the north or south coasts, through their travel agency, Parewa Travel, on Jl Sumbawa. They can also provide you with an English-speaking guide, and pack you a lunchbox. They offer a cultural events tour, including dances, rice sowing and harvesting demonstrations, and methods of traditional fighting, including ram-like head-butting. Standard fan $10; VIP w/AC $17.50.

The hotel also owns a 50-ton ship, *Komodo Shalom*, which is available for up to 20 passengers to see the dragons of Komodo island. There are 8 bunks and a sit-down toilet and shower. The trip takes 4 hrs each way, and overnight facilities are provided on the island. None of the other ships available for charter to Komodo approaches this boat's standards. Reserve early as the ship is often booked ahead. $200 upwards, depending on the number of passengers (food extra). The boat can also be chartered for trips elsewhere.

Sumbawa 2

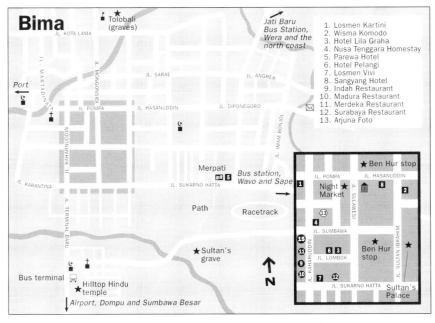

Bima

1. Losmen Kartini
2. Wisma Komodo
3. Hotel Lila Graha
4. Nusa Tenggara Homestay
5. Parewa Hotel
6. Hotel Pelangi
7. Losmen Vivi
8. Sangyang Hotel
9. Indah Restaurant
10. Madura Restaurant
11. Merdeka Restaurant
12. Surabaya Restaurant
13. Arjuna Foto

Wisma Komodo Jl St. Ibrahim 5, between Hotel Sanghyang and the royal palace. ☎ 2070. Simple but clean. Has a small dining-room. The only budget *losmen* that we can recommend in Bima. $5/night, including breakfast.

Also: **Kartini**. Jl St. Kaharuddin, in front of the market. 20 rms. Only in an emergency. $1.50/night. **Pelangi**, Jl Lombok 8. **Vivi**, Jl Sudirman 24. **Penginapan Bahagia**, Jl Karantina 3. **Putra Sari**, Jl Sukarno Hatta. All mostly patronized by locals.

BEACH RESORTS

Lawata Beach Hotel Jl Sultan Salahuddin. ☎ 3696–7, Fax: 3698. 23 rms. A newly built hotel and restaurant with a swimming-pool on the very edge of Bima Bay, surrounded by beautiful scenery and facing the Donggo highlands. The first *real* tourist resort in Bima, as far as facilities and standards are concerned. An ideal place to relax, though bathing conditions, as elsewhere around Bima, are disappointing (no beach). An open pavilion looking onto the pool shelters a pleasant restaurant, serving good Indonesian and western food at reasonable prices. The nice little cottages with terraces overlook the sea. All rooms w/AC. Bar at the pool, laundry, drugstore and room service open 16 hrs, parking lot, satellite TV, card telephone, credit cards accepted. Booking can also be made through Varianusa Tours & Travel, Jl Bung Karno no. 3A, Mataram, Lombok. ☎ (364) 25832, 34515, or directly to the hotel. Since Bimanese are still quite disapproving of the rampant display of human skin—such as wearing a bikini in a public bathing area—it's a good idea to stay here if you find such sensiblities difficult to cope with while on holiday. Standard $20 S, $22 D. Deluxe $27.50 S, $30 D. Suite $32.50 S, $35 D. Presidential suite $50.

Sonco Tengge Beach A small hotel located on the road to Lawata, facing the bay. A little obsolete and nothing to really dream about, including the restaurant. Economy $6.20. Standard $8.50. VIP $15.

Dompu

There are a few *losmen* in Dompu, but there is no reason for you to do anything but pass through this sleepy little city. The better accommodation is near the highway. All cost around $3–$4.

Karijawa Jl Sudirman 5. 6 rms.
Wisma Praja Jl A. Yani 9. 8 rms, restaurant.
Kotabaru 9 rms.

Sape

There are two *losmen* here for those not wishing to rise in Bima at an ungodly hour to catch the 8 am ferry to Komodo. Both are basic but cheap, provide meals and have built extensions to accommodate the July–August crowds.

Friendship 9 rms w/shared facilities, 6 rms w/attached facitlies and AC. $2–$7.
Give 14 rms. $1.50/person. 2 new rms w/enclosed facilities, $3/person. You can find someone here to charter a small motorized canoe for a look around.

The *losmen* keep minibuses that can run up to 9 passengers to Lamere village. *Benhurs* (horse and cart) to the *losmen* or bus station area charge 30¢ minimum for the 2 km trip to the harbor. The harbormaster's office at the docks can also help you to find a small boat with an outboard, minimum $10 for a half day.

LOCAL TRANSPORTATION

Outside Sumbawa Besar and Bima, local transportation is still difficult, although the main highway linking the two cities is now in good condition almost all the way along, especially in West Sumbawa. Smaller roads are being slowly improved, but *bemos* from one village to another are still scarce and are often replaced by trucks on rough inland tracks. The latter often break down, but people will always be ready to help, including giving you a lift. People here are accustomed to walking for miles across country, and even though an area may seem remote and empty, there are always passers-by.

Horses and carts (*cidomo* in Sumbawa, and *benhur* in Bima) were formerly the most common means of transport in town. They still operate around town, and on short village-to-village runs. Standard fare is around 15¢, which may be raised if you go further than normal, even in town. Nowadays *bemos* run along the dusty streets of Subawa Besar, and between the twin cities of Bima (historical and business center and harbor) and Raba (administrative hub).

West Sumbawa

The terminal for public buses to Bima has recently moved from Brang Bara to Labuhan, near the harbor. Fares, Sumbawa Besar–Bima, $5. (Note also that the Seketeng terminal in Sumbawa Besar has moved to Air Bari.) Both the Tambora Hotel and the Suci Hotel can help book and/or buy your ticket.

The ferry terminal at Labuhan Tano can be reached from Sumbawa Besar quite easily by public buses, such as Langsung Jaya and Tirtasari (many buses, mostly running before noon). Fare: $1.20.

Many other buses are available to Alas, Taliwang, Plampang and Empang (30¢–$1.20). Those buses even run late into the night, especially those arriving at Tano around 8 pm. Despite that the vehicles look worn-out and over full, and the drivers reckless, you needn't worry about your safety.

Bungin island, the abode of Bajo fishermen, opposite the now dozing Alas harbor, is only 15 min from the mainland by motorboat (20¢ minimum). Boats leave as they fill up, especially at market time. You can also charter (around $10 for up to 6 persons).

In the hilly countryside people still ride their own little horses bareback, boys live with their horses, take baths with them, and horses are used to carry almost everything. If you're keen for a ride, try making friends and ask them to let you have a go, especially in West Sumbawa. Inexperienced riders will find it difficult, if not impossible, to ride bareback.

Some remote areas, such as Tepal village, 36 km south of Batu Dulang, can still only be reached on horseback (8 hrs minimum in the dry season, 3 to 4 *days* during the rainy season!). To get to Batu Dulang, take a truck from Sumbawa Besar terminal (check on arrival, as terminal locations are being modified for all directions). 40¢ for the 1.5-hr trip.

Access to another interesting destination for tourists, Batu Tering, with its caves and sarcophagus remains, is also by truck (the road has yet to be asphalted). 50¢, 1.5–2 hrs. The trucks leave Sumbawa Besar very early and come back a later in the morning, before noon. *Bemos* can also be chartered for around $15.

From Taliwang to Sejorong on the south coast, trucks charge about $1.50. To Sekongkang Atas, 80¢. These are basically standing room only. A few have hard wooden seats, but it's more comfortable to stand, unless you can wrangle your way into one of the front seats next to the driver, a spot usually kept for pretty girls.

Bima

In Bima, the main terminal is Dara, at the entrance of the city. To find the small buses which run to Wawo and Sape in the east, you have to go to Kumbe, east of Raba. Usual fares from Bima (displayed in Raba terminal): Dompu ($1), Sila (50¢), Donggo, via Sila ($1), Hu'u ($1.50).

You can shorten the trip to Donggo by crossing Bima Bay on a small motorboat (50¢). It only takes 15 min to cross to Bajo harbor, where you now have two alternatives: waiting for the bus from Sila to Donggo, or take an *ojek*, a taxi motorbike. The *ojek* is to be preferred, as the bus still starts out from Bima at dawn and is invariably overcrowded. Horseback riding seems to have declined in the Bima region, and travelers wishing to visit the Donggo mountains can count on climbing after getting off the bus at Donggo.

Note: the road to Donggo is now asphalted as far as Sangari, which makes things much easier, if less picturesque. To reach Padende, take the road to Dompu, and, at Sila, turn right to Rora.

Many tracks are still in very bad condition, even very close to Bima town. Just try to go to Ule and Songgela beaches from the surrounding hills, just 5 km north of the city, and you will understand why almost all vehicles are helpless

in this rugged landscape. Many places are only accessible by boat, such as Kolo fishing village on the eastern shore of Bima Bay, near the neck (take a small passenger boat at the harbor; usually easier in the morning at market hours).

Destinations east and northeast of Bima other than Wavo and Sape (situated along the main highway east) are still quite difficult to reach, even by jeep. The north coast road is very pleasant, leading through the teak woods, but beyond Jatiwangi and Jatibaru, becomes dust and potholes. Any journey to the remote Wera district in the northeast opposite Gunung Api, could turn into a nightmare if you're not prepared.

Car and minibus rental

Since public transport seems so tenuous in Sumbawa, it may be a good choice to hire a car. In view of road conditions and the distances to be covered, you should not think about a self-drive car of a motorcycle.

In Sumbawa Besar, contact **Hotel Tambora**. For a jeep with a capacity for 6 persons, rates from Sumbawa Besar are: Alas ($40), Tano ($45), Taliwang ($60), Dompu ($80), Bima ($90). You can also choose to go overland from Tano to Sape ($150 minimum). Minibuses are cheaper ($40/day). Full-sized buses can be charterd, but can be twice the price of minibuses.

Renting motorcycles to travel throughout the countryside is not a very good idea. It is not without out reason that it is difficult to find places that have motorbikes for hire; you may try at **Mekarsari**, one of the *losmen*, if you really think you can manage alone.

In Bima, the **Parewa Hotel** and **Surya Kencana** (Jl Lombok 44. ☎ 2568) can arrange vehicle rental. **Hotel Sanghyang** offers a "taxi service" along fixed routes: Bima to Sape ($20), city tour ($25), one-day rental ($25). You can also arrange something with public *bemo* drivers, as all the vehicles are privately owned.

Although most outfits are nervous about renting self-drive vehicles, **Parewa Hotel** rents Kijang utility vehicles or Suzuki minibuses for $5/hr, or around $35/day (a little more w/AC), plus gas. Bringing along a local driver can be safer and much more pleasant anyway. Many places in Bima are isolated, and the people are not at all accustomed to seeing foreigners. A local driver can often smooth the way for you.

DINING

Sumbawa Besar

Sumbawa is not famous for its restaurants, but you will not starve. In Sumbawa Besar, you can still eat decently at **Hotel Tambora**, which offers a whole range of Indonesian and Chinese dishes. Next door to the hotel, two delicious Javanese restaurants owned by the same family, **Cirebon I** and **Cirebon II**, are highly recommended. They offer a whole range of traditional Javanese and Sundanese dishes. The DAMRI buses stop there for lunch. Also try **Surabaya**, Jl Diponegoro 39 ☎ 21433, which serves simple and tasty East Javanese food, **Aneka Rasa Jaya**, Jl Hasanuddin 10, which serves Chinese and seafood, and **Puspawarna**, on Jl Kartini.

If you'd like to try hot Sasak food, you can eat the famous *ayam Taliwang* at **Selera Taliwang**, on Jl Gurami, above Seketeng market. These types of restaurants are becoming increasingly popular throughout Bali and West Nusa Tenggara (around $3 for a delicious meal of grilled whole chicken, rice, and spicy sidedishes). Also try **Muchsin**, on Jl Wahidin, serving Sasak food, and two simple *rumah makan* located next to each other in Jl Garuda, **Ojo Lali** which serves Javanese cuisine, and **Parewa**.

For a late breakfast or early lunch, try mixed rice or vegetables in sauce at the food stalls (usually owned by Balinese housewives) in **Seketeng market**. It is a real treat (50¢ a plate). At night, the **stalls along Jl Setiabudi** are the place for *es campur*, *saté* and other delicacies. A *cidomo* can take you to all these places.

The beach at **Kencana** (contact Hotel Tambora for information, or ☎ 22555), is a great place to rest and enjoy lunch: Chinese, Indonesian and Samawa food are available—try the *sepat* and *singang*, fish cooked in tamarind. Special dinner and dances at night on order.

Bima

In town, the three main hotels offer restaurant facilities, with Chinese and Indonesian cuisine. Apart from these, there is **Padedoang**, a Sassak restaurant on Jl Martadinata, the street leading to the harbor, which serves the well-known *ayam Taliwang* either grilled, fried or *pelecing* (in sauce)—for $1.50 to $3, or grilled or fried *bandeng* fish. *Bandeng* is a very tasty fish appreciated all over Indonesia (despite its bones!), and it is a delicacy that you should not miss in Bima, as it is very easy to get here. Padedoang can also prepare you tasty lunch boxes of *nasi ayam* (chicken rice) for $1 to $1.50. ☎ 2155.

Apart from *bandeng*, Bimanese cuisine is based on all sorts of delicious fish dishes, such as *palumara* (fish in sauce), which are always eaten alongside *bohidungga*, a sauce made of chillies, lime and tomatoes, but you are unlikely to taste this unless you visit a Bimanese home. However you can buy bottled *bohidungga* at the market, as well as the famously sweet and mellow *bingka dolu*—egg custard cakes.

There are several simple **Padang restaurants** along Jl Kaharuddin (where the bus offices are), and Jl Sumbawa. **Sekedar** on Jl Pasar, near the market, sells Madurese dishes including *sate* and *gule kambing* (goat stew) for about $1.

Also try **Anda**, a very simple Chinese *rumah makan* on Jl Kaharuddin. **Sebelas Maret**, a "cafeteria" formerly in Raba, has now moved to Jl Soekarno Hatta along the palace square. Most restaurants are open all day.

For a light drink with friends, try the little cafelike **Mawar**, in one of the lanes leading to the market behind Jl Sumbawa, near the bakery. They serve many kinds of *es* (iced drinks) and are mainly patronized by young Bimanese, who have few other places of entertainment.

In the evenings the **night market** is the place to go for *mie goreng* (fried noodles), *sate*, *gule* and other delicacies such as *ubi goreng* (fried manioc, eaten with chili sauce), or local cakes.

The restaurant in **Lawata Beach Hotel** is highly recommended, for its tasty and cheap food, friendly service, and atmosphere. Diners sit in an open pavilion overlooking the glittering waters of Bima Bay: *the* place for relaxing and feeling like a tourist in Bima! ☎ 3696, 3697.

For food shopping, go to the new Lancar Jaya supermarket next to Hotel Sanghyang on Jl Hasanuddin, and to **Toko Ardjuna**, on the corner across the street, which offer the most complete range of food and household items. For fresh cakes go to the small bakery on Jl Sumbawa, opposite the police station. A wide selection of goods is also available in the Raba shopping complex.

Between Sumbawa and Bima, there are few places we can recommend. In Plampang, there is one restaurant right where the night buses usually stop. In Empang, there is **Surabaya** (East Javan food). In Banggo, at the crossroads to Sanggar and Tambora, there is **Banyuwangi** (East Javan food). In Dompu: **Rumah Makan Jawa Timur**, in front of Losmen Karijawa; **Wisma Praja**, Jl A. Yani 9; **Nasional**, Jl Sudirman 64; and **Damai**, Jl Melati 1. All these restaurants serve mainly Javanese cuisine.

Moyo Island

Moyo island, with an area of some 300 sq km, is located 15 km off the coast of Sumbawa, and has been a wildlife reserve since 1976. Some 85 out of the 124 species of birds living in Sumbawa are found inside its tropical forest and highland meadows, and the snorkeling off Tanjung Pasir, on the island southernmost tip, is some of the best in the region.

Recently, everything has changed on Moyo. Up until 1993, you had to get a permit issued by the KSDA (Nature Conservation Office), undertake a tortuous journey to the park, report to the rangers in Moyo, and thereafter you were left pretty much to your own devices.

Things have become a little more regimented, to say the least. Firstly because half of the island has been monopolized by the **Amanwana** resort (see "Accommodations" below); Secondly because access to the rest of the island is now through a company called **P.T. Moyo Safari Abadi** (Jl Garuda, Sumbawa Besar. ☎ 21838). They have set up accommodations at Labuhan Cedal, (Air Manis camp), including six tents and a restaurant serving simple dishes such as *nasi goreng* and *mie goreng*. You can also contact them directly at Air Bari, the jump-off village northeast of Sumbawa Besar, where they have a counter. A package including transportation by boat, entrance fee for one day, but not food, costs $17.50. You can also contact **Hotel Tambora**'s travel agency, which will arrange a voucher, including the boat trip.

ACCOMMODATIONS

Amanwana Moyo Island, Sumbawa. ☎ (0371) 22233, Fax: (371) 22288. Amanwana, which means "peaceful forest," is a brand new holiday resort built by the Aman resorts international hotel group. The resort is a self-contained complex, even reservations have to be made through the International Reservations Center in Amanusa, Bali, or from abroad. It is virtually impossible to book it from Sumbawa mainland.

The resort provides 20 luxury tents, all of the same design, including full AC, kingsize bed, a sitting area w/luxury divans and desk, and an outdoor terrace. Bathrooms are fitted w/shower and toilet. The tents are scattered on a secluded beach, and comprise "beach tents" and "jungle tents." There's a bar, library and shop. Watersports facilities include windsurfing, snorkeling, catamaran sailing, boat hiring and diving. Diving packages available, including certification courses.

Cruises can be organized aboard the four boats owned by Amanwana. The boats can also be used to drop off and pick up guests at any of the beaches on Moyo island at no extra charge. Roundtrip between Bali and Amanwana, by Merpati and the resort's boat, $100/person. Tickets can be collected at Amanusa in Bali.

Ocean tent: $300 S, $400 D. Jungle tent $200 S, $300 D; extra person $100. Rates include all food, beverages and most activities. Bali Central Reservations Office, c/o Amanusa Resorts, Nusa Dua, Bali. ☎ (361) 71267, Fax: (361) 71266.

Hu'u

Hu'u is said to be "the new paradise for surfers." It was included in tourism development programs as early as 10 years ago, but not really "discovered" until the beginning of 1988 by young Australians.

ACCOMMODATIONS

There is a package offered by the Balinese-Australian Paul King Surf travel of Sydney, including transportation from Bima airport and all transfers as well as no language hassles. Some surfers say this is overpriced.

If you go on your own, most people recommend the Mona Lisa for those with a bit of spare cash and the Intan Lestari for thinner wallets. **Mona Lisa**. 22 rms. Billiards, volleyball, souvenir shop and an inexpensive restaurant. $4 S–$6 D for each of the economy rooms. $8.50 S–$12 D for each of the deluxe rooms, w/ attached toilet/bath and mosquito nets. Write to Mona Lisa, Lakey Beach, Hu'u, Dompu, NTB for reservations. Or try to contact them through the Toko Mona Lisa in Dompu (☎ 170, 422), or the Toko Metro in Bima (☎ 2550). These stores are owned by the same Chinese family that built the Mona Lisa Cottages. Remember that the postal service is slow in Indonesia, especially to out-of-the-way places like Hu'u.

Intan Lestari Cottages 14 rms. Their restaurant has the reputation for serving the best and most plentiful meals. $3/person w/ shared facilities, $5/person w/attached facilities.

There are several other *losmen* here. The first to be built was **Unicorn Camp**, and there is **Anton Camp**, **Donis Camp** and **Lakey Camp**. Rates are usually around $10/person per day, incl. 3 meals, drinks and laundry. These traditional Bimanese cottages may be followed by larger hotels, as the beautiful white sand beach—far from the nearest village—is now being eyed by investors. 300 ha of land are available for the building of minimum 50-rm hotels, and Bima wants to get its share of the tourist boom.

Things get crowded at Hu'u from early June through August. During this time, the rooms fill up and only a relatively uncomfortable beach-sleep remains. The best waves crash at the beginning of the month and at full moon. They split in three in the middle of the sea, which is a fabulous challenge for surfers. New names have been given to surf locations, such as: Pipe Peak, Lakey Peak, Nanga Peak and Priscop Peak.

Note: Although the surfing locations are far from the nearest village, remember that Bima is a very traditional area, and most of the people living there are devout Muslims. You are not obligated to bathe in full dress like them, but try not to do so in the nude or behave indecently.

Climbing Tambora

Gunung Tambora dominates the northern peninsula of Sumbawa. It is 2,851 m high, heavily wooded, and surrounded by a thick belt of rain forest, a strange contrast to the aridity of the remainder of the peninsula. A 20,000 ha timber concession has stripped much of the mountain's southern slopes. The lumber is trucked to Calabai on the coast, then shipped out to Java.

Note: a working knowledge of Indonesian is essential in the peninsula. Few tourists come here, and little English is spoken. You may be able to find an interpreter in Sumbawa Besar or Bima to accompany you on the climb.

Calabai The base for the ascent is Calabai, a small logging town on the coast, and the only town of consequence in the whole peninsula. Food and equipment are expensive here, so stock up in Sumbawa Besar or Bima.

There is only one place to stay, the guesthouse belonging to the local timber corporation. It is a pleasant place, a small wooden building on the waterfront, with excellent views of the sunset over Moyo island from an outside veranda. You need written permission from the production manager to stay here, but there should be no difficulty in obtaining this on arrival. The price of a night's stay is negotiable, maybe $5.

There are a number of ways to get to Calabai. From Sumbawa Besar (at Badas harbor), you can hire a speedboat to Calabai for $30 minimum. It is also possible to go to the fishing village of Air Bari, where a fishing boat can be chartered for around $10 if the sea is calm, and $15–$20 if it is rough. The wind gets usually up round about 11 am until late afternoon, so to take advantage of the lower fare, get a very early start from Sumbawa, or stay overnight at Air Bari.

From Bima, a bus leaves daily at 7 am for Calabai. It is a 13-hr ride, as it stops at every single *kampung* en route, and is packed to the gunwales. The road runs along the main road past Dompu to Soriutu, then follows a bush track up the coast to Calabai. It is a bumpy ride, although the authorities appear to be making an effort to repair some of the worst bridges and sections. Trucks also run from Calabai to Dompu. These land routes are the only practicable way to leave the peninsula, as there is no shipping—except for timber—in Calabai.

Pancasila The footpath to the summit of Tambora starts from the village of Pancasila, 15 km from Calabai. Before leaving Calabai, it is essential to register with the local police. This is for your own protection, as it will be they who have to bring you back if you get lost.

To get to Pancasila, you can walk, or take a motorcycle or horse and cart. An occasional truck also runs there in the early morning. There are a number of men in Pancasila who will offer their services as guides. You *must* take a guide if you want to reach the top. The mountain is separated from Pancasila by 12 km of rain forest, and even if the vegetation were not so thick, Tambora is obscured by low clouds most of the time anyway. It is very difficult to keep your bearings in the forest if you should accidentally step off

the path—easy to do, as so few people use it that it is overgrown in many places. A number of groups who did not take guides are reported to have gotten lost for up to several days on Tambora. The guides are inexpensive; bargain them to about $5/day, plus food. This will be basically rice and fish (if you want to eat anything else, bring it along from Sumbawa Besar or Bima). They will act as porters at the same time, carrying the food and jerrycans of water.

The ascent It is recommended to leave Pancasila in the early morning, as it usually rains on the mountain in the afternoon; you should aim to get as far as possible and camp in the afternoon if necessary. You will initially follow a cart track towards the tiny *kampung* of Tambora for 4–5 km, before branching off onto a smaller path, almost completely overgrown, which often has to be cleared with a *parang* (machete).

After about two hours, you reach thicker woodland, where trees grow taller and denser, with thinner undergrowth; here one occasionally comes across deer, wild boar, monkeys and snakes. The terrain on this stretch can be terrible, very muddy and slippery, with deep gullies cutting across the path at points, which is itself very faint. The forest is also thoroughly infested with leeches.

After another 4 hrs, climbers reach the only stream that can be found during the climb. At this point, a change in the forest becomes almost immediately apparent. It is drier, and pine trees replace the hardwoods. The undergrowth thins out and the leeches disappear. Actually this is the point where you reach the base of the mountain. The path rises steeply through temperate forest and thickets of giant nettles. The *parang* still proves very useful in this terrain.

If you wish to reach the crater of the mountain at sunrise, you have to camp high enough on its slope, although it can be very cold because of the wind, and leave the camp before dawn, carrying only a light load. The climb through the pine forest is relatively easy, and then up along a spine of bare volcanic rock to the top.

The crater is an awesome, gigantic hole 3–4 km across and about 300 m deep with sheer cliff sides leaking steam from a dozen vents. The rim is an eerie place; several hundred meters wide, it is a wilderness of cracked and gouged volcanic rock. Nothing green grows there. Although it looks as if a descent would be suicidal, some guides say that it is possible to climb down to the crater floor, and camp by an unattractive lake at the bottom, which apparently contains fresh water. The summit itself is only a hundred meters higher than the rim. To the west, the coastline and Moyo island can be seen, as well as Mount Rinjani in Lombok, but only if it is not too cloudy.

The descent is far quicker than the ascent, although the greasy footing makes some of the path treacherous.

Conclusion: This is a *very* difficult climb with a lot of hazards, and may be disappointing as the view at the top is not always worth it. This should be tried *only* by very, very experienced and physically well-prepared climbers.

Recommended clothing includes: long-sleeved shirts and long heavy trousers, strong, ankle-length boots with a good grip, and if possible, some waterproof clothing and a warm sweater to provide protection against the cold wind and rain when camping on the mountain.

—*Chris Thring*

SHOPPING AND SOUVENIRS

Textiles Traditional textile handicraft is probably the best thing to buy in Sumbawa. The Ministry of Industry has recently encouraged and subsidized weaving, which had disappeared for almost two generations. Modern fabrics take their inspiration from the patterns and motifs formerly favored by noble classes.

There are no *ikat* fabrics here, but you will find *pelekat*—checkered, brightly coloured cloths—and red-and-black sarongs and scarves with the 8-branch star motif (once a royal privilege).

In West Sumbawa, it is best to go to the production sites, which are relatively easy to get to: **Poto** and **Malili**, are in the Moyo Hilir district, some 11 km east of Sumbawa. Prices here range from $20 to $75, depending on the size (scarf, headdress, sash or sarong). Actually the items are overpriced, even if it does take many days to make one piece of cloth. To go there, take a *bemo* to Poto just north of Seketeng market (fare: about 10¢); it takes about 20 min on a recently asphalted road. Alternatively, take a minibus to Moyo town from Sumbawa Besar at Brang Bara, and from there walk about 8 km through the countryside to reach Bekat and Poto from the east. This is a very pleasant trip enabling you to see everyday village life.

Pamulung, a little village off the main road west from Sumbawa Besar to Utan (about 5 km from town), also offers good fabrics. To reach Pamulung, go west as far as Tirtasari Cottages, and turn left where the main road branches. The formerly terrible track leading to Pamulung is being upgraded. Hotel Tambora in Sumbawa Besar organizes tours there which include weaving demonstrations and a traditional buffalo race. Many of the fabrics are also on sale at the hotel itself as well as their restaurant at Kencana Beach.

In Bima, the most typical textile item is the *weri*, a brightly colored scarf formerly used by men as a loincloth, and which can be used as a tablecloth, scarf, wall decoration, or cut and sewn to make dresses, pillowcases etc. These usually fetch $4 to $6. You will find a wide range of colors in Bima market, in the Raba shopping complex, but Siti Sundari's souvenir shop

Mutmainah definitely has the best choice is in souvenir shop. This very enterprising young woman employs a lot of weavers in several workshops and also sells the products of weavers working at their homes in Rabadompu (in the suburbs east of Raba) and in the little village of Ntobo, about 10 km from Raba. You can go directly to this village to see them made (the road is not very good). Located opposite **Toko Arjuna** in the main street, the shop also sells purses, handbags, hats and other articles, as well as Muslim clothes and T-shirts.

Other modern fabrics (much like *songket* brocades, but without silver or gold thread) are also available in Bima, at cheaper prices than in Sumbawa Besar. Fabric quality is now improving both in Sumbawa and Bima, although colors may fade when the items are washed.

Other craft items You can find local pottery and basketry in **Seketeng** market, Sumbawa Besar, at cheap prices, or acquire a *parang*—a machete-like knife used by farmers and hill people when working—for around $8. Cassettes of traditional music are sold in several shops.

Wild honey Gourmets will not forget to bring back jerrycans of Sumbawa's delicious wild honey. It is really special: local lore has it that you can test honey by spilling a few drops on the ground; if it does not attract ants, it is the genuine article, otherwise it is mixed with sugar or syrup!

In Sumbawa, **Lantung** honey is famous; in Bima, the best honey is collected in **Kore**, **Sanggar** or **Tambora** (a dangerous job). The price is at least $2 for one bottle. People also often speak of "white honey," which costs at least six or seven times more. In Sumbawa, ask in the market, or buy it from Hotel Tambora. In Bima, honey is sold in many houses, indicated by a wooden sign *"Disini jual madu"* ("Honey sold here"). Make sure you punch small holes into the container, to prevent it from bursting, especially if you go back by plane.

Other delicacies you will find in West Sumbawa are *kue manjareal*, funny dry cakes in the shape of a clover leaf, made of ground peanuts and brown sugar, and *dodol susu*, a kind of toffee made with buffalo milk.

SERVICES

Post Office In the harbor area of Sumbawa Besar, in Bima, in Jl Gajah Mada (take a *ben-hur* from the center of the city).

Telephone Office In Bima in Jl Sukarno Hatta, near Raba. There is also a *wartel* (telephone service counter) in Jl Lombok.

Hospitals In Sumbawa Besar, opposite Tambora Hotel (recently upgraded). In Bima, located in Jl Langsat in Raba (☎ 3142).

Police In Sumbawa Besar, near the Tambora Hotel, opposite the square. In Bima, in Jl Sukarno Hatta (☎ 110).

Money changing In Sumbawa Besar, go to Bank Rakyat Indonesia (BRI), in Jl Wahidin, and Bank Negara Indonesia (BNI 46), in Jl Kartini. In Bima, go to BNI 46 in Jl Hasanuddin (☎ 2345). They will usually only change US dollars.

Film 35mm color print and slide film can be purchased in **Dynasty** and **Sahabat** shops in Sumbawa Besar, and in **Dewi** and **Farida** in Bima. Prices are not much higher than in Bali.

MUSEUMS

Sultan's palace in Sumbawa Besar Recently renovated, the old wooden palace, located on a square near Pasar Seketeng market (accessible through a side street), is open daily to the public. Dance rehearsals usually take place every Sunday morning. The building is intended to be turned into a museum, but it is still practically empty. Open: 8 am-11:30 am, and 2:30 pm–6 pm daily, except Fri., 8 am–11 am. Visitors are asked for a 30¢–60¢ donation. The sultan's heirlooms are kept in the **Bala Kuning**, the late Sultan's daughter house, and can only be seen with special permission.

Sultan's palace in Bima Located in the very center of the city, in front of the main square. Local artifacts are displayed in several rooms on the ground floor; the sleeping quarters upstairs have been reconstructed as they originally were. The family heirlooms are also kept at Prince's Kahir house on the other side of the square, and can only be seen with (difficult to obtain) permission. Open every day 7:30 am–5:30 pm. Entrance fee: 50¢.

AGENCY TOURS

In Sumbawa, Hotel Tambora (see above) has its own travel agency, **Tambora Duta Wisata Tours & Travel**. They can organize all kinds of tours in the area, including city tours (visits to the market and old wooden palace, or to the Sultan's daughter's house to see the heirlooms). They also arrange two handicraft village tours. The first one is to **Pamulung**, a little village off the main road west of Sumbawa Besar, where dances, traditional weaving, metal-working and, on request, buffalo races can be shown. The second one is in **Perung**, a newly opened up hamlet 12 km south of Sumbawa Besar, off the road to Semongkat, where the same activities can be seen. It is situated near a holy spring, the water of which is sought by those who wish to remain young or have children. Tambora can also arrange fishing parties to Moyo island or Tanjung Menangis, traditional dances at the hotel or at Kencana Beach, and overland trips.

Perama Tourist Information in Jl Hasanuddin, next door to **Losmen Saudara**, as well as in Hotel **Tirtasari,** can organize a 7-day land/sea adventure tour from Mataram to Flores via Sumbawa and Komodo.

In Bima, two hotels have agencies: Hotel Sanghyang, **Komodo Tours**; and Hotel Parewa, **Parewa Tours & Travel**, in Jl Sumbawa, ☎ 2440, Fax: 2304. The latter can arrange a cultural events tour, including dances, rice-sowing and harvesting demonstrations, and methods of traditional fighting, including ram-like head-butting. Both agencies have city, Wawo and Komodo packages. Other travel agents are located along Jl Soekarno Hatta.

Grand Komodo Tours & Travel ☎ 2018, Fax: 2812. They also have an office in Bali, P.O. Box 3477, Denpasar 80034. ☎ (361) 287166, Fax: (361) 287165. The most well-known operation. They offer a whole range of packages in both West and East Nusa Tenggara, such as: Rinjani trekking, Flores, Komodo (3 or 4 days), as well as trips to the Baliem valley in Irian Jaya. A tour to Komodo (via Bima) from Denpasar costs $250 for 3 days and $275 for 4 days, including transfers, accommodation and meals.

Kalpataru Tours & Travel Jl Soekarno Hatta, ☎ 2824. Specializes in wildlife and adventure.

Ora Tours & Travel Jl Soekarno Hatta, ☎ 3339

Limbunan Tours & Travel Jl Rambutan 10A. ☎ 2824, 3543.

Perama Tourist Information Jl Lombok, ☎ 2886 and 3510.

Floressa Tours Jl Wira 2, Bali. ☎ (0361) 289253, 289254. Specializes in Nusa Tenggara.

CULTURAL EVENTS

Islamic rituals Most of the circumcision rituals, the Muslim *sunatan*, take place during the month before Maulud (around October), while the wedding month is the one between the end of Ramadan (Lebaran) fasting month, and the Idul Adha festival (commemorating Abraham's son sacrifice). These are private ceremonies, but you may be invited to one of them.

Dances A few dance troupes are now emerging both in Sumbawa Besar and in Bima. In Sumbawa, dances performances can be arranged—again by **Hotel Tambora**, and in Bima, by **Hotel Sanghyang** (Donggo dances are the favorite). Also watch for special events, including the HUT Kabupaten (Regency anniversary) and the PORSENI (Sports & Arts Week), which takes place in each regency (district) of the Nusa Tenggara Barat province in rotation.

Horse races The track is in front of the Hotel Parewa on Jl Sukarno Hatta, Bima. Racing is common in August and September, and during local or national celebrations. Normally on Sundays.

Buffalo races In Sumbawa, these usually take place before planting rice, after the previous harvest, but can be organized especially by Hotel Tambora for you in a village. Very entertaining and exciting.

—*Agnès Korb*

3 Komodo PRACTICALITIES

INCLUDES RINCA

Although the dry, rocky island of Komodo now attracts thousands of tourists a year to see the world's largest lizard, this is still one of the most interesting trips one can make in Nusa Tenggara. The landscape is strangely beautiful, reminiscent more of something from the North Pacific than the tropics, and the blue, coral-filled water makes a stunning setting for the rugged islands. The dragons are, indeed, impressive animals: whether they are in the process of tearing a goat into pieces with their strong jaws, or even—post slaughter—just licking their bloody chops in the sunshine.

GETTING THERE

There are a number of ways to get to Komodo island to see the dragons. Travel agencies in Jakarta, Bali and even Lombok and Bima can set up a tour for one, or a group. The price depends on the length of the trip and on the number of persons going, but each individual should be prepared to pay plenty for a agency-organized trip to Komodo. On the other hand, the boat is chartered, the food is all taken care of, and you have an English-speaking guide.

Grand Komodo Tours & Travel. This experienced outfit runs tours to Komodo on the *Komodo Plus*, a 17-m traditional wooden boat built in the Bugis style. Accommodations on the ship are simple, but comfortable, and tours run directly from Bali, by plane to Bima, Sumbawa, then overland to Sape where the boat is docked. 3-day tour, all inclusive: $250/person. 4-day tour, $275/person. Grand Komodo can also arrange other tours of the region, and offers live-aboard diving packages in the very rich waters around Komodo and Rinca.

Main office: P.O. Box 3477, Denpasar 80034 Bali. ☎ (361) 287166, Fax: (361) 287165, Tlx: 35513 KOMODO IA. In Bima: Jl Sukarno Hatta, Bima NTB. ☎ (374) 2018, Fax: 2812.

If you have some money, but aren't inclined to follow a tour group, fly to Labuhanbajo, Flores or Bima, Sumbawa, then take a bus to Sape. There are scheduled ferries or boat charters from either Labuhanbajo or Sape to Komodo.

Travelers with a sense of adventure and time on their hands can make their way overland and by ferry from Bali all the way to Komodo.Set aside at least 10 days for the overland round-trip; more if you intend to visit other islands.

FLIGHTS

Merpati flies six times a week from Denpasar, Bali to Labuhanbajo (via Bima, $100) on the eastern tip of Flores but flights are often cancelled or over-booked (Bima–Labuhanbajo only, $30).

From Labuhanbajo, one can rent a motorboat or catch the ferry to Komodo. Because of the small, unreliably scheduled airplanes to Labuhanbajo, agencies fly their clients to Bima.

Merpati flies daily—often twice or more daily—from Bali to Bima, Sumbawa ($70). From the airport, 15 km from town, takes a *bemo* to Bima town ($3.50 charter), then catch the bus or charters a *bemo* ($10–$15 charter) to Sape, 45 km (1.5 hrs) away. At Sape take a horse-drawn "Ben Hur" to the harbor for the Komodo ferry.

FERRY

Ferries run daily (except Friday) between Sape, Sumbawa and Labuhanbajo, Flores, via Komodo (10–11 hrs, $5). To Komodo only, $4 (6–7 hrs) from Sape, $2 (4 hrs) from Labuhanbajo. The ferry leaves around 8 am. At Komodo, the ferry anchors offshore, but local boats will land you on the island for a small fee ($1).

All of the above is the way things work most of the time. But one of the two ferries could be pulled off its route for a month and sent to Surabaya for overhaul without advance notice—and there would then be only 3 ferries a week between Sape and Labuhanbajo.

BOAT CHARTER

If several people travel together, the headaches of scheduling can be avoided by chartering a boat out of Sape or Labuhanbajo. Although Komodo Island looks almost equidistant from Sape and Labuhanbajo on the map, because you have to land at Loh Liang on the eastern side of Komodo, it is much closer (about 50 km) to Labuhanbajo than to Sape (around 120 km). The Sape Strait is also more open and featureless than the island-dotted Lintah Strait.

This is reflected in boat charter prices. From Sape, figure $125–$250 round trip, depending on the boat and your ability to bargain in Indonesian. From Labuhanbajo, an equivalent charter would run $35–$75.

Be aware that there are some extremely strong currents in these waters, and at times a motorboat, even with its engine running at full throttle, will actually go backwards. The local boatmen know the conditions so don't worry about your safety, but respect the captain's time of departure—it is based on the tides and currents.

ACCOMMODATIONS

The PHPA (Park Service) administrative site of Loh Liang has several large cabins with a total capacity of 40 beds. Each cabin has two toilet/baths. Overnight stays: $4 single bed, $6.50 double bed (the rats, which are plentiful, are free). Simple meals ($1.50), tea, coffee, soft drinks, and beer ($1.50) are available most of the time. The food available is simple Indonesian fare (mostly rice), so if you require something else you better bring it from Bima.

The majority of the 5,000-odd yearly visitors come in June, July and August, and it's very difficult to obtain a room. Up to 75 persons have to sleep in a large dining area (no mattresses).

In addition to the crowds, this is also the worst period to see the dragons as it is their mating season and they often "disappear" from the easy viewing spot. It usually rains in January and February so you might want to avoid these months as well. The best time is just after the rains, say from mid-March through early May, when the island is dry, but a beautiful, velvety green.

KOMODO NATIONAL PARK

Komodo Island as well as adjacent waters and islands are part of the Komodo National Park, managed by the PHPA (Perlindungan Hutan dan Pelestarian Alam, "Forest Protection and Nature Conservation"). When arriving in either Sape or Labuhanbajo, check with the local PHPA office for current information. It might be useful to know, for example, if all the beds are taken on Komodo.

Upon arriving in Komodo, you must report to the PHPA office in Loh Liang (where all the boats stop), register, and pay a $1 entrance fee, good for 7 days. Any time you leave the PHPA compound, you must be accompanied by a guide. It's about a 30–45 min walk to the feeding site, called Banu Nggulung.

Guides

There are some 10 guides on the island, and for the usual dragon-viewing jaunt, they charge $1.50/group. One guide will lead groups up to 5; two guides for groups of 6 to 10. Guides can also take you to Komodo village ($1.50); Poreng, for scenery and perhaps wild water buffalo, boar and deer ($4); Gunung Ara ($5, add $8 for overnight, add $13 for two extra nights to Mt. Satalibo); Loh Serikaya ($5); and Sebita ($5). A porter for any of these trips runs $2–$3.

Through the PHPA office you can charter a boat for a 3-hr jaunt to Pulau Lasa and Pulau Kalong, up to 5 persons, $8–$12. Same for Pantai Merah (Red Beach), a good snorkeling beach not too far from the current dragon watching site. (Guide fee $1.50; add 60¢/hr past 3 hrs.)

Dragon Feeding

As of this writing, the dragons were being fed only on Saturdays. There are also plans for a water hole viewing area, and the organized feedings might be halted altogether in 1994.

Fruit Bats

The colony of flying foxes on Kalong Island can be easily seen from a boat after a short ride from Komodo village. There is another colony on Rinca, close to and west of Rinca village.

WEATHER

During the January–March rainy season, a scant 500–600 mm of rain falls on the island, and storms during these months can make the sea quite dangerous. The best time to visit Komodo is April–June or Oct–Nov. From Sept to Dec it is quite hot—often 40°C—but the seas are quiet. Seas can be rough July–Aug.

HEALTH

Bring a hat, sunscreen, long-sleeved shirts and long pants. And take malaria pills, even if you are there just for a short time. (See "Travel Advisory," pg 241.) The hospital in Labuhanbajo is used to treating malaria-stricken tourists.

Rinca

This island is smaller than Komodo, some 20,000 ha, and has fewer dragons, perhaps 600. The PHPA center is at Loh Buaya— "Crocodile Bay." Troupes of monkeys live nearby, and the island is also home to deer, horses, buffalo, pigs and megapode birds. Basic accommodations and simple meals are available at Loh Buaya (same prices as Komodo). Round trip charter from Komodo to Rinca: $60.

Rinca's 860 residents live in two small villages: Kerora (the smaller one) and Rinca. On market days in Labuhanbajo (Wednesday and Saturday) boats go both ways from Rinca (2 hrs).

There are several nice walks from Loh Buaya, one following a river (2 km) and another—quite scenic—leading up over some hills (5 km). Seeing wildlife requires luck. You can also walk to Rinca village (3 hrs) or Golo Kode (2 hrs), where there are 60 cm stones of more or less human shape, and to the pearl farm at Loh Kima.

4 — Flores PRACTICALITIES

Travel to the ruggedly beautiful and culturally rich island of Flores is no longer difficult, and the trans-Flores highway, in good condition for most of the way, provides a reliable land route across the island's 360-kilometer length. Maumere is the most well-served city for tourists, and Ende is the island's largest city. Either of these towns will provide a good base for explorations, as will some of the other district capitals. This section, like the main text, is organized from West to East, beginning with Labuhanbajo and working across the length of the island to Larantuka.

THE TRANS-FLORES HIGHWAY

The trans-Flores highway winds some 700 km through the scenic mountains of the island, from Labuhanbajo in the west, to Larantuka on the island's eastern tip. Most of the road is paved, and it passes through all 5 of Flores' district capitals.

Segment	Distance	Time
Labuhanbajo–Ruteng	126 km	4 hrs
Ruteng–Bajawa	130 km	5 hrs
Bajawa–Ende	126 km	5 hrs
Ende–Moni (Keli Mutu)	52 km	1.5 hrs
Moni–Maumere	96 km	3 hrs *
Maumere–Larantuka	137 km	4 hrs

This stretch is prone to washing out, which means a very long detour via Kota Baru.

Public buses—cheap, reliable, and crowded—shuttle continuously back and forth along the highway. Most of the buses run during the day, although there are a few night expresses. No single bus makes the entire run; usually they are based in one district capital, and just run to the next and back. Although some bus companies have begun longer runs, such as Labuhanbajo–Ende, it is best to take one hop at a time, so as not to travel at night and miss the scenery.

Always try to reserve one of the two front seats, next to the driver, as these places offer the best vantage points for viewing. Your *losmen* or hotel can arrange this for you, but give them time—say one day. If you can't get a front seat (the local bigwigs also favor this spot) try for a window seat on the right of the bus—as, traveling east, most of the panoramas unfold on this side. Although buses usually stop for the mid-day meal, bring some bottled drinking water ("Aqua") on board.

The most enjoyable way to cross the island is in a chartered vehicle with driver, which costs about $40–$60/day. Several western-sized bodies can be accommodated in relative comfort, and you can then split the cost. Charter-ing your own vehicle allows you to leave when you want, and stop anywhere along the way. Side-trips depend on the type of vehicle, your driver's confidence, and the state of the roads. Remember that map distances often have little relevance to travel time.

The ferries between Sumbawa and Flores are large enough to accommodate cars and *bemos,* so vehicles rented in Bali or Lombok can be brought into Flores (motorcycles too.) A few vehicles are available for several-day charters in Labuhanbajo. You could also bargain with the driver of a public *bemo*/minibus for at least the first hop, to Ruteng, or perhaps all the way to Ende. Most drivers do not like to travel beyond their usual run, but can sometimes be persuaded to do so with more cash. A few vehicles with driver are available for rent in Ende and Maumere for one day or longer.

Labuhanbajo

If you arrive by ferry, simply walk to the *losmen* of your choice. The various out-of-town seaside hotels have boats which whisk you off to beach-side seclusion. If you arrive by bus from Ruteng, the bus will drop you wherever you say. The airport is a couple of kilometers out of town, $3 charter, 60¢ for a collective minibus.

TRANSPORTATION

By Air Until Merpati increases the reliability of its scheduled flights, it's tough to get in and out of Labuhanbajo by plane. Reserve early and re-confirm. The landing strip was paved and extended (to 1,400 m) in early 1994, but only small planes were servicing this strip when we went to press. There are at the moment 6 flights a week ($105) reaching Labuhanbajo

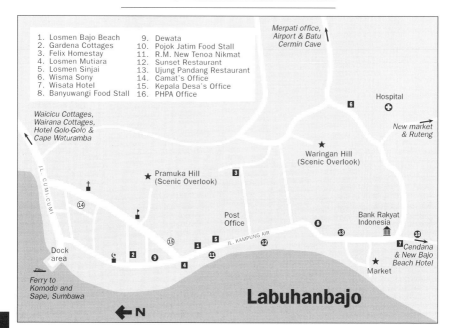

1. Losmen Bajo Beach
2. Gardena Cottages
3. Felix Homestay
4. Losmen Mutiara
5. Losmen Sinjai
6. Wisma Sony
7. Wisata Hotel
8. Banyuwangi Food Stall
9. Dewata
10. Pojok Jatim Food Stall
11. R.M. New Tenoa Nikmat
12. Sunset Restaurant
13. Ujung Pandang Restaurant
14. Camat's Office
15. Kepala Desa's Office
16. PHPA Office

Merpati office,
Airport & Batu
Cermin Cave

Hospital

New market
& Ruteng

Waringan Hill
(Scenic Overlook)

Waicicu Cottages,
Wairana Cottages,
Hotel Golo-Golo &
Cape Waturamba

Pramuka Hill
(Scenic Overlook)

Post
Office

Bank Rakyat
Indonesia

Dock
area

Cendana
& New Bajo
Beach Hotel

Market

Ferry to
Komodo and
Sape, Sumbawa

Labuhanbajo

←N

JL. CUMI-CUMI

JL. KAMPUNG AIR

on the Kupang to Bima route. Great scenery in clear weather. There are connecting flights out of Bima and Kupang, to Bali and elsewhere.

By Bus and Ferry Buses connect Labuhanbajo to Ruteng, and the ferry runs via Komodo to Sape, East Sumbawa. (See "Komodo Practicalities," pg. 281, for more on the ferry.) Buses to Ruteng run 3 times daily ($3, 4–5 hrs). Charter minibus to Ruteng, $50–$75. Night buses direct to Ende, $7, 15 hrs. Going the other way, at Labuhanbajo you can book a direct ride on the Langsung Indah bus line to Jakarta ($55), Surabaya ($35) and Bali ($28). These buses start their run in Bima.

ACCOMMODATIONS

While most places are geared for the low end of the budget travel market, a few hotels have opened recently for somewhat upscale tourists. Until there are larger airplanes and/or more reliable flight schedules, these hotels will have plenty of available rms and their prices will stay low.During the high season, when getting a room is sometimes difficult, prices usually rise 10%–25%. On the other hand, from around October through May, prices go down and you could reduce the asking price by bargaining.

Lodgings in or Near Town

Golo Hilltop Out of town to the north, a short ride on a dirt road in the hotel's vehicle, available to guests. 10 cottages on a hillside. Excellent panoramic view from their restaurant and from a vantage point just outside it. Views from

the cottages marred by electrical cables. $13–$32 S; $16–$39 D.

New Bajo Beach The best in Labuanbajo, located about a kilometer south of town, but with free transportation for guests. ☎ 41047, 41069. 16 very large rms, 10 cottages and a dining room in a nicely landscaped area with a beach. Tours can be arranged. Fan cooled rms, $18 S or D; AC rms $25 S or D; cottages $16 S or D.

Bajo Beach Same owner as the above. ☎ 41009, 41008. 27 clean rms with attached facilities. Large dining room serving good meals, $1–$4. This *losmen* can arrange tours to Komodo, snorkeling jaunts, visits to the petrified wood area, visits to Batu Cermin cave and *caci* whip fighting. Vehicles available for rental, both for the vicinity or a tour of all Flores. With enclosed facilities $5–$6.50 S, $5–$8.50 D; shared facilities $2.50 S, $4 D. Compressor and tanks available for scuba diving but they are looking for a dive master before launching the business.

Wisata ☎ 41020, very nice new place with 23 rms, all with enclosed facilities. Restaurant serves good Indonesian meals $1.50–$3. Larger rms, $5 S, $7.50 D; smaller rms $3.50 S, $5 D.

Gardena With 8 cottages, a bit of a steep climb but worth it. Restaurant. With enclosed facilities, $7.50 S or D; shared facilities $5 S or D.

Sinjai Next to the Post Office. 10 rms, dark but not dirty, $4–$7 S or D.

Sony On a hill, a short walk from town. 8 rms. Nice breezes and view of the bay from across the road. Meals available. Nearby creek with a pristine waterfall. Run by a nice lady, Ibu Maria Fabiola. $5/room, S or D, with breakfast.

Mutiara Near the shoreline. 23 rms. Simple, inexpensive meals, 75¢–$3. Excellent views over the harbor from the upstairs rms and dining area, but plenty of garbage underneath and to the sides. With attached facilities, $3.50/person; w/shared facilities, $2.50 S, $4 D.

Chez Felix Close to the Sony but enclosed by vegetation, 10 rms of which 6 have enclosed facilities and fans, $2.75/person. Rooms with shared facilities, $1.75/person. Meals $2.

Beachside Lodgings

Aside from the above accommodations, either in town or easily reached by road, there are several beachside places, accessible only by (free) motorboat rides. Mosquitoes can be fierce during and just after the rainy season. Nets usually provided, but bring repellent.

Batu Gosok 40 min boat ride from Labuhanbajo, just around the northwest tip of Flores. In a hill-enclosed valley and fronted by wide white sand beach. 10 cottages so far, but up to 50 planned. The dock extends out 350 m, so it's an easy, dry landing. Good topside views of marine life in clear waters, or snorkeling off the pier, with squids and fishes, a bit of coral. A swimming pool is planned. The simple but tasteful cottages erected so far go for $10–$15 S or D. The upcoming VIP ones will rent for $50–$100.

Waecicu About 5 min further from town than the Wai Rana (below), with 18 cottages, snorkeling, volleyball, restaurant. Very relaxed atmosphere, but it's almost like camping out until piped water reaches the place. So far, only a well. The toilets don't work, but the young Europeans who stay here love the place. Good view of Kukusan Island. Tours to Komodo, $15 for 2-day trip. $4–$8/person, meals included.

Wai Rana On the beach, 15 min boat ride from town. Several bungalows and dining area. Nice beach and view of nearby islands. Good coral for snorkeling fairly close to the beach, just past a sandy stretch with seagrass. $4 per person with breakfast or $5.50 with three very basic meals. This place offers scuba diving with a dive master said to be qualified (he was not around when we checked, however, so we can't judge). All inclusive (boat, equipment, lunch) for two dives at nearby locations, $65/person. There's gear for up to 8 persons. If only one person dives, it's $85.

Kanawa Island Cottages About 30 min by boat west of Labuhanbajo, on an otherwise deserted island, with white sand beach. 10 cottages, $4/person w/breakfast. Other meals available.

The **Losmen Bajo Beach** serves the best food in town. Otherwise, try the **Nikmat**. The **Sunset Restaurant** serves Chinese and Indonesian, good chow and, as the name implies, sunset views. The **Dewata**, run by a Balinese cook

who used to work at the Bajo Beach, serves European, Chinese, Indonesian and Balinese food at a good location with a view—albeit, through electrical cables—of the harbor and beyond. Javanese style meals are dished up at the **Banyuwangi**, the **Pojok** and the **Bintang Karya** (50¢ to $3). Amazingly, fish is not always available in this fishing town. There are three Padang restaurants, of which the **Minang** is the best.

TOURIST SERVICES

The **Losmen Bajo Beach** or the **PHPA Information Center**. Boat rentals to Komodo or nearby can be arranged through these parties or wherever you are staying. An outboard-powered outriggered fishing boat, holding 5–6 persons and ideal for nearby snorkeling and exploring islands nearby, runs $7–$20 for a day; it can take 4 to 6 passengers. They can drop you off and pick up at a prearranged time. Charter boats to Komodo, $30–$75 for inboard motorboats; $75–100 for speedboats. Or you can take the daily (except Friday) ferry, $2.

Guides Varying levels of English and general knowledge, $7.50–$10/day.

HEALTH

A good hospital, with two doctors speaking some English. They are used to treating tourists with malaria.

SNORKELING

Best May–June and September– November.

Ruteng

Telephone code 385
The landing field is close to town. Some *losmen* send out a car to meet the planes, offering free rides if you stay at their place. Otherwise, it's 60¢ for the short ride to town. If you arrive by bus, the driver will drop you off at the *losmen* of your choice.

By Air The Merpati office is on a no-name dirt street in an area called Paukaba, near the Pertamina station. (☎ 21147; airfield ☎ 21518). 6 direct weekly flights by 18-passenger planes to Kupang ($70); 6 weekly flights to Bima ($51, with connection to Bali) of which two stop at Labuhanbajo on the way ($25). Frequent cancellations due to weather, but great scenery.

By Land There are several buses a day, all early morning departures. Labuhanbajo ($2), Bajawa ($2), Ende—a long, tough 10 hrs— ($3.50). The best bus line for the Ende run is Bis Agogo.

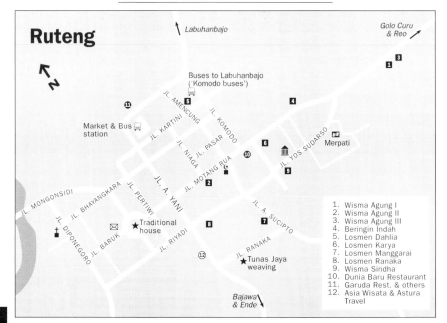

Ruteng

Labuhanbajo

Golo Curu & Reo

Buses to Labuhanbajo ('Komodo buses')

Market & Bus station

JL. AMENCUNG
JL. KARTINI
JL. NIAGA
JL. KOMODO
JL. PASAR
JL. MOTANG RUA
JL. YOS SUDARSO
Merpati

JL. MONGONSIDI
JL. BHAYANGKARA
JL. PERTIWI
JL. A. YANI
JL. DIPONEGORO
JL. BARUK
JL. RIYADI

★Traditional house

JL. A. SUCIPTO
JL. RANAKA

★Tunas Jaya weaving

Bajawa & Ende

1. Wisma Agung I
2. Wisma Agung II
3. Wisma Agung III
4. Beringin Indah
5. Losmen Dahlia
6. Losmen Karya
7. Losmen Manggarai
8. Losmen Ranaka
9. Wisma Sindha
10. Dunia Baru Restaurant
11. Garuda Rest. & others
12. Asia Wisata & Astura Travel

4 Flores

ACCOMMODATIONS

The highest priced rms have hot water—a godsend on cold mornings and evenings.

Dahlia ☎ 21377. With 27 rms, of which 6 VIP. VIP rms come with TV, hot water shower, sit down toilets, toilet paper, and space. Standard rms are smaller, but have everything else except the TV and hot water. A good dining room offers a variety of dishes (chicken, pork, squid) at $2–$4, and cheaper Indonesian and Chinese standards. Economy $4 S, $5 D; standard $7.50 S, $10 D; VIP $18 S or D.

Agung III ☎ 21083. New, best in town. An extension of the Agung I, same owner. With 9 large, clean, very pleasant rms, all with sit-down toilets, lacking only hot water (there are plans to add hot water, at which time prices will rise slightly). The top "penthouse" room has a good view to the east: sunrise, rice fields, landing strip. Restaurant. $13 S or D.

Sindha ☎ 21197. 21 rms, 14 w/attached facilities. Good Indonesian and Chinese meals, $2.50–$3. With attached facilities, $6.50–$7 S, $9–10 D; w/shared facilties, $3.50 S, $5 D.

Agung II ☎ 21835. Downtown, off a main street. 19 rms. Same owner as other Agungs. With attached facilities, $5.50 S, $7 D; w/shared facilities, $3.50 S, $5 D.

Manggarai ☎ 21008. Quiet, with 10 large, airy rms. No restaurant. With attached facilities, $4 S, $6 D; w/shared facilities $2.50 S, $4 D.

Agung I About a half-kilometer from downtown, by the road to Reo. 33 rms. ☎ 21080. Popular with foreigners. The losmen is next to rice paddies, and offers good sunrises and sunsets. (Although there is a lot of building going on nearby) A small restaurant serves Indonesian and Chinese dishes for less than $1. The owner and staff are quite helpful, but their knowledge of English is limited. With attached facilities, $4 S, $5 D; w/shared facilities, $3 S, $4 D.

Ranaka ☎ 21353. 12 rms. A somewhat seedy, run-down place, being upgraded. The owner, Pak Yosef, speaks English well. $2.50–$4/room, some with enclosed facilities. No food available.

Karya 5 rms. Food can be ordered, except for pork, which is not allowed in this Muslim-owned losmen. Next to the Bamboo Den (good *ayam paggar*—grilled chicken—$2/person). All shared facilities. $3.50 S, $4 D.

Asia Wisata Jl A. Yani 14, ☎ 21795, same owner as Astura Tours, to be completed in late 1994. 12 rms, all with shared facilities, $2.50 per person. Agent for bus tickets, and can arrange interesting tours at reasonable prices.

DINING

Best eating at the *losmen*. The 5-table **Dunia Baru** serves simple Indonesian and Chinese dishes, 75¢–$2. Lots of beer drinking by locals here late at night, some fights. There are several Padang style restaurants in the market area, of which the **Garuda** is the cleanest and best. In back of the market, opposite the bus station, several little restaurants serve dog meat, called "RW," pronounced "airway." At the market, pigs and dogs are sold on the far side of the bus terminal, in deference to Muslim sensibilities.

SERVICES

Agency Tours

Astura Tours Jl A Yani 14, ☎ 21795. This Jakarta-based company has an office in town to handle overland tours of Flores. Main office in Jakarta: Jl Soleh 36A, ☎ (21) 548 1879 Fax: (21) 530 0064. Owned by Drs. Ginting. Local operator, knows area well, with inexpensive tours for small groups to traditional areas and panoramic locations. These include the Tengkulese waterfall about 18km from Ruteng and the all-thatch-roof village of Tebo. If there is enough interest, they set up a *caci* (whip fight) with music and the works (and occasionally blood) on Wednesday and Saturday afternoons, $5/person. The total payment must be $50—so if you are willing to foot the whole bill, the event can be performed for an individual or a couple.

Souvenirs

Tunas Jaya Jl Ranaka, ☎ 21815. This is also a weaving center, women working from 8 am to 5 pm. Nice local sarong type cloth with distinctive Manggarai design ($33) along with ties, hats, purses with local motifs.

Reo

By Land Two small buses shuttle back and forth between Ruteng and Reo, covering the 60-odd km in about 2.5 hrs. There is no fixed schedule; they leave when full, or when the driver feels like it ($1.50).
By Sea Reo's port, Kedindi, lies 5 km west of town, across rice fields (fairly frequent *bemos,* 15¢). Most of Kedindi's shipping goes to Surabaya, with a boat leaving on average every 3 days. A mixed freighter, the *Elang,* calls at Kedindi, leaving about twice a month to Maumere and once a month to Labuhanbajo.

ACCOMMODATIONS

The **Losmen Teluk Bayur** in Reo offers lots of staring adults and children, and it's next to the mosque, with 4:30 am wake-up loudspeakers. Anyway, if this doesn't bother you, it's close to the Phone and Post Office, with 12 rms, all shared facilities, $2.50 S, $4 D. The **Nisang Nai**, 9 rms at the edge of town on the road to Kedindi, in front of the police station, among rice fields, is much better. The frog chorus will serenade you at night. It's a good deal—$3.50 S or D.

The **Warung Rumah Makan** in Reo has "nasi Padang," including huge fish and lots of vegetables, for $1.

LOCAL TRANSPORTATION

Irregular small boats shuttle to various coastal villages east and west of Kedindi. A daily truck takes passengers along a coastal road west of Reo, for about 3 hrs and 50 km ($1.25).

Bajawa

Telephone code 384
If you arrive during the day by bus from Ende or Ruteng, you have to get off at the Watujaji terminal, on the main road, 3 km from town. From there it's by *bemo* (25¢) to get dropped off at the *losmen* of your choice. If you arrive after 6 pm, the bus can drop you off in town—wherever you like—at no extra charge. If arriving by plane, the 26-km ride from the airport, near Soa, costs $1 in a collective vehicle, $10–$15 for a charter.
By Air Merpati (☎ 20212) offers three flights weekly to and from Kupang ($70), stopping at Ende ($25); and two flights weekly to Bima ($41) connecting to Bali (additional $72).
By Land Buses from Ruteng take 5–6 hrs ($2); from Ende, 4–5 hrs ($2).

ACCOMMODATIONS

Kembang Jl Martadinata, ☎ 21072. 10 rms. Slightly upscale, catering to government officials. $9/room, all with attached facilities.
Korina Jl A. Yani, ☎ 21162. 12 rms, owned and operated by multi-lingual Pak Kornelis (English, Dutch, a little German) and his wife, Ibu Mariana. Pleasant and clean. Guides available, restaurant close by. With enclosed facilities, $5.50 S, $9 D; w/shared facilities, $4 S, $6.50 D.
Anggrek Jl Haryono, ☎ 21172. 15 rms, and restaurant next door. The rms and toilets very clean, pleasant; guides available. $5.50 S or D.
Virgo Jl Panjaitan, ☎ 21061. Around the corner from the Kambera, 8 rms. $4 S, $5 D, all w/ attached facilities.
Losmen Kambera Jl El Tari, ☎ 21166. 16 rms. None of the staff speaks much English. Dining room with simple meals (75¢–$1.50) can get very crowded in peak season, leading to long waits. Noisy at night, until 10–11 pm. The management can help you hire local day transportation, but it helps if you speak some Indonesian. With attached facilities (6 rms), $4.25 S, $5.50 D; w/shared facilities, up to 3 per rm, $1.75/person.
Kencana Jl Suprapto. 13 rms, all w/facilities. On a quiet street, meals available. $2.75–$5.50.
Johny Jl Gajah Mada, ☎ 21079. 16 rms, all with enclosed facilities. Friendly, English (some, anyway) speaking staff. Meals available with one hour's notice. $2.25–$5.50/room.

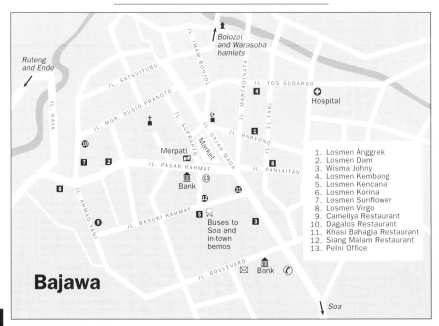

Bajawa

1. Losmen Anggrek
2. Losmen Dam
3. Wisma Johny
4. Losmen Kembang
5. Losmen Kencana
6. Losmen Korina
7. Losmen Sunflower
8. Losmen Virgo
9. Camellya Restaurant
10. Dagalos Restaurant
11. Khasi Bahagia Restaurant
12. Siang Malam Restaurant
13. Pelni Office

Sunflower Jl H. Wuruk, ☎ 21236. 12 rms. Hidden from the street, in back of the Dagalos. Tourist information center and the current favorite with foreigners. The town's best guide, Lukas, works here (from 9 am) and the other guides are also good. Meals can be ordered, including pasta and sandwiches. With attached facilities $2.75 S, $3.25 D; w/shared facilities, $2.25 S, $3.75 D.
Dam Jl Gereja, ☎ 21045, with 11 rms. $3.50/person w/attached facilities; $2.50/person w/shared facilities.
Dagalos Jl A. Yani, ☎ 21230. 9 rms, meals available. With attached facilities, $2.25/person; w/shared facilities, $1.75/person.

Overnighting in Villages

For most families, who are poor, guests are a burden. They feel obliged to leave their work to keep you company and will probably even kill one of their very few chickens to feed you. If you insist on staying, to be fair, pay as much for room and board as you would in Bajawa.

DINING

Many of the *losmen* serve meals, or try one of the restaurants around the market. Chinese and Indonesian dishes (75¢–$2), Javanese food (75¢–$2), the **Beringin** and several other Padang style restaurants, (75¢–$2).
Camellya, on Jl A. Yani. Best place in town. Friendly owner and family. Some western dishes, along with lots of Chinese and Indonesian. Lasagna ($2.50), spaghetti Bolognese ($2), Swiss rösli (potatoes) and egg ($1.75).

LOCAL TRANSPORTATION

Your hotel can help arrange transportation for half- or full-day trips. Prices depend on the state of the roads and your bargaining abilities. "Normal" price for minibus runs about $30/day for a minibus. Somewhat more expensive ($25/half day, $40/full day) is Ebet Henry, at the Sutdio Foto Gaya Baru, whose jeep can take 5 rather squeezed passengers. Motorcycles are hard to find and expensive (about $1/hr).

SIGHTS AND SERVICES

Guides

Guides available, often working at tourist-oriented *losmen*, with varying levels of English ($3–$7.50 per day). One of the best is Lukas, a licensed guide with a good command of English and knowledgeable about local culture. He works at the Sunflower and charges $3–$6 a day, including lunch with local dishes. Well worth it.

Market

Most active on Sundays, in the morning after church lets out.

Dress and behavior

Don't show too much flesh, which embarrasses the locals. Even worse for their sensitivities is seeing tourists kissing and fondling each other—save it for later.

MOUNTAIN CLIMBING

Climbing Gunung Inerie This 2245-m volcano is not a difficult climb, leads along a clear path, and in good conditions yields an excellent view of central Flores. You begin the climb from the top of the saddle between the villages of Langa and Bena. You can hire a guide in Bena, or go on your own. You can't really get lost. Take a *bemo* from Bajawa to Bena, and ask the driver to set you down at the beginning of the path to the summit—he'll know where it is. Ask directions until you are clear of the cultivated area.

Follow the path up a steep grassy slope and through a wide belt of gnarled and twisted trees before clambering onto the lava cone itself. Climb steeply to the summit but watch your step (especially on the way down); the slope is composed of fine volcanic scree and it's like walking on ball-bearings. The crater at the summit is a deep hole, rather like a giant ice-cream scoop. Pick your way round the crater rim to climb the peak on the far side. The summit yields a magnificent 360° view of central Flores, and on a really clear day you can see Sumba.

The summit often clouds over by mid-morning, so get an early start. You could arrange to overnight in Bena with a local family, or bring a tent. Alternatively, you could climb the mountain in the late afternoon, by which time the clouds have often lifted, and catch the last bemo back to Bajawa. Climbing time from the road to the crater is about 2–4 hrs, depending on what shape you're in, plus another 30–45 min to the summit. If you begin in Bena, figure on a bit more time, as you have to walk along the road to the start of the path.

Climbing Gunung Ebulobo 2149-m Ebulobo, split by a giant crater on its northward slopes and perpetually leaking steam and smoke, is one of Flores' more spectacular mountains. Start the climb from the hamlet of Mulakoli, 4 km up an awful track (barely passable by motorcycle) south of Rega, which is on the main Bajawa–Ende road, 3 km east of Bouwae.

It is advisable to get onto the summit at sunrise or shortly afterwards, both to be sure of a good view and also because by mid-morning a northerly breeze often pushes volcanic gases from the crater back over the summit. Inhaling these is at best unpleasant and can be downright dangerous. You will want to overnight in Mulakoli to get an early start, and you can ask the kepala desa about accommodation.

Locals will point the way to the start of the path up the mountain, and although there are a few turnings, if you keep to the most well-trodden track you won't get lost. You could hire a guide if desired in Mulakoli. The climb leads through steep forest for 1.5 hrs before exiting onto the lava cone. The path becomes a bit indistinct at this point, but since generations of Indonesian college groups have thoughtfully left graffiti on every large rock near the path, route-finding is not exactly a problem. It should take another half hour to the top.

The summit is broad and heaped with sulphur and volcanic slag. On the north side it falls gradually away into Ebulobo's huge crater; be very careful walking on this side as the footing is composed of brittle lava that crumbles into dust when you tread on it. You get good views of the central Flores plain between the Bajawa highlands and the mountains northwest of Ende.

—*Chris Thring*

Riung

There are occasional small boats from Reo (5–7 hrs) and from Maumere (9–12 hrs). A road, opened in 1994, connects Riung to Bajawa via Soa (4 hrs, $2 by bus), good panoramic views. Coming from the east, the way to Riung is from Aegela, on the main trans-Flores highway, 56 km from Ende towards Bajawa. A well-paved road heads north from Aegela to Danga and Mbay.

Note: The Friday night/Saturday market at Danga draws great crowds: coastal Buginese, Javanese and Bajawa locals. There is a *losmen*, the Mandiri, near the market, with 9 rms and 4 toilet/baths ($2.25/person).

From Danga, a 13-km paved road leads to the port of Marapokot whence you might catch coastal ships or a bigger boat to Surabaya. Following the road 5 km, a turn to the left leads towards Riung. A short way down this road, you cross the Aisesa River. From the river, it's 48km to Riung. More traffic moves this way just before and during Riung's Monday market. Towards the end of this road, there are several villages and some panoramic views of the islands off Riung.

ACCOMMODATIONS

There are 5 small *losmen* in Riung, all $4/person for room and board: the **Madona**, the **Ikhlas**, the **Tamri Beach**, the **Florida** and the **Liberty**. The last two are the best. All can arrange a boat and connect you with the local PHPA office.

Ende

Telephone code 381
There is no official price for transportation from the airport to town, so bargaining is in order. Asking price might be $2, but you can get this down to about $1. It's 50m from the terminal to the main road, where you can catch the normal *bemos* to town for 15¢ (Note: *Bemo* drivers

in Ende arguably the worst on Flores for over-charging foreigners, often demanding 25¢ on up). Easy walk with backpack. You can also walk to the Ikhlas or Safari *losmen* from the terminal.

TRANSPORTATION

By air

After Maumere, Ende has the most frequent land and sea communication on Flores. Still, keep your plans flexible as you might not be able to get to Ende—or get away—on the day you wish. **Merpati** Jl Nangka, ☎ 21355. Theoretically open from 8 am to 1 pm and 4 pm to 7 pm, but phone first before going to the office. 9 direct flights weekly to Kupang ($50, none on Thursdays); 5 flights weekly to Bima ($50) continuing to Mataram ($100) and Bali ($110); 4 flights weekly to Labuhanbajo ($55); and 3 flights weekly to Bajawa ($25).

By Sea

Pelni The only reliable sea transportation is by ferry or Pelni's *Kelimutu,* a large passenger ship which makes scheduled swings between Java, Kalimantan and the Lesser Sundas, to Kupang and Waingapu. The Pelni office is near the old port, Pelabuhan Ende, although the ships leave from the new port, Pelabuhan Ipi.
Inter-island boats Once or twice a month, you could catch another—unscheduled—ship to Waingapu. During the northwest monsoon, Oct/Nov through March/April, shipping activity shifts from the old port to Pelabuhan Ipi.
Ferry The ferry motors once a week to Kupang, 16 hrs, $8–$11; once a week to Waingapu, 11 hrs (night) $6–$8. Departures and the ticket office are at Pelabuhan Ipi. Tickets can be purchased one day ahead of departure.
Local Boats Daily motor boats to Ende Island, 50¢. Also an early morning boat (except on Fridays) to Nggela, the weaving village, 2.5 hrs with stops, then returning to Ende. Occasionally there's transportation out of Nggela, otherwise it's about a 3.5-km walk to Wolojita from where there's public transportation to Wolowaru, on the main Ende–Maumere road, relatively close to Moni, the take-off village for Keli Mutu.

By Land

Buses to Bajawa to the west, and Moni and Maumere to the east, are frequent, reliable, cheap and crowded. $2.50 to Maumere, $2 to Bajawa. Consider buying two seats for yourself. Try for the front to see all the scenery. There's also an early morning bus straight to Ruteng and Labuhanbajo, and another to Riung.

Smaller buses, trucks and minibuses go to just about every village in the district that can be reached by road. Their frequency depends on market days and the size of the village. Fares are cheap. To Nuabosi, 4–5 public minibuses each day, 50¢ (round-trip charter, $15).

Buses to the west leave from Terminal Ndao on the outskirts of town on the way to Bajawa. Buses leave here for Labuhanbajo ($7, 8 am–10 am); and Ruteng ($5, 8 am–5 pm). Buses to the east leave from Wolowana village, 4 km out of town on the road towards Maumere. Bus to Maumere: 4–5 hrs (once you get under way), $4. **Chartering a bus to Keli Mutu** Your hotel or *losmen* can arrange this. Round-trip, w/English-speaking guide: $80 for up to 6–8, 3–4 am departure to catch dawn at the top. We especially recommend the Losmen Ikhlas for this. The Dwi Putra Hotel can arrange for multi-day minibus charters, including to Labuhanbajo ($225).

ACCOMMODATIONS

There are two fairly good hotels with AC rms, several in the medium price range and lots of cheap ones in varying states of squalor. *Bemo* drivers know all the locations. There is lots of daytime and early evening transportation around town (15¢) so it's always easy to get back and forth to and from your *losmen*, unless you stay out late at night doing God knows what.
Dwi Putra ☎ 21685. New, 43-room hotel. Huge restaurant with Indonesian, Chinese and European dishes (75¢–$3). Post Office across the street. All rms w/attached facilities. Fan-cooled, $7.50 S, $10 D; AC rms $15 S, $18 D; VIP rms $40 S or D.
Bitta Beach (See below under Dining.) Bungalows planned by late 1994: $25 S or D.
Flores ☎ 21075. 19 rms, quite pleasant. Restaurant, all rms with enclosed facilities. Economy rms (squat toilet), $6/person; standard AC rms $18 S or D; VIP rms, $25 S or D.
Wisata ☎ 21368 19 rms. Restaurant, cold beer available. All rms large, with enclosed facilities, some with showers. The more expensive rms have AC. $6–$13 S, $8–$16 D. Good value.
Nirwana ☎ 21199. 24 good-sized rms, under renovation. All w/attached facilities $7.50–$13.
Safari ☎ 21499. 12 rms, all clean, bright and airy. Restaurant. All rms w/attached facilities. $6–$8 S, $8–$12 D, including breakfast.
Melati 10 rms. Neither spotless nor awful, close to the airport but no other redeeming features. All rms w/attached facilities. $3.50–$5 S, $6.50–$8 D.
Ikhlas. ☎ 21695. 33 rms. This *losmen* is frequented by many travelers partially because the owner, Pak Jamal, speaks English and German and is the town's top source of travel information. Money changing and tours (including trekking) for individuals or small groups. One day tours to interesting areas close to Ende, including Nuabosi, weaving at Woloare or Ndona,

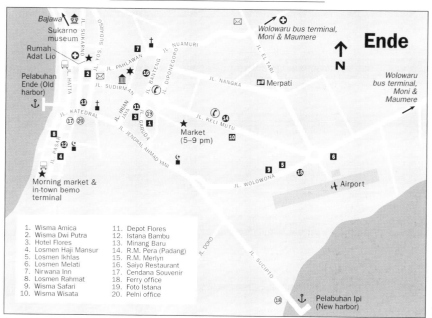

Map of Ende showing Bajawa, Sukarno museum, Rumah Adat Lio, Pelabuhan Ende (Old harbor), Wolowaru bus terminal, Moni & Maumere, Merpati, Market (5–9 pm), Morning market & in-town bemo terminal, Airport, Pelabuhan Ipi (New harbor). Streets labeled JL. SUKARNO, JL. YOS SUDARSO, JL. NUAMURI, JL. EL TARI, JL. PAHLAWAN, JL. HATTA, JL. SUDIRMAN, JL. BANTENG, JL. DIPONEGORO, JL. NANGKA, JL. KATEDRAL, JL. IRIAN, JL. GARUDA, JL. KELI MUTU, JL. PASAR, JL. JENDRAL AHMAD YANI, JL. WOLOWONA, JL. DOKO, JL. SUCIPTO.

1. Wisma Amica
2. Wisma Dwi Putra
3. Hotel Flores
4. Losmen Haji Mansur
5. Losmen Ikhlas
6. Losmen Melati
7. Nirwana Inn
8. Losmen Rahmat
9. Wisma Safari
10. Wisma Wisata
11. Depot Flores
12. Istana Bambu
13. Minang Baru
14. R.M. Pera (Padang)
15. R.M. Merlyn
16. Saiyo Restaurant
17. Cendana Souvenir
18. Ferry office
19. Foto Istana
20. Pelni office

Flores 4

and lots more. Costs can be split among up to 6 people. For the vehicle, driver and fuel, it's $40/day, plus $10 for English-speaking guide. If you want the *losmen* to fix a box lunch and bring bottled water, it's $2.50 more per person. An attached restaurant at the Ikhlas serves Indonesian and European food (50¢–$1.50). Rms w/attached facilities, $3 S, $4.50 D; w/shared facilities, $1.75 S, $3 D. Recently built, very nice rms, some with AC, $5 S, $7.50 D. **Amica** ☎ 21683. 10 rms. None to clean, but renovation planned. All rms with enclosed facilities. $3.50/person.

There are also several small *losmen* in the noisy downtown area: **Sandalwood, Haji Mansur, Sinar Harapan**. All have 8–10 rms, not of very high standards, but they're cheap at $1.50/person. All shared facilities.

DINING

Nothing too fancy here. Near the Losmen Ikhlas, the **Merlin**, small and clean, has good Chinese cooking (85¢–$2.50). Near the old port, a series of adjacent mini-restaurants offer very inexpensive Indonesian dishes. Also in the downtown area, the **Istana Bambu** offers very good Chinese cooking and seafood: chicken dishes $2, pork $2.50, fish $5–$7.50, lobster (when available) $7.50–$10. There are several good Padang style restaurants, especially the **Minang Baru**. The small, clean **Saiyo**, located further out, also specializes in Padang cooking.

We recommend the **Bitta Beach**, a bit off the road to Maumere, reached by a side road which heads for the sea at the far end of the landing strip (see map above). A large bamboo building faces the sea, just in back of a busy bit of black sand beach which is usually okay for swimming. There are fishing *prahu* here and motor boats heading east in the morning to various coastal villages, including Nggela. A sea breeze cools the area when the rest of Ende swelters. Open from 10 am to 1 am, with karaoke. On Saturday nights, it's also a disco, the only one between Senggigi and Kupang, staying open till 3 am. Live music that one night. Traditional dances can be arranged here. The restaurant is located at the start of the seaside walk to Wolotopo. A good variety of Indonesian and Chinese dishes: soups $1–$3, pigeon $2.50, chicken $2, noodles $1, veggies $1, fresh fish $2.50–$5 ($5/kg), lobster when available $12.50/kg, special hot plates of beef or chicken, $2. Cold beer ($1.75/bottle) and whiskey ($1.25). Try to be there to catch the moonrise. Favored by locals, especially on weekends, when the beach gets crowded.

SERVICES AND SIGHTS

Money Exchange

The **Bank Rakyat Indonesia** will change major travelers' checks in U.S. and Australian dollars, Deutchmarks and Yen. Also cash from those countries, as well as Singapore dollars, but only if the bills are in perfect shape. The Losmen Ikhlas has money changing facilities, a godsend on weekends.

Keli Mutu

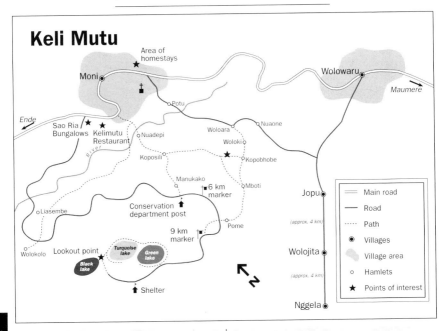

Photo Supplies

Ende is the only place we know of between Bima and Kupang where you can purchase slide film and camera batteries. The **Apollo** and the **Istana** are very close to each other, and also offer print film processing.

Guides

About $8/day, plus their expenses. Ask at your *losmen*.

Festivals/Rituals

Planting (November–December) and harvesting (June–July) are marked by rituals in many villages. You have to ask around as there are no fixed dates until a week or so before the events, decided by the elders who take the moon phase into consideration. One of the best planting rituals, lasting two days and two nights, takes place at Kampung Saga, a short way from Ende, towards Maumere.

Pulau Ende Island

This nearby island, with 12,000 inhabitants, rarely sees tourists. A hundred kids and not a few adults are likely to follow you, but not if you walk all the way around the island, which takes about a day. There's boat building to see, along with the women's rhythmic cutting up of cassava, the staple root crop. Almost all the men fish for a living. Good snorkeling in a couple of places. Boats from Ende town, 50¢.

Souvenirs

Itinerant salesmen of *ikat* cloth (from Flores and elsewhere) come out of the woodwork at some of the hotels and *losmen* when foreigners show up. Bargaining is crucial. If you go to the villages, you can purchase directly from the lady weavers but bargaining is also expected—unless you are Japanese. In the downtown area, there are several large, adjacent stands displaying cloth for sale, with an average cost per cloth of $20, antique ones $50–$125. The only souvenir shop is the close by Cendana, located downtown, near the Pelni office. New cloths from Flores sell for $25–$30, old ones go for $125–$200. They also sell purses and bags made from local ikat cloth.

CLIMBING MEJA AND IYE VOLCANO

Climbing Gunung Meja To climb the low, table-like Gunung Meja, take the road to the new harbor, Pelabuhan Ipi, and turn right on Jl Doko which leads to the path, well marked, to Meja, about 1.5 hrs walk.

Climbing Gunung Iye This 659-m still active volcano lies just a short walk south of Ende. You begin this climb from your losmen in Ende, either early in the morning or late in the afternoon. The humidity is high, so take a lot of water along.

A good path—the same one that leads to Meja—runs off the end of Jl I.H. Doko (off the road to Pelabuhan Ipi), skirts the foot of Gunung Meja, then follows the ridge-tops to Iye. There are a lot of branches in the early stages, but there are usually plenty of people around to point the way. It takes 2–4 hrs from downtown Ende to reach the crater rim. (Note: Some sources will tell you can climb Iye from the vulcanology station at Rate village, but don't try it—the path disappears halfway up, leaving you lost and struggling on loose scree.)

If you are trying to arrive at the summit for sunrise, it would be a smart idea to prospect the first part of the route the day before, or to take a guide. You might also feel more secure with a guide who can carry your camera gear and some water. $5 should cover his fee.

Iye has two craters. The smaller is at the mountain's summit, a small horseshoe open on the eastern side, and filled with small pine trees. Be sure to walk right round the horseshoe to the seaward side where you can peer over the edge of a massive crater (completely invisible from the town). This is the site of Iye's last eruption in 1969, and still looks very raw and unfinished. There are good views back over Ende. You can camp in the small crater if you desire.
—*Chris Thring*

Keli Mutu

To see the colored lakes of Keli Mutu, stay in Wolowaru, or in Moni, which is much closer.

STAYING IN WOLOWARU

The **Losmen Kelimutu** has 12 rms, of which two have attached facilities. $3–$3.50 w/attached facilities, $1.50/person w/shared. The **Losmen Setia** has similar facilities and prices.

The **Jawa Timur** restaurant serves Indonesian food (50¢–80¢), western food ($2.50–$3), and beer or soft drinks. The **Selera Kita** and the **Bethania** serve Indonesian food (50¢–80¢).

Transportation in general is in short supply here, so—if it's even available—a round trip to Keli Mutu costs about $30, much more than it costs from Moni. Wolowaru's weekly market is on Saturday.

STAYING IN MONI

The **Moni Bungalow Sao Ria** is about 1.5 km out of Moni, on the way to Ende, just before the turnoff to Kelimutu. There are 12 rms, $8S, $10D. The rms have attached facilities, but no hot water. Sao Ria is next to the **Kelimutu Restaurant**, with long waits and so-so food, but it is the only restaurant nearby. Simple Indonesian dishes (60¢–$1), fish, beef, and shrimp ($3), and pigeon ($2).

In Moni itself, there is the **Losmen Friendly** (7 rms, $2.25/person) and 6 homestays: **Amina Moe**, **Daniel**, **Hidayah**, **John**, **Nusa Bunga**, and **Regal Jaya**. 2–3 per room, and cold water–only

facilities are outside and shared. About $1.50/person at all establishments. All the *losmen*/homestays can arrange traditional dancing ($24 for an hour or two). There are several small restaurants, including the **Wisata** (Chinese), **Ankermi** (Javanese) and the **Moni Indah** (Indonesian). All cheap. Simple Indonesian meals can also be ordered (50¢–$1).

Transportation to Keli Mutu

Every morning, around 4–5 am, a large truck (followed by others if there are enough tourists) goes up to Keli Mutu, $1.50 each way. The Kelimutu Restaurant has a jeep (6 can squeeze in) which can be chartered to go up Keli Mutu for $14 round-trip. All vehicles get you to within about 1 km of the lakes.

TRADITIONAL VILLAGES

In Moni, check out the "adat" house in back of Daniel's Homestay. There is also a *rumah adat* at Koanara village, in front of the market, and at Wolowaru, and at Watunaga. You can also, if the time is right, see funeral and agricultural rituals here. Special masses are held on August 31 (Moha Kudus) and October 28 (Bunda Maria).

For most of the traditional areas of relatively easy access, head back towards Ende. About 12 km from Nduria, a good side road (okay for *bemos*) heads to nearby Wologai and, a bit further on, to Detukeli. You might have to walk the last 2–3 km, depending on the state of the roads. It's worth it: there are large stone altars for the ancestors, and the mummy of a long-deceased chief. Seeing the mummy requires negotiations with its keeper.

Maumere

Telephone code 382

Luggage unloading at the airport is not the most efficient, but it gets to you eventually. You can purchase taxi tickets while you wait, $3 for the short ride to Maumere and $5 to the two diving resorts. (The Sao Wisata usually has transportation for guests holding reservations). You can probably get lower prices if you go outside the terminal and bargain directly with the drivers, if the law of supply and demand is in your favor. Say $3 to the dive resorts, but you must know a bit of Indonesian to bargain. The drivers understand numbers in English, however. If you are going to Maumere and don't have much luggage, you can walk the half-kilometer or so to the main road and catch a 10¢ ride on a crowded minibus heading southwest (left). It's not worth taking a public *bemo* to the dive resorts, as you have to change 3 times.

TRANSPORTATION

By Air Merpati (Jl Don Tomas, ☎ 21342) has daily flights to and from Ujung Pandang ($65), Kupang ($35), Bima ($55) and Bali ($105) with connections to Surabaya and Jakarta.

Bouraq (Jl Nong Meak, ☎ 21467) has 3 weekly flights to and from Kupang as well as Bali, at the same prices as Merpati.

By Sea Check at the Pelni office near the Losmen Bogor, or go the docks to inquire if anything is going your way in the near future.

By Land There are several daily buses, all crowded, to both Larantuka ($2.50, 3–4 hrs) and Ende ($2.50, 6 hrs). The buses to Larantuka leave from the Waioti terminal, 3 km from town, just off the main road past the airport turnoff. The buses to Ende leave from the Ende terminal, 1.5 km from downtown Maumere. The first buses of the day leave around 8–9 am and the last ones—bis malam, "night bus"—head out at 4–5 pm. You miss the scenery with the night buses and they arrive at inconvenient times.

It's also possible, however, that your hotel can arrange to have you picked up. Smaller buses heading to intermediate towns or villages also leave from one of these two terminals, depending on which direction they're going. They usually wait until they fill up before leaving Town bemos charge about 10¢.

ACCOMMODATIONS

Permata Sari Jl Sudirman, just off the main road where it is joined by the airport road, ☎ 171, 249.

20 rms plus 10 cottages. Attached restaurant with a variety of meals (75¢–$1.75). Lobster and shrimp ($4–$5). A nice hotel, but there is no sense staying here unless you have your own transportation. A small shop sells *ikat*, cigarettes and other knick-knacks. Back of the hotel opens on a black sand beach, good for sunsets. All rooms have attached facilities. $8–$30 S, $12–$40 D, the more expensive rooms w/AC.

Maiwali Jl Don Thomas, ☎ 21220. 24 rms, 14 w/AC. There is a bar handy. This hotel is geared to foreign travelers. They can arrange a variety of chartered transportation: *bemo* charters in the area ($3/hr, $25/day); round-trip to Keli Mutu, 3am departure ($45); two-day round trip to Keli Mutu, overnight in Moni ($90); one-way charter to Ende ($92); same day round-trip to Ende ($70). These costs are for transportation only. All rooms w/attached facilities. Fan-cooled, $5–$10 S, $12–$25 D; w/AC, $16–$27.

Wini Rae Jl Gajah Mada, on the road heading out of town to Ende, ☎ 21388. 27 rms. Indonesian and Chinese meals available ($1–$3). Front rooms tend to be noise, but it's fairly quiet in the back. Good service. Car rental, in town $40, out of town $50/day, with driver. With shared facilities, $3.75/person; w/attached facilities, $10–$12.50 S, $12.50–$15 D; w/AC, $17.50–$20 S, $20–$22.50 D.

Bogor I Jl Slamet Riyadi, ☎ 21191. 30 rms. Chinese-owned. Top value for budget travelers. Restaurant with excellent Chinese dishes. With shared facilities, $2.75–$3.50 S, $4.50–$5 D; w/attached facilities $3.75–$5 S, $6.25–$7.50 D; w/AC $17.50–$22.50 S or D.

Bogor II Jl Slamet Riyadi, ☎ 21137. 19 rms. Chi-

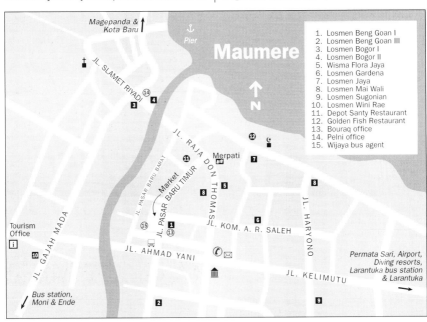

1. Losmen Beng Goan I
2. Losmen Beng Goan III
3. Losmen Bogor I
4. Losmen Bogor II
5. Wisma Flora Jaya
6. Losmen Gardena
7. Losmen Jaya
8. Losmen Mai Wali
9. Losmen Sugonian
10. Losmen Wini Rae
11. Depot Santy Restaurant
12. Golden Fish Restaurant
13. Bouraq office
14. Pelni office
15. Wijaya bus agent

nese-owned, Top value for budget travelers. A Padang style restaurant is attached. Can be noisy Same room prices as Bogor I (above).

Senja Wair Bubuk Jl Yos Sudarso, ☎ 21498. 20 rms. A pleasant, clean, family-run place, located a bit out of central Maumere. Meals available ($1.25–$2). With attached facilities, $5.50 S, $8.50 D; w/AC $14 S, $19 D.

Flora Jaya Jl Don Thomas, ☎ 21333. 4 rms. A tiny place, friendly and close to the central part of town, famous for Mama Jo's meals, $2.25 a shot. Closed for renovations when we checked.

Beng Goan III Jl K. S. Tubun, ☎ 21283, 21532. 28 rms. Simple Indonesian-style lunch and dinner, $1.25. With shared facilities, $2.50 S, $4.50 D; w/attached facilities, $4 S, $7.50 D; w/AC $12.50 S, $17.50 D.

Beng Goan I Jl Moa Toda, in front of the central market, ☎ 21041. Rebuilt after the earthquake with 22 rms. The owner runs buses, and there is a Bouraq agency in front. The owner practices traditional herbal medicine, claims to have found a cure for hepatitis B and is working on an Aids treatment. Fan-cooled, $4 S, $7.50 D; w/AC $12.50 S, $17.50 D.

Gardena Jl Pattirangga 5, ☎ 21489. 10 rms, 5 w/AC. A quiet, friendly place, just a bit out of the way of the downtown area. Breakfast (75¢) and other meals ($1.75) served. All rooms w/attached facilities. $5 S, $7.50 D, fan-cooled; $12.50 S, $15 D, w/AC.

Jaya Jl Hasanudin 26, ☎ 21292. 5 rooms. A new hotel, in front of a mosque. All rms w/attached facilities. $4/person; w/AC, $15/person.

Sugonian Jl Dua Toru, ☎ 21692. 10 rms. Quiet, but a bit far from "downtown." Some of the toilets are the squat-type, others the sit-down variety. With shared facilities, $3 S, $4.50 D; w/attached facilities, $6 S, $7.50 D.

Losmen Flores Froggies Located at Wodong, near Waiterang village, 28 km out of town toward Larantuka. Lots of public minibuses to town, 25¢. For backpackers and back-to-nature lovers. Built and run by an English-speaking Corsican, Michel Colombini, with a dozen bungalows at the juncture of a creek and the sea, just off a sunken WWII Japanese boat. It's like this: swinging suspension bridge, thatched huts on stilts, $4 for a cabin for two, with breakfast. Lunch and supper available on request, about $1.50 or so, depending on what you want. Michel hopes eventually to offer scuba diving, also at ridiculously low prices, if he can ever get his gear out of customs in Jakarta. Canoes, small boats available. Also trips to Gunung Egon. Highly recommended. We hope the place thrives.

Diving Clubs

Both of Maumere's dive clubs are about 12 km east of town, just off the main road to Larantuka. All-inclusive dive packages—including airport pickup, meals, accommodations and two dives a day—cost $75–$140/day, depending on the type of accommodations. Although both places have dive shops and equipment for rent, the Sao Wisata is better organized, has more and better gear, and a qualified divemaster. The best diving is from April to December. Both resorts also offer land tours.

Sao Wisata Jl Sawista, Maumere, Flores, NTT, ☎ 21555, Fax: 21666. With luck only will the phone and fax work. Also, in Jakarta: Sao Wisata, Room 68, 2d Floor, Borobudur Hotel, Jl Lapangan, Banteng Selatan, Jakarta 10710. Fax: (21) 359740.

Sao Wisata offers 4-day/3-night scuba packages (2 diving days) for $260–$320 (per person, based on a group of two), depending on the type of accommodations. If you want to extend your stay, figure $80–$100 a day, depending on your room. For non-divers, the basic 4-day/3-night package is $175–$245, and extra days cost $55–$70.

Sea World Club P.O. Box 3, Jl Nai Noha, Km 13, Maumere, Flores, NTT, ☎ 570. Sea World, owned by the Catholic mission, provides single rooms at $10–$25, doubles at $15–$30 and meals for $4–$5. Snorkeling equipment, $3.50/day. They have some scuba gear available. Boat rental for 2 hrs, $12; all day, $75. They run tours to Kelimutu; Sikka, Ledalero Museum, Wuring fishing village; Watublapi for weaving demonstration, cacao and clove plantation; Ende; and Larantuka. Six passenger minimum for tours. Costs depend on number of passengers. Guide fee, $9 per day.

DINING

All the *losmen* in Maumere provide meals, but at some you have to order ahead and/or are limited to set mealtimes. There are a dozen restaurants downtown, and lots of *warungs* serving *saté*, goat soup and basic Indonesian dishes.

For a full range of Indonesian, Chinese and (some) western dishes, try the restaurant **Rumah Makan Depot Shanty** on Jl Nangka. For Padang food, try the **Surya Indah** downtown. For Chinese food, go to the **Losmen Bogor's restaurant**, and you will get large, delicious portions. Meals are about $1–$3 everywhere. Only heavy beer drinking—$1.40 for a bottle, 90¢ a can, often served over ice—will run up your bill. Lobster is available at the better places (if ordered ahead) for $5–$15, depending on size. For the best seafood around, try the **Golden Fish**, Jl Hasanudin, ☎ 21667. Pick your dinner from the holding tanks in back. Fresh lobster, $12.50/kg; red snapper $4–$5/kg. depending on size.

SERVICES

Tourism Office The Kantor Pariwisata is inconveniently located at Jl Wair Klau, ☎ 21652.

Bodewyn da Gama can arrange tours for you and the tourism office could help with brochures and information. Otherwise, try the hotel at which you are staying.

Guides There are several in town, with varying levels of fluency in English. Ask at your losmen. The best, Antonius, hangs out at the Losmen Beng Goan I and charges $10/day. He is familiar with lots of places, including Keli Mutu, Ende and Riung.

Arranging Tours Grand Komodo Tours, based in Bali and Bima (Sumbawa), have a local agent, Agus, who can be contacted at Jl Nong Meak, ☎ /Fax: 21523. Free information.

There are no other travel agents worthy of the name in Maumere, but your hotel can usually phone to book an seat for you on an airplane or bus. Make reservations as far in advance as possible for any flights.

Your hotel can also arrange tours to the *ikat* weaving villages of Nita (14 km), Sikka (27 km, 45min by minibus) and Watublapi (18km on a partially paved road). You get to see the *ikat* process, and receive a welcome dance as well. A day's notice is required, and figure about $75–$100.

Money Exchange As usual, only at the Bank Rakyat Indonesia. Their Maumere office is on Jl Sukarno-Hatta, in front of the bupati's office. They are open for exchange Mon–Sat, 8–11 am. Don't get there too early, or they won't yet have the day's rates. Major travelers' checks accepted, as well as bills in perfect condition. The **Harapan Jaya** will also exchange money any time they are open, but at 6% less than the bank rate. The Sao Wisata, Sea World and the Harapan Jaya souvenir store will accept Visa, Mastercard and Data (Indonesian) credit cards.

Post Office Jl Pos, in front of the Kantor Daerah. Open Mon.–Thurs. 8 am–2 pm; Fri. 8 am–11 am; Sat. 8 am–12:30 pm.

Souvenirs and Shopping

There is a great selection of *ikat* cloths at the Harapan Jaya store which forms a part of the block of shops enclosing the downtown market. Also ivory items carved from old tusks—avoid these, as they are now illegal to bring into most countries—and *ikat* bags, like those sold in Bali. The asking prices are quite reasonable, but you might be able to bargain a little. Also try the Kota Pena for a wide selection and good prices.

Larantuka

Telephone code 383
By air. There is a scheduled weekly flight from Kupang to Larantuka to Lewoleba, Lembata and back to Kupang, but don't rely on it. It's often canceled. The local Merpati agent may or may not know if it is on. Try him anyway at ☎ 121.

By Land There are several buses daily from Maumere to Larantuka, all crowded ($2). Although it's less than 140km, figure on 5hrs or more from the time you get on the bus until it drops you off in Larantuka, wherever you want. There is a 30–45min break about halfway, on the outskirts of Boganatar village, where some passengers grab a meal, 75¢.

By Sea Two weekly ferries to/from Kupang, more if there are enough passengers. Leaves Larantuka on Tuesday and Friday afternoon, 14–21hrs ($6). Contact ☎ 245 for the ferry. For information on boats going elsewhere, try phoning the Pelni office, ☎ 201, if you speak Indonesian. Otherwise just walk to the docks and ask around.

ACCOMMODATIONS

Tresna ☎ 21072. 16 rms. The best in town. Prices include morning and afternoon tea or coffee. Meals can be ordered: breakfast 60¢, lunch or dinner, $1.25. Cold beer available. Laundry service. With shared facilities, $4 S, $6 D; w/attached facilities, $6 S, $9 D; for the two best rooms up front, $20 S or D.

Rulies ☎ 21198 Next door to the Trisna. 8 rms. Favored by young foreign travelers. None too clean, but beds have mosquito netting. All shared facilities. $11/person.

Kartika ☎ 21083. Next to the harbor entrance and *bemo* terminal. 16 rms. Noisy, and none too clean. $2.50/person.

Fortuna 2 km from the harbor (15¢ on frequent—daytime only—*bemos*), just beyond the gas station. 19 rms. Breakfast ($1), lunch or dinner ($1.50) served. With shared facilities, $3 S, $4.50 D; w/attached facilities, $5.50 S, $8 D.

Sederhana In front of the shop Toko Sumber Murni, 8 rooms, $3/person.

Syaloom Jl Lalamentik 35, ☎ 21464. Located on the hillside towards the back of town. 22 rms, all clean and quiet, fan-cooled. Meals available, 50¢. With shared facilities, $2.50–$4/person; w/attached facilities, $7.50/person.

DINING

If you do not eat at your *losmen,* try the **Nirwana**, in the downtown shops area, for a good meal. Chicken prepared several different ways (well explained on the English menu) $2.50, *capcai* $1.75, Indonesian dishes, $1. Cold beer $1.50, cold soft drinks 60¢.

LOCAL TRANSPORTATION

Mini- and medium-sized buses cover the East Flores area out of Larantuka. 25¢–80¢ for the crowded rides. You can also negotiate a charter ($3–$4/hr).

5 Lembata & Alor PRACTICALITIES

INCLUDES PANTAR

Lembata and Alor, the two largest islands in the dry, rugged little archipelago just east of Flores, are little-visited, and still quite traditional. Lewoleba, Lembata, can be easily reached by air or boat from Flores or Timor. You can even make a phone call from Lembata now. Alor is still a bit more off the beaten path, but in recent years has become much more accessible by both air and sea. Real explorers will want to take a boat to Pantar. A Kupang-based diving operation has recently pioneered the waters between Alor and Pantar, which are very rich.

Lembata

Telephone code 383
Warning: Merpati flights are often canceled; boat and airplane schedules change.

By Air

On Mondays and Thursdays Merpati flies to Lewoleba from Kupang (via Larantuka, Flores) and then directly back to Kupang. Kupang–Lewoleba ($45); Larantuka–Lewoleba ($20). The landing strip is just 3 km from Lewoleba, a $4 taxi ride or 50¢ by public transportation.

By Sea

Regular boats Boats leave twice a day from Larantuka, Flores to Lewoleba. The trip takes about 3 hrs, and costs $1.50. Once a week, small boats leave from Larantuka to Lamalera, the whaling village on Lembata's south coast. The 8-hr journey costs $1.75. The boats (usually) leave Larantuka on Friday and Saturday (8 am) and return on Wednesday. On Mondays, there's usually a boat from Lamalera to Lewoleba, returning the same night.

Ferry A twice weekly ferry from Kupang (it leaves the capital on Sunday and Thursday) calls at Larantuka the next morning, then makes a quick round-trip to Lewoleba before returning to Timor the next day. Kupang–Larantuka–Lewoleba ($7.75); just Larantuka–Lewoleba ($1.75). This ferry gets very crowded, and you're better off trying to hire one of the crew's cabins (you have to negotiate, but around $5–$6 for the 14-hr overnight journey) because there may not be enough room on the passenger deck to stretch out and sleep.

Mixed Freighters Irregularly, 2–3 times a month, the locally owned *Karya Mandiri* motors to Sinjai in South Sulawesi. The trip takes 48 hrs, and costs $16, food included.

ACCOMMODATIONS

Lewoleba

Rejeki I and II. Jl Lembata No. 1193, ☎ 41028 (Rejeki I). The Rejeki I has 14 rms; the Rejeki II, 10 rms. Both are owned by the very pleasant Alex Chandra, who will give you a map of the island and help arrange things if you wish. All rooms have mosquito nets, and include morning and afternoon coffee or tea and cakes. Meals cost $1.25–$1.50. The food is delicious and plentiful. The hotel will exchange US bills for rupiah, and offers locally woven cloths and other craft items. Rooms with shared toilet/baths $3/person; with enclosed facilities $3–$5 S, $5.50–$7.50 D, $8.50–$10 T.
The Rejeki I will change money, and serves as the Merpati agent.
Rahmat. 5 rms. Meals available. $2/person.

Other villages

At Balauring there is a small, inexpensive *losmen* that can provide meals. At Lamalera, There are three homestays—**Capt. Yos**, **Abel Beding**, and **Ben Ebang**, all with room for about 8 guests ($4 for room and board). Capt. Yos, in a conspicuous house overlooking the beach, has a couple rooms with attached facilities, but the rest are shared. Some 500 foreigners overnighted in the whaling village in 1993.

LOCAL TRANSPORTATION

The road network in Lembata is fast improving, and boats from Lewoleba go to the coastal villages that trucks can't reach. Public transportation is more frequent on Monday, during the big market in Lewoleba. An all-weather (but bad and often barely passable) dirt road circles the peninsula formed by the Ile Api volcano, and another follows the island's north coast to Bal-auring, then cuts inland to the eastern port village of Wairiang, about 75 km from Lewoleba. Passenger trucks make the journey from Lewoleba to Balauring (54 km, $2) and on to Wairiang (70 km, $2.50) on average 5 times a week—but never on Monday. The trip takes 8–12 hrs, including stops.

You can also rent a jeep or truck, which runs $40–$110/day, with a driver, depending on the condition of the vehicle. Pak Alex at the Losmen Rejeki will rent you a motorcycle for $8.50–$12.50/day with driver, plus fuel. It is almost impossible to rent a motorcycle if you insist on driving yourself. Too many tourists have rented motorcycles, banged them up, then refused to pay for repairs.

To Lamalera

A regular/irregular boat leaves for this whaling village late Monday night and returns the next day ($2). Although the boat doesn't leave until 2 am, board between 11 and 12 pm if you want any space. The boat arrives in Lamalera 7–8am Tuesday morning. Chartering a boat—if one is available—costs about $125. This is the same as it would cost to take a jeep, which can make the trip only in the dry season. Daily, except Thursdays, trucks go from Lewoleba to Boto for $1.50, often continuing to Imolong for another 50¢. From there, it's about a 1.5–2 hr walk to Lamalera. This road is scheduled to reach Lamalera as soon as funds are available.

To Points East

For travelers heading east, the weekly small wooden boat *Diana Express* leaves Lewoleba early Tuesday mornings, headed for Kalabahi, Alor. The first leg of the trip offers nice views of the Ile Ape volcano. Around mid-day, the boat pulls into the seaside village of Balauring where it stays until the following morning. There are two little *losmen*, very basic, in Balauring, each charging $2.50 for the night, including dinner, tea, coffee. We recommend the one just off the dock, cooler and cleaner than the other (which is a bit inland, next to the road to Lewoleba). The following morning, the *Diana Express* calls at some coastal villages, including a fairly long stop at Wairiang, before the 6-hr final leg to Kalabahi, arriving around sunset. The seas can be rough off the northeast coast of Pantar. Passage from Lewoleba to Kalabahi, $6. If you want a bunk for body and gear just behind the helmsman, add $1–$1.50.

FERRY TO ALOR

A ferry runs 3 times weekly from Balaurang to Kalabahi, stopping at Baranusa on Pantar in between (7 hrs, $5).

Offering one of the best panoramas in Nusa Tenggara, this 1450-m mountain can be climbed from the village of Lamagute on its northern side. Get there from Lewoleba by motorcycle, infrequent truck (market days only) or even walk, if you have a day to spare (24 km). Pak Alex from the Rejeki (see above) can fix you up with extended family in Lamagute if necessary. Take a guide on this climb, as the path is rather indistinct, and there are lots of turn-offs into cultivated areas. It costs about $2.50 per guide—usually you have to hire two, as the locals often refuse to climb without a friend along.

Basically it's a fairly easy climb, through coconut groves and dried-out bush, and takes about 3.5–4 hrs. Humidity at sea level is high, so aim to arrive at the summit shortly after sunrise to avoid climbing in the heat of the day. Note the belt of charred stumps at the treeline, where the forest has been set on fire by sparks drifting down from the peak.

The top yields excellent all-round views of Lembata, eastern Flores, and the islands in between, the whole landscape studded with volcanoes. Api's peak, a bright yellow sulphurous cone, pours out smoke in a sometimes almost continuous stream. This can be an eerie sight, particularly if it is mixed with clouds streaming over the crater rim, in which case the whole crater looks like a giant, boiling cauldron.

—*Chris Thring*

Alor

Telephone code 397

By Air Merpati schedules 4 flights per week to Alor from Kupang ($50), but the average is closer to twice a week.

By Sea Ferry service to Alor is reliable: twice weekly to and from Kupang (14 hrs, $7.50); twice weekly to and from Atambua ($4). Pelni's *Kelimutu* calls on Alor twice monthly on route to Dili, and and twice to Maumere. (For more on Pelni, see "Transportation" pg. 253, and "Timor Practicalities" pg. 310.) There are also an average of three mixed freighters a month to and from Dili, taking about 13 hrs to make the trip. Every 28 days, a scheduled mixed freighter leaves for Ambon, taking about a week to get there (Deck passage is cheap, but bring food. You can negotiate for a crewmember's bunk).

Every 15 days another mixed freighter makes a run through the Moluccan islands to the east of Alor, along with southeast Sulawesi, including Buton and the Tukang Besi Islands. This ship often calls at Ambon on its regular run.

It is also likely that a traditional *pinisi* freighter,

a few still under sail-power only, could get you to Buton, but this could take 8 days at sea. No setups for fussy foreigners. These ships could leave from Kokar, a village on the northwest coast of Alor. For departure information, go to the office of the harbormaster, the *syahbandar*. Chartering a small boat for a tour around Kalabahi Bay, about $30–$35 a day.

ACCOMMODATIONS IN KALABAHI

Melati Jl. Dr Sutomo 2, ☎ 21073. 15 rms, 2 w/AC. Also on the waterfront, a bit closer to the harbor, but next to a (noisy) mosque. $3–$13 S, $6–$15 D

Marlina Jl. El Tari 3, ☎ 21141. 10 rms. Clean and quiet, but located a half-hour's walk from downtown. $4–$7.50 S, $8–$11 D.

Adi Dharma Jl. Martadinata 26, ☎ 21280. 16 rms and 6 more coming on line. On the waterfront and clean. Owned and run by Pak Abu Salim, who speaks excellent English, is always in good humor, and is a mine of information about Alor. His Alorindo Travel, at the hotel, can set up tours of Alor and Pantar. Or just vehicle rental. Traditional dances organized at the hotel for groups. Nice view of the harbor and Kalabahi Bay, especially at dawn and dusk. Almost all foreign visitors stay here. $3–$5 S, $5–$10 D.

A new, more up-market hotel, the Pelangi, was scheduled to open in Kalabahi in mid 1994, on Jl Sudirman, near the downtown area (☎ 21251, fax: 21305). Half the rooms will be AC, and a good restaurant and car rentals are planned.

All the hotels provide meals ($1–$3), but they have to be ordered in advance. Ask way ahead of time if you want cold beer ($2). Small restaurants serving inexpensive meals are concentrated around the harbor area and around the central market. Indonesian meals, 50¢–$2.

LOCAL TRANSPORTATION

Land In-town *bemos* cost 15¢. For out-of-town transportation, there are inexpensive public minibuses which leave when full from the station next to the main market. These run fairly often on the paved roads, and infrequent trucks take passengers to the more remote areas. You can rent a minibus for about $30–$50 per day, and a jeep for $50–$80. Complete with driver and fuel. Very little moves on the roads of town after dark and in-town *bemos* stop around 8pm.
Sea Some towns along the south coast of Alor, as well as all the coastal villages on Pantar, are only accessible by small boat, which are fairly frequent and inexpensive. Irregular, but frequent passenger/cargo boats leave Kalabahi for Pantar Island: Kabir takes about 2.5 hrs, and Baranusa, Pantar's principal town, 5 hrs. Occasional boats also head to Lembata, Kupang, and even Surabaya.

SERVICES

Post Office Open 6 days a week, 7am–2pm.
Telephone The office is open 24 hours, 7 days a week, theoretically for country-wide and international phone calls. Good connections to Kupang, but awful to anywhere else.
Money Exchange Bank Rakyat Indonesia has a money exchange office on the street running in back of the harbor, close to the entrance. US dollars only. The main office in town will change Australian dollars and American Express traveler's checks. The rates are awful.
Electricity 24 hrs a day, but with wild fluctuations and fluorescent lights constantly struggling to light back up.
Medical Kalabahi has a general hospital (*rumah sakit umum*) and 3 drug stores.
Movies Surya Theater, shows at 8pm.
Guides Speaking varying levels of English, these can be arranged by your hotel for about $20/day.

DIVING

Alor offers some spectacular diving, mostly in the strait between Alor and Pantar, which can be arranged by Pitoby Water Sports in Kupang, with two weeks' advance bookings. Contact Graeme or Donovan Whitford in Kupang.
Pitoby Watersports Jl Jend. Sudirman 118, Kupang NTT. ☎ (391) 32700, Fax: 31044. Or: P.O. Box 1120, Kupang NTT. ☎ /Fax: (391) 31634. Eight days/7 nights dive package (10 dives) $645 plus airfare ($100 rt), minimum 4 pax, with own dive gear (10% more if gear rental from Pitoby's). If your group has less than 4, there is a 50% surcharge.

Pantar

In addition to the Balaurang, Lembata–Baranusa, Pantar–Kalabahi, Alor ferry mentioned above ($5, three times a week), a twice weekly wooden boat makes the run from Kalabahi to Baranusa (6 hrs, $1.50).

You can also rent a speedboat from Kalabahi (several days' notice is required) for $200 round-trip (1.5 hrs each way). Chartering a wooden motor boat (6 hrs each way) costs $50–$100.

From Baranusa to the Gunung Siring volcano takes 4 hrs by jeep ($40 round-trip, if one is available) plus another 1 hr of hiking.

Sumba PRACTICALITIES

Sumba is one of the most traditional islands in Nusa Tenggara, with an estimated 65 percent of the population, mostly in the west, adhering to the animist Merapu religion. There are two main towns on the island, Waingapu in the East (by far the larger of the two) and Waikabubak in the West. Although there is a small airport in the West, the best way to enter is to fly or take a boat into Waingapu, and from there take a vehicle over Sumba's good road system to Waikabubak. West Sumba is more populous, and sees three times the rainfall of East Sumba.

East Sumba

Telephone code 386

By Air

Flying to Waingapu, from either Bali or Kupang, is the most efficient way to reach Sumba. Bouraq offers four weekly flights from Bali ($90) and an equal number from Kupang ($66). Merpati schedules —and sometimes actually flies— 3 times weekly direct from Bali ($90) and 3 times direct from Kupang ($66). Merpati also flies the following milk run, 3 times weekly: Bali ($90)— Bima, Sumbawa ($45)—Tambolaka, West Sumba ($30)—Waingapu—Kupang ($66) and then returns. (Fares are to/from Waingapu.)

The taxi from Mauhua Airport to town (6 km) costs $6.

Bouraq Jl Yos Sundarso 57, ☎ 21363, 21906, 21671.

Merpati Jl A. Yani 73 (part of the Elim Hotel), ☎ 21323.

By Sea

FERRIES

The ferries are quite reliable. Once a week (Fridays, at last notice) to Savu $9 top class, $6 economy, 16 hours. (then continuing to Kupang) Once a week (Wednesdays) to Ende, $7.50 and $5, 11 hrs. Ferry office: Jl Yos Sundarso 4, ☎ 21211.

PELNI LINES

The passenger ship *Kelimutu,* run by Pelni Lines (Jl Yos Sudarso, ☎ 21027) calls at Waingapu on its weekly route, on Wednesdays, continuing on to Ende, Kupang, Dili, Kalabahi, Maumere and Ujung Pandang, and returning by the same route. In economy class to Ende, $7.50 (7 hrs), to Kupang $12 (19 hrs). On Thursdays, from Waingapu, another Pelni ship heads to Bima, $9 (10 hrs), Mataram $16 (24 hrs), Surabaya,

and Banjarmasin. On the way back, the ship stops at Benoa Harbor in Bali but not in Mataram.

ACCOMMODATIONS

In Waingapu

Merlin Jl Panjaitan 25, ☎ 21300, 21490. 19 rms, the more expensive rms with AC. All with attached facilities and breakfast. New, comfortable, with an excellent restaurant which offers panoramic views. Satellite-receiving TVs, vehicle rentals. $9–$22 S; $11–$28 D.

Elim Jl A. Yani 73, ☎ 21462. Next to the Merpati office, which is a part of the hotel grounds. 28 rms, including 8 VIP rms, which are the best in town. Mosquitoes are a major problem, but nets are provided and rms sprayed whenever you ask. We would suggest also lighting a green coil—*obat nyamuk*—or two. Restaurant has a fair variety of inexpensive dishes. A very nice couple runs the place. They have a large map of Sumba, and information is freely given. All rms with attached facilities. $3–$17 S, $10–$21 D.

Sandlewood Jl Panjaitan 25, ☎ 21199. 25 rms. (Should be "Sandalwood" but the tourism department in Kupang imposed the wrong spelling.) Good restaurant and an incredible quantity and variety of *ikat* cloths for sale, along with other souvenirs. Supermarket, bus terminal nearby. The cheaper rms have shared facilities. $6–$14 S, $8–$20 D, all w/breakfast.

Surabaya Jl El Tari 2, ☎ 21125. Opposite the bus terminal. 7 rms. Near supermarket. Cheaper rms w/shared facilities. Motorcycle for rent. $4–$6 S, $7–$10 D.

Kaliuda Jl Marisi, ☎ 21272. 8 rms, some w/shared facilities. $6 S, $5–$7.50 D.

Lima Saudara Jl Wangameti 2, ☎ 21085. In the harbor area. 13 rms. All rms with attached facilities. A good value for the budget traveler. Meals $1. $2.50–$4.50 S, $4.50–$7.50 D.

Permata Jl Kartini 8, ☎ 21516. 5 rms, all w/attached facilities. Recommended for budget travelers. $2.50 S, $4.50 D.

Pink Palace Jl Hatta 9, ☎ 21006. 7 rms, all w/attached facilities. $2.40–$4.40 S or D.

Outside of Waingapu

In Melolo you can stay at **Losmen Hermindo** (5 rms, $4 S, $8 D w/shared facilities) and in Baing there are cottages, with a capacity for 14 people ($25–$100). Outside of these, arrange to sleep in the home of the *kampung* heads.

DINING

The best restaurants are at the hotels: **Merlin**, **Sandlewood**, **Elim**. If you feel like stepping out, there are several decent, but not fancy restaurants in Waingapu. The **Rajawali** serves seafood and other dishes, Chinese and Indonesian style; the **Urip Santoso** specializes in Javanese dishes, the **Handayani** (formerly Mahameru) also features Javanese cooking and the **Padang** (near the bus terminal) serves exactly what its name suggests. Two newer restaurants, the **Mini Indah** and the **Bu Jaenab**, also serve Javanese cooking at modest prices.

TRANSPORTATION

Bemos in town cost 15¢ a ride. Public transportation follows all relatively decent roads, then you have to rely on trucks. There is not much traffic out of town—weekly market days are the best time to reach many places. Buses to Melolo (75¢) are fairly frequent, and there is a daily bus to Baing ($2). To the north coast, there are daily buses to Mondu ($1), to Kadahang ($1.25), and, if road conditions permit, to Wunga ($1.50). You can get to Lenang and Mamboru only during the dry season, and by jeep. There is a twice daily bus to Waikabubak ($2.50).

For exploring, it is most efficient to hire your own transportation, which is not too expensive if you can share the cost among several people—as many as 8 can fit in most minibuses or jeeps. Many vehicles (with a driver) can be hired for out of town jaunts: $5–$6/hr, $35–$50/day, depending on distance and road conditions, plus fuel. You can also arrange a round-trip rate: to and from Melolo, for example, might run $35–$40, including waiting time, fuel included. You can also bargain for a charter directly with the *bemo* drivers at the bus terminal. *Bemo* charter to Waikabubak, about $65.

SERVICES

Agency tours The Elim or Sandlewood arrange tours, usually for large groups or cruise ship tourists. A fairly good series of dances with lots of performers runs $50–$100. Same price to see the "horse dance" with the animals prancing to the beat of gongs.

Ikat Weaving demonstrations, showing all phases for the *ikat* technique (almost impossible to see on your own unless you have unlimited time) cost $40–$80, depending on how many natural dyes you want to see prepared.

Guides English-speaking guides are also available through the Elim or the Sandlewood, about $10/day.

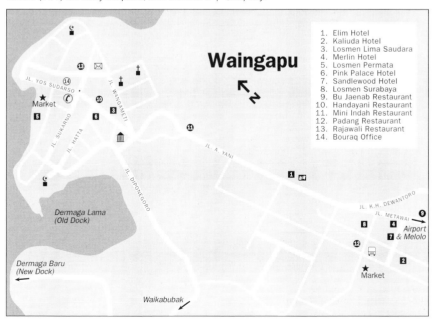

Waingapu

1. Elim Hotel
2. Kaliuda Hotel
3. Losmen Lima Saudara
4. Merlin Hotel
5. Losmen Permata
6. Pink Palace Hotel
7. Sandlewood Hotel
8. Losmen Surabaya
9. Bu Jaenab Restaurant
10. Handayani Restaurant
11. Mini Indah Restaurant
12. Padang Restaurant
13. Rajawali Restaurant
14. Bouraq Office

JL. YOS SUDARSO
Market
JL. WANGAMETI
JL. SUKARNO
JL. HATTA
JL. A. YANI
JL. DIPONEGORO
Dermaga Lama (Old Dock)
Dermaga Baru (New Dock)
Waikabubak
JL. K.H. DEWANTORO
JL. METAWAI
Airport & Melolo
Market

Sumba 6

West Sumba

Telephone code 387

By Air

Although service is irregular, Merpati is scheduled to fly three times a week to Tambolaka, West Sumba, from Bima, Sumbawa ($29) and from Waingapu ($28). Tambolaka is on the north coast, about 40 km from Waikabubak. The ride to the western capital costs $20, split among the passengers. The airport is only a couple of km from the main road, but public transportation to the capital is infrequent, and always crowded. You might be able to get a ride to town with the Merpati agent.

By Land

It's much easier to get to Waikabubak overland from Waingapu. Buses frequently make the 5 1/2-hr run (the first hour is spent rounding up passengers in Waingapu) over a good road ($2.50). The bus will drop you off at the hotel/*losmen* of your choice. A chartered vehicle costs $55–$65, although you can share the cost.

ACCOMMODATIONS

Mona Lisa Hotel Jl Adyaksa 30, ☎ 21364. A couple of km from the center of town, on the road to Watabula. With 9 two room-cottages, all with enclosed facilities. Nice, but the last time we checked there was no hot water, no excuse at their prices. Cottages in local style. Motorcycle or horse rental $5/day for guests. $30 S, $40 D.
Manandang Jl Pemuda 4, ☎ 21197, 22192. 31 rms. A nice, clean, new hotel. Rated the best in town, with a restaurant serving excellent meals. All rms include breakfast. The restaurant serves Indonesian and Chinese dishes ($1–$2). Vehicles for rent. Will change U.S. dollars. The cheaper rms have shared facilities. Prices include breakfast. $4.50–$20 S, $7–$22 D.
Artha Jl Veteran 11, ☎ 21112, about a kilometer on the road to Waingapu. 11 rms, all w/attached facilities. $5.50–$14 S, $11–$14 D.
Aloha (formerly Mona Lisa) Jl Gaja Mada 14, ☎ 21024. 9 rms. This is a traveler's haven, with lots of information including a wall full of photos showing what you can see and where (things look much better than in these snapshots). Lobby restaurant. Vehicles and motorcycles for rent. English-speaking guides, $6/day. The place is often full during the summer months. The cheaper rms have shared facilities. $3.50–$5.50 S, $4.50–$7 D w/breakfast.
Pelita Jl Bhayamangara, ☎ 21104. 23 rms. A bit noisy and somewhat seedy, but OK for budget travelers. Motorcycle rental, $10/day. $2.50–$8 S, $4–$11 D.

Outside Waikabubak

There is now a luxury beach resort on Tanjung Karoka, near Rua beach.
Sumba Reef Lodge A bungalow-style, 5-star international resort opened in 1992. The American investor who picked this site chose well: there is a large, fine beach, and excellent waves for surfing, although swimming a bit rough. The access road has been completed and activity there indicates work is proceeding.

In Kodi, you can stay at the **Penginapan Stori**, 5 rms, all shared facilities, $5/person. In Waitabula, **Beni Dopo's house**, $4/person.

Homestays

For travelers with a bit of time to spare, and who are not finicky as to western creature comforts, we highly recommend homestays as the best way to get some insight into West Sumba's fascinating culture. In fact, homestays are the only way to overnight near the traditional villages.

In most hamlets you can arrange for a homestay through the *kepala desa* (village chief) and/or the *kepala kampung* (hamlet chief). There are no fixed prices, and you should pay according to what you get—or don't get—such as a mattress, a room for yourself, and any food besides rice. Count on $2–$6 a day, w/board.

The only semi-official places we've seen are at Kabunduk village near Anakalang, run by the *kepala desa*, and the home of Mr. and Mrs. Hoga, a fine couple, at Lamboya/Kabukarudi. The Hoga's home is usually frequented by travelers only at Pasola time.

DINING

Your hotel will provide suitable meals, but for a change, you might want to try the *warungs* along A. Yani Street. There is nothing special here, however, and the area is none too hygienic. The only restaurant worthy of the name is the new **Gloria**, Jl Bayang Karang 147. This is a Chinese seafood restaurant, with fresh fish daily. You can also try the **Idola**, the **Ronita** or the **Ande Ate**, the last one specializing in pork dishes.

TRANSPORTATION

Buses, of varying sizes, and trucks offer cheap access to most of West Sumba where there are roads of any kind. Prices vary depending on distance and the state of the roads, but will never exceed $2. They are, however, crowded and not always convenient. Out-of-the-way places are usually serviced only on their market days, which usually fall on Saturday or Wednesday. Only trucks travel the worst roads.

States of discomfort on public transportation vary from being packed like livestock on the back

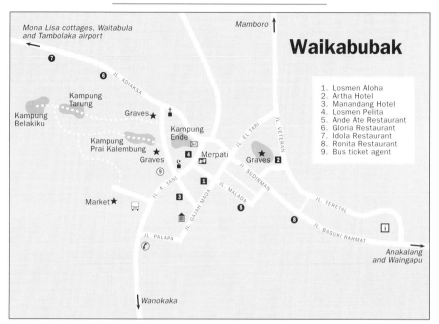

Mona Lisa cottages, Waitabula and Tambolaka airport

Mamboro

Waikabubak

Kampung Tarung
Kampung Belakiku
Graves
Kampung Ende
Kampung Prai Kalembung
Graves
Merpati
Graves
Market
JL. ADJAKSA
JL. EL TARI
JL. VETERAN
JL. SUDIRMAN
JL. A YANI
JL. GAJAH MADA
JL. MALADA
JL. TERETAL
JL. BASUKI RAHMAT
JL. PALAPA
Wanokaka

Anakalang and Waingapu

1. Losmen Aloha
2. Artha Hotel
3. Manandang Hotel
4. Losmen Pelita
5. Ande Ate Restaurant
6. Gloria Restaurant
7. Idola Restaurant
8. Ronita Restaurant
9. Bus ticket agent

of a truck to a comfortable seat, but also squeezed in, on a minibus. The problem is that the vehicles don't stop along the way. If you get an early morning start, however, you will have most of the day to look around the market area, and perhaps explore part of the area on foot before squeezing back into one of the vehicles (or the only vehicle) returning to Waikabubak in the late afternoon.

If you are an experienced rider, you could also rent a motorcycle ($5–$10/day) which offers very good mobility and relative comfort. You could also hire a motorcycle and an English-speaking guide (in short supply, however) for a total expenditure of $12–$18/day.

The ideal solution is to charter a vehicle (jeep or minibus) with a driver to see West Sumba according to your own schedule. Your *losmen* can arrange this for you. Rates depend on the trip undertaken, about $30–$40 each to the popular destinations close-by—Wanukaka, Anakalang or Lamboya—and a bit more, around $50, to the Kodi area.

Jeeps can go to the out-of-the-way places on some pretty tough roads, carrying up to 6 passengers. Minibuses (up to 10 passengers) have to stay to the good roads, although these now reach—or come close to—all the popular areas.

Some *losmen* have their own vehicles, as well as drivers and guides with varying amounts of experience. Try the Manandang, the Monalisa or the Artha for jeeps ($50/day). Same price for a clean *bemo* at the Manandang, or test your Indonesian bargaining skills at the *bemo* terminal.

During our last trip to West Sumba, we hired an independent, Pak Man Bamualin (Jl Ahmad Yani, ☎ 191) who charged a very reasonable $37 per grueling 10–11 hr day. He was also willing to take his aging, but very tough jeep on the roughest tracks. He speaks some English, and could save you the cost of a guide. An ethnic Arab born in Waikabubak, he knows his territory well. Contact him directly or through your hotel.

SIGHTS AND SERVICES

Guides Guides, whose knowledge of English and the local traditions varies widely, are available for $6/day. Have your hotel/*losmen* find one. It's best to get somebody who can speak the language of the subdistrict where you are heading. **Visiting Fees** Many of the traditional villages charge a fee for visiting, and some keep guest books. There is no set rate, and you can expect to pay about 60¢–80¢ (In rupiah, of course). Remember that this is the only tangible benefit that tourism brings to the villagers and, of course, without them there would be nothing to visit. **Performances** The better hotels can arrange a good dance for you. With about 30 participants, the event costs $140. They can even arrange for a mini-Pasola with 40 or more riders for about $550. These events require at least 3 days—and maybe a week—to arrange. **Markets** *Bemos* and buses make the Waikabubak–Anakalang run, especially on Saturday. Traffic is also regular south to Waikelo. More distant areas see little traffic except on market days: Saturday for Gaura and Laihuruk/Praibaku (Wanakaka area); and Wednesday at Padedewatu (Rua and Lamboya regions). Both Kodi's and Waiha's market days are Saturday.

Sumba 6

Savu & Roti PRACTICALITIES

7

Few people visit these small, drought-prone islands, and there is little available here in the way of creature comforts or organized traveler's services. But the tradition and history of Savu and Roti, and their tiny companion islands of, respectively, Raijua and Ndao, are much more interesting than their size would suggest. These are not places to pop into for a day and a quick look around, but if you have time, and willing to take the initiative, a visit to these islands can be very rewarding. It also really helps here to be able to speak some Indonesian, even if your skills are very basic.

Savu

For flights and scheduled boats to Savu, see "Timor Practicalities," pp. 310–311.

Seba is the only town and a small one at that. The airport is close by, as is the ferry landing. Two non-official *losmen*/homestays are here, **Makarim** and **David Kido**, plus a government rest house. About $3 for the room, $3/day for food. There is a nice beach near Seba. Savu's roads are generally good, and there is some public transportation available, but it is still best to travel to the outlying areas on their market days, when there will be more traffic.

Roti

Missionary Aviation Fellowship (MAF) pioneered flights to Roti in the 1970s but gave up its reliable service in 1987 at Merpati's request. Now there is an unreliable weekly (Sat.) flight from Kupang. The number of passengers and available planes determines whether you can get on the 20-min flight ($23).

Ferries usually run 6 days a week ($2–$3, 4 hrs), although the schedules are occasionally restricted when one of the Kupang-based ships disappears for a few weeks of R&R or an overhaul in Ujung Pandang. The ferry ride is an absolute mess, poorly organized and with no crowd control. Just grin and bear it.

When the ferry reaches the narrow Roti Strait, currents can cut the boat's forward speed from the usual 8 knots to 1.5 knots. It gets very rough here January–February.

The ferry lands at Pante Baru (see map pg. 195), inside bottle-necked Korbafo Bay. At the dock, passengers rush off to squeeze into *bemos*, buses and trucks heading to various points on the island. Most head to Ba'a ($1).

ACCOMMODATIONS

Ba'a, Nambrela and Papela offer lodgings. The only decent place to sleep is **Ricky's** in Ba'a—15 rms, 3 with AC, at $7.50/person; fan-cooled rooms $5 S, $7.50 D. The meals at Ricky's ($1.75) are quite passable, and there is the possibility of lobster for $3.50 extra. Ricky's can arrange expensive, but reliable, transportation for touring Roti. There are two other joints in town, the **Kisia** (6 rms), and the **Pondok Wisata** (5 rms). Both w/shared facilities, $2.25/person.

In Namberela, there are several homestays, $4–$5 for room and board, cold beer extra at $2 a bottle. The food is good, if a bit monotonous.

Papela has a mini-*losmen*, the **Pondok Wisata**, and three homestays. $2–$3/night plus meals 50¢–80¢. Try to stay at **Vonny Helberg's** place—she's a Tasmanian woman trying to develop tourism in Papela and can arrange boat rides, dances and touring.

LOCAL TRANSPORTATION

Most of Roti's coastal roads and fine scenery can be covered in a grueling 12–14 hr day. But neither the frequency of public transportation nor the state of the roads favor seeing Roti quickly and on the cheap. Hiring your own transport can be reasonable for a small group: $40–$60 a vehicle. Motorcycles, $10–$15/day. Forget about getting around Roti during the rainy season (Dec–March), except on the best roads.

MARKET DAYS

Batutua (Mon), Bokai (Sat), Busalangga (Wed, Sat), Daurendale (Thurs), Kuli (Thurs), Lalao (Tues), Nemberala (Tues), Nggodimeda (Sat), Oela (Fri), Oelaba (Thurs), Oelue (Fri), Oenitas (Sat), Oesili (Wed), Pante Baru/Olafulihaa (Mon), Papela (Daily), Seda (Mon).

8

Timor PRACTICALITIES
INCLUDES EAST TIMOR

Kupang, the capital of Nusa Tenggara Timur (NTT) province is the largest city and the easiest point of entry to the island of Timor. You can even fly to Australia from here. From here you can explore the various districts of West Timor, and make your way to the islands of Savu or Roti, or Alor. Kupang has star-rated hotels and good communications. East Timor—a separate province—still attracts few visitors, but the capital, Dili, offers good accommodations and services. Because of the island's generally good system of roads, travel around Timor is easiest by bus or chartered vehicle.

West Timor

Telephone code 391
El Tari airport is 15 km east of downtown Kupang. The taxi ride costs $4/person, whatever the destination in town, so try to get a taxi for yourself or you could waste a lot of time while others are dropped off before you. When you tell the taxi driver the name of the hotel you want to be dropped off at, he will probably tell you that it is full. Don't believe him. He gets a commission from another hotel.

ACCOMMODATIONS

In Kupang

Kupang has several star-ranked hotels, along with a good range of less expensive accommodations. English is spoken at most of the better establishments which also charge 10–21% tax. Construction has begun on a new hotel, the Palm Beach, with 160 rms planned beachside, aiming for 4-star ranking, the highest in Kupang. Planning a 9-hole golf course, jogging track, squash. Negotiations for management by the Grand Hyatt chain, scheduled opening 1995.
Orchid Garden Jl Fatuleu 2, ☎ 32004, 33707; Fax: 33669. 40 rms. All AC, a 3-star hotel. Swimming pool, television, restaurant with European, Chinese and Indonesian cuisine, tours, tennis, car and driver ($5/hr in city). $56 S, $64 D; suites $84–$125; including taxes and breakfast.
Sasando Jl Kartini 1, ☎ 33334–7; Fax: 33338. 46 rms. Excellent view from this hilltop hotel, all rooms facing the sea. Inconveniently located, unless you have your own transportation or pay $4 for a taxi ride. Good restaurant with Chinese and Indonesian food ($3–$5) and spaghetti, chicken and sandwiches. Bar with lots of different beers, disco ($2.50 entrance), and expensive drinks at both ($4–$6). Travel agent

on premises for tours and airline bookings. Major credit cards accepted. Disco, tennis, nice pool. $60–$72 S, $72–$84 D with all taxes.
Flobamor II Jl Sudirman 21, ☎ 33476, Fax 32560. 33 AC rms. This is a one-star hotel with good, attentive service. The restaurant serves steaks as well as Indonesian food. Swimming pool. The hotel also owns very nice cottages on Semau Island (see "Flobamor Beach Cottages" below). $15–$40 S; $20–$40 D, with breakfast and taxes included.
New Ausindo Jl Pahlawan, about 1.5 km west of downtown towards Tenau harbor, ☎ 32873, Fax: 31736. 18 rms. Spacious AC or fan-cooled rooms with fridges and TV. The bar-restaurant on the top floor offers superb view of the water. Lots of *bemos* running in front (but not at night). Transportation and tour service available. Fan cooled $15 S, $18.50 D; AC $20–$28 S, $24–$36 D, taxes included.
Keli Mutu Jl Keli Mutu 38, ☎ 31179. 20 rms, half AC, all clean and new. Restaurant serving Indonesian food. $8–$15 S, $14–$17.50 D, $28–$35 suite.
Charvita Jl Lalamentik 30, ☎ 22676, 21221. 58 rms. Mini-fridge, color TV. $16–$30, depending on room.
Astiti Jl Sudirman, ☎ 21810. 35 rms. This one-star hotel is in the process of adding a new, big wing. Convenient location and a good value. Chinese and Indonesian food at the restaurant. $13–$23 S, $16–$26 D.
Cendana Jl El Tari 23, ☎ 21541. 54 rms. The Cendana is 4 km from downtown, but in an area with frequent public transportation, close to the governor's office. Large souvenir shop. Staff none too efficient; restaurant has meals, but no menu. Prices include breakfast and taxes. With shared facilities $8 S, $11 D; fan and attached facilities $10 S, $14 D; AC and TV $14 S, $20 D.
Pantai Timor Beach ☎ 31651 Jl Sumatra, 1 km east of downtown. 22 rms. The outdoor restaurant offers a good view of the sea and sunset; indoor restaurant as well with a good selection

of food (about $2 per dish). Fan-cooled $6 S, $7.50 D; AC $11–$14 S, $14–$17 D. Plus 12%.

Komodo Jl Keli Mutu 40, ☎ 21913. 12 rms, some AC. New place, good location. $8.50–$15 S; $14–$17.50 D.

Laguna Inn Jl Kelimutu 36, ☎ 21559. 55 rms. Clean place with no frills, few foreigners. Inexpensive Indonesian food. $3–$6 S, $5–$15 D.

Maliana Jl Sumatra 35, ☎ 21879. Opposite the Pantai Timor, near the BNI bank and next to the Wisma Susi. 12 rms. No restaurant. Satellite TV in more expensive rooms. All AC and attached facilities. $10–$12 S, $12–$14 D.

Mariana Jl A. Yani. ☎ 22566, next to the Sempati Airlines office. 12 rms. Nice, but on a noisy street. Fan and shared facilities $9 S, $11 D; AC and attached facilities $12 S, $14 D.

Susi Jl Sumatra, ☎ 22172, 33421. 21 rms. No restaurant. Good view from the roof but not from the top floor, due to cables. All w/attached facilities. AC rooms, $10 S, $13 D; fan-cooled rms, $5–$8 S, $12–$14 D.

King Stone Jl Timor-Timur, 6 km east of downtown, ☎ 22014. Looks clean enough. Said to be decent snorkeling off the beach here. Inexpensive Indonesian food available. Popular Pondok Bamboo restaurant (see below). Disco every night, 8pm to 2am, $2.50 entrance, drinks lots cheaper than the Sasando. Sunday party, 2–6 pm. $2 entrance fee for males, ladies free. Drinks reasonably priced. All AC, $12 per room.

Kupang Indah Jl Kelimutu 25, ☎ 22638. 20 rms. Meals available. $3.50–$8 S, $4–$10 D.

Taman Ria Beach ☎ 31320. Jl Timor-Timur, 3 km east of downtown. Just off a sand-and-stone beach, in an amusement park setting of fading colors. The bar on the premises can get quite noisy at night. Restaurant with Indonesian dishes. Dorm-type rooms $2; w/attached facilities, $4.50–$7 S, $5–$9 D.

Fatuleu Jl Fatuleu, in front of the Orchid Garden, ☎ 31374. 15 rms. Attached restaurant, meals $1.25. With shared facilities $4 S, $5 D; w/attached facilities, $5–$6 S; $6–$7.50 D.

Eden Off Jl Kancil, next to a public pool. 13 rms. The large, pleasantly rustic pool gets crowded only during vacation times and on weekends. Quite basic and far from downtown but has a nice atmosphere. Favored by travelers on a tight budget. $1.50–$3/person, higher priced rooms have enclosed facilities.

Backpackers Jl Kancil 38 B, Air Nona. 6 rms. Part of an international group, but open to anyone. Out of the downtown area. $2/person.

Semau Island

There are two bungalow-type hotels and a *wisma* in front of Uiasa village on Pulau Semau, 11 km west and a 50-min boat ride from Kupang. Nice, peaceful island. Expect a wet landing. Not recommended Jan–Feb when the waves are high.

Flobamor Beach Cottages Run by the Flobamor Hotel in Kupang. 6 single, 8 double rms in 3 units with thin walls—not so good for privacy if the place is full. More modern than the Uiasa. Well-organized management. They will find a local guide for the 3-km climb to the lighthouse—bring good shoes as there's lots of sharp coral. They have a glass-bottom boat on order for the trip from Kupang. Snorkeling and diving possible. Excellent meals. $40 S or D including meals.

Uiasa Hotel 10 thatched roof, detached bun-

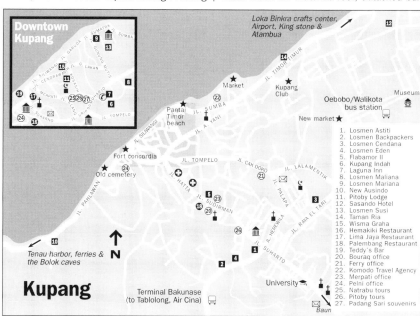

Downtown Kupang

Loka Binkra crafts center,
Airport, King stone &
Atambua

Market

Kupang Club

Museum

Oebobo/Walikota bus station

New market

Pantai Timor beach

Fort concordia

Old cemetery

JL. TOMPELO

JL. CAK DOKO

JL. LALAMENTIK

JL. PALAPA

JL. HEREWILA

JL. RAYA EL TARI

JL. SUDIRMAN

JL. HATTA

JL. PAHLAWAN

JL. SILIWANGI

JL. A. YANI

JL. SUHARTO

Tenau harbor, ferries & the Bolok caves

N

Kupang

Terminal Bakunase (to Tablolong, Air Cina)

University

Baun

1. Losmen Astiti
2. Losmen Backpackers
3. Losmen Cendana
4. Losmen Eden
5. Flabamor II
6. Kupang Indah
7. Laguna Inn
8. Losmen Maliana
9. Losmen Mariana
10. New Ausindo
11. Pitoby Lodge
12. Sasando Hotel
13. Losmen Susi
14. Taman Ria
15. Wisma Graha
16. Hemakiki Restaurant
17. Lima Jaya Restaurant
18. Palembang Restaurant
19. Teddy's Bar
20. Bourag office
21. Ferry office
22. Komodo Travel Agency
23. Merpati office
24. Pelni office
25. Natrabu tours
26. Pitoby tours
27. Padang Sari souvenirs

galows 100 m from Flobamor. Owned by Teddy's Bar in Kupang. Bottle beer is only $2, but other booze is expensive, so bring your own. Tours available. Meals, included, could be improved. $17.50 S, $30 D.

Wisma UM Intene Between the others, 100 m back from the beach. 4 dbl rms. Hard roof, spacious rooms w/clean tile floors. Good view of harbor. Attached facilities. Friendly, local owner (Mr. Pong, the *kepala desa*). $5/person including full board.

Elsewhere in West Timor

Losmen, from fairly decent to quite desperate, are found in the district capitals of Soe, Kefamenanu ("Kefa"), and Atambua, and the towns of Pante Macassar and Betun. The better places throw in a free breakfast. The buses will usually drop you off at the *losmen* of your choice, or you can find local transportation at the bus station—all the *bemo* drivers will know where the few *losmen* are. These towns also have Padang-style restaurants where you can eat your fill for about $3 plus drinks.

CAMPLONG

Oemat Honis 28 rms. Run by the church. Next to a local park with a cave, an artificial lake and lots of weekenders. $4/person including 3 meals. Two better rooms, $5/person.

SOE

Bahagia II Newest and best in town, Jl Gajah Mada at the entrance from Kupang, ☎ 21095. 15 rms, fine restaurant serving Chinese and Indonesian food, about $3/meal. $13 S, $15 D.

Mahkota Plaza ☎ 21050. In front of the bus station. 20 rms. Dining room with decent if slightly expensive meals. Several Padang-style restaurants nearby. $4 S, $7 D, $14 VIP.

Bahagia I Jl Diponegoro, ☎ 21015. 12 rms. Clean and bright, with an attached restaurant—meals $1–$3. Souvenirs, including *ikat,* sold here, but a bit expensive. Other shops nearby. Cheaper rooms have shared facilities. $5–$10.

The most inexpensive options are the **Cahaya** (Jl Kartini, ☎ 21087) with 17 rms, $3/person with attached facilities, $2.50/person with shared ones, the **Anda**, which has a multi-lingual boss (Yohannes) and similar prices, and The **Sejati** (Jl Gajah Mada, ☎ 21101).

KEFAMENANU

Cendana Jl Sonbai, ☎ 21168. Near the petrol station on the road to Atambua. 13 rms, restaurant. Best hotel in town. Fan-cooled rooms, $7 S or D; AC rooms, $18 S or D.

Ariesta Jl Basuki Rahmat, ☎ 21007. 13 rms. The deluxe rooms are very spacious and a good value. The restaurant is okay. A long, gaudy dragon and fish pond in back garden. $15/room.

Sederhana ☎ 21029. On the exit road to Ambeno. $3/person.

Soko Windu 10 rms. Family run and pleasant enough. Near the market. $2.75/person w/breakfast.

Also the **Bahtera**, on a quiet street, a ways from the market. Basic but cheap. Same for the **Sederhana** and the **Setankai**.

Restaurants with Chinese cooking and a bit of seafood: **Stella Maris**, the **Elim** and the **Citra Rasa**, all $1–$2.50/meal.

ATAMBUA

Intan Jl Merdeka, ☎ 21343. Near the market, 18 rms. Best in town. Restaurant in back with Chinese and Indonesian meals. Non-AC $7.50/person; w/AC $20 S or D.

Nusantara On the main road from Kefa, near the edge of town. Best value, but often full. A couple of Padang restaurants a short walk down the street. One of these, the Kalpataru, also has rooms in the back ($3/person). All rms w/attached facilities $4 S, $7 D.

Merdeka Jl Mekat, ☎ 21197. 15 rms. Quiet and clean. $3.25 S, $6.50 D.

Liurai Jl Satsuitubun, ☎ 21084. Near the gas station. Dirty lobby and unpleasant attendant. Rms are okay, toilets dirty. With shared facilities, $2/person; w/attached, $4/person.

Klaben Jl Dubesinanat, ☎ 21079. 10 rms. On a quiet side street. All beds have mosquito nets; all rooms w/attached facilities. $3/person.

You can also try the **Sahabat**, and the **Ramayana** at prices similar to those above. Near the Sahabat there is a restaurant called **Sinar Kasih** which looks clean and decent enough. For cheaper places to sleep, try the **Kalpataru**, the **Slamat**, or the **Minang**.

PANTE MACASSAR

Aneka Jaya 10 rms. The only *losmen* in town. Clean rms w/attached facilities. $4 S, $6.50 D.

BETUN

Two *losmen*: the **Adi Indah** and the **Cinta Damai**, all $5/person. The latter two have small restaurants where Chinese and Indonesian dishes are served.

DINING IN KUPANG

Western

Teddy's Bar Downtown, right along the water, ☎ 21142. Seafood and chicken at $2.50–$3. Aussie meals $2–$6. Pleasant, seaside, outdoors place, but with reeking toilets.

Kupang Klub This place has its ups and downs. Up: the beer is cheaper than at Teddy's. Down: you need transportation to get there and back. Aussie chow, $2–$2.50, Indonesian $1.25.

Western food also at the **Rotterdam**, located way out in the middle of nowhere (car needed), 1 km past the Sasando Hotel. Highlights: steaks $2.50–$4, ice-cream combinations $1.50. The better hotels also serve western food.

Chinese

Pantai Laut Next door to Teddy's, (see above). Considered one of the best, but certainly the slowest Chinese restaurant in town, serving fish, squid, chicken and pork dishes at $2–$6. With some notice, they can prepare local specialties such as *daging se'i* (smoked beef), *jagung bose* (corn with coconut milk) or *lawar* (a vegetable dish). For "RW" (dog) they need a full day's notice, so they can buy a suitable beast.

Palembang Jl Sudirman. Our favorite, and also the most popular with the locals for good, fast service. Excellent food, moderate (for Indonesia) prices: pigeon $4, seafood, including prawns $2.50–$3.50, grilled fish according to size $3–$5, chicken $2–$3, grilled beef $2 and lots of other goodies.

Hemaliki Jl Sukarno. Serves seafood, Chinese and Indonesian style, and offers a pleasant, open setting. A fine place for a meal. Figure $3–$6 per person, plus drinks.

Lima Jaya Just past the downtown bus terminal. Has a very full selection of Chinese dishes $1.75–$3. Good, fast service. Second-floor bar, open from 7:30 to whenever, with an entrance fee of $1. (For those with delicate sensibilities: There could be working girls wandering around up there.)

Other Chinese restaurants of note include the **Mandarin** on Jl Sudirman, the **Karang Mas** downtown—good sunset views but so-so food, small portions—and the **Surabaya Indah**, Jl Tombelo 19, along with the **Tanjung**, on the same street.

Indonesian

Pondok Bamboo At King Stone hotel, 6 km from downtown on Jl Timor-Timur. Fish, beef, lamb, squid, prawn and crab dishes $1.75–$2.50. Indonesian meals, $1.50. One of Kupang's best restaurants and many locals make the trip out.

There are lots of Padang-style restaurants around town. The best we found was the **Bundo Kanduang** on Jl Tompelo. Other good bets are the **Surya**, about 200 m from the downtown bus station towards the sea, the **Beringin Jaya** near the seaside market and the **Bundo Kanduang** on Jl Sudirman downtown. About $1–$3 excluding canned or bottled drinks. The cheapest place, **Murah** (literally "Cheap"), serves good *nasi campur* and other Indonesian dishes for 30¢–75¢. Near the downtown bus terminal.

REGIONAL TRANSPORTATION

By Air

Be prepared for schedule changes, canceled flights and overbookings. Note: For the twice weekly Merpati flight to Darwin, Australia, most nationals need a visa before a ticket can be issued, and you cannot get one in Kupang.

Merpati offers lots of flights, with the longer hauls on reliable F27s and F28s. Shorter hops, on 18-passenger Twin Otters and Indonesian-built Cassas, are more dodgey. Round-trip fares twice the one-way fare, except for Darwin.

F27/28 flights: Twice daily to Bali ($115), daily to Bima ($112), three times weekly to Dili ($44), 8 times weekly to Surabaya ($152), 4 times weekly to Jakarta ($223), 11 times weekly to Maumere ($40), 3 times weekly to Ujung Pandang ($91), 3 times weekly to Balikpapan ($178), 3 times weekly to Tarakan ($251). On Wednesdays and Saturdays to Darwin, Australia ($150 ow; $250 rt). Most non-Australians need a visa to get on this flight, available from their consulate in Bali (1–2 days) or embassies world-wide. You need proof of financial solvency and must swear on your grandmother's tomb that you won't work in Australia.

Twin Otter and Cassa flights: 20 flights weekly to Bima ($112); 9 weekly to Ende ($51); 6 weekly to Labuhanbajo ($105); 6 weekly to Ruteng ($71); 3 weekly to Waingapu ($70) and Tambolaka ($95); 3 weekly to Bajawa ($70); 4 weekly to Kalabahi, Alor ($51); once weekly to Larantuka ($45) and Lewoleba, Lembata ($65); once a week to Roti ($23) and Savu ($43); and once a week to Dili ($44). Some of these flights are direct, others are "milk runs," stopping in several places. In good weather, these flights provide great aerial scenery.

Merpati Main office: Jl Kosasih 2, ☎ 33205, 33654. Open 7:30 am–7pm. Another office at the Flobomor II, ☎ 33221, 21961, and Fax: 33500 (same hrs).

Sempati Jl A. Yani, next to the Marina Hotel, ☎ 31612, Fax: 33500. This airline flies to Bali 5 times weekly, with the flight continuing to Surabaya and Jakarta. Same prices to these destinations as Merpati.

Bouraq Jl Sudirman 20, ☎ 21421. You can also fax Pitoby's (see below under "Tour agencies"). Open 7 days a week from 8 am to 4 pm. Three weekly flights Kupang–Maumere–Denpasar, Bali–Surabaya, Java–Jakarta; 4 weekly flights Kupang–Waingapu, Sumba–Denpasar, Bali. Same prices as Merpati.

By Land

Regional buses for the various district capitals and points in between leave from the Walikota terminal in the eastern part of the city. Although several buses leave for key inland towns during the day (and there are even night buses to Atambua), most of the departures are in the early morning, particularly to the more distant places.

The buses are quite reasonable. Kupang to Dili, East Timor, for example, a 12-hr run, costs $7, including meals and a bus change at Atambua. To Soe, $2; Kefa, $3.50; Atambua, $4.50.

By Sea

FERRIES

There are several ferries operating out of Kupang, each with two classes for passengers and large enough to take several trucks and other vehicles. They are fairly reliable, but the schedules are not set in concrete, so check at the office, either by phone (Indonesian only) or in person. At last notice, the following ferries were running: To Roti island every day except Wed (4 hrs, $2.50–$3); to Larantuka, Flores and Lewoleba, Lembata twice a week (13–15hrs, $6–$8); to Waingapu, Sumba once a week ($5–$7), making a round-trip to Savu from there, then to Ende and back to Kupang before doing the same trip but in reverse, starting from Kupang to Ende ($8–$11); and to Kalabahi, Alor twice a week ($8–$11). During the height of the western monsoon, Jan–Feb, the ferries "climb waves like mountains" according to one skipper. Everyone, including the crew, gets seasick.
Ferry office Jl Cak Doko 20, ☎ 21140.

PELNI LINES

The state shipping line's large passenger ships, the *Kelimutu* and the *Dobonsolo*, call at Kupang. These boats are generally set up according to Indonesian—not western—travel standards.

The *Kelimutu* follows the following route: Kupang; Ende, Flores; Waingapu, Sumba; Bima, Sumbawa; Lembar, Lombok; Surabaya, Java; Banjarmasin, Kalimantan and return by the same route. The ship has 7 first-class cabins for two people, 10 second-class cabins for 4 people, and lots of space in economy (except during vacation times).

The *Dobonsolo* goes from Kupang to Dili, Ambon, Sorong, Manokwari, Biak and Jayapura before returning and including Kalabahi, Maumere, Ujung Pandang, Surabaya and Jakarta's Tanjung Priok on its route.

Pelni also operates mixed deck passenger/cargo ships that stop at Kupang. The crowded ships cover the routes to Flores and other islands on the average of once or twice a month. They are deck passage only, but you can try to negotiate with one of the crew members for his bunk. Small cargo and passenger boats irregularly motor to many a harbor, some not even on maps. Check at the harbormaster's office at the Tenau docks for possible departures.
Pelni Jl Pahlawan 3, opposite Fort Concordia, ☎ 21944.

SERVICES

Travel agencies

Pitoby Tour and Travel Jl Sudirman 118, ☎ 32700. Fax: 31044. Branch office: Jl Sili-

wangi 75, ☎ 21222, 21333.

This is the oldest and largest travel agency in NTT, opened in 1972. They have many package tours, for example:

1. Komodo Island 3 days and 2 nights via Labuhanbajo or Bima. One person, $500; for two, $325/ea; 4–6, $290/ea; larger groups, $260/ea. All inclusive except airfares.

2. East Timor and Dili 4 days and 3 nights, one person $347; two, $260/ea; 4–6 persons, $222/ea; 15–19, $180/ea.

They have many more packages including Kelimutu and Central Flores tours with scuba diving in Maumere; Bali plus Lesser Sundas tours that are competitive with tours originating in Bali; Sumba tours; Japanese memorial tours; and even a Darwin and North Australia tour (7 days, 6 nights: $889–$996/person depending on accommodations, airfare extra).

On a more local scale, the agency runs Kupang City tours, Semau Island tours, and even a special "Timor night" with traditional dances. The agency regularly presents local dances and cultural shows on request at their upstairs Pitoby Balelebo Hall. For just one person, $123; but for a group of 20, $8/person.

Floressa Wisata Jl Mawar, ☎ 22012, 22594
Ultra Jl Sukarno 15A, ☎ 31064, 21796

GUIDES

Tours arranged by travel agencies always have an English-speaking guide. If you want a freelance guide, your hotel or *losmen* can arrange for one. The best individual we found is **Aka Nahak**. He speaks several Timorese languages and the local traditions thoroughly. He can set up tours of varying lengths with the widest range of budgets, from backpackers to oil company executives. Travel is either by public transportation of chartered vehicle. He charges $15/day either for an individual or groups of up to 8 persons. In Kupang, you can try to contact him at ☎ 32278. Or, best, write ahead to him and have him meet you upon arrival: Jl Soeprapto, Kefa 85612, Kabupaten TTU, Timor, NTT Indonesia. You could also try to contact **Willy Kadati**, another free-lance guide, at the same Kupang telephone number.

Diving

Pitoby Watersports Jl Sudirman 118, ☎ 32700. Fax: 31044. This outfit, a division of Pitoby Tours (see above), is very professionally run by an experienced Australian father and son team, Graeme and Donovan Whitford. (Direct contact: P.O. Box 1120, Kupang NTT, Indonesia, ☎ /Fax: 31634.) They offer a variety of packages for diving around Kupang, around Kupang and Roti Island, and even to Alor. The diving, particularly around Roti and Alor, is absolutely first-rate. Examples of pricing (all per person for a group of 4; add 50% for smaller group):

Kupang 4 days, 3 nights: 4 day dives, 1 night dive, city tour, cultural show, island tour. $245.
Kupang and Roti 8 days, 7 nights: 9 day dives, 1 night dive, city tour, cultural show, island tour, escorted 3-day dive and tour of Roti. $645.
Roti 6 days, 5 nights: Escorted 4-day dive and tour of Roti, 4 day dives and 1 night dive. $475.

All accommodations, transport (except for flight to Kupang), boats, board (except for drinks) and gear is included in these prices. (Deduct 5% if you bring your own dive gear). Trips to Alor—probably the very best diving in the area—can be arranged with notice, for similar prices.

Health

For traveling in Timor (and elsewhere in Nusa Tenggara) make sure you take malaria pills. This is very important. (See "Travel Advisory," pg. 241) Should you get sick, we recommend the **Rumah Sakit Polisi** (Police Hospital), Jl Nanga 84, ☎ 21273. $20 a day for VIP rms. Try to see Dr. Hadi Sulisuyanto, who speaks some English. The General Hospital, **Rumah Sakit Umum** on Jl M. Hatta, also has some English-speaking doctors:
Gynecologist Dr. Heru Tjahyono, Jl Sudirman 30, ☎ 22015
Neurologist Dr. Harry Hartono, Jl Cak Doko 53, ☎ 22626.
Internist Dr. Iksan, Jl Sudirman, ☎ 21340.
Apotik Pelengkap Drugstore open 24 hours at Kompleks R.S.U. Kupang, ☎ 21356.

Souvenirs and Shopping

Primitive Art and Ceramics This store, in a private home, is run by Ibu Sulastri, who speaks English. She has lots of wood carvings from Timor as well as ceramics and more. By appointment only. ☎ / Fax: 31634.
Dharma Bakti Jl Sumba 19–32, about 2 km from downtown on the main coast road going east, ☎ 21154. Open 8am–3pm and 6pm–9pm, closed Sundays. A tremendous selection of cloths, including *patola* ($550–$1,500), old *ikat* cloths ($150–$300), new *ikat* ($6–$120), and shirts made from local *ikat* ($22–$55).
Ie Rai Ikat Weavers Cooperative Jl Hati Mulia 41, in back of the Cendana Hotel, has the best selection of new Savu weavings, at very reasonable prices. Their fully traditional cloths, in standard 3-meter lengths, cost $40—with discounts possible with the purchase of several pieces. Their wall hangings feature three or four identical-patterned cloths sewn together.
Padang Sari Jl Suharto 57. This shop, run by a Balinese couple, it has some surprisingly fine cloths, and interesting odds and crafts.

You could also try **Toko Sinar Baru**, near the downtown *bemo* terminal, the **Kartika** on Jl Hati Suci (Aebobo), and the **Krisnawati** on Jl El Tari.

Itinerant cloth sellers, not too bothersome, hang around tourist watering holes such as Teddy's. Their wares are usually inferior and the initial asking price is beyond reason, so bargain like hell. For the best general shopping—for anything except antiques—go to the **Loka Binkra**. *Ikat* weaving demonstrations and sale at Osmok village, on the way to Tenau Harbor, near the cement factory, about 8km from downtown.

For antiques: **Dharma Bakti**, the **Padang Sari** and **Goris Timora**, the latter on Jl Tim-Tim.

ENGLISH LANGUAGE NEWS
Toko Buku Semangat Jl Sudirman 152, open 7am to 12pm, ☎ 31034. The only place in town where you can get the *Jakarta Post* and the *Observer*. (One day to three weeks old, depending. No other English language newspapers or news magazines are available in Kupang.

MARKET DAYS
Kupang district Baun, Saturday; Camplong, Saturday; Baumata, Sunday; Buraen, Tuesday; Oeakabiti, Wednesday; Takari, Monday (especially good for cattle and all kinds of animals); Oesao (the busiest) Thursday and Friday.
Soe district Kapan, Thursday; Niki Niki, Wednesday; Batuputih, Sunday; Oenlasi, Tuesday (this is the biggest in West Timor); Tono (one of the very best), Tuesday.
Kefa district Eban, Tuesday; Maubesi, Thursday; Oelolok, Wednesday; Manufui, Saturday; Noemuti, Wednesday; in Kefa itself, daily, but best on Sundays; Oenopu, Tuesday.
Atambua/Belu district Betun, Wednesday; Hailulik, Thursday; Besikama, Sunday; Bolan, Thursday; Klitik, Friday; Boas, Tuesday; Fatubesi, Monday; Nurobo, Monday; Nenuk, Monday.

East Timor

Telephone code 390
With the fast-improving road system in East Timor, the Merpati flights that had linked the district capitals to Dili have been discontinued for lack of passengers. Instead, there are now daily buses out of Dili leaving every morning for the district capitals: Aileu, Ainaro, Ermera, Liquica, Los Palos, Maliana, Manatuto, Same, Suai, Viqueque and Baucau.

The Timorese are friendly and helpful. Many of the people in the countryside do not yet speak Indonesian (they speak a local language), so forget about communicating in English. Although few men wear beards, many sport handsome mustaches or great Van Dykes.

The province's lingua franca, Tetun, is spoken by about 75% of the inhabitants. The Portuguese language is still used by some 10,000 persons, the former elite in colonial times. But, like Dutch for elder Indonesians generally, Portuguese here is slowly fading. The government closed the last Portuguese language (private) schools in the late 1980s.

We suggest traveling around East Timor to those with some initiative. Basically, it's easy: there's a good network of paved roads and a fair number of *losmen*. No Bali-type (or any-type) of foreign crowds. The official figure was 7,000 tourists in 1993, which could be, but on one trip to Dili, we only saw 3 foreign faces; on another, none. Outside of Dili, we never met another foreigner. It's you, the very nice locals and the scenery—often stunning sea or mountain views. The most isolated of the districts, Viqueque (no *losmen*) can only be reached by paved road from the north, via Baucau.

Dili

A visit to the port of Dili gives a good idea of the province's subsidized economy. All the essentials are imported: asphalt, cement, wood, rice, eggs and most food, you name it. Coffee is the only export of real value. Small quantities of rotan, marble, sandalwood oil and *kemiri* nuts are also shipped out. But the value of imports far outweigh that of the exports. While at the port, check out the graceful freighter—schooners, bringing wood from Kalimantan, anchored next to freighters, new and rusting.

GETTING THERE

BY AIR

Merpati flies direct to/from Bali 5 times weekly ($140) and 3 times weekly to/from Kupang ($40); Sempati has a twice weekly Kupang flight, same price. There are, on the average, 5 buses daily to Kupang (9–10 hrs, $5) as well as Atambua (4 hrs, $2.50). Taxi from Comoro airport to Dili, $2.50.

Merpati Jl Madeiros, next to the New Resennde Inn, ☎ 21881, ☎ 21880 (no fax).

Sempati. Jl Carmona, at the Turismo Hotel, ☎ 22651, Fax: 22822.

BY SEA

Three large ships, belonging to the Pelni lines, each call every two weeks at Kupang. The *Kelimutu* heads for Kalabahi, Alor on one journey and to Kupang the following week. The *Tatamailau* connects Dili with western Indonesia, as well as Saumlaki, Tanimbar; Tual, Kei; Dobo, Aru; and Merauke, Irian Jaya, to the east. The *Dobonsolo*, starting from Tanjung Priok (Jakarta) and Surabaya makes for Kupang, then Dili, whence to Ambon (the capital of the Moluccas) and the ports of Irian Jaya's north coast, returning by the same route a week later.

Pelni. Jl Alexio de Corterial, ☎ 22478, Fax: 21415.

Two freighters, with plenty of deck-only passengers, the *Duta Nusantara* and the *Daya Nusantara*, sail fascinating 3-week round-trips out of Kupang and Dili to the small, hard to reach

islands of the south-east Moluccas: Lirang, Wetar; Kisar; Romang; Damar; Tepa, Babar; Saumlaki, Tanimbar; Tual, Kei; and Ambon, returning on the same route. It's about a week from Dili to Ambon. Deck passage on these ships is for dirt-poor budget travelers (it also helps to be young and/or tough) and the trip will be less than enchanting. It will be a tremendous improvement if you can bargain with a crew member for the use of his bunk. (Figure $5–$10 a day.)

ACCOMMODATIONS

Dili

There is not a very large range to choose from. Nothing like an international grade hotel is planned, but the prices are reasonable.

Turismo Avenida Marechal Carmona, ☎ 22029, Fax: 22284. 48 rms. The building fronts the sea, but is out-of-the-way, towards the end of the seafront drive. Anyway, trees block the view of the sea for the few rms actually facing the water. There is an outdoor, coin-operated phone for guests. Also a restaurant. Pretentious and overpriced with lousy service. $10–$34 S, $12–$37 D.

Mahkota Timor Jl Alves Aldea, ☎ 21662, 21664; Fax: 22499. 44 rms. Three-story building near downtown and seafront. Restaurant serves Indonesian, Chinese, Portuguese dishes. $25–$30 S, $27–$33 D, includes taxes and breakfast.

New Resende Inn Jl Avenida Bispo Medeiros, ☎ 22094, 21768. 22 clean, modern, AC rms. Good location near downtown and seafront. The restaurant, the Diak Kliu, is perhaps the best around. $20–$25 S, $22–$27 D, with taxes and breakfast.

Wisma Cendana Jl Americo Thomas (next to the Crafts Center), ☎ 21141. 10 rms. Clean, pleasant lobby and beautiful rms. Just off a traffic-laden street. No employees and little service. $18–$27 S or D.

Dili Jl Carmona, ☎ 21871. 12 rms. Renovated place on the seafront. Fan-cooled, $11, AC $17, S or D.

Wisma Taufik Jl Americo Thomas, ☎ 21934. 15 noisy rms in the downtown area. Shared facilities $5 S, $8 D; w/attached facilities and fan, $7.50–$11.

Basmery Indah Jl Villa Verde, ☎ 22151 towards the cathedral. 10 rms. Agents for the Gemilan bus company, which offers service to Atambua and Kupang. $4–$8 S, $7–$8 D.

Vila Harmonia In Becora, a suburb of Dili, 4 km from downtown. 5 rms, shared outside facilities. Attached to the Mona Lisa restaurant. $4 S, $7 D.

Elsewhere in East Timor

There are small *losmen* in several of the district capitals, nice, simple places, charging about

Dili

Selat Wetar

Lighthouse

Motael church

Port

Integration monument

Branca Beach

N

5

JL. ALVES ALDEIRA

JL. JOSE MARIA MARQUEZ

1

Merpati JL. Virgin Mary statue

JL. COMORO

JL. AMERICO TOMAS

6 ★

Comoro Airport, market, Atambua, Tasitolu bus terminal and Kupang

15

9 **7** **12** **3**

10

14

JL. JACINTO CANDIDO

JL. MADEIRUS

13

4

8

Cathedral

2

JL. KAIKOLI

16

Tourism office

Municipal market

★

Becora, Baucau and Los Palos

Becora market ★

Portuguese war monument ★

Australian war monument, Aileu and Ainaro

1. Dili Hotel
2. Losmen Basmery Indah
3. Mahkota Timor Hotel
4. New Resende Inn
5. Turismo Hotel
6. Wisma Cendana
7. Wisma Taufik
8. Audian Restaurant
9. Beringin Restaurant
10. Jakarta Restaurant
11. New Tropical Restaurant
12. Pantai Laut Restaurant
13. Governor's Office
14. Multi Prona Maya Tours
15. Pelni Office
16. Telecoms Office

Lahane bus terminal

$2.50 per person: 2 *losmen* in Maliana, 2 in Suai, pleasant ones in Tutuala and Los Palos, one with a spring-fed pool at Same, one in Maubessi (Ainaro District) and one at Matubuilico, departure point for the 3-hr horseback ride to the top of Tatamailau. The only hotel-type place to stay outside of Dili, the Flamboyant at Baucau, charges $8/person. Where there's no *losmen*, sleep at the school teacher's house, the village headman's house, or the police station.

DINING

With well over 30 restaurants, Dili offers a good choice of dining possiblities. There are plenty of Padang style places, others with the usual Chinese or Indonesian dishes. Plus, in a very few restaurants, you can find Portuguese meals and traditional Timorese ones. For careful, finicky eaters, we suggest the restaurants in the better hotels, the Mahkota Timor and the Paradiso. They offer a fair range of Indonesian and Chinese cuisine, along with a bit of Portugal. Figure on $5–$10 per meal, with beer squeezed in. At the other places below, the prices are somewhat cheaper for basically the same things, but in not quite so sanitized a setting.

There are two basic local dishes, traditionally eaten only during celebrations. The coastal dwellers' *saboko* resembles the Indonesian *ikan pepes* but with different spices. The fish or squid and spices are wrapped in sago leaves and cooked over an open fire. The mountain dwellers' speciality is *tukir* (or, sometimes, *tukil*) with spices and meat stuffed into bamboo tubes which are rotated over an open fire until done.

(The Toraja of Sulawesi also prepare traditional dishes this way.) The meat is usually chicken or goat, occasionally pig, and best of all, deer. Phone a day ahead if you want to try one or both of these two traditional dishes. For dog meat, you have to cadge an invitation to someone's home, during a special occasion.

Audian Jl 15 Octubre. Has the reputation of being the best seafood restaurant in town. Chinese, European and Indonesian dishes.

Fajar Jl 15 Octubre. The longest menu in town, probably the best Chinese restaurant. Depending on quality, the birds's nest soup could be up to $50. Abalone, expensive anywhere, $25 here. Sharks' fin soup at $5. Sea cucumber $3–$6; fish fillets (seasonal) $3–$6, pigeon $4–$5, frog $2–$3, shrimp $3–$4, crab $4–$6; squid or oyster $3–$4; beef or pork $2–$4. Or gorge on a good-sized lobster on a bed of vegetables, mushrooms and asparagus, $14–$20. Highly recommended.

Jakarta Jl Colmera. Excellent seafood, Chinese and Indonesian cuisine.

Lima Jaya Jl 15 Octubre. Indonesian and especially Chinese cooking. Very extensive menu, most dishes $2–$5 with lobster to about $10. Also: pigeon, frog, sea cucumber and goodies cooked in fish bellies. Excellent seafood and lots more. Recommended.

Massao Jl Massao, ☎ 22599. Phone to make sure your diver knows how to get there, as it's on a small back street. Worth the effort. Grilled chicken, $5; squid $3–$4. Fish cooked Portuguese style (with oil, butter and potatoes), according to size and species, $5–$10, lobster $7–$20. On Wednesdays and Saturdays, *tukir*-

style beef or *calderirada sapi* (beef stew, sort of), both $4. Live local music on Saturday nights. Highly recommended.

Mona Lisa In Becora, 4 km from downtown Dili. Central Javanese cooking.

New Tropical Jl Raya Becora. Padang-style.

Pantai Laut Jl Gov. Alves Aldeia. Indonesian and Chinese.

Totonito Jl Taibesse (Lahane Timur) ☎ 21560. Well worth the 50¢ taxi ride. A good, but not over-whelming choice of Portuguese dishes, including chicken (*frango*), fish (*peixe*), squid (*lula*), crab (*carangueijo*), shrimp (*camarao*), goat stew (*caldeirada de cabrito*) and traditional goat (*tukir de cabrito*).

REGIONAL TRANSPORTATION

The best way around East Timor is by bus, and the departures are usually in the early morning. The buses leave from three inter-city terminals outside town; to get to the proper terminal, catch a local bus (10¢) or by taxi, at the Mercado Municipal in Dili. The three terminals are at the edge of town, each hosting buses heading in the same general direction.

Terminal Tasitolu (on the way to the airport; $1.50 by taxi). For buses to the west.

To	Buses daily	Time	Fare
Kupang	5	9–10	$5
Atambua	5	4	$2.50
Maliana	6	5–6	$4
Liquica	Lots	0.5	$.75
Ermera	Lots	3	$1
Pante Makassar (Oecussi)	1	9	$7.50
Suai (via Atambua)	2	7	$7.50

Terminal Lahane (taxi, 50¢) buses going south:

Ainaro	6	5–6	$2
Same	2	6	$2.25
Suai (via Ainaro)	2	11–12	$4.50

Terminal Becora (taxi $1) buses going east:

Manatuto	4	1.5	$1.25
Baucau	12	2.5	$2
Viqueque	4	6	$3
Los Palos	4	7	$3.50

Note: Most buses leave in the early morning 6:30 am–9 am, taking off when (very) full; get there early for a good seat.

SERVICES

TRAVEL AGENTS

Multi Perona Maya Jl Marques 23 (next to a big shop of the same name) ☎ 21444; Fax: 23066. Here you can buy tickets for Merpati and Sempati flights, as well as tickets on the Pelni ships—their ship tickets are a bit more expensive, but a lot less hassle to obtain than directly from the Pelni office. Here you can also change

bills (if in good condition) from the US, Australia, Singapore, Sterling Pounds and Yen. Car rental, with driver, $50/day, you pay for the gas. English-speaking guide, $17–$25/day (depends on his level of English).This agency plans to build a 50-room seaside hotel, with golf, tennis courts, swimming pool.

Tourism Dept Jl Caicoli, ☎ 21350. See if Pedro Lebre is around, their best English-speaker.

SNORKELING

There are reports of decent snorkeling around Metinaro (about 40 km east along the coast from Dili) and Tutuala (way on the far eastern tip of the island).

MONEY EXCHANGE

Bank Rakyat, Bank Dagang Negara, Bank Danamon and Bank Summa. Multi Prona Maya travel agency (see above).

CRAFTS AND RITUALS

IKAT AND CRAFTS

The Manufahi district (capital: Same) is reputed to produce the best *tais* back-strap weavings. Natural fibers and dyes are sometimes still used, alongside more modern materials. For wood or water-buffalo horn carvings, go to the Manatuto district and ask around to find the craftsmen at work. (Look for views of Mt. Tatamailau from this area. For the best views, take a pre-dawn, 3-hr horseback ride to the summit, starting from the *losmen* at Hatubuilico village. Try this only in the dry season, Aug–Nov.)

Handspun thread and natural-dye *ikat* costs up to $100 a cloth whereas the store-bought thread and artificial dye versions go for as little as $15. Weaving is most common in the Ermera and Los Palos districts.
Horseback riding

TRADITIONAL RITUALS

Timing and luck are essential here. There's one called "*Extracção de Sal de Laga*" to celebrate the salt harvest at Danau Laga Lake, near Baucau, beginning in early or mid-October, stretching for some 2 weeks and including sacrifices of goats and water buffalo. Also (usually) in October, the Cavala fish festival (*sescarià*), performed in the Lantern, Bobonaro and Covalima districts. Or, the most interesting (name-wise, anyway), the Cuci Kaki Kerbau ("Washing Water-Buffalo Feet"), a harvest/thanksgiving rite, performed in the Bobonaro District around August. There are probably lots more, so ask around. The dates are set by the local *kepala adat*, chief of traditions. You might also check at the Tourism Office in Dili (see above).

For sanitized song-and-dance (but with fixed dates), try Kupang during one of the celebrations: 17 July (Anniversary of East Timor), 17 August (National Independence Day), and 15 October (Anniversary of Dili).

Further Reading

Adams, Marie-Jean. "System and Meaning in East Sumba Textile Design: a Study in Traditional Indonesian Art." New Haven: Southeast Asia Studies Cultural Reports Series #16, Yale University, 1969.

Auffenberg, Walter. *The Behavioral Ecology of the Komodo Monitor Lizard*. Gainsville: University of Florida Press, 1988.

Banks, Joseph. *The Endeavour Journal of Joseph Banks, 1768-1771*. London: Angus and Robertson, 1962.

Barnes, R. H. "Lamalerap." *Indonesia* #17, April 1974.

Bellwood, Peter S. *Man's Conquest of the Pacific: the Prehistory of Southeast Asia and Oceania*. New York: Oxford University Press, 1979.

————. *Prehistory of the Indo-Malaysian Archipelago*. Sydney, NSW; Orlando, FL: Academic Press, 1985.

Bickmore, A. S. *Travels in the East Indian Archipelago*. New York: D. Appleton, 1869.

Boxer, Charles Ralph. "The Topasses of Timor." Koninklijke Vereeniming Indisch Instituut, Mededeling No. 73, Afdeling Volkenkunde No. 24, 1957.

————. *Fidalgos in the Far East 1550-1770*. The Hague: Martinus Nijhoff, 1948.

————. *The Portuguese Seaborn Empire 1415-1825*. London: Hutchinson, 1969.

Brackman, Arnold C. *A Delicate Arrangement*. New York: New York Times Books, 1980.

Campagnolo, Henri. *Fataluku I: relations et choix: introduction methodologique a las description d'une langue "non-Austronesienne" de Timor Oriental*. Paris: SELAF, 1979.

————. *La Langue des Fataluko de Lorehe (Timor Portugais)*. Paris: SELAF, 1973.

Cenderroth, Sven. *The Spell of the Ancestors and the Power of Mekkah*. Gotenborg: Acta Universitatis Gothenburgensis, 1981.

Cool, Wouter. *With the Dutch in the East: Outline of Military Operations Against Bali and Lombok*. London, 1897.

Djukatana, N.G. *Pasola: A Religious Magical Ceremony*, mimeographed document, no date.

Du Bois, Cora Alice. *The People of Alor: a Social-Psychological Study of an East Indian Island*. With analyses by Abram Kardiner and Emil Oberholzer. Cambridge, MA: Harvard University Press, 1969

Earl, George Winsor. *The Eastern Seas*. With introduction by C.M. Turnbull. [Orig.: *The Eastern Seas, or Adventures in the Indian Archipelago in 1832–33–34*. W.H. Allen: London, 1837.] Singapore, New York: Oxford University Press, 1971.

Fisher, Joseph. *Threads of Tradition*. Berkeley: University of California at Berkeley, Lowie Museum of Anthropology, 1979.

Forbes, Henry O. *A Naturalist's Wanderings in the Eastern Archipelago*. Singapore; New York: Oxford University Press, 1989.

Forth, Gregory L. *Rindi: an Ethnographic Study of a Traditional Domain in Eastern Sumba*. Verhandelingen van het Koninklijk Instituut voor Taal-, Land- en Volkenkunde No. 93. The Hague: Martinus Nijhoff, 1981.

Fox, James J. *Harvest of the Palm: Ecological Change in Eastern Indonesia*. Cambridge, MA: Harvard University Press, 1977.

————, ed. *The Flow of Life: Essays on Eastern Indonesia*. Cambridge, MA: Harvard University Press, 1980.

————, ed. *To Speak in Pairs: Essays on the Ritual Languages of Eastern Indonesia*. Cambridge: Cambridge Studies in Oral and Literate Culture, Cambridge University Press, 1988.

Franca, Antonio Pinto da. *Portuguese Influence in Indonesia*. Jakarta: Gunung Agung, 1970.

Gittinger, Mattiebelle. *Splendid Symbols: Textiles and Tradition in Indonesia*. Washington, D.C.: The Textile Museum, 1979.

Glover, Ian C. *Archaeology in Eastern Timor, 1966–67*. Canberra, ACT: Dept. of Prehistory, Research School of Pacific Studies, Australian National University, 1986.

————. "The Late Stone Age in Eastern Indonesia." *Indonesia Circle*. March 12, 1977, London, pp. 6-20.

Goethals, Peter R. *Aspects of Local Government in a Sumbawan Village*. Ithaca, NY: Southeast Asia Program, Dept. of Far Eastern Studies, Cornell University, 1961.

Groeneveldt, W.P. Notes on the Malay Archipelago and Malacca Compiled from Chinese Sources. *Verhandelingen van het Bataviaasch Genootschap van Kunsten en Wetenschappen* 39, 1:1-144, 1880.

Guillemard, Francis Henry Hill. *The Cruise of the Marchesa to Kamschatka and New Guinea*. J. Murray, London, 1889.

Heekeren, H.R. van. *The Bronze Age of Indonesia*. The Hague: Martinus Nijhoff, 1958.

————. *The Stone Age of Indonesia*. 2d rev. ed.

With contribution by R.P. Soejono. The Hague: Martinus Nijhoff, 1972.

Hilir, Ismail M. *Peranan Kesultanan Bima dalam Perjalanan Sejara Nusantara.* Private Printing, Bima, 1988

Hill, Hal. *Unity and Diversity: Regional Economic Development in Indonesia Since 1970.* Singapore: Oxford University Press, 1989.

Hiorth, Finngeir. *Timor Past and Present.* Townsville, QL: James Cook University of North Queensland, 1985.

Holmgren, Robert J. and Anita E. Sperties. *Early Indonesian Textiles from Three Island Cultures: Sumba, Toraja, Lampung.* New York: Metropolitan Museum of Art: Distr. by Harry N. Abrams, 1989.

Jolliffe, Jill. *East Timor, Nationalism and Colonialism.* University of Queensland Press, 1978.

Kahlenberg, Mary Hunt, ed. *Textile Traditions of Indonesia.* Contributers include Alpert, S.G., "Sumba." Los Angeles: Los Angeles County Museum of Art, 1977.

Kartomi, Margaret J., ed. *Five Essays on the Indonesian Arts.* Clayton, Victoria: Centre of Southeast Asian Studies, Monash University, 1981.

Kraan, Alfons van der. *Lombok: Conquest, Colonization, and Underdevelopment, 1870-1940.* Singapore: Pub. for the Asian Studies Association of Australia by Heinemann Educational Books (Asia), 1980.

Kuipers, Joel C. *Power in Performance: The Creation of Textual Authority in Weyewa Ritual Speech.* Philadelphia: University of Pennsylvania Press, 1990.

Lebar, Frank M. (ed.). *Ethnic Groups in Insular Southeast Asia.* New Haven: Human Relations Area Files Press, 1972.

Leur, J. C. van. *Indonesian Trade and Society.* W. Van Hoeve, The Hague, 1955.

Lewis, E. Douglas. *People of the Source: The Social and Ceremonial Order of Tana Wai Brama on Flores.* Verhandelingen van het Koninklijk Instituut voor Taal-, Land- en Volkenkunde No. 135. Dordrecht, Holland: Foris Publications, 1988.

Mackie, J.A.C., ed. *Indonesia: the Making of a Nation.* Canberra: Australian National University, Research School of Pacific Studies, 1980.

Needham, Rodney. *Mamboru: History and Structure in a Domain of Northwestern Sumba.* Oxford: Clarendon Press; New York: Oxford University Press, 1987.

———. Sumba and the Slave Trade. Melbourne: Centre of Southeast Asian Studies, Monash University, 1983.

Noorduyn, J. Makassar and the Islamization of Bima. *Bijdragen tot de Taal-, Land- en Volkenkunde* 142: 312-342, 1987.

Ormeling, F.J. *The Timor Problem.* Jakarta and Groningen: J. B. Wolters, 1956.

Pigafetta, Antonio. *Magellan's Voyage: A Narrative Account of the First Navigation,* trans. and ed. by R.A. Skelton from the original manuscript at Yale University. London: The Folio Society, 1975.

Pires, Thome. *Summa Oriental.* London: Hakluyt Society, 1944.

Poortenaar, Jan. *An Artist in Java and Other Islands of Indonesia.* Singapore; New York: Oxford University Press, 1989.

Renard-Clamagirand, Brigitte. *Marobo: Une société ema de Timor.* Paris: SELAF, 1982

Schulte Nordholt, H. G. *The Political System of the Atoni of Timor.* Verhandelingen van het Koninklijk Instituut voor Taal-, Land- en Volkenkunde 60. The Hague: Martinus Nijhoff, 1971.

Sherlock, Kevin. *A Bibliography of Timor: Including East (Formerly Portuguese) Timor, West (Formerly Dutch) Timor and the Island of Roti.* With a forward by James J. Fox. Canberra: Research School of Pacific Studies, Australian National University, 1980.

Stokhof, W.A.L. *Preliminary Notes on the Alor and Pantar Languages.* Canberra: Dept. of Linguistics, Research School of Pacific Studies, Australian National University, 1975.

Sutton, Annabel. *The Islands in Between.* London: Impact, 1989

Tasuku Satu, *I Remember Flores.* Trans. from the Indonesian by P. Mark Tennien. New York: Farrar, Strauss and Cudahy, 1957.

Tate, D.J.M. *The Making of Modern South-East Asia.* Rev. ed. Kuala Lumpur; New York: Oxford University Press, 1977.

Traube, Elizabeth G. *Cosmology and Social Life: Ritual Exchange among the Mambai of East Timor.* Chicago: University of Chicago Press, 1986.

Wallace, Alfred Russel. *Australasia.* London, 1879.

———. The Geographical Distribution of Animals. London; New York: Hafner, 1962.

———. The Malay Archipelago. Singapore: Oxford University Press, 1986.

Waterson, Roxanne. *The Living House: An Anthropology of Architecture in South-East Asia.* Singapore: Oxford University Press, 1990.

Whitmore, Timothy Charles, ed. *Biogeographic Evolution of the Malay Archipelago.* Oxford: Clarendon Press; New York: Oxford University Press, 1987.

———, ed. Wallace's Line and Plate Tectonics. Oxford: Clarendon Press; New York: Oxford University Press, 1981.

Wolters, O. W. *Early Indonesian Commerce.* Ithaca, NY: Cornell University Press, 1967.

Index

Map Index